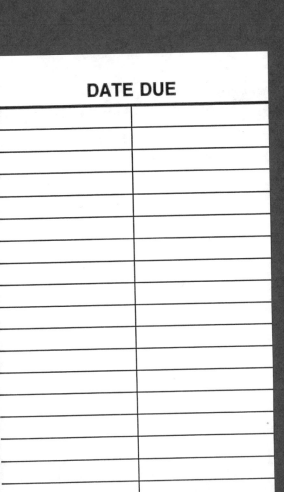

DATE DUE

	PRINTED IN U.S.A.

TRUE THAI

with Theresa Volpe Laursen
and Byron Laursen

Photographs by E. K. Waller

TRUE THAI

The Modern Art of Thai Cooking

Victor Sodsook

William Morrow and Company, Inc.

New York

Copyright © 1995 by Victor Sodsook, Theresa Volpe Laursen, and Byron Laursen

All rights reserved. No part of this book may be reproduced or utilized in any form or by any means, electronic or mechanical, including photocopying, recording, or by any information storage or retrieval system, without permission in writing from the Publisher. Inquiries should be addressed to Permissions Department, William Morrow and Company, Inc., 1350 Avenue of the Americas, New York, N.Y. 10019.

It is the policy of William Morrow and Company, Inc., and its imprints and affiliates, recognizing the importance of preserving what has been written, to print the books we publish on acid-free paper, and we exert our best efforts to that end.

Library of Congress Cataloging-in-Publication Data

Sodsook, Victor.
    True Thai : the modern art of Thai cooking / Victor Sodsook with Theresa Volpe Laursen and Byron Laursen.
        p.   cm.
    Includes bibliographical references and index.
    ISBN 0-688-09917-3
    1. Cookery, Thai. I. Laursen, Theresa. II. Laursen, Byron. III. Title.
TX724.5.T5S63   1995
641.59593—dc20   94-40234
                                                                       CIP

Printed in the United States of America

First Edition

1 2 3 4 5 6 7 8 9 10

BOOK DESIGN BY RICHARD ORIOLO

To my mother, Savad Sodsook

—VICTOR SODSOOK

Thanks to my lifetime business partner and friend,
Chris Chapman, for his patience and assistance

—VICTOR SODSOOK

To the Thai people—especially those here in America.
Their generous, welcoming spirit is as easy to fall in love
with as their elegant, sumptuously flavorful cooking.

—THERESA AND BYRON LAURSEN

First, our deepest appreciation is for the trust, wisdom, and guidance of our agents, Eric and Maureen Lasher. Thank you for believing in us, and in this project, from the beginning. We needed your many talents and great sensitivity all the way through. Our editor, Ann Bramson, whose intelligence, foresight, and patience were vital ingredients, deserves the medal of valor. Then there were the other terrific talents at William Morrow who helped edit, shape, and design this book—among them Bob Aulicino, Richard Oriolo, and M. Pearl.

Special thanks to our dear friend, E. K. Waller, whose vision and artistry in photography were matched only by her faith and long-term commitment to bringing this cookbook beautifully to life. Thanks also to E. K.'s photography assistant, Carleen Sweeney, and to stylist Alice M. Hart of Food For Film Stylists.

Many thanks to Hugh Carpenter, whose remarkable openness and encouragement did much to launch this project. And to our families and friends on both coasts, who, after the first couple of years, learned not to say "How close are you to being finished?"

For helping to provide key visual elements, thanks to Vibul and Patchara Wonprasat, of the Thai Community Arts and Cultural Center. They coordinated contributions from many sources, including the monks of the Wat Thai (Thai Buddhist Temple) of Los Angeles, who sweetly guided us in depicting an authentic Thai spirit house. The beautiful antique silver Thai bowl and spoons were loaned by Mr. and Mrs. R. J. Kelley. The exquisite vegetable carvings were created by Saowapa Albright, Walapa Lee, and Petchara Tseng.

Julie Sanders of Cyclamen Studio in Berkley kindly provided beautiful serving dishes for the cover photo. Tesoro and Freehand, two outstanding Los Angeles galleries, were the sources of several striking props and accessories.

On the editorial side, we're grateful to Nancy Elder for generously sharing her expertise in tropical ingredients. Others who gave timely assistance include Dick Bennett, Laura Maisch, Angela Birch, Patty Krause, and Rae Newman.

Loving thanks to Nancy Doyne for her wise counsel. And a big hug and kiss to cousin Joe Taccarino, patron of the arts. Finally, we appreciate the tireless appetites of our Beachwood Canyon and Malibu Beach Taste Testers, as willing a crew as ever folded a spicy salad into a lettuce leaf.

—Theresa and Byron Laursen

CONTENTS

FOREWORD
"THE SPIRIT HOUSE"

In a certain corner of my restaurant, as in almost every Thai home or place of business, you will find a tiny structure called a spirit house. In accordance with old beliefs, I privately pay tribute every day to the original occupants of the space I now inhabit.

A spirit house may be a modest little replica of a traditional Thai house or—befitting a grand establishment—it may be a large, elaborately decorated shrine. In the front of it can be found small dishes of rice and other foods, and slender red sticks, which are the remains of incense offerings. We give offerings at our spirit houses both to show respect for any spirits displaced by our daily activities and to request their powerful protection and guidance.

In that tradition, I want this Foreword to serve as the spirit house of this book, an honored dwelling place for the spirits of all those down through the ages who have kept and advanced the art of Thai cooking. They have been at work as far back as the first people who cultivated rice. Even the kings of old Siam long ago wrote cycles of poetry about cuisine and sent for the finest chefs in the country to join their royal courts. And every day, for centuries, talented women and men throughout Thailand have devoted themselves to making mealtime as stimulating and refreshing to the eye and to the soul as it is to the body.

The long and richly evolved traditions of the Thai kitchen are a source of pride, not only to me but to all the people of my native country, and one of our most important legacies.

My wish is that this book will honor all those people who nurtured Thai cooking through the long ages and will prove how grateful I am to have been given such a rich background from which I could emerge as a chef.

It's also my great privilege to welcome you to the ever-evolving traditions of taste and beauty in Thai cuisine. I hope you enjoy all the culinary adventures that lie ahead and that when you share the Thai food you've created with your friends and family, you feel as much happy pride as I do now.

INTRODUCTION

I've lived and worked in America for more than twenty years, a little bit more than half of my life. During that time, a handful of good Thai cookbooks for Americans have been published, most rather recently, as the popularity of Thai cuisine has spread from the great cities to the small towns of America. But I was spurred to write a book that would impart a sense of how Thai culture and cuisine have evolved together, each nourishing the other, one that would provide both those recipes Americans have come to know through visits to Thai restaurants and cafés, and those that have not yet made it to these shores but are deeply loved and an essential part of the cuisine as it's enjoyed in Thailand. At the same time I felt Thai cuisine could be made easier to understand, and to produce in American home kitchens, without sacrificing the flavors, textures, and colors that make it so characteristically Thai.

The book begins with a chapter on ingredients and equipment and moves on to chapters on the "building blocks" of Thai cuisine, such as curry pastes, soups, rice and noodle dishes, poultry and meat, and seafood.

Thai regional specialties are interspersed through the chapters, with descriptions of how the regions, and their varying topographies, climates, and foods, contrast with one another.

The introductions to the recipes show how various dishes fit into the Thai lifestyle, what traditions they reflect, and what the food reveals about the people themselves.

I'm especially proud of the chapter devoted to Thai vegetarian cooking. Every recipe in this chapter is free of animal products, whether meat, dairy, or eggs. It is really a cookbook in itself, offering all types of recipes, from vegetarian curry pastes to vegetarian appetizers, soups, side dishes, main courses, and one-dish meals.

Another lengthy chapter, one that reveals a great deal of what makes Thai cooking traditions so distinctive, is devoted entirely to salads. Westerners are always amazed at how we serve one or more salads with almost every meal, how many different salads we have, and how many surprising things—ranging from minced fish to potato chips—are found in them. We simply have a different, more inclusive concept of salads. It places Thai cooking among the healthiest, yet most appealing, cuisines on the planet.

Additionally, I've highlighted some distinctly Thai traditions, such as the foods of the royal court and the surprisingly sophisticated and satisfying cuisine of Thailand's many street-food vendors. Both these categories have their own chapters, complete with explanations of how these traditions evolved and how they fit into daily life.

In all chapters, I strive to help you understand facts that a native Thai would consider essential. For example, some Thai dishes are appropriate for lunch and some only for dinner—while certain other dishes, especially some soups, are right for any meal, day or night. Many Thai restaurants in this country offer the same menu at lunch and dinner. In Thailand, this would be as silly and inappropriate as offering peanut butter–and–jelly sandwiches alongside a roast rack of lamb. The Menu-Planning Guide on page 375 shows you how to pull together complete Thai meals, from simple lunches to multi-dish feasts.

"Fruit and Vegetable Carving and Thai Favors" is a chapter on making the garnishes and floral adornments Thais traditionally use to beautify their tables.

Two concepts are particularly important in this book: *authentic* and *modern*. Let me tell you why.

Being "authentic" doesn't mean making everything from scratch. It does mean using the freshest and choicest ingredients available—based on well-informed, selective shopping—in ways that are compatible with Thai traditions. Because refrigeration is a comparatively new part of life for many Thai people, we are still a nation of everyday shoppers. One reason our food is so healthful and appealing is that we always begin with the freshest, most fully flavored ingredients. So should you.

"Modern" means that you are free, once you have a good foundation of traditional knowledge, to branch out and be expressive in your cooking—just as Picasso mastered realism before he went on to produce his wonderful abstract art. Modern means knowing what came before, while continuing to evolve and adapt: going back to the Stone Age and using a mortar and pestle for certain tasks, but using a food processor for many others. It means knowing which time-saving, modern-day prepared ingredients will allow you to produce high-quality dishes and which, unfortunately, will not.

In keeping with modernism, and the constant evolution of Thai food, I've supplied a chapter entitled "Cooking with a Thai Accent." It shows you how to take the knowledge you've gained from this book and use it in new ways, creating your own dishes. The terrific Thai-American recipes in this chapter were evolved by my co-authors, Byron and Theresa Volpe Laursen, as they applied what I had taught them to their own American and Italo-American cooking traditions.

Before long, you'll be evolving your own recipes too.

This, then, is the book I've always wanted on the kitchen shelves of Americans who love Thai food. I've been watching you since I was a very young man, seeing what thrilled you about Thai cuisine and sensing how many more things you might eventually come to love—if given the right introduction. I think you're ready for a complete picture, including an understanding of the culture that invented Thai food, and of how to make this very exciting, pleasurable, healthful way of cooking a part of your life.

INGREDIENTS *and* EQUIPMENT

INGREDIENTS

BASIL

No other people love basil as much as Thais do. We use several varieties, cooked into curries, stir-fries, and other dishes, as well as raw in salads and vegetable platters. Although substitutions are permitted, certain basil varieties are just right for certain dishes. All varieties of basil are tender annuals that are easy to grow outdoors during summer or year-round in a sunny window. Keep them pinched back; the leaves will have more flavor.

HOLY BASIL   *Bai kaprao*   Ocimum sanctum
All basils are related to mint, and this variety is especially mintlike. The leaves are small and green, rough-textured like mint, with a purplish tinge. They release an intense flavor when cooked. Holy basil is found in Asian markets during spring, summer, and early fall. Fresh mint can be substituted.

THAI BASIL   *Bai horapha*   Ocimum basilicum
The leaves are pointy ovals, with purple stems and a strong anise flavor.

THAI LEMON BASIL   *Bai mangluk*   Ocimum canum
As the name suggests, this variety carries a hint of citrus in both its aroma and flavor. The leaves are small and pungent.

CHILI PEPPERS, DRIED *Phrik haeng*

CALIFORNIA CHILI Capsicum annuum

This mild variety of long red chili has a beautiful, rubylike color. I use dried California chilies in various curry-paste recipes, often in combination with dried Japanese chilies.

GUAJILLO CHILI Capsicum annuum

This is a sweet, moderately hot, long chili of brick-red color that I use, in dried form, in many curry-paste recipes, often combined with dried Japanese chilies.

JAPANESE CHILI Capsicum annuum

This hot, thin chili is very similar to both the cayenne and the Mexican variety called *chili de árbol*. It is about 2 inches long and is usually sold dried in cellophane packs. I use it in curry pastes, to contrast with the mellower flavors of other chilies.

NEW MEXICO CHILI Capsicum annuum

Except for a slightly earthier taste, the New Mexico chili is much like the **California chili**—a mild, long red chili, sold in dried form, good in various curry-paste recipes.

CHILI PEPPERS, FRESH *Phrik*

BANANA PEPPER or HUNGARIAN WAX PEPPER *Phrik yuak*
Capsicum annuum

This flavorful, mildly hot chili is smaller than a bell pepper and just large enough for stuffing. Yellow bell peppers may be substituted.

SERRANO CHILI *Phrik khee nu kaset* Capsicum annuum

The serrano is a hot green chili common in Latin markets that is now grown in Thailand and very popular with Thai cooks. It's somewhat plump, around 2 inches in length, and very easy to handle and slice, with the perfect spice and flavor for Fresh Chili Curry Paste (page 28).

THAI CHILI, LONG *Phrik chee fa* Capsicum annuum

These slender, bright red chilies have less fire than the more frequently used *phrik khee nu*, or **small Thai chilies**, but they still pack a respectable punch. They're not yet available in the United States, so I substitute red jalapeño chilies. *Phrik chee fa* can be found in pickled form, packed in jars, labeled *Thai red pickled chilies* or *phrik daeng dong*. They make a great table condiment and are also found in the filling for Panang Curry Omelet (page 141).

Recommended Brand of Pickled Chilies: Bee Brand

THAI CHILI, SMALL *Phrik khee nu* Capsicum annuum

Sometimes called a "bird" or "bird's-eye" pepper, the little *phrik khee nu* is among the world's hottest varieties. They're about 1 inch long, usually green, sometimes red. We use them freely in curries, soups, stews, and sauces, and even thin-sliced in vinegar as a table condiment. Substitute **serrano** chilies if *phrik khee nu* aren't available.

CHILI-TAMARIND PASTE   *Nam phrik pao*

This hot and spicy seasoning paste is the heart of many Thai soups, salad dressings, and stir-fries. Its depth of flavor comes from frying the garlic, shallots, and chilies before blending them with tamarind sauce. Good ready-made versions are available, but I urge you to try making your own (page 46).

CHINESE CHILI-GARLIC SAUCE

This condiment for cooking will quickly add a jolt of chili heat and garlic flavor. Vietnamese sometimes spoon it on at the table; Thais use it more sparingly.

Recommended Brand: Lee Kum Kee

CILANTRO   *Pak chee*   Coriandrum sativum

Known also as "Mexican parsley" or "Chinese parsley," this is the most-used fresh herb in the world and is indispensable for hundreds of Thai recipes. Its leaves are thin and flat, with a refreshing herbal scent. They are full-favored, more savory than the seeds, which are the familiar spice coriander. The roots of the cilantro plant are also used, but since most stores in America chop off the roots, I use cilantro stems instead. Cilantro accents faint flavors while tempering the richness of others. It is an annual that can be grown outdoors or in a window box. Plant some seeds every few weeks and you'll have a steady supply. Let some plants go to seed and you'll be supplied with coriander, an important ingredient in many Thai curry pastes. When you harvest the plants, pull them up, roots and all. Then you can try using the roots in recipes calling for cilantro stems.

COCONUT   *Maprao*   Cocos nucifera

COCONUT MILK AND CREAM   *Nam kati*
Coconut milk is an essential of Thai cuisine, adding flavor and creamy thickness to curries and other dishes. To make it at home from grated coconut meat is a very time-consuming job, so I recommend buying a good quality canned coconut milk. If you open a can without shaking it up, the cream will be at the top.

Recommended Brands: Mae Ploy, Chaokoh, Chef's Choice

COCONUT-PALM SUGAR   *Nam tan peep, nam tan maprao*
This is the maple sugar of the tropics. With its mild caramel-like flavor, it's as enjoyable in a cup of tea as it is in curries, stir-fries, and sweets. It is made from the sap of young coconut trees, which is boiled down into a semisoft paste, or to a firmer consistency, and is sold in cans or jars. Golden-brown sugar may be substituted.

COCONUTS, YOUNG GREEN   *Maprao on*

Very young coconuts are filled with a refreshing liquid. Their meat is soft and jellylike, perfect for custards and other desserts. A few specialty markets carry fresh young coconuts, which have pale-colored shells. Young coconut flesh is also available frozen and canned.

DRIED COCONUT   *Maprao haeng*

Flakes of dried, unsweetened coconut can often be used in place of fresh grated coconut. They're available in most health food stores.

DRIED FISH

Before refrigeration, people preserved fish by packing them in salt. Salt-preserved fish have interesting, useful characteristics: They're crispy; dunking them into dipping sauces makes for a nutritious snack. In a soup, they soften into tasty morsels, while their saltiness enhances the overall flavor of the broth. Several kinds of dried fish are found in Asian markets, including squid, rabbit fish (*gourami*), mackerel, and herring.

DRIED SHRIMP   *Kung haeng*

An important source of both flavor and protein, sun-dried shrimp are salty and intense, like a seafood version of bacon. Dried shrimp are usually cellophane-packed. They should be a light orangy-pink. Squeeze them to test for plumpness and resiliency. They should still have enough water content to "give" slightly under pressure.

FISH SAUCE   *Nam pla*

No ingredient is more vital to Thai cooking than this thin, flavorful, vitamin-rich sauce. Its aroma may seem strong, but *nam pla* quickly cooks down to a demure undertone that helps to "marry" various flavors within a dish. Since it is made from salt-packed, fermented fish, there's no need for a salt shaker on a Thai table. Ancient Romans made a similar sauce and used it in nearly every dish, as Thais do today. *Nam pla* can be made from various types of fish. Like olive oil, it is available in different levels of quality—the lesser are for cooking and the best for table use. Better grades, usually made with shrimp or anchovies, are pale amber in color.

Recommended Brands: Squid, Tiparos

GARLIC   *Kratiem*   Allium sativum

In recent years, Americans have really embraced this pungent, healthful herb. Gilroy, a California farm town, now attracts hundreds of thousands to its annual Garlic Festival. French and Italian cooks use garlic liberally, but Thais exceed them all. You may be surprised at how much garlic some of this book's recipes call for, but Thai spices and the dishes' multiple flavors somehow subdue the herb's pungency. Pickled

Garlic (page 64), Golden Garlic (page 65), and Fried Garlic Chips (page 66) are popular condiments for soups, salads, noodles, and other dishes.

GINGER   *Khing*   Zingiber officinale

Ginger ale and gingersnap cookies give only a hint of this herb's stimulating pungency and celestial aroma, which can only be experienced from the fresh herb. Choose heavy, firm-skinned pieces and peel them with a light hand—the flesh nearest the skin is the most flavorful. Avoid ginger with a low moisture content and darkened, withered skin.

BABY GINGER   *Khing on*   Zingiber officinale

The best fresh ginger in American markets arrives in early summer, flown in from Hawaii. The young shoots are full of peppery-sweet juice, with tender, opalescent, pinkish skins that need no peeling. The flavor is milder than that of mature ginger. Because it is picked at the moment of perfection, much of the baby ginger crop is preserved by pickling.

LESSER SIAMESE GINGER   *Krachai*   Kaempferia pandurata

This relative of ginger has a mildly spicy flavor, perfect for fish curries. It is quite aromatic, with a light brown skin and yellow interior. *Krachai* is often sold fresh in Thai markets, and also found powdered or frozen under the name "rhizome."

SIAMESE GINGER   *Kha*   Alpinia galanga siamensis

Also called galangal or galanga this is the type of ginger Thai cooks use most. The flavor is both more lemony and more peppery than that of common ginger, and it has a richer aroma. The skin is pale yellow, with pink-tinged knobs; the interior is cream-colored. *kha* is never eaten alone; it is used as a flavoring component. We float large slices into soups or chop and pound pieces into curry pastes. Sliced and dried *kha*, available in cellophane packs, is the best substitute when the fresh variety is unavailable. Otherwise, use common ginger.

JACKFRUIT   *Kanoon*   Artocarpus heterophyllus

Related to durian and breadfruit, jackfruit grows so large that it anchors itself around the trunk of its tree, rather than out on the limbs. Markets and street vendors usually sell it in chunks; it is also available canned. The rind is green and covered with little spines; the flesh is yellow and juicy, with a delightful taste and a pineapple-like odor.

KABOCHA   *Fak thong*   Cucurbita moschata

This goldfish bowl–sized squash probably came to Thailand centuries ago with Spanish and Portuguese traders. Its greenish, usually mottled skin is tough. You'll find yourself carving off chips rather than long peels. But the flesh inside is sweeter and finer in flavor than that of the common pumpkin. In California, kabocha is now popular enough to appear in nonethnic supermarkets.

KAFFIR LIME   *Magroot*   Citron hystrix

Imagine a cousin to the common lime—smaller and covered with a dark, thick, wrinkly skin. The peel, the zest, and the leaves of the Kaffir lime are used for cooking, not its perfumy juice. Kaffir lime trees grow well in southern California and Florida.

KAFFIR LIME LEAF   *Bai magroot*   Citron hystrix

The intensely aromatic leaves of the Kaffir lime tree grow in pairs, end to end, and are sold fresh in small plastic bags. Use them whole in soups and curries, as an aromatic ingredient not meant to be eaten. Or slice them into very fine, edible slivers. Either way, they add a wonderful flowerlike fragrance and taste.

LEMON GRASS   *Takrai*   Cymbopogon citratus

One of the most-used herbs in Thai cuisine, lemon grass adds a lemony flavor and aroma without acidity or sharpness. A thin, reedy plant, it grows in long, sheathlike stalks. The usable inner core is about the thickness of a finger. When finely sliced, it can be eaten; larger pieces are used just for flavor and aroma. Lemon grass is also pounded into curry pastes and used, in dried form, for beverages. In mild climates, lemon grass will grow outdoors year-round, spreading to form clusters of stalks. It can also be grown in pots in a sunny window. Cut the plants off at ground level when you harvest.

LONGAN   *Lam yai*   Euphoria longana

Longans grow on trees in northern Thailand, in grapelike clusters, and they're the most popular fruit of the region. Their taste is light and sweet, something like a muscat grape, but more mellow. Canned longans are available, as are raisinlike blocks of dried longan pulp. One of Thailand's favorite drinks is Sweet Longan Drink with Whole Fruits (page 351).

Recommended Brand: Concord Foodstuffs Dried Seedless Longan

MANGO   *Mamuang*   Mangifera indica

Mangoes grow abundantly in Thailand, with more than 100 varieties available. Many Americans have never tasted mangoes, but they are the most popular fruit worldwide. Southeast Asian people have cultivated them for sixty centuries. When unripe, mango flesh is pale green and very tart and can be used as a vegetable. When ripe, the flesh is yellow-gold and extremely luscious, like a peach but far more heavenly.

NOODLES   *Mee*

BEAN-THREAD VERMICELLI   *Woon sen*

These fine noodles, made from the starch of mung beans, are white when dried but nearly translucent when cooked. Variously called "cellophane noodles" or "silver noodles," they're flavorless and take on the taste of their accompanying sauce or broth. Bean-thread vermicelli is usually sold in bundles of individually wrapped 2-ounce packets.

KHANOM CHINE *Khanom chine*
At the Suan Pakkad Palace, an ancient mural depicting Buddha's last earthly meal shows a woman making these noodles. Made of white-rice flour, they resemble white angel hair pasta. They're made and sold fresh daily in Thailand. In America we substitute Japanese *somen* noodles or angel hair pasta. In several dishes *khanom chine* are whirled into nests and adorned with a curry sauce, condiments, and chopped fresh vegetables.

RICE NOODLES, DRIED *Kwaytiao sen lek, sen jahn, sen mee*
Dried rice noodles come in various shapes and widths. They are sometimes cooked after being softened in water, and sometimes by being dropped directly into hot oil. *Sen lek* and *sen jahn* are thin, flat noodles often called "rice sticks." They're opaque and white and come in a variety of shapes and thicknesses. I prefer to use flat, fettuccinelike rice sticks about ⅛ inch wide for stir-fries like *phat Thai*. This size of noodle is sometimes labeled *chantaboon*. *Sen mee* are very narrow and brittle, like vermicelli. They must be softened before cooking, or else crisp-fried right from the packet—in which case they'll explode into a crispy mass that's perfect for *mee krob*.

RICE NOODLES, FRESH *Kwaytiao*
Sometimes called "fat noodles," these are soft, thick, ribbonlike, chewy noodles made of rice flour. You'll find them in plastic "wet packs," either presliced or in folded sheets that you can cut into wide strips prior to unfolding. When presliced, they are called *sen yai*, which means "big path."

PANDANUS *Toey hom*

The long, slim leaves of this pretty tropical tree are useful both for weaving and for cooking.

PANDANUS ESSENCE *Krin bai toey* Pandanus amaryllifolius
The extract of the pandanus leaf has a sweet, floral quality with a hint of smokiness. It's especially refreshing in drinks, such as Pandanus Leaf Iced Tea (page 350).

PANDANUS LEAF *Bai toey* Pandanus amaryllifolius
Chicken in Pandanus Leaves with Sweet Black Bean Sauce (page 132) is an example of how Thai cooks wrap food in this fragrant leaf during cooking to infuse the dish with its flavor. We also use pandanus as an aromatic herb, placing one or two leaves in a pot of sticky rice before cooking, then removing them before serving the rice. Frozen fresh leaves are sometimes available in Asian markets.

PAPAYA *Malakaw* Carica papaya

There are many varieties of papaya, some growing quite large. Those found in most American markets come from Hawaii and weigh about 1 pound. In Thailand, we eat papayas when they're green and when they're ripe, just like mangoes. Green Papaya Salad (page 245)—shreds of unripe papaya flesh with peanuts and lime juice—is among Thailand's most popular dishes. Ripe papayas are very fragrant, with a mild flavor we sometimes enhance with lime juice.

PEPPERCORNS   *Phrik Thai*   Piper nigrum

Until Europeans introduced chili peppers, peppercorns were the most important hot spice in Thai cooking. Our name for them literally means "Thai pepper." Fresh green peppercorns grow on vines that climb the trunks of coconut palms and other trees. Best when fresh-picked, they are also available bottled and canned. When dried, their husks turn black and they become the black pepper familiar in America. White pepper comes from the largest black peppercorns, with their outer skins removed.

PICKLED CHINESE MUSTARD CABBAGE
Hua pak kad dong

This condiment from the Szechuan province of China, made of mustard cabbage pickled with salt, chilies, and garlic, has found a home in Thai cooking. Thais love its wonderful sour taste, either as a side dish or as a condiment. It is usually sold in 24-ounce jars.

POMELO   *Som o*   Citrus maxima

The largest citrus fruit of all, about the size of a small cantaloupe, the pomelo is the ancestor of the grapefruit. It originated in or near Thailand and grows abundantly in our tropical lowlands. Pomelos appear in Asian markets around January and February. Look for a firm, taut skin and a nice aroma. They're sweeter, less acidic, and more fragrant than grapefruits.

RICE   *Khao*

The most basic ingredient of all, rice is part of nearly every Thai meal.

BROKEN RICE   *Prai khao*
Prized for its ability to absorb liquid quickly, broken rice, added to soups and broths, creates a comforting, nourishing, porridge-like meal.

JASMINE RICE   *Khao hom mali*
The favorite of central and southern Thailand, jasmine rice is white, long-grained, and slightly translucent, with a delicate, flowerlike scent.

STICKY RICE   *Khao niao*
Also called "glutenous rice," sticky rice is usually white and less translucent than **jasmine rice**, with a round, plump grain. Some varieties are black and look like wild rice. Sticky rice is high in gluten, so the cooked grains tend to adhere to one another—convenient

for finger-style eating and for dipping into curries and sauces. The preferred rice of our northern-dwelling people, sticky rice is also used for dessert making throughout Thailand.

SALTED RADISH   *Hua pak kad kem*

Used in soups and stir-fries, these are gold-colored matchstick shreds of radish that have been sun-dried and then cured in salt. They add a salty-sweet flavor and a bit of chewy texture. You will find them packed in cellophane bags, sometimes labeled *preserved turnip*.

SALTY EGGS   *Khai khem*

Before there was refrigeration, Thai people preserved eggs by curing them with a long immersion in heavy brine. The tradition has continued into modern times. Salty eggs are sold both hard-boiled and uncooked in Asian markets. Thais serve them with snacks or in sauces to flavor plain steamed rice. They should not be confused with the Chinese preserved duck eggs known as "thousand-year-old eggs," which are cured by being packed in charcoal ash and do not require cooking.

SHALLOTS   *Hom lek*   Allium ascalonicum

The large onions found in American kitchens adapt well to Thai cooking, but we prefer this milder, smaller, subtler member of the onion family. American markets consider them a specialty item, and price them accordingly. They are less expensive in Asian markets.

SHRIMP PASTE   *Kapi*

This blend of salted and fermented shrimp, sold in little plastic jars, is among the most intense of all Thai ingredients. A small amount of the thick, soft paste, when dry-roasted, adds a fundamental note to nearly all curry-paste recipes.

SHRIMP POWDER WITH CHILI   *Kung phrik pon*

This spice, based on dried shrimp, is sprinkled over various dishes as a condiment, adding protein and crunchiness, along with mild chili heat.

SPRING-ROLL WRAPPERS   *Poh pia*

Found in the frozen-foods section of Asian markets, these are paper-thin 8-inch pastry squares. A 1-pound package holds about twenty-five wrappers. They are sometimes labeled *spring-roll pastry* or *spring-roll skins*.

SRIRACHA CHILI SAUCE   *Sriracha*

Just as genuine Parmesan cheese must come from around Parma, this sweet and hot table condiment, loved throughout Southeast Asia, must come from Sriracha, a seaside village in the south of Thailand. Splash this sauce on any dish you want to accent.

Recommended Brand: There is no English translation of the brand name on the slim, long-necked bottle, but the Thai script looks like *FISSION*.

SWEET BLACK SOY SAUCE   *See-eu wan*

A blend of dark soy sauce and molasses, this sauce provides both sweetness and a wood-toned hue. It's sometimes labeled *Dark Sweet Soy Sauce.*

TAMARIND   *Makham*   Tamarindus indica

Tamarind comes from the long, beanlike fruit of the tamarind tree, which was brought from India to Thailand centuries ago. The indefinable sweet-sour flavor of tamarind is obtained by soaking and straning blocks of tamarind pulp or simply by buying prepared liquid tamarind concentrate. It is the basis of many sauces used to flavor stir-fries and other dishes, such as Royal Son-in-Law Eggs (page 314) and Grilled Catfish with Sweet and Bitter Herbs and Savory Tamarind Sauce (page 198).

Recommended Brand of concentrate: P. Pra Teep Thong (sold in plastic jars)

THAI CHILI POWDER   *Phrik pon*   Capsicum annuum longum

Thailand's favorite dried chili pepper in coarsely ground, dried form is known as *phrik chee fa.* It is full-flavored and lively. All powdered chili peppers lose their spark over time, so buy only the amount you'll be likely to use within two or three months. If you can't find Thai chili powder, substitute New Mexico, or any other lively red chili powder.

THAI COFFEE AND TEA   *Oliang* and *Cha Thai*

Thai people love Western-style coffee, but we seldom let a basic flavor go unspiced. Corn, chicory, rice, sesame seed, and sugar are used to flavor the fine-ground Thai coffee used for Thai Iced Coffee (page 354). We also like to "nudge" tea into a slightly different flavor realm. Powdered tea leaves are mixed with cinnamon, vanilla, and enough food coloring to ensure the rounded flavor and amber-orange color of Thai Iced Tea (page 353).

THAI EGGPLANTS

Eggplants originated in or near Thailand, and we still have more varieties than anyone else, ranging from pea-sized specimens to large globes.

PEA EGGPLANT   *Makbua puang Solanum torvum*
These tiny eggplants are tart and grow in berrylike clusters. We use them in curries and *nam phriks*, spicy dipping sauces.

SMALL ROUND EGGPLANT   *Makbua khun Solanum melogena*
These range from the size of a Ping-Pong ball to the size of a hen's egg, and may be white, pale green, or yellow. We eat them raw with *nam phriks* or cook them in curry dishes.

THAI SOY SAUCE WITH MUSHROOM   *See-eu khao het hom*

The woodsy essence of straw mushrooms is blended with light, thin soy sauce to make this very useful condiment. A few dashes add a wonderful depth of flavor to a simple broth or vegetarian stir-fry.

Recommended Brand: Healthy Boy

THAI THIN SOY SAUCE   *See-eu khao*

Light in color, neither thick nor sweet, thin soy sauce is wonderfully subtle in flavor. Substitute any good light soy sauce, but not so-called lite or low-sodium soy sauce.

TOASTED RICE POWDER   *Khao kua pon*

This is a traditional ingredient in the country-style salads of the northeastern provinces. It is made by dry-roasting grains of uncooked rice until they develop a nutty, golden color, then grinding them to a coarse, crunchy powder (page 63).

TOFU   *Tao hoo*

Americans are becoming more aware of this high-protein, cholesterol-free, easy-to-digest soybean product. Tofu—also known as bean curd—has been loved in Asia for more than two thousand years. There are several varieties, each with a slightly different texture or flavor.

DEEP-FRIED TOFU
Cut into small cubes and deep-fried, tofu puffs up into tasty yellow-gold pillows. Sold ready-made in the refrigerator sections of Asian markets, the cubes are about 1½ inches across. They are often used in vegetarian cooking. You can also make your own deep-fried tofu, as in Home-Fried Tofu Squares with Savory Tamarind Sauce (page 269).

FIRM, PRESSED, and SOFT TOFU

Weights placed on fresh tofu squeeze out moisture. Depending on the amount of weight, and how long it is applied, the tofu becomes "firm" (about the consistency of fresh mozzarella), "pressed" (compact cakes), or "soft" (somewhat custardlike).

RED TOFU

Small cakes of tofu, pickled in a red-hued vinegar, come in jars and are sometimes labeled *preserved bean curd (red)*. They are an essential part of a wonderful soup dish known as *yen ta fo* (page 294).

SAVORY BAKED TOFU

Firm cakes of tofu, processed with soy sauce, develop a savory brown coating, contrasting with the white interior. Sliced into matchsticks, they are perfect for stir-fries.

WATER SPINACH   *Pak bung*   Ipomoea aquatica tetrogonolobus

With all its waterways, Thailand produces a great deal of this very nutritious leafy green vine. It's related to morning glory vine, not to spinach, but its taste is similar to spinach. When stir-fried, the soft, arrowhead-shaped leaves contrast nicely with the crunchy, hollow stems. Water spinach is sometimes called "morning glory vine" or "swamp cabbage."

WINGED BEANS   *Tua phu*   Psophocarpus tetrogonolobus

Winged beans are the long legumes of a climbing plant. They vary in length from about 3 inches to 1 foot and have four frilly-edged wings running their full length. Like green beans, they can be eaten raw or cooked, by themselves or in various salads and other dishes. They have a delicate flavor, similar to asparagus, and are sometimes called "asparagus peas." You can substitute green beans, but winged beans will give your dishes a showy and exotic appearance.

WONTON WRAPPERS

These are very thin sheets of dough, about 3½ inches square, sold in 1-pound packets. They are used for dumplings as well as wontons. (See, for example, Tropical-Fruit Wontons with Green Peppercorns, page 259, and Steamed Dumplings with Minced Chicken and Shrimp, page 277).

YARD-LONG BEANS   *Tua fak yao*   Vigna sinensis

Darker than green beans, and slightly stronger tasting, yard-long beans really do grow as long as 3 feet, though most you'll find in the market are about half that long. Probably the most popular bean in Thai cooking, they hold up well in curries, stews, and other dishes with long cooking times. They are also called "Chinese long beans." Look for fresh, plump beans with a crisp snap.

YELLOW BEAN SAUCE, CRUSHED   *Tao jiew dam*

Sometimes called "brown bean sauce," this condiment—usually found in tall, long-necked bottles—gives dishes an earthy background flavor. It's made by salting and fermenting split and crushed soybeans.

YELLOW BEAN SAUCE, WHOLE   *Tao jiew khao*

Usually packed in jars, this sauce is made of fermented whole soybeans. It is sometimes labeled *white bean sauce,* or *yellow bean sauce.*

EQUIPMENT FOR THAI COOKING

About five years ago, after being absent from my homeland for nearly twenty years, I made my first return visit. So many aspects of daily life had changed. One of the most striking changes was in household kitchens. The ones I knew as a boy had only the most elementary equipment. Thai kitchens of today, by comparison, are richly equipped with conveniences. Still, the style of cooking remained very much the same as the one I had learned so many years before.

However complex its flavors may be, Thai cuisine evolved in simplicity. Knives, simple cookware, and a one-burner charcoal stove are practically all a Thai cook ever really needs. Chances are, your own kitchen is already equipped with most of what you'll require for every recipe in this book.

My advice: Don't be overly fussy about equipment. Use whatever leaves you free to concentrate on the food itself.

The key pieces, in alphabetical order, include:

BARBECUE GRILL, OR STOVETOP GRILL

Although these are really optional, there will be times when you cherish the added smokiness and flavor of grilling. Inexpensive stovetop grills are just big enough for certain jobs, such as quickly grilling a half pound of shrimp or sliced beef tenderloin. If you have no grill, use your oven's broiler.

BLENDER

Though not a necessity, a blender will help you enormously with salad dressings, fruit drinks, and many other recipes.

FOOD PROCESSOR

I use these wonderful machines frequently, especially when making curry pastes. Sometimes I crush ingredients lightly using a mortar and pestle, then let the food processor complete the job of reducing them to creamy smoothness. Occasionally, the small type of food processor known as a "mini-chop" will be just right for the task at hand. For example, just a few quick pulses in a mini-chop will help you make perfect Golden Garlic (page 65).

FRYING PAN

Almost any large, heavy frying pan can successfully take the place of a wok. Cast-iron skillets work particularly well. They can be preheated, just like woks. You can use a small one for dry-frying spices and coconut flakes and a large one for stir-frying and shallow-frying.

KNIVES

Don't frustrate yourself by trying to work with poor-quality knives. Equip your kitchen with a high-quality chef's knife and cleaver.

MORTAR AND PESTLE

When I flew to America at the age of twenty, I carried a large stone mortar and pestle on my lap all the way across the Pacific Ocean. I still use that mortar and pestle today. For bringing out the full flavors of garlic, cilantro, lemon grass, pepper, and many other spices, it's simply the best tool available. Instead of slicing something to small bits, a mortar and pestle crushes its cell walls and releases all the flavorful essences within. Their aromas suffuse your kitchen, and their flavors blend into your recipe more quickly and subtly.

I prefer a stone mortar and pestle for durability and for ease of cleaning. You'll find them at Thai markets. Buy one at least 8 inches wide—the larger the better. A heavy pestle actually makes the work easier, minimizing the force you need to apply.

RICE COOKER

Of all the modern conveniences that have arrived in Thai kitchens in recent years, the most popular by far is the electric rice pot. Any large saucepan with a tight-fitting lid can be used to cook rice, but these appliances make it so convenient. Once you've measured your water and rice and flipped the "on" switch, there's nothing more you need to worry about. Asian groceries and cookware stores have rice cookers in a variety of sizes, at reasonable prices. They last through years of steady use.

SAUCEPAN

What you call a saucepan I think of as a curry pot. The 4-quart size is good for most uses.

STEAMER

Steaming is the most healthful cooking method of all. The little fold-out steaming baskets found in many American kitchens are too small for Thai cookery. Get a tiered aluminum steamer (available in Thai markets or by mail order) equipped with a large base pot and a high-domed lid, with racks big enough to hold at least a medium-sized fish. Bamboo steamers are hard to clean, unless you always put the food on plates while steaming it. I've given Thai-style steamers to many American friends, who've found that they become among the most useful items in their kitchen.

WOK

Because Thai cuisine evolved from a tradition of stovetop cooking, the most-used implement is the wok. The small bottom and sloping sides of a wok distribute heat evenly and let you cook with less oil. The high sides are also perfect for stir-frying.

Many Asian chefs will use only carbon-steel woks that have been carefully seasoned. But you have to use a wok like that almost every day to keep it in good shape. I think almost any wok—steel or brass, nonstick or plain—can do a fine job. I'm partial to large woks, at least 14 inches in diameter, with nonstick finishes. They're great for the easy handling of crêpes, omelets, and similar dishes. They're deep enough for deep-frying, and they hold lots of vegetables for a family-size stir-fry. And—if you tend to them reasonably soon after cooking—they clean up nicely with just hot water and a soft scrubbing pad. Whatever size or type of wok you use, warm it on the burner first, then drizzle your cooking oil down the sides. Let the oil get nice and hot before adding your next ingredient, but never allow the oil to overheat and smoke. That would add a bitter flavor to your dish.

MISCELLANEOUS IMPLEMENTS

A *wire skimmer* is invaluable when you're blanching vegetables or retrieving food from a deep-fryer. These skimmers usually have a bamboo handle and a flattened, wide-open wire spoon bowl, designed to let hot oil or water drain quickly away.

Kitchen shears are useful when you want to cut lime leaves or other herbs into slivers.

For homemade sausages, you'll want a *pastry bag* and *tips.*

Bamboo skewers are needed for satays and other grilled entrées.

A sock-like *Thai coffee and tea strainer* is useful for making various kinds of steeped brews.

You may want a *candy thermometer* to ensure the right oil temperature for deep-frying.

The kind of soup server sometimes called a *Mongolian hot pot*, which features a central chimney and is designed to be placed over a heat source, allows you to enjoy warm soup throughout a meal.

GLOSSARY OF THAI FOOD TERMS

Some of the phrases Thai people use to describe food are sweetly poetic. For example, when shrimp is at its very freshest, we call it *kung ten,* which means "dancing shrimp." *Laab,* the name of a salad featuring minced, cooked meat and crushed, toasted rice, literally means "good fortune." But many ingredients and recipes are named literally. *Nam pla,* the thin sauce made from fish, is a combination of *nam* ("water") and *pla* ("fish").

As you see from the above example, in Thai the modifier comes after the noun it modifies. For example, baby ginger is *khing* ("ginger") *on* ("young"). Beef Stir-Fried with Baby Ginger is *neua* ("beef") *phat* ("stir-fried") *khing on.*

The facing page glossary will help you understand the names of many other Thai ingredients and recipes.

LANGUAGE NOTES

You may already have noticed, on visiting different Thai restaurants, that a favorite dish will be spelled very differently on different menus. *Mee krob,* the popular crispy and sweet noodle dish, might be spelled *mee grob. Tom yum kung,* the spicy shrimp soup, may be spelled several different ways, including *dom yum goong.*

The Thai language is a member of the same linguistic family as Chinese. Like Chinese, it is a tonal language with many different dialects.

The Thai alphabet is traditionally written with a script form that originated in southern India. Changing Thai words over to English-language letters, a process called transliteration, is not an exact science. That's why different menus, and different books, often employ vastly different spellings.

In transliterating Thai words for this book, we've tried to make it easy for you to pronounce them as closely as possible to the way a native speaker would.

Just a bit of explanation may be needed:

When a consonant is followed by the letter *h,* give that consonant its normal sound, with a slight, soft breathiness after. That's why *Thailand* sounds like *tie-land* and not *thigh-land.* Similarly, *phat,* the first word in the name of the popular noodle dish called *phat Thai,* is pronounced much like *pot.*

Vowels are pronounced as follows: *a,* as in *raw; ae,* as in *gang; e,* as in *lend; i,* as the double *e* in *green; o,* as in *flow; u,* as in *cut.*

Overall, Thai tends toward a pleasing, soft sound.

THAI	ENGLISH	THAI	ENGLISH
ahan	food	*nam phrik*	spicy dipping sauce; literally "water pepper"
ahan talay	seafood		
bai	leaf	*nam pla*	Thai fish sauce
dom	boiled	*nam som*	vinegar; literally "water sour"
dong	pickled		
haeng	dried	*neua*	beef
het	mushroom	*on*	young, baby
hom daeng, hom lek	shallot; literally "onion red" or "onion little"	*pak*	leafy greens
		pak chee	cilantro
kaeng	liquid, as in a curry or soup	*phat*	stir-fried
		phet	spicy
kai	chicken	*phrik*	pepper
kha	galanga, Siamese ginger	*phrik khee nu*	small Thai chili
		phrik Thai	black pepper
khai	egg	*piew*	peel
khao	rice	*pla*	fish
khao niao	sticky rice	*pu*	crab
khao phod	corn	*sod sai*	stuffed
khing	ginger	*som*	orange, sour
kluay	banana	*supparod*	pineapple
krachai	lesser Siamese ginger	*takrai*	lemon grass
		thaeng kwa	cucumber
kratiem	garlic	*tom*	boiling
krob	crispy	*tum*	pounding with a mortar and pestle
kung	shrimp		
kwaytiao	fresh rice noodle	*wan*	sweet
magroot	Kaffir lime	*yai*	large, wide
makham	tamarind	*yam*	salad; literally "to mix with the hands"
mamuang	mango		
manao	lime		
maprao	coconut	*yang*	roasted, grilled
mu	pork		
nam	water		

Ingredients and Equipment

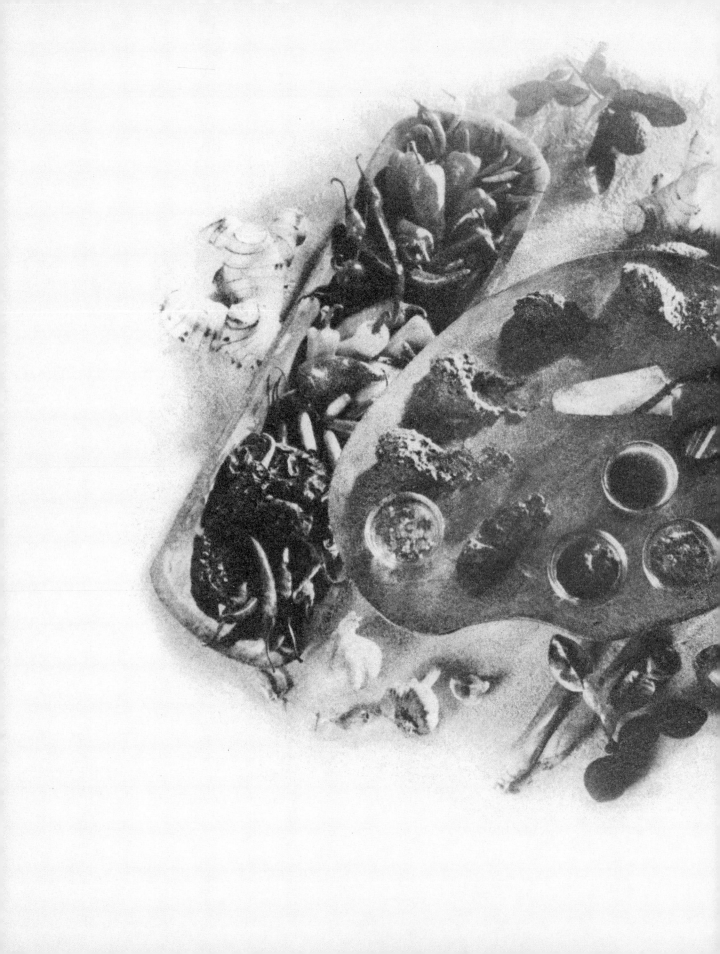

CURRY PASTES, SAUCES, and CONDIMENTS

Kaeng Phed, Nam Phrik, leh Kreung Prung Ahan Bontho

My earliest kitchen memory is the afternoon my mother let me stand on a stool to help prepare a fresh curry paste. I was so small that I had to wrap one arm around the bowl of our stone mortar as I thumped its pestle on the heady mix of chili peppers and spices. But I felt very grown up to be trusted with such important work.

Curry pastes, sauces, and condiments are the building blocks of Thai cooking. They're like money in the bank—rich flavors you can draw upon to make quickly prepared dishes taste like something that took many hours to produce.

Recipes throughout the book will call upon the curry pastes, sauces, and condiments you'll learn about in this chapter. Many of these concoctions can be bought in ready-made form, but Thai cooks take great pride in creating their own—which are always fresher, more aromatic, and more satisfying than any taken from a store's shelves.

Thai curry pastes are moist, intense blends of chilies and other fresh ingredients, mostly herbal, such as lemon grass, Kaffir lime, ginger, cilantro stems, garlic, and shallots. The ingredients vary remarkably little from recipe to recipe, but altering the proportions can create great differences in taste.

The flavors of these curry pastes infuse a dish instantly. Mixed with coconut milk or broth, then combined with meat, fish, or vegetables, they create some of the most distinctive and sensual dishes in Thai cuisine.

We classify our curry pastes by their colors, which range from brick red to goldenrod yellow to soft green, and by their usage. Some, like Classic Red Curry Paste, can be found in a great many dishes. Others are specialized, used in only one dish or with one particular type of main ingredient, such as gingery Chu Chee Curry, which accompanies only fish and seafood.

You'll find a dozen curry pastes in this chapter, representing a wide spectrum of colors and flavors. But these are really just a beginning. There are dozens more within the Thai tradition.

Refrigerated or frozen, most homemade curry pastes will last for weeks or months. They take some effort to make, but every time you concoct a rich, multi-flavored curry dish in just minutes, you'll know that your effort has been well rewarded.

Sauces and condiments are simpler preparations, but they are just as versatile and useful. They let your family and guests customize the dishes before them, adding exactly the degree of piquancy, sweetness, or savor they desire. Some sauces and condiments have multiple uses—as dipping sauces, as toppings, and as the centerpieces of a meal.

Toasted Coconut is sprinkled over savory and sweet dishes, from salads to ice cream. Chili-Tamarind Paste, known as *nam phrik pao*, can be used as a seasoning in soups, stir-fries, and salad dressings and can be spread on rice cakes or toast points. Golden Garlic and Crispy Shallots are toppings that can accent scores of dishes.

Finally, there is a family of sauces that come very close to being complete meals in themselves. These are the *nam phriks*, assertively flavored dipping sauces that are eaten in millions of Thai homes every day, by everyone from prosperous Bangkok professionals to mountain-dwelling villagers. Served alongside platters of raw or steamed vegetables, sometimes with pieces of fried fish, and always with lots of rice, they provide a very low-fat meal with exceptional nutrition.

The three *nam phrik* meals I've included in this chapter are typical of the everyday favorites of Thai people. Classic Shrimp Paste–and–Chili Sauce, *nam phrik kapi*, is the one I grew up on. Every family has a version of this simple, pungent sauce based on roasted shrimp paste. *Nam phrik ong*, Country-Style Tomato Sauce with Ground Pork and Red Curry, is like a moderately spicy, decidedly flavorful *chili con carne*. The more unfamiliar taste of pickled fish punctuates a fiery regional specialty called *nam phrik het*, Issan-Style Spicy Mushroom Sauce.

This chapter will bring new depths of flavor and spice to your cooking. I guarantee that you'll feel, as I did on the day I made my first curry paste, that you've taken a wonderful step forward as a cook.

A FEW WORDS ON
MAKING CURRY PASTES

The first recipe I teach in my cooking classes is Classic Red Curry Paste. I always make it in the great stone mortar I carried on my lap on the flight that brought me to America more than twenty years ago. When the rhythmic pounding begins, the aromatic essences of the spices are released instantly and permeate the room. My students always respond enthusiastically to this seemingly magical process. Many of them troop off eagerly to a nearby Thai market right after class to buy their own mortars and pestles.

Making curry pastes this old-fashioned way is a sensual, satisfying experience. If you'd like to try it, here are a few guidelines: First, grind any whole or dried spices, such as coriander seed or peppercorns. Next, add the fibrous herbs and spices, such as fresh lemon grass, ginger, and Kaffir lime peel. When these are thoroughly pulverized and blended, add the tender herbs and spices, such as garlic and soaked dried chilies. Scrape down the sides of the mortar occasionally with the pestle, and continue grinding and pounding until a moist paste begins to form. Lastly, add the roasted shrimp paste (if called for) and grind with the pestle to create a smooth, moist paste.

Quite often, however, I'll use both a mortar and pestle and a food processor to make curry pastes.

The mortar and pestle are simply unequaled for crushing and pulverizing herbs and spices like ginger root, cilantro stems, and lemon grass, while the food processor makes quick work of blending the myriad ingredients into a moist paste. (A little of the chili-soaking liquid should be reserved to ease the blending in the food processor.)

This is the method I've given in my recipes. It yields a quickly made, yet fragrant, smooth paste in the best Thai tradition.

If your modern kitchen doesn't yet include a big stone mortar, you can still make wonderful homemade Thai curry pastes. Use a spice mill or mini-chop food processor to grind the whole or dried spices. Combine them with the rest of the ingredients in a food processor. Spoon in as much of the chili-soaking liquid as needed to ease the grinding.

If you have a complement of curry pastes in the freezer to draw upon, you'll always be ready to create a complexly flavored gourmet Thai meal in a very short time.

One cup of paste is the usual requirement for a curry dinner for six. You can easily double the recipes and freeze some curry paste for a later meal. If you do, freeze the extra paste in 1-cup portions.

CLASSIC RED CURRY PASTE

Krung Kaeng Phed

Makes about 1½ cups

P rized for its depth of flavor and great versatility, this is the most basic and widely used Thai curry paste. It's also among the hottest, even though filled with aromatics such as lemon grass and Kaffir lime peel. We use red curry in chicken, duck, beef, and pork dishes, with all manner of seafood, and in soupy noodle curries as well as in dips, sauces, and marinades.

1 package (3 ounces) dried red New Mexico chilies

12 small dried Japanese chilies

1 tablespoon whole coriander seed

1½ tablespoons shrimp paste (*kapi*), wrapped neatly in a double layer of aluminum foil

¾ cup chopped shallots

½ cup peeled whole garlic cloves

½ tablespoon minced fresh Kaffir lime peel or domestic lime peel

2 large stalks lemon grass, tough outer leaves discarded, lower stalks trimmed to 3 inches and finely sliced

⅓ cup finely chopped, peeled fresh Siamese ginger (galanga or *kha*) or common ginger

With kitchen shears or a chef's knife, stem the New Mexico chilies and shake out most of the seeds. Cut the chilies in half lengthwise and remove any tough, dried ribs. Cut crosswise into ¾-inch pieces and put them in a bowl. Stem the Japanese chilies, shake out most of the seeds, and cut them into small pieces. Put them in the bowl with the New Mexico chilies. Add water to cover and soak the chilies for 30 minutes.

Meanwhile, dry-roast the coriander seed in a small skillet over medium heat for 3 to 5 minutes, until toasty and aromatic, shaking the pan often to prevent burning. Transfer the coriander seed to a small bowl and set aside to cool.

Set the skillet back over medium heat. Place the foil-wrapped shrimp paste in the skillet and cook for about 5 minutes, until aromatic, turning the packet over once or twice. Remove the packet from the skillet and set it aside to cool.

Combine the shallots and garlic in the skillet and dry-roast over medium heat until tender and slightly browned, about 5 minutes, stirring often. Remove from the heat and set aside to cool.

Put the roasted coriander seed in a large, heavy mortar and grind to a powder. Transfer the ground coriander to the bowl of a food processor fitted with a metal blade.

Combine the minced lime peel, lemon grass, and ginger in the mortar and pound for a minute or so to break down the fibers. Transfer the crushed mixture to the food processor.

Pound the roasted shallots and garlic in the mortar just until crushed and transfer them to the food processor.

Unwrap the shrimp paste and add it to the food processor.

Drain the chilies, reserving about ½ cup of the soaking liquid. Add the chilies to the food processor.

Process the ingredients until a rich, moist paste forms. Stop occasionally to scrape down the sides of the work bowl. Add a few tablespoons of the chili-soaking liquid now and then, if needed, to ease the grinding.

This paste can be stored in an airtight container in the refrigerator for 1 month, or in the freezer for up to 3 months.

Curry
Pastes,
Sauces, and
Condiments

FRESH GREEN CHILI CURRY PASTE

Krung Kaeng Khiew Wan

Makes about 2 cups

The queen of all curry pastes, this is sublimely herbal, complex, and sensual in flavor, a deceptively cool-appearing, delicate jade green in color, and at the same time almost the hottest curry preparation of all.

½ tablespoon whole coriander seed

½ teaspoon whole anise seed

1½ tablespoons shrimp paste (*kapi*), wrapped neatly in a double layer of aluminum foil

12 whole white peppercorns

2½ teaspoons minced fresh Kaffir lime peel or domestic lime peel

⅓ cup chopped cilantro stems

2 stalks lemon grass, tough outer leaves discarded, lower stalk trimmed to 3 inches and finely sliced

⅓ cup finely chopped, peeled fresh Siamese ginger (galanga or *kha*) or common ginger

¼ cup chopped garlic

1 cup chopped shallots

½ cup sliced green serrano chilies (about 16)

6 ounces fresh lettuce (about 6 large leaves of romaine, for example), with good green color

Dry-roast the coriander and anise seeds in a small skillet over medium heat for 3 to 5 minutes, until toasty and aromatic, shaking the pan often to prevent burning. Transfer the roasted seeds to a small bowl and set aside to cool.

Set the skillet back over medium heat. Place the foil-wrapped shrimp paste in the skillet and cook for about 5 minutes, until aromatic, turning the packet over once or twice. Remove the packet from the skillet and set it aside to cool.

Put the roasted seeds and the peppercorns in a large, heavy mortar and grind to a powder. Transfer the ground spices to the bowl of a food processor fitted with a metal blade.

Combine the minced lime peel, cilantro stems, lemon grass, and ginger in the mortar and pound for a minute or so to break down the fibers. Transfer the crushed mixture to the food processor.

Pound the garlic and shallots in the mortar just until crushed and transfer them to the food processor.

Unwrap the shrimp paste and add it to the processor with the green chilies.

Rinse the lettuce, shaking off the excess moisture. Roughly tear the leaves into pieces and add them to the food processor.

Process the ingredients until a rich, moist paste forms, stopping occasionally to scrape down the sides of the work bowl.

This paste can be stored in an airtight container in the refrigerator for 1 week, or in the freezer for up to 1 month.

Curry
Pastes,
Sauces, and
Condiments

YELLOW CURRY PASTE

Krung Kaeng Kari

Makes about 1 cup

This curry paste is closest in taste and color to what Westerners think of when they hear the word *curry*. That's because this mellow, sweetly spiced paste is based on Indian-style seasonings: turmeric and mild yellow curry powder. But even though this paste shows the influence of our neighbor across the Bay of Bengal, it also carries a distinct Thai identity in its lemon grass, shrimp paste, dried red chilies, and shallots.

Thai people especially love this curry paste with chicken, onions, and potatoes, as in Yellow Chicken Curry with Spicy Cucumber Relish (page 124).

1 package (3 ounces) dried red California chilies

1 tablespoon whole coriander seed

1 tablespoon whole cumin seed

1½ tablespoons shrimp paste (*kapi*), wrapped neatly in a double layer of aluminum foil

3 tablespoons curry powder

2 tablespoons ground turmeric

2 stalks lemon grass, tough outer leaves discarded, lower stalks trimmed to 3 inches and finely sliced

2 tablespoons finely chopped, peeled fresh ginger

2 tablespoons chopped garlic

⅓ cup chopped shallots

With kitchen shears or a chef's knife, stem the chilies and shake out most of the seeds. Cut the chilies in half lengthwise and remove any tough, dried ribs. Cut them crosswise into ¾-inch pieces and put them in a bowl. Add water to cover and soak for 30 minutes.

Meanwhile, dry-roast the coriander and cumin seeds in a small skillet over medium heat for 3 to 5 minutes, until toasty and aromatic, shaking the pan often to prevent burning. Transfer the roasted spices to a small bowl and set aside to cool.

Set the skillet back over medium heat. Place the foil-wrapped shrimp paste in the skillet and cook for about 5 minutes, until aromatic, turning the packet over once or twice. Remove the packet from the skillet and set aside to cool.

Put the roasted spices, curry powder, and turmeric in a large, heavy mortar and grind to a powder. Transfer the ground spices to the bowl of a food processor fitted with a metal blade.

Put the lemon grass and ginger in the mortar and pound a minute or so to break down the fibers. Transfer the crushed mixture to the food processor.

Pound the garlic and shallots in a mortar just until crushed and transfer them to the food processor.

Unwrap the shrimp paste and add it to the food processor.

Drain the chilies, reserving about ½ cup of the soaking liquid. Add the chilies to the food processor.

Process the ingredients until a rich, moist paste forms, stopping occasionally to scrape down the sides of the work bowl. Add a few tablespoons of the chili-soaking liquid now and then, if needed, to ease the grinding.

This paste can be stored in an airtight container in the refrigerator for 1 month, or in the freezer for up to 3 months.

Curry
Pastes,
Sauces, and
Condiments

PANANG CURRY PASTE

Krung Kaeng Panang

Makes about 1²/₃ cups

P anang is an island off the west coast of Malaysia in the Strait of Malacca, just
south of Thailand. Although this paste derives its name from another country,
it's a perfect example of what Thai cooks aspire to—many distinctive flavors held in
a beautiful balance, with no single taste predominating.

A Panang curry dish will be moderate in heat and will often contain crushed
peanuts, which are very popular in Malaysian cooking.

1 package (3 ounces) dried red New
Mexico chilies

1 tablespoon plus 1 teaspoon whole
coriander seed

2 tablespoons shrimp paste (*kapi*),
wrapped neatly in a double layer of
aluminum foil

2 fresh Kaffir limes (*magroot*), or 1 small
domestic lime

10 (5 pairs) fresh Kaffir lime leaves (*bai
magroot*), or ½ teaspoon grated
lime zest

2½ tablespoons chopped cilantro,
including the stems

1 large stalk lemon grass, tough outer
leaves discarded, lower stalk trimmed
to 3 inches and finely sliced

2 tablespoons finely chopped, peeled
fresh Siamese ginger (galanga or *kha*)
or common ginger

⅓ cup chopped garlic

⅓ cup chopped shallots

With kitchen shears or a chef's knife, stem the chilies and shake out most of the
seeds. Cut the chilies in half lengthwise and remove any tough, dried ribs. Cut them
crosswise into ¾-inch pieces and put them in a bowl. Add water to cover and soak
for 30 minutes.

Meanwhile, dry-roast the coriander seed in a small skillet over medium heat for
3 to 5 minutes, until toasty and aromatic, shaking the pan often to prevent burning.
Transfer the coriander seed to a small bowl and set aside to cool.

Set the skillet back over medium heat. Place the foil-wrapped shrimp paste in the
skillet and cook for about 5 minutes, until aromatic, turning the packet over once or
twice. Remove the packet from the skillet and set it aside to cool.

Put the roasted coriander seed in a large, heavy mortar and grind to a powder.
Transfer the ground coriander to the bowl of a food processor fitted with a metal
blade.

Peel the Kaffir limes. Mince the peel and set aside.

If using fresh Kaffir lime leaves, stack them and cut them into fine slivers with kitchen shears or a sharp knife.

Combine the minced lime peel, lime leaves, cilantro, lemon grass, and ginger in the mortar and pound for a minute or so to break down the fibers. Transfer the crushed mixture to the food processor.

Pound the garlic and shallots in the mortar just until crushed and transfer them to the food processor.

Unwrap the shrimp paste and add it to the food processor.

Drain the chilies, reserving about ½ cup of the soaking liquid. Add the chilies to the food processor.

Process the ingredients until a rich, moist paste forms, stopping occasionally to scrape down the sides of the work bowl. Add a few tablespoons of the chili-soaking liquid now and then, if needed, to ease the grinding.

This paste can be stored in an airtight container
in the refrigerator for 1 month,
or in the freezer for up to 3 months.

Curry
Pastes,
Sauces, and
Condiments

PHRIK KHING CURRY PASTE, COUNTRY STYLE

Nam Phrik Khing, Chow Na

Makes about 1¼ cups

───────────

This paste is used to make what are called "dry-style curries." Instead of being blended into a creamy sauce with coconut milk, dry curries are just barely liquefied with a bit of chicken stock.

A *phrik khing* curry sauce features a smooth, peppery taste and concentrated flavor that's especially good with pork, chicken, and fried fish.

Pork cracklings, crushed and blended into the paste, give this recipe its country identity. They add a bit of flavor and a lot of texture. Omit them, and you've made Phrik Khing Curry Paste, Bangkok Style.

6 large dried red Guajillo chilies

I teaspoon shrimp paste (*kapi*), wrapped neatly in a double layer of aluminum foil

I teaspoon whole black peppercorns

½ teaspoon salt

½ tablespoon minced fresh Kaffir lime peel or domestic lime peel

I large stalk lemon grass, tough outer leaves discarded, lower stalk trimmed to 3 inches and finely sliced

1½ teaspoons finely chopped, peeled fresh Siamese ginger (galanga or *kha*) or common ginger

¼ cup chopped garlic

½ cup chopped shallots

I small package (2½ ounces) pork cracklings (optional)

With kitchen shears or a chef's knife, stem the chilies and shake out most of the seeds. Cut the chilies in half lengthwise and remove any tough, dried ribs. Cut them crosswise into ¾-inch pieces and put them in a bowl. Add water to cover and soak for 30 minutes.

Meanwhile, set a small skillet over medium heat. Place the foil-wrapped shrimp paste in the skillet and cook for about 5 minutes, until aromatic, turning the packet over once or twice. Remove the packet from the skillet and set it aside to cool.

Put the peppercorns in a large, heavy mortar and grind them to a powder. Transfer the ground pepper to the bowl of a food processor fitted with a metal blade. Add the salt.

Combine the minced lime peel, lemon grass, and ginger in the mortar and pound for a minute or so to break down the fibers. Transfer the crushed mixture to the food processor.

Pound the garlic and shallots in the mortar just until crushed and transfer them to the food processor.

Unwrap the shrimp paste and add it to the food processor.

If using the pork cracklings, crush them with the pestle and add them to the food processor.

Drain the chilies, reserving about ½ cup of the soaking liquid. Add the chilies to the food processor.

Process the ingredients until a rich, moist paste forms, stopping occasionally to scrape down the sides of the work bowl. Add a few tablespoons of the chili-soaking liquid now and then, if needed, to ease the grinding.

This paste can be stored in an airtight container in the refrigerator for 1 month, or in the freezer for up to 3 months.

Curry
Pastes,
Sauces, and
Condiments

MASSAMAN CURRY PASTE

Krung Kaeng Massaman

Makes about 1½ cups

This rich, mild curry paste gets its name from the Muslim people of southern Thailand. Its exotic perfume comes from sweetly fragrant spices such as cloves, cardamom, and cinnamon. Thai cooks use this paste in hearty stewlike dishes and as the principal ingredient of Curried Peanut Satay Sauce (page 55), the dipping sauce for grilled meat satays.

1 package (3 ounces) dried red California chilies

2 cardamom pods, husked

1¼ teaspoons whole cumin seed

1½ tablespoons whole coriander seed

1½ teaspoons shrimp paste (*kapi*), wrapped neatly in a double layer of aluminum foil

¼ teaspoon whole black peppercorns

2 whole cloves

¼ teaspoon ground cinnamon

1 large stalk lemon grass, tough outer leaves discarded, lower stalk trimmed to 3 inches and finely sliced

1 tablespoon finely chopped, peeled fresh Siamese ginger (galanga or *kha*) or common ginger

¼ cup chopped garlic

⅓ cup chopped shallots

With kitchen shears or a chef's knife, stem the chilies and shake out most of the seeds. Cut the chilies in half lengthwise and remove any tough, dried ribs. Cut them crosswise into ¾-inch pieces and put them in a bowl. Add water to cover and soak for 30 minutes.

Meanwhile, combine the cardamom, cumin, and coriander seeds in a small skillet. Dry-roast the spices over medium heat for 3 to 5 minutes, until toasty and aromatic, shaking the pan often to prevent burning. Transfer the spices to a small bowl and set aside to cool.

Set the skillet back over medium heat. Place the foil-wrapped shrimp paste in the skillet and cook for about 5 minutes, until aromatic, turning the packet over once or twice. Remove the packet from the skillet and set it aside to cool.

Combine the peppercorns, cloves, cinnamon, and the roasted spices in a large, heavy mortar and grind to a powder. Transfer the ground spices to the bowl of a food processor fitted with a metal blade.

Put the lemon grass and ginger in the mortar and pound for a few minutes to break down the fibers. Transfer the crushed mixture to the food processor.

Pound the garlic and shallots in the mortar just until crushed and transfer them to the food processor.

Unwrap the shrimp paste and add it to the food processor.

Drain the chilies, reserving about ½ cup of the soaking liquid. Add the chilies to the food processor.

Process the ingredients until a rich, moist paste forms, stoping occasionally to scrape down the sides of the work bowl. Add a few tablespoons of the chili-soaking liquid now and then, if needed, to ease the grinding.

This paste can be stored in an airtight container in the refrigerator for 1 month, or in the freezer for up to 3 months.

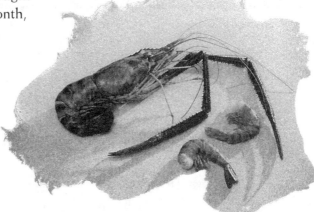

Curry
Pastes,
Sauces, and
Condiments

SOUR CURRY PASTE

Krung Kaeng Som

Makes about ¾ cup

---

*S*om has two meanings: "orange" and "sour."

This curry paste is orange in color but isn't really sour. However, it is traditionally combined with tart ingredients such as tamarind sauce or vinegar so that the finished dish has the pleasingly sour tang that's the hallmark of a fine *kaeng som*.

This paste is used primarily in seafood soups and soupy fish curries such as Curried Tamarind-Shrimp Soup (page 75) or Steamed Swordfish with Sour Curry and Yard-Long Beans (page 162). It is one of the simplest curry pastes to prepare.

5 large dried red New Mexico chilies	½ teaspoon salt
1 teaspoon shrimp paste (*kapi*), wrapped neatly in a double layer of aluminum foil	2½ tablespoons chopped garlic
3 medium shrimp	½ cup chopped shallots

With kitchen shears or a chef's knife, stem the chilies and shake out most of the seeds. Cut the chilies in half lengthwise and remove any tough, dried ribs. Cut them crosswise into ¾-inch pieces and put them in a bowl. Add water to cover and soak for 30 minutes.

Meanwhile, set a small skillet over medium heat. Place the foil-wrapped shrimp paste in the skillet and cook for about 5 minutes, until aromatic, turning the packet over once or twice. Remove the packet from the skillet and set it aside to cool.

Clean and peel the shrimp. Fill a small saucepan with lightly salted water and bring to a boil. Add the shrimp. Cook for 1 minute, then drain. Chop the shrimp into small dice and set aside.

Drain the chilies, reserving about ½ cup of the soaking liquid.

Work the ingredients to a paste using a mortar and pestle or food processor:

Mortar-and-pestle method: Pound the chilies with the salt until mashed. Unwrap the shrimp paste and add it to the mortar with the diced shrimp, garlic, and shallots. Pound for several minutes to make a moist, well-mixed paste.

Processor method: Combine and process all the ingredients until a moist, nearly smooth paste forms. Scrape down the sides of the work bowl now and then, and add a few tablespoons of the chili-soaking liquid, if needed, to ease the grinding.

This paste can be stored in an airtight container for 1 week, or in the freezer for up to 1 month.

RED CURRY PASTE, SOUTHERN STYLE

Krung Kaeng Phed, Meng Dai

Makes about 1 cup

Southern Thai cooking is often blazingly hot, but this curry paste is mild and aromatic, featuring only a handful of chilies. When it's mixed with coconut milk, a pretty red-orange color emerges.

With its short list of ingredients, this moderately spicy curry paste is among the easiest to make.

3 large dried red Guajillo chilies

5 small dried Japanese chilies

2 stalks lemon grass, tough outer leaves discarded, lower stalks trimmed to 3 inches and finely sliced

3 tablespoons finely chopped, peeled fresh Siamese ginger (galanga or *kha*) or common ginger

1½ tablespoons chopped garlic

½ cup chopped shallots

2 tablespoons ground turmeric

With kitchen shears or a chef's knife, stem the chilies and shake out most of the seeds. Cut the chilies in half lengthwise and remove any tough, dried ribs. Cut them crosswise into ¾-inch pieces and put them in a bowl. Add water to cover and soak for 30 minutes.

Meanwhile, combine the lemon grass and ginger in a large, heavy mortar and pound for a minute or so to break down the fibers. Transfer the crushed mixture to the bowl of a food processor fitted with a metal blade.

Pound the garlic and shallots in the mortar just until crushed and transfer them to the food processor.

Drain the chilies, reserving about ½ cup of the soaking liquid. Add the chilies and turmeric to the food processor.

Process the ingredients until a rich, moist paste forms, stopping occasionally to scrape down the sides of the work bowl. Add a few tablespoons of the chili-soaking liquid now and then, if needed, to ease the grinding.

This paste can be stored in an airtight container in the refrigerator for 1 month, or in the freezer for up to 3 months.

Curry Pastes, Sauces, and Condiments

JUNGLE CURRY PASTE

Krung Kaeng Pha

Makes about 1⅓ cups

In the wilds of northern Thailand, people gather herbs, leafy greens, edible flowers, and young shoots and vines throughout the day. At evening, these become dinner ingredients for a robust curry.

Jungle curry paste is wild in another sense, too. With three different types of chili adding flame, it is by far the hottest curry paste in Thai cuisine. Yet liberal quantities of sweet, pungent greens—such as Italian and Thai basils, tarragon, chives, and arugula—make it as intensely herbal in flavor as it is hot in character.

½ cup small dried Japanese chilies

1 tablespoon shrimp paste (*kapi*), wrapped neatly in a double layer of aluminum foil

1 large stalk lemon grass, tough outer leaves discarded, lower stalk trimmed to 3 inches and finely sliced

½ cup chopped cilantro stems

6 tablespoons finely chopped, peeled fresh lesser Siamese ginger (*krachai sod*) or fresh ginger, or 2 tablespoons dried lesser Siamese ginger (*krachai*) (see Note)

⅔ cup chopped shallots

10 medium serrano chilies, stemmed and chopped

6 small Thai chilies (*phrik khee nu*), stemmed and chopped

2 cups mixed fresh herbs:

   ½ cup roughly torn Italian basil

   ½ cup roughly torn Thai basil (*bai horapha*) or purple or Italian basil

   ½ cup chopped tarragon

   ¼ cup chopped chives

   ¼ cup roughly torn arugula

Stem the Japanese chilies and shake out most of the seeds. Cut the chilies into small pieces and put them in a bowl. Add water to cover and soak for 30 minutes.

Meanwhile, set a small skillet over medium heat. Place the foil-wrapped shrimp paste in the skillet and cook for about 5 minutes, until aromatic, turning the packet over once or twice. Remove the packet from the skillet and set it aside to cool.

Combine the lemon grass, cilantro stems, and lesser Siamese ginger in a large, heavy mortar and pound for a minute or so to break down fibers. Transfer the crushed mixture to the bowl of a food processor fitted with a metal blade.

Pound the shallots in the mortar just until crushed and add the serrano and Thai chilies. Pound until the chilies are smashed and blended with the shallots. Transfer the mixture to the food processor.

Unwrap the shrimp paste and add it to the food processor.

Drain the chilies, reserving about ½ cup of the soaking liquid. Add the chilies to the food processor.

Process until the mixture is well blended but still coarse. Add the mixed herbs and process until a rich, moist paste forms, stopping occasionally to scrape down the sides of the work bowl. Add a few tablespoons of the chili-soaking liquid now and then, if needed, to ease the grinding.

This paste can be stored in an airtight container in the refrigerator for 1 week, or in the freezer for up to 1 month.

N O T E : Dried lesser Siamese ginger is also known as "dried rhizome powder."

CHU CHEE CURRY PASTE

Krung Kaeng Chu Chee

Makes about 1¼ cups

Chu chee is an especially fragrant curry paste, infused with Kaffir lime, lemon grass, and the even more exotic note of *krachai*—a sweet-and-pungent Asian ginger. This curry paste is used only in fish and seafood dishes.

4 large dried red California chilies

6 small dried Japanese chilies

½ tablespoon whole coriander seed

1 tablespoon shrimp paste (*kapi*), wrapped neatly in a double layer of aluminum foil

16 whole black peppercorns

10 (5 pairs) fresh Kaffir lime leaves (*bai magroot*), or ½ teaspoon grated lime zest

½ tablespoon minced fresh Kaffir lime peel or domestic lime peel

1 tablespoon chopped cilantro stems

1 large stalk lemon grass, tough outer leaves discarded, lower stalk trimmed to 3 inches and finely chopped

3 tablespoons finely chopped, peeled fresh Siamese ginger (galanga or *kha*) or common ginger

1½ tablespoons finely chopped, peeled fresh lesser Siamese ginger (*krachai sod*) or fresh ginger, or 1½ teaspoons dried lesser Siamese ginger (*krachai*) (see Note)

¼ cup chopped garlic

½ cup chopped shallots

With kitchen shears or a chef's knife, stem the California chilies and shake out most of the seeds. Cut the chilies in half lengthwise and remove any tough, dried ribs. Cut them crosswise into ¾-inch pieces and put them in a bowl. Stem the Japanese chilies. Shake out most of the seeds and cut the chilies into small pieces. Put them in the bowl with the California chilies. Add water to cover and soak for 30 minutes.

Meanwhile, dry-roast the coriander seed in a small skillet over medium heat for 3 to 5 minutes, until toasty and aromatic, shaking the pan often to prevent burning. Transfer the coriander seed to a small bowl and set aside to cool.

Set the skillet back over medium heat. Place the foil-wrapped shrimp paste in the skillet and cook for about 5 minutes, until aromatic, turning the packet over once or twice. Remove the packet from the skillet and set it aside to cool.

Put the roasted coriander seed and peppercorns in a large, heavy mortar and grind to a powder. Transfer the ground spices to the bowl of a food processor fitted with a metal blade.

If using fresh Kaffir lime leaves, stack and cut them into fine slivers with kitchen shears or a sharp knife.

Combine the minced lime peel, lime leaves or zest, cilantro stems, lemon grass, ginger, and lesser Siamese ginger in the mortar and pound for a minute or so to break down the fibers. Transfer the mixture to the food processor.

Pound the garlic and shallots in the mortar just until crushed and transfer to the food processor.

Unwrap the shrimp paste and add it to the food processor.

Drain the chilies, reserving about ½ cup of the soaking liquid. Add the chilies to the food processor.

Process the ingredients until a rich, moist paste forms, stopping occasionally to scrape down the sides of the work bowl. Add a few tablespoons of the chili-soaking liquid now and then, if needed, to ease the grinding.

This paste can be stored in an airtight container in the refrigerator for 1 month, or in the freezer for up to 3 months.

N O T E : Dried lesser Siamese ginger is also known as "dried rhizome powder."

LIANG CURRY PASTE

Krung Kaeng Liang

Makes about ¹/₂ cup

This rich, nourishing paste has a bright and salty seafood flavor that is a delicious counterpoint to vegetable curries. It is especially tasty with pumpkin, as in Curried Pumpkin-Coconut Soup with Thai Basil (page 307).

¼ cup large dried shrimp (*Kung haeng*) (see Note)

1 teaspoon whole white peppercorns

4 serrano chilies, a combination of green and red if possible, stemmed and sliced

1 large clove garlic, chopped

½ cup chopped shallots

Put the dried shrimp in a small bowl and add hot water to cover. Soak for 10 minutes.

Meanwhile, pound the white peppercorns to a powder in a mortar, or coarsely grind them in a spice mill.

Drain the dried shrimp.

Work all of the ingredients to a paste using a mortar and pestle or a food processor:

Mortar-and-pestle method: Mix the dried shrimp and ground pepper in the mortar and pound until the shrimp are crushed and blended with the pepper. Grind the chilies into the shrimp mixture until blended. Add the garlic and shallots and pound for several minutes to make a moist, well-mixed paste.

Processor method: Combine all of the ingredients in the bowl of a food processor fitted with a metal blade. Process until a moist, nearly smooth paste forms, stopping occasionally to scrape down the sides of the work bowl.

This paste can be stored in an airtight container in the refrigerator for 1 week, or in the freezer for up to 1 month.

NOTE: Look for packages of large dried shrimp that have good color. The shrimp should be somewhat plump and yield to a gentle pressure when pressed through the package.

KUA CURRY PASTE

Krung Kaeng Kua

Makes about I cup

M ade with mild red chilies and only a touch of shrimp paste, this is an earthy, moderately hot curry that takes on a golden shade when you mix it with coconut milk. It's a specialty curry paste, used in fish and seafood dishes such as Curried Mussels with Kabocha and Thai Basil (page 166).

I package (3 ounces) dried red California chilies

I teaspoon whole coriander seed

I teaspoon whole cumin seed

2 teaspoons shrimp paste (*kapi*), wrapped neatly in a double layer of aluminum foil

I teaspoon minced fresh Kaffir lime peel or domestic lime peel

2 tablespoons chopped cilantro stems

I stalk lemon grass, tough outer leaves discarded, lower stalk trimmed to 3 inches and finely sliced

I teaspoon finely chopped, peeled fresh Siamese ginger (galanga or *kha*) or common ginger

3 tablespoons chopped garlic

2 tablespoons chopped shallots

With kitchen shears or a chef's knife, stem the chilies and shake out most of the seeds. Cut the chilies in half lengthwise and remove any tough, dried ribs. Cut them crosswise into ¾-inch pieces and put them in a bowl. Add water to cover and soak for 30 minutes.

Meanwhile, dry-roast the coriander and cumin seeds in a small skillet over medium heat for 3 to 5 minutes, until toasty and aromatic, shaking the pan often to prevent burning. Transfer the roasted spices to a small bowl and set aside to cool.

Set the skillet back over medium heat. Place the foil-wrapped shrimp paste in the skillet and cook for about 5 minutes, until aromatic, turning the packet over once or twice. Remove the packet from the skillet and set it aside to cool.

Put the roasted spices in a large, heavy mortar and grind to a powder. Transfer the ground spices to the bowl of a food processor fitted with a metal blade.

Combine the minced lime peel, cilantro stems, lemon grass, and ginger in the mortar and pound for a minute or so to break down the fibers. Transfer the mixture to the food processor.

Pound the garlic and shallots in the mortar just until crushed and transfer to the food processor.

Unwrap the shrimp paste and add it to the food processor.

continued

Drain the chilies, reserving about ½ cup of the soaking liquid. Add the chilies to the food processor.

Process the ingredients until a rich, moist paste forms, stopping occasionally to scrape down the sides of the work bowl. Add a few tablespoons of the chili-soaking liquid now and then, if needed, to ease the grinding.

This paste can be stored in an airtight container in the refrigerator for 1 month, or in the freezer for up to 3 months.

CHILI-TAMARIND PASTE

Nam Phrik Pao

Makes about 1 cup

The spicy tang of Hot-and-Sour Shrimp Soup (page 74), and that of numerous stir-fries and piquant Thai salad dressings, is derived from this savory chili paste.

Although the word *pao* translates as "roasted," the key ingredients here are deep-fried for a richer flavor, then blended into a paste with tamarind sauce and simmered with coconut-palm sugar.

Good ready-made versions of this frequently used condiment are available on store shelves. In fact, most Thai restaurants use store-bought pastes. But the following recipe will give you a paste that's much more flavorful and mellow, making your dishes more distinctive than those of most restaurants!

½ cup large dried shrimp (*kung haeng*)

1¾ cups vegetable or peanut oil

⅓ cup sliced garlic

1 cup sliced shallots

12 small dried Japanese chilies

3 tablespoons Tamarind Sauce (page 61) or liquid tamarind concentrate

3 tablespoons coconut-palm sugar or golden brown sugar

1 tablespoon Thai fish sauce (*nam pla*)

Put the dried shrimp in a small bowl and add water to cover. Swish around a few times for a brief rinsing, then drain. Set aside.

Pour 1½ cups of the oil into a wok or heavy saucepan set over medium-high heat and bring the oil to 360°F. (To test the oil temperature, dip a wooden spoon in the hot oil. The oil should bubble and sizzle gently around the bowl of the spoon.)

Add the garlic and cook until golden brown, about 1 minute, stirring occasionally. Remove with a wire skimmer or slotted spoon to a bowl lined with paper towels. Return the oil temperature to 360°F before adding each of the next three ingredients.

Fry the shallots, stirring often, until they begin to brown, about 2 to 3 minutes. Add them to the bowl with the fried garlic. Fry the shrimp, stirring occasionally, for 1 minute. Add them to the bowl. Fry the chilies until they darken and become brittle, about 30 seconds. Add them to the bowl of fried ingredients.

Transfer the fried ingredients to a blender or the bowl of a food processor fitted with a metal blade. Add the remaining ¼ cup of oil and the tamarind sauce and blend until a moist, nearly smooth paste forms. Stop occasionally to scrape down the sides of the blender or work bowl.

Transfer the chili paste to a small, deep skillet or saucepan and set over medium heat. Add the sugar and fish sauce and cook, stirring occasionally, until the color deepens to a rich dark brown, about 5 to 8 minutes. Remove from the heat and cool to room temperature.

Transfer the chili paste to a glass jar with a tight-fitting lid.

This paste will keep for about 3 months if stored in the refrigerator.

Curry
Pastes,
Sauces, and
Condiments

CLASSIC SHRIMP PASTE AND CHILI SAUCE

Nam Phrik Kapi

Serves 4 to 6

No dining table, from the royal palace to the poorest country hut, could be more decidedly Thai than when it displays an inviting bowl of *nam phrik kapi* surrounded by steamed rice, fresh vegetables, herbs, and the fried fish known as *pla tu.* This may well be the national dish of Thailand.

However, *nam phrik kapi* can be overly strong for Western tastes. I offer it here in a slightly toned-down version that both Thais and Americans should enjoy.

3 tablespoons shrimp paste (*kapi*), wrapped neatly in a double layer of aluminum foil

14 peeled whole cloves garlic

½ cup large dried shrimp (*kung haeng*) or small pickled crab (*pu khem*)

3 tablespoons coconut-palm sugar

A few slices fresh green mango, peeled and chopped (optional)

2 tablespoons Thai fish sauce (*nam pla*)

20 small Thai chilies (*phrik khee nu*), stemmed

1 cup fresh lemon juice

2 tablespoons shrimp powder with chili (*kung phrik pon*)

1 pound catfish fillets, grilled, or 4 small salted mackerel (*pla tu*), fried

Assorted raw or steamed vegetables, such as 1 small cucumber, sliced into rounds, a wedge or two of green cabbage, and a handful of green beans or baby corn

Set a small skillet over medium heat. Place the foil-wrapped shrimp paste in the skillet and cook for about 5 minutes, until aromatic, turning the packet over once or twice. Remove the packet from the skillet and set aside to cool.

Put the garlic in a large, heavy mortar and pound with the pestle just until crushed. Grind the dried shrimp or pickled crab into the crushed garlic until blended, about 2 minutes. Unwrap the shrimp paste and add it to the mortar with the coconut-palm sugar. Pound until the ingredients are well mixed, about 1 minute. If using green mango, lightly crush it into the mixture. Add the Thai fish sauce and chilies. Stir with the pestle and pound gently to prevent splashing and to crush the chilies without pulverizing them. Add the lemon juice and stir it into the mixture with the pestle. Lightly grind the ingredients in with the lemon juice to keep it from splashing. When blended, the sauce should resemble a soupy, coarse purée.

Transfer the sauce to a serving bowl, sprinkle the shrimp powder on top, and set it on the table.

Arrange the fish and vegetables on a large serving platter and set it alongside the bowl of classic shrimp paste and chili sauce.

Serve at room temperature with hot steamed rice.

Any leftover sauce can be stored in a tightly sealed jar in the refrigerator for 2 or 3 days.

CLASSIC CHILI DIPPING SAUCE

Nam Pla Phrik Khee Nu

Makes about ⅓ cup

One of the most popular of all our condiments, *nam pla phrik khee nu* is found almost anywhere Thai food is served. This spicy, aromatic sauce is a smooth blend of fresh hot chilies, fish sauce, fresh lime juice, and a bit of minced garlic. We spoon it over just about everything—soups, salads, noodles, curries, stir-fries, grilled meat, and seafood.

6 tablespoons fresh lime or lemon juice

2 tablespoons Thai fish sauce
   (*nam pla*)

6 small Thai chilies (*phrik khee nu*) or 3 serrano chilies, finely sliced

1 small clove garlic, minced

Combine all of the ingredients in a small bowl and serve. Covered and refrigerated, this sauce will keep for 2 weeks.

COUNTRY-STYLE TOMATO SAUCE WITH GROUND PORK AND RED CURRY

Nam Phrik Ong

Serves 4 to 6

Nam phrik ong is a specialty of the northern Thai provinces, where tomatoes are plentiful. Spicy meat sauces like this one are traditionally served as dips, with a full complement of raw vegetables, balls of sticky rice, and crispy pork skins.

3 tablespoons vegetable oil

¾ cup Classic Red Curry Paste (page 26)

3 plum tomatoes, chopped

1 pound ground pork

¾ teaspoon white pepper

1½ cups tomato juice

6 tablespoons golden brown sugar

2½ tablespoons Thai fish sauce (*nam pla*)

3 tablespoons fresh lemon juice

Assorted fresh vegetables, such as 1 small cucumber, sliced into rounds, a wedge or two of green cabbage, and a handful of green beans or mushrooms

1 recipe Issan Sticky Rice (page 90)

Crispy pork skins (optional)

Place all of the ingredients except the vegetables, sticky rice, and pork skins within easy reach of the cooking area.

Set a wok or heavy iron skillet over medium-high heat. Add the oil. If using a wok, rotate it a bit so the oil coats the sides. When the oil is hot, add the curry paste and cook for 2½ minutes, stirring briskly to keep it from burning.

Add the tomatoes and stir-fry for 1 minute. Add the ground pork and white pepper and stir-fry for 1½ minutes.

Mix in the tomato juice. Add the golden-brown sugar and fish sauce and stir-fry for 1 minute. Add the lemon juice and cook for 2 minutes, stirring occasionally as the mixture boils. Remove from the heat and let cool.

Transfer the sauce to a serving bowl and place the vegetables on a platter. Serve the sauce warm or at room temperature with the vegetables, bite-size balls of sticky rice, and pork skins, if desired.

ISSAN-STYLE SPICY MUSHROOM SAUCE

Nam Phrik Het

Serves 6

"It makes a tiger cry." That's what people in the rural northeast of Thailand say of a searingly hot dish like this many-chilied dipping sauce. Mudfish, which is quite similar to American catfish, provides a bit of pungency, while the mushrooms, garlic, and shallots give this sauce an earthy base.

Crisp raw vegetables dipped into this sauce create a delicious combination of cool and hot, mild and intense.

6 shallots, peeled and halved lengthwise

10 peeled whole cloves garlic

12 serrano chilies, stemmed and halved lengthwise

4 tablespoons sugar

2 tablespoons Thai fish sauce (*nam pla*)

1 can (14.8 ounces) straw mushrooms, drained

3 tablespoons pickled mudfish with chili (*pla ra pla chawn*)

½ cup fresh lemon juice

Assorted fresh vegetables, such as 1 small cucumber, sliced into rounds, and a few handfuls of green beans, cherry tomatoes, or scallions

1 recipe Issan Sticky Rice (page 90)

Dry-roast the shallots, garlic, and chilies in a small, heavy skillet over medium heat, stirring the mixture and shaking the pan occasionally so everything cooks evenly. Cook until the garlic and shallots are softened and browned and the chilies begin to blister, about 10 to 12 minutes.

Coarsely chop the dry-roasted ingredients and transfer them to a large, heavy mortar. Pound for a minute until crushed, then add the sugar and fish sauce. Continue pounding until the chilies are mashed and roughly blended, about 1 to 2 minutes. Add the mushrooms and pound until crushed and blended, about 1½ minutes. Add the pickled mudfish and lemon juice. Stir with the pestle, then pound gently, just until the liquid is well mixed, making a moist, coarse blend.

Transfer the sauce to a serving bowl and set it on a large platter along with the fresh vegetables. Serve at room temperature with bite-size balls of sticky rice.

Any leftover sauce can be stored in a tightly sealed jar in the refrigerator for 2 or 3 days.

CHILIES-IN-VINEGAR SAUCE

Phrik Dong Nam Som

Makes about ½ cup

This basic, easy-to-make condiment consists of sliced fresh chilies floating in a clear, amber-colored liquid of white vinegar mixed with a splash of fish sauce. It is part of the condiment display set on every Thai table, to be spooned over noodle dishes like our classic, *phat thai* (page 114), or added to almost any dish for a spicy tang.

The sliced chilies are meant to be eaten, as much for their crisp bite as their heat, but you can use just the liquid for a more moderately spiced sauce.

½ cup distilled white vinegar
½ tablespoon Thai fish sauce (*nam pla*)

12 small Thai chilies (*phrik khee nu*), or 3 serrano chilies, finely sliced

Combine all of the ingredients in a small serving bowl. Let stand for 15 to 20 minutes for the flavors to develop.

The sauce will keep for 3 to 4 days if covered and stored at room temperature, or 2 weeks if refrigerated.

SPICY CUCUMBER RELISH

Nam Thaeng Kwa

Makes about 3 cups

This cool and crunchy, spicy relish is a traditional accompaniment to dozens of Thai dishes. Crisp sliced cucumber and cilantro are bathed in a sweet-and-sour dressing, then studded with crushed peanuts and chopped chilies.

These bright, lively flavors welcome the seared-meat taste of grilled satays (pages 280 to 283) or barbecued chickens (pages 298 to 302). Dainty appetizers like Sweet Corn Fritters (page 261) or salmon toasts (page 278) enjoy the company, too.

You can also serve this relish with many all-American favorites. Try it with smoked salmon and toast points, fried chicken, or catfish with fresh corn pudding.

I cup distilled white vinegar

I cup golden brown or white sugar

I teaspoon salt

I large cucumber, hothouse or common variety, or I pound small pickling cucumbers

4 to 6 small Thai chilies (*phrik khee nu*), or 2 to 3 serrano chilies, finely chopped

½ cup roasted unsalted peanuts, crushed in a mortar or finely chopped

⅓ cup loosely packed chopped cilantro, including the stems

Combine the vinegar, sugar, and salt in a small saucepan over medium heat. Bring the mixture to a boil, stirring to dissolve the sugar and salt. Cook for 1 minute at a gentle boil, stirring occasionally. Remove from the heat and cool to room temperature.

When ready to serve, peel the cucumber and cut it in half lengthwise. (If using a common cucumber, scrape out the seeds with a spoon.) Cut the halved cucumber crosswise into thin slices. Place the cucumber, chilies, peanuts, and cilantro in a mixing bowl. Pour the cooled vinegar dressing over the relish ingredients and mix gently.

NOTE: You can make the dressing and refrigerate it up to 1 day in advance. Add the relish ingredients just before serving so the cucumbers and peanuts stay crisp and the cilantro stays lively.

SWEET-AND-SPICY DIPPING SAUCE

Nam Jeem Kai Yang

Makes about 1½ cups

This is a wonderful sweet, hot, sticky chili sauce that always accompanies the charcoal-scorched flavor of Thai barbecued chicken. It goes well with crispy, deep-fried foods as well, particularly appetizers like spring rolls, fried squid, and stuffed crabs.

½ cup distilled white vinegar
1 cup sugar
½ teaspoon salt

1 tablespoon Chinese-style chili-garlic sauce, preferably Lee Kum Kee brand

In a small saucepan, combine the vinegar and ½ cup of the sugar. Bring to a low boil over medium-high heat, stirring occasionally. Lower the heat to medium and stir in the rest of the sugar. Cook for 2 minutes, stirring frequently as the mixture comes to a boil. Reduce the heat to low and add the salt. Simmer for 5 minutes, stirring occasionally. Stir in the chili-garlic sauce and remove from the heat.

Let cool and serve at room temperature.

Covered and refrigerated, this sauce will keep for 2 to 3 weeks.

SWEET-AND-SPICY DIPPING SAUCE WITH PEANUTS

Nam Jeem Kai Yang Kap Tua Lisong

To accompany certain dishes—especially grilled seafood—add 1 to 2 tablespoons of crushed peanuts to the cooled sauce.

CURRIED PEANUT
SATAY SAUCE

Nam Satay

Makes about 2¹⁄₂ cups

—————

S atay sauce is a sophisticated blend of tropical flavors, including one that's an American childhood favorite. Maybe that's why Americans take so quickly and wholeheartedly to this rich, creamy dip, flavored with fresh Massaman curry paste and cooked with coconut milk, brown sugar, and chunky peanut butter.

This recipe makes a large quantity, enough for a mixed grill of beef, lamb, chicken, and pork satays for 16 people. Any leftover sauce can be used as a dip for raw vegetables or warmed and spread on toast for a quick, delicious snack.

1 can (14 ounces) unsweetened coconut milk	⅔ cup chunky peanut butter
6 tablespoons Massaman Curry Paste (page 36)	7 tablespoons dark brown sugar
	2 tablespoons Thai fish sauce (*nam pla*)

Put the coconut milk in a medium saucepan and slowly bring it to a gentle boil over medium heat, stirring occasionally. Add the curry paste and stir until well blended and fragrant, about 3 minutes. Add the peanut butter and cook, stirring constantly, for 1 minute. Reduce the heat to low and add the brown sugar. Cook, stirring frequently, until the sauce is smooth and well blended, about 2 minutes. Remove from the heat and stir in the fish sauce.

Cool slightly and serve warm or at room temperature.

This sauce will keep for at least 3 weeks if refrigerated in a covered container.

QUICK STREET-
VENDOR'S HOT SAUCE

Phrik Nam Som

Makes about ⅔ cup

When street-food vendors run low on *sriracha*, the omnipresent hot-and-savory Thai chili sauce, they're likely to mix up a quick batch of this easy, tasty substitute. This sauce is tart, thin, and spicy. It goes well with everything from stir-fries to soups, noodle dishes, scrambled eggs, and even fried chicken.

1 heaping tablespoon Chinese-style chili-garlic sauce, preferably Lee Kum Kee brand	½ cup distilled white vinegar

Combine the ingredients in a small bowl and serve. Covered and refrigerated, this sauce will keep for about 2 weeks.

THAI PLUM SAUCE

Nam Jeem Boi

Makes about 1¼ cups

Here's my homemade version of the popular bottled sweet-and-sour plum sauces available in Asian markets. This recipe yields a tart, tangy sauce, the kind Thai people prefer.

⅓ cup finely chopped, pitted, preserved plums (about 22 plums from a 12-ounce jar)

⅔ cup distilled white vinegar

⅔ cup water

⅓ cup sugar

2½ tablespoons honey

A splash or two of bottled Thai chili sauce (*sriracha*) or any good Mexican or Louisiana-style hot sauce (optional)

Process the plums, vinegar, water, sugar, and honey in a blender until smooth and liquid. Put the mixture in a small saucepan and gradually bring to a boil over medium-high heat. Cook at a gentle boil for 1 minute, then lower the heat and simmer until the sauce reduces slightly and begins to thicken, about 12 to 15 minutes. Stir in a little Thai chili sauce, if desired.

Remove from the heat and cool to room temperature. Serve with your choice of prepared dishes.

This sauce will keep for 6 to 8 weeks if refrigerated in a covered container.

VIETNAMESE-STYLE PLUM SAUCE

Nam Jeem Boi Yuan

Makes about 1½ cups

This recipe gives a Thai accent to the sweet-and-spicy dipping sauce traditionally served with salad rolls, a Vietnamese specialty, as well as with such Thai dishes as spring rolls, wontons, Sweet Corn Fritters (page 261), and Golden Money Bags (page 310).

1 cup bottled sweet plum sauce

½ cup rice vinegar

4½ tablespoons sugar

1½ tablespoons bottled Thai chili sauce (*sriracha*), or season to taste with any good Mexican or Louisiana-style hot sauce

½ tablespoon quick-mixing flour

Combine the plum sauce, vinegar, sugar, and chili sauce in a small saucepan and gradually bring to a boil over medium-high heat. Boil gently for 3 minutes, stirring occasionally. Stir in the flour and return to a boil. Boil gently for 1 minute, stirring occasionally.

Remove from the heat and let cool to room temperature. Serve with your choice of prepared dishes.

This sauce will keep for 6 to 8 weeks if refrigerated in a covered container.

VIETNAMESE-STYLE DIPPING SAUCE

Nam Phrik Yuan

Makes 1½ cups

Nam phrik yuan is typical of the clear, liquid dipping sauces of Vietnam. It is notable for its subtle sweetness and tang.

1 cup water

⅔ cup sugar

1 teaspoon Chinese-style chili-garlic
    sauce, preferably Lee Kum Kee brand

½ cup rice vinegar

¼ cup grated carrot

Bring the water to a boil in a medium saucepan. Stir in the sugar until it dissolves, then add the chili-garlic sauce and rice vinegar. Boil gently until the mixture reduces slightly, about 2 minutes. Remove from the heat and let cool to room temperature.

Transfer the sauce to a serving bowl. Mix in the grated carrot and serve.

This sauce will keep for several days if refrigerated in a covered container.

Curry
Pastes,
Sauces, and
Condiments

FRESH LEMON-CHILI SAUCE

Nam Manao Phrik Sod

Makes about 1 cup

___

This bracing sauce is especially good with grilled fish. It's an invigorating blend of chilies, lemon, and herbs—hot, yet refreshing and well balanced.

10 cloves garlic

8 to 12 small Thai chilies (*phrik khee nu*), preferably red for color, finely sliced

3½ tablespoons chopped cilantro, including the stems

¾ cup fresh lemon juice

Mortar-and-pestle method: Pound the garlic, chilies, and cilantro into a smooth paste. Stir in the lemon juice with the pestle to make a well-blended, liquid sauce.

Blender method: Crush the garlic with the side of a chef's knife and chop. Combine the garlic, chilies, and cilantro in the blender with half of the lemon juice. Process to a well-blended, liquid purée. Add the remaining lemon juice and whirl once to mix.

This sauce can be made a day or two in advance and kept refrigerated in a tightly sealed jar.

SWEET BLACK BEAN SAUCE

Nam Jeem See-eu Dam

Makes ¾ cup

___

Sweet black soy sauce, with its molasseslike edge, is the foundation of this dark and earthy dipping sauce. We drizzle this thin but rich sauce over street-vendor specialties, such as steamed dumplings and rice-noodle rolls, and it always accompanies Chicken in Pandanus Leaves with Sweet Black Bean Sauce (page 132).

½ cup sweet black soy sauce (*see-eu wan*)

¼ cup distilled white vinegar

¼ cup golden brown sugar

Combine all of the ingredients in a small saucepan and set over high heat. Stir until the sugar dissolves, then bring the mixture to a boil. Boil gently for 1 minute, stirring occasionally.

Remove from the heat and cool slightly. Serve warm.

This sauce will keep for a week or more if refrigerated in a covered container. Rewarm before serving.

Sauces

The vegetarian version of Savory Tamarind Sauce is a great accent for scrambled eggs. Add Crispy Shallots if desired.

TAMARIND SAUCE

Nam Som Makham

Makes 1 cup

R ipened seed pods of the tropical tamarind tree give us nature's own sweet-and-sour sauce. Tamarind sauce is the color of dark raisins, with a clean, inviting, fruity sourness. Thai people use this tangy essence in everything from curries, soups, and sauces to beverages and sweets.

You can buy a prepared sauce, liquid tamarind concentrate, but it's easy to make your own.

2 ounces seedless tamarind pulp   1 cup warm water
   (see Note)

Put the tamarind pulp in a medium bowl and add the warm water. Soak until soft, about 20 minutes. Break the pulp apart with your fingers, then mash and stir with a wooden spoon to help it dissolve.

Pour the mixture through a fine mesh strainer into another bowl. Stir and mash the soft pulp against the strainer to extract all the thick sauce. Scrape the sauce clinging to the bottom of the strainer into the bowl.

Discard the fibrous pulp collected in the strainer.

This sauce, if refrigerated in a tightly sealed container, keeps indefinitely. For best flavor, however, use it within 1 week.

NOTE: Sold in packets in Thai, Indian, and other Asian markets.

TOASTED COCONUT

Maprao Kua

Makes about ²/₃ cup

There is no oil in our sweet-hot, citrus-based salad dressings, so we like to shower these sweet, nutty flakes over our salads for a little richness and crunch.

Toasted coconut can be a pleasing addition to other dishes as well. Try it as a topping for Coconut Ice Cream (page 340) or a fruit salad.

1 cup dried, unsweetened coconut flakes,
    chopped to nearly uniform size
    (see Note)

Toast the coconut in a heavy, dry skillet over low heat until fragrant and golden brown, about 8 to 10 minutes. Shake the pan frequently, tossing and stirring so the flakes brown evenly without burning. Remove from the heat and continue stirring for a minute or two as the pan cools. Set aside to cool completely.

Stored in an airtight container at room temperature, toasted coconut will keep indefinitely.

NOTE: Many health food stores carry the unsweetened dried coconut I like to use when making *maprao kua*. Sometimes labeled "coconut chips," these small, curling flakes are generally sold in 8-ounce plastic bags.

TOASTED RICE POWDER

Khao Kua Pon

Makes about ¼ cup

T o accent their famous *laab* salads, made of minced spiced meat served in lettuce cups, the Issan people of Thailand's northeastern provinces roast raw rice until it takes on a subtle aromatic quality reminiscent of roasted nuts, then grind it to a delicate, crunchy powder. It's a wonderful complement to *laab*'s characteristic herbal notes of lemon grass, mint, and fresh citrus juice.

In the provinces they use raw sticky rice for *khao kua pon*, but any raw rice will work perfectly.

¼ cup raw sticky rice (*khao niao*) or any other raw rice

Toast the rice in a small, dry skillet over medium-high heat for about 3 minutes. Shake the pan constantly, so the grains color evenly on all sides. When the grains turn a deep golden color, remove from the heat and set aside to cool.

Transfer the toasted rice to a stone mortar and pound to a gritty, sandy powder. (An electric spice grinder also works well.)

Store at room temperature in a tightly sealed jar until ready to use.

Curry
Pastes,
Sauces, and
Condiments

PICKLED GARLIC

Kratiem Dong

Makes about 1 pint

You'll be surprised at the sweetness and tenderness of these Thai-style pickles. *Kratiem dong* is traditionally served on the side with soups, curries, fried rice, and noodle dishes.

Pickled garlic is available ready-made in Asian markets, but it's easy and enjoyable to make your own. Select the smallest, youngest bulbs available. It isn't necessary to peel the garlic. The paperlike coverings will soften in the sweet brine and slip off easily as you slice the garlic pickles for serving.

6 small bulbs fresh garlic, unpeeled	2 cups sugar
3 cups water	1½ tablespoons salt
1½ cups distilled white vinegar	

Trim off the garlic stems without cutting into the cloves.

Bring the water to a boil in a medium saucepan. Add the garlic, reduce the heat, and simmer for 10 minutes. Drain and set aside.

Combine the vinegar, sugar, and salt in a small saucepan and bring the mixture to a boil. Boil vigorously for 1 minute, stirring occasionally. Reduce the heat and simmer until the pickling solution begins to thicken, about 6 to 8 minutes.

Remove the pan from the heat and cool to room temperature.

Place the garlic in a glass jar with a tight-fitting lid and pour in the pickling solution to cover. Seal tightly and store at room temperature in a cool, dark place for 2 weeks or more before using.

To serve, remove one head and cut it crosswise into thin slices. Return any leftover garlic to the sweet brine.

GOLDEN GARLIC

Kratiem Jiew

Makes about ½ cup

———

What cook doesn't love the heady fragrance of fresh garlic sizzling in the skillet? Thai cooks capture the robust flavor and crunchy texture of fried garlic for use as a condiment.

We love to spoon it into our soups or over noodle dishes and steamed dumplings. The toasty bits of garlic are used together with the perfumed oil for a silky-crisp infusion of fresh-fried garlic taste.

6 tablespoons vegetable oil	4 tablespoons finely chopped garlic (about 12 large cloves; see Note)

Heat the oil in a small cast-iron skillet over medium heat. Drop a bit of garlic into the oil. If it sizzles right away, the oil is ready. Add all of the garlic and stir-fry until it becomes aromatic and turns a pale golden color, about 1½ minutes.

Remove from the heat and continue stirring for a minute or two as the pan cools.

Let cool and transfer to a glass jar with a tight-fitting lid. Refrigerate if prepared more than a day in advance. This will keep for about 1 week in the refrigerator.

NOTE: You can chop the garlic by hand or whirl it briefly in a mini-chop food processor. It should be finely chopped to nearly uniform size. If using the mini-chop, be careful not to overprocess, or the garlic will become so moist that it's likely to burn. Just three or four quick pulses should do it.

FRIED GARLIC CHIPS

Kratiem Tod

Makes about 3 tablespoons

This wonderful condiment provides lush garlic flavor in a crispy, crunchy form. We like to scatter small handfuls of these chips over prepared dishes such as Chiang Mai Noodle Curry (page 289), Pink Pomelo and Grilled Shrimp Salad (page 308), and Home-Fried Tofu Squares with Savory Tamarind Sauce (page 269).

1 cup vegetable oil	¼ cup thinly sliced garlic (about 12 cloves)

Pour the oil into a wok or a small cast-iron skillet set over medium-high heat and bring the oil to 360 °F. (To test the oil temperature, dip a wooden spoon in the hot oil. The oil should bubble and sizzle gently around the bowl of the spoon.)

Add the garlic and cook until golden brown, stirring occasionally, about 1 minute. Remove with a wire skimmer or slotted spoon and drain on paper towels. (Let cool, then strain and reserve the flavored oil for stir-frying or sautéing, if desired.)

Cool to room temperature and serve with your choice of prepared dishes. The chips will keep for about a week or two if stored at room temperature in a tightly sealed jar.

CRISPY SHALLOTS

Hua Hom Tod

Makes about ½ cup

These tasty fried shallot rings add a pleasing, delicate crunch and rich fried-onion flavor to various Thai dishes, including rice, soupy noodle curries, and sauces. They are paired with Fried Garlic Chips (page 66) in such dishes as Pink Pomelo and Grilled Shrimp Salad (page 308), Royal Son-in-Law Eggs (page 314), and Grilled Catfish with Sweet and Bitter Herbs and Savory Tamarind Sauce (page 198).

Try them with American dishes too. Sprinkle some over mashed or home-fried potatoes.

1 cup vegetable oil	⅔ cup thinly sliced shallots (about 5 or 6)

Pour the oil into a wok or a heavy saucepan set over medium-high heat and bring the oil to 360°F. (To test the oil temperature, dip a wooden spoon in the hot oil. The oil should bubble and sizzle gently around the bowl of the spoon.)

Add the shallots and fry, stirring frequently, until crisp and brown, about 2 minutes. Remove with a wire skimmer or slotted spoon and drain on paper towels. (Let cool, then strain and reserve the flavored oil for stir-frying or sautéing, if desired.)

Cool to room temperature and serve with your choice of prepared dishes.

The shallots will keep for a week or two if stored at room temperature in a tightly sealed jar.

SOUPS

Kaeng Chued, Kaeng Tom Yum, leh Tom Kha

"**R**ap pra taarn."

These are the traditional words we say when a Thai family and its guests seat themselves for the evening meal: "Sit down to share this food." Before the gathering is a small but wonderfully varied feast. Fragrant jasmine rice might sit beside a platter of seasonal vegetables and crisply fried fish, accompanied by *nam phrik kapi,* an earthy chili sauce. A spicy meat or seafood curry is usually on the table as well, along with an artfully composed salad.

But perhaps the most inviting sight of all is the steamboat, the traditional serving vessel for Thailand's aromatic soups. Glowing charcoals radiate heat beneath the steamboat's metal bowl, keeping the soup hot and fragrant no matter how long dinner lasts.

In Western cooking, soup is a first course, a prelude to the main meal. In Thailand, soup holds the central place among a mosaic of dishes served all at once. The Thai custom is to savor dinner slowly, and the comforting warmth of soup urges you to linger over the meal, perhaps to ladle a second bowl, while you relax and enjoy the company of family and friends.

In other chapters of this book you'll find specialty soups that are complete meals in themselves. For example, *yen ta fo,* Pink Soup Noodles with Mixed Seafood and Thai Condiments, is a great favorite at lunchtime. It is a specialty of street vendors, so I have placed it in the "Bangkok Street Cooking" chapter.

Khao tom, Late-Night Soup with Four Special Condiments, is perfect at the end of a long evening. In fact, shops that specialize in *khao tom* are usually the liveliest places in Bangkok between midnight and dawn. Because it is a one-dish meal based on rice, you'll find *khao tom* in the "Rice and Noodles" chapter.

The recipes in this chapter, however, are for "dinnertime" soups, most often served at the evening meal with a complement of other dishes. But there is no need to feel bound by rules when it comes to serving and enjoying these soups. An elegant dinner soup like *tom yum kung,* combined with a dish of rice, makes a wonderful light lunch. And I find that a hot bowl of *tom kha kai* is very calming when I need to relax after a busy evening in my restaurant's kitchen.

There are three main categories of Thai soups:

Kaeng tom yum soups feature a spicy, tart, highly aromatic broth. *Tom yum kung,* Hot-and-Sour Shrimp Soup, is a favorite of both Americans and Thais. The broth is a lively blend of chicken stock, lime juice, and chili-tamarind paste, punctuated with crushed hot chilies and aromatic leaves and herbs. It's a soup that changes its flavors subtly while it continues to simmer throughout dinner, almost like a wine that becomes fuller in flavor as it breathes.

Kaeng chued soups evolved from the clear broth soups of Chinese cuisine. Clear Broth Soup with Ground Pork, Garlic, and Water Spinach is heady with garlic and pleasingly spiced with a splash of fish sauce and a dash of white pepper. It looks Chinese, but the taste is Thai.

Tom kha soups are aromatic and mildly spiced, with a broth that's rich in coconut milk. Anyone who loves Thai food is probably already familiar with *tom kha kai,* Chicken-Coconut Soup with Siamese Ginger and Lemon Grass. Many people will choose a favorite Thai restaurant, and stick with it faithfully, because of a fondness for their *tom kha kai* recipe. I promise that you'll soon be able to make a *tom kha kai* that will rival, or perhaps even surpass, any you've tasted before.

In addition to the three soups above, I've chosen recipes that will give you an idea of the range and variety of Thai soups. Some are simple, home-style soups like those my mother made. Others, like Rain Forest Soup, showcase ingredients that will seem quite exotic.

I hope you, and your friends and family, will sit down to share some of these soups very soon. It's my privilege to share these recipes and to say to you, *"Rap pra taarn."*

A Few Words on Serving Soup Thai Style

You have access to a Thai or Chinese grocery, buy an inexpensive steamboat (or Mongolian hot pot, as they are often called). But I also love to serve my soups from a handsome soup tureen when I'm entertaining, or to ladle them right from the pot into individual soup bowls for a casual get-together. No matter how elegant or humble the occasion, I like to have Asian-style porcelain soup spoons. They stay cool and pleasant to the touch, and they hold just the right amount—a perfect mouthful.

CHICKEN STOCK

Soup Kai

Makes about 8 cups

C ilantro stems, garlic, and peppercorns give this light, flavorful broth its Thai identity. Chicken stock is a versatile mainstay in Thai kitchens, used not only as the base for our homemade soups, but also in curries and stir-fries. I like to make two or three batches at a time. Some will go in the freezer; the rest will find its way into my favorite recipes in no time at all. Chicken stock can lighten and balance the richness of a coconut-based curry, and when you stir a few spoonfuls into a stir-fry sizzling with garlic, chilies, fish sauce, and sugar, a delicious sauce is born.

You can get chicken backs and necks from the supermarket, or ask your butcher to save you the bones from chicken breasts. They make a particularly light, elegant stock.

2 pounds chicken backs and necks, or bones from chicken breasts	I bunch cilantro, stems only (reserve leaves for another recipe)
I medium onion, halved	6 cloves garlic, lightly crushed
3 large carrots (about ¾ pound), halved	I teaspoon whole black peppercorns
½ pound Japanese radish (daikon) or 3 stalks celery, cut into thirds	

Put the chicken backs and necks in a large stockpot. Add the vegetables, seasonings, and water to cover. Gradually bring to a boil over medium-high heat. Skim off any foam that collects on the surface. When the stock reaches a boil, reduce the heat and simmer, covered, for 2 hours.

Strain the stock through a fine-mesh sieve into a medium saucepan or heatproof bowl. Discard the solids. Cool the stock to room temperature, then chill in the refrigerator. When the stock is thoroughly chilled, the fat will form a thin layer on the surface. Defat the stock before using it in soups or other recipes.

Covered and refrigerated, this stock will keep about 1 week. You can also freeze it for several months.

CHICKEN-COCONUT SOUP WITH SIAMESE GINGER AND LEMON GRASS

Tom Kha Kai

Serves 4 to 6

In one rich, ivory-colored bowlful, *tom kha kai* brings together the creaminess of coconut milk and the spiciness of Thai chilies with the sweetness of coconut-palm sugar and the tang of lemon juice, all infused with the woodsy perfume of Siamese ginger. Newcomers to Thai cooking love *tom kha kai* from the first spoonful. It's the perfect introduction to our cuisine. Some customers, no matter how many visits they make to my restaurant, order this satisfying, vividly flavored soup every time. Chances are that you will also find yourself being asked to make it again and again.

3 cups Chicken Stock (page 72) or canned chicken broth

8 large slices unpeeled Siamese ginger (galanga or *kha*), about 5½ ounces, or common ginger

1 large stalk lemon grass, tough outer leaves discarded, trimmed to 12 inches and angle-cut into 2 inch pieces

12 (6 pairs) fresh Kaffir lime leaves (*bai magroot*), or strips of peel from 1 small lime

2 cans (14 ounces each) unsweetened coconut milk

1 pound boneless, skinless chicken breast, cut into bite-size pieces

2 tablespoons Chili-Tamarind Paste (page 46), or 1½ tablespoons commercially made chili-tamarind paste (*nam phrik pao*)

¼ cup fresh lemon juice

2½ tablespoons coconut-palm sugar or golden brown sugar

2½ tablespoons Thai fish sauce (*nam pla*)

½ pound mushrooms, sliced

5 small Thai chilies (*phrik khee nu*), stemmed and lightly crushed

Put the stock, ginger, and lemon grass in a soup pot. If using Kaffir lime leaves, tear each leaf in half and add to the pot. If using lime peel, add to the pot. Gradually bring the stock to a boil over medium-high heat. Boil for 1 minute, stir in the coconut milk, and return to a boil. Stir in the chicken and return to a boil. Add the chili-tamarind paste, lemon juice, sugar, and fish sauce. Stir until the chili-tamarind paste and sugar are dissolved and blended. Add the mushrooms and simmer just until tender, about 1 minute.

Float the chilies on top and turn off the heat. Ladle the soup into a steamboat, a soup tureen, or individual serving bowls.

NOTE: Frequent customers of Thai restaurants know that the Siamese ginger, lemon grass, and lime that flavor Thai soups are not meant to be eaten. Eating the chilies is optional.

HOT-AND-SOUR
SHRIMP SOUP

Tom Yum Kung

Serves 4 to 6

N o two spoonfuls of this tangy soup ever taste exactly alike: The first might contain a sweet, juicy shrimp, the next might be full of lemon-lime pungency. As the aromatic leaves and roots gradually release more of their perfumes, the soup's flavors blend into new patterns. The spiciness, at first a surprise, becomes more familiar and welcome.

Try spooning a bit of *tom yum kung* over rice, creating a contrasting mildness, like a pale shade of a favorite color. Then return to the full impact of the tart, herbal broth.

6 cups Chicken Stock (page 72) or canned chicken broth

1 large stalk lemon grass, tough outer leaves discarded, trimmed to 12 inches and angle-cut into 2-inch pieces

10 (5 pairs) fresh Kaffir lime leaves (*bai magroot*), or strips of peel from 1 small lime

2 tablespoons Chili-Tamarind Paste (page 46), or 1½ tablespoons commercially made chili-tamarind paste (*nam phrik pao*)

4 tablespoons Thai fish sauce (*nam pla*)

½ cup fresh lime juice

¼ cup coconut-palm sugar or golden brown sugar

1 pound medium shrimp

½ pound oyster mushrooms or button mushrooms, wiped clean and sliced

5 small Thai chilies (*phrik khee nu*), stemmed and lightly crushed

Sprigs of cilantro

Put the stock and lemon grass in a soup pot. If using Kaffir lime leaves, tear each leaf in half and add to the pot. If using lime peel, add to the pot. Gradually bring to a low boil over medium-high heat. Keep at a low boil for 1 minute. Stir in the chili-tamarind paste. Add the fish sauce and lime juice. Add the sugar and stir until it is dissolved and blended. Add the shrimp and mushrooms and simmer just until cooked, about 1 minute.

Float the chilies on top and turn off the heat. Ladle the soup into a steamboat, a soup tureen, or individual serving bowls. Tear a sprig or two of cilantro over each serving.

N O T E : This soup is the classic form of a very popular soup style called *kaeng tom yum*. Replace the shrimp with chicken and you will create another version, *tom yum kai*.

Frequent customers of Thai restaurants know that the lemon grass and lime leaves that flavor Thai soups are not meant to be eaten. Eating the chilies is optional.

CURRIED TAMARIND-
SHRIMP SOUP

Kaeng Som Kung Sod

Serves 4 to 6

I prefer to use freshly made curry pastes and stocks no matter what I'm cooking, but here they are absolutely essential. The overall flavor of this soup depends so much on the quality of these two ingredients. I'm generous with the curry paste in my recipe because a fine *kaeng som kung sod* should have a saucy broth with a lively cinnabar hue and a texture somewhere between a soup and a curry.

I large head Napa cabbage (about 1¾ pounds)

3½ cups Chicken Stock (page 72)

⅔ cup Sour Curry Paste (page 38)

1½ tablespoons coconut-palm sugar or golden brown sugar

2 tablespoons Thai fish sauce (*nam pla*)

¼ cup Tamarind Sauce (page 61), liquid tamarind concentrate, or fresh lemon juice

½ pound medium shrimp, peeled, butterflied, and deveined

Remove the large outer leaves from the cabbage. Chop the tender inner leaves. You should have about 5 cups. Set aside.

Pour the stock into a soup pot and set it over high heat. Add the curry paste and stir constantly until blended, about 2 to 3 minutes. Cover and bring to a boil, about 2 minutes. Reduce the heat to medium and bring the broth down to a simmer.

Add the sugar and stir until it is dissolved and blended. Stir in the fish sauce and tamarind sauce and simmer for 2 minutes. Add the shrimp and stir in the cabbage. Cover and simmer just until the shrimp and cabbage are cooked through, about 1 minute.

Ladle the soup into a steamboat, a soup tureen, or individual serving bowls.

BANGKOK FISHERMAN'S SOUP

Tom Kha Talay

Serves 4

Thailand has more than 1,600 miles of coastline, almost as much as California, Oregon, and Washington put together. The center of the country is an enormous basin of many rivers, covering thousands of miles. In Bangkok, located near the sea on the most important river of all, the Chao Phraya, the rich and various seafood resources of the country come together. This soup is an expression of Bangkok's abundance. It shares coconut milk and fragrant herbs, such as lemon grass and Siamese ginger, with *tom kha kai*, Chicken-Coconut Soup, but it has a lighter broth, infused with the ocean-flavored liquors of scallops, mussels, and shrimp.

3½ cups Chicken Stock (page 72) or canned chicken broth

1 large stalk lemon grass, tough outer leaves discarded, lower stalk trimmed to 12 inches and angle-cut into 2-inch pieces

3 large slices unpeeled Siamese ginger (galanga or *kha*), about 2 ounces, or common ginger

1 can (14 ounces) unsweetened coconut milk

3 teaspoons Chili-Tamarind Paste (page 46), or 2 teaspoons commercially made chili-tamarind paste (*nam phrik pao*)

¼ cup fresh lemon juice

2½ tablespoons coconut-palm sugar or golden brown sugar

3 tablespoons Thai fish sauce (*nam pla*)

8 New Zealand mussels, placed in a bowl or sink full of cold water

½ pound scallops

8 medium shrimp, peeled, butterflied, and deveined

5 small Thai chilies (*phrik khee nu*), stemmed and lightly crushed

Sprigs of cilantro

Put the stock, lemon grass, and ginger in a soup pot. Gradually bring to a boil over medium-high heat. Boil for 1 minute. Stir in the coconut milk and return to a boil. Add the chili-tamarind paste, lemon juice, sugar, and fish sauce. Stir until the paste and sugar are dissolved and blended. Reduce the heat and simmer gently while you prepare the mussels.

Agitate the water in which the mussels are soaking. (Live mussels open and close to breath. Any mussels that don't eventually close should be discarded.) Scrub and debeard the mussels. Drain and gently pry the mussels open, breaking them apart at the hinge ends. Discard the upper shells, reserving the mussels on their half shells.

Return the soup to a boil. Add the mussels, scallops, and shrimp. Do not stir. Bring back to a boil and cook just until the seafood is cooked through, about 1 minute.

Float the chilies on top and turn off the heat. Ladle the soup into a steamboat, a soup tureen, or individual serving bowls. Tear a sprig or two of cilantro over each serving.

N O T E :   Frequent customers of Thai restaurants know that the lemon grass and Siamese ginger that flavor Thai soups are not meant to be eaten. Eating the chilies is optional.

CLEAR-BROTH SOUP WITH JULIENNED OMELET, SHRIMP, AND GOLDEN GARLIC

Kaeng Chued Khai Jiew

Serves 4 to 6

E very night, families throughout Thailand make this soup the center of their evening meal. It's as much a family favorite in our country as chicken-noodle soup is in America. Like most of our clear broth–style soups, it's very simple and nutritious, made with just a few ingredients added to homemade chicken stock. In this way it is faithful to its Chinese origins, but Golden Garlic, white pepper, and a good splash of our salty fish sauce give it a distinctly Thai personality. At home we would serve a mellow *kaeng chued* like this with a spicy curry for contrast and balance. This soup could also highlight the menu of a Sunday brunch.

1 tablespoon vegetable oil	1 tablespoon sugar
3 eggs, lightly beaten	1 teaspoon white pepper
4 cups Chicken Stock (page 72) or canned chicken broth	½ pound medium shrimp, peeled, butterflied, and deveined
1 medium onion, cut in half and finely sliced	3 tablespoons Golden Garlic (page 65)
2 tablespoons Thai fish sauce (*nam pla*)	Sprigs of cilantro

To make the omelet: Add the oil to a medium nonstick or cast-iron skillet and set over high heat. Tip the skillet so the oil coats the surface. When the oil is sizzling hot, add the beaten eggs and rotate the skillet so the whole surface gets coated with egg. As the omelet begins to set, gently push the cooked edges back with a spatula and tip the skillet so that any liquid can reach the skillet's surface. Turn off the heat when the omelet is just set on the bottom, then slide it onto a cutting board. Slice into julienne strips and set aside.

To make the soup: Put the stock and onion in a soup pot and set over medium-high heat. Gradually bring to a boil, stirring occasionally. Add the julienned omelet, fish sauce, sugar, pepper, and shrimp. By the time you reach for the golden garlic and stir it in, the shrimp will be cooked.

Ladle the soup into a steamboat, a soup tureen, or individual serving bowls. Tear a sprig or two of cilantro over each serving.

TOMATO AND SARDINE SOUP
WITH THAI CHILI AND MINT

Tom Yum Pla Ka Pong

Serves 2 to 4

S ardines packed in spicy tomato sauce, a staple found in almost every Thai cupboard, can help a busy Thai cook bring a simple broth out of the ordinary. Fresh tomatoes, lemon grass, and lime juice enliven this pretty, cinnabar-colored soup, and it all comes to the table in just a few minutes.

Add a stir-fry like Pork-Fried Rice (page 94), some fresh vegetables, and a dipping sauce for a quick home-style Thai dinner.

2¼ cups Chicken Stock (page 72) or canned chicken broth

3 large shallots, peeled and halved

1 large stalk lemon grass, tough outer leaves discarded, lower stalk trimmed to 12 inches and angle-cut into 2-inch pieces

6 (3 pairs) fresh Kaffir lime leaves (*bai magroot*), or two strips of lime peel, about 1 inch wide

2 cans (5½ ounces each) sardines in tomato sauce with chili

2 small tomatoes, cut in half and sliced into thin wedges

½ cup fresh lime juice

1 tablespoon Thai fish sauce (*nam pla*)

½ teaspoon white pepper

6 small Thai chilies (*phrik khee nu*), lightly crushed

1 cup loosely packed fresh mint

Put the stock, shallots, and lemon grass in a soup pot. If using Kaffir lime leaves, tear each leaf in half and add to the pot. If using lime peel, add to the pot. Gradually bring to a low boil over medium-high heat. Keep at a low boil for about 3 minutes. Add the sardines with their sauce. Return to a low boil. Keep at a low boil for 1 minute. Add the tomatoes, lime juice, fish sauce, and white pepper. Return to a low boil.

Float the chilies on top and turn off the heat. Ladle the soup into a steamboat, a soup tureen, or individual serving bowls. Tear a small handful of mint leaves over each serving.

N O T E : Frequent customers of Thai restaurants know that the lemon grass and lime leaves that flavor Thai soups are not meant to be eaten themselves. In this soup, the same is true of the shallots. Eating the chilies is optional.

COUNTRY-STYLE SWEET-AND-SALTY MACKEREL SOUP

Pla Thu Tom Khem

Serves 4 to 6

Although it's so humble that it is rarely found in restaurants or cookbooks, *pla thu tom khem* is a wonderful example of Thai country cooking. Unlike our city cooking or royal cuisine, in which multiple flavors are delicately balanced, this soup has two strong notes: richly sweet and aggressively salty.

As you might expect of a country-style dish, it needs only a few ingredients, the kind that are always on hand. *Pla thu,* a variety of mackerel that is one of the most common fishes in Thai cookery, is often packed in salt for preservation. You'll find ready-steamed, frozen, salt-preserved mackerel in your Thai market, or you can substitute fresh mackerel or red snapper fillets and add a few tablespoons of fish sauce to create the authentic salty taste needed to balance this soup's sweet broth.

½ pound ready-steamed, frozen, salt-preserved mackerel (*pla thu*) (about 3 small whole fish), defrosted

3 cups Chicken Stock (page 72) or canned chicken broth

3 tablespoons coconut-palm sugar

6 cloves garlic, sliced

2 large shallots, sliced

½ teaspoon white pepper

2 tablespoons Thai soy sauce with mushroom (*see-eu khao het hom*) or a Chinese brand, such as Pearl River Bridge

Sprigs of cilantro

Cut each fish in half with kitchen shears, a cleaver, or a chef's knife. Set aside.

Put the stock and sugar in a soup pot. Gradually bring to a boil over medium-high heat, stirring to dissolve the sugar. Stir in the garlic, shallots, and pepper. Return to a boil and add the fish. Simmer for 1 minute. Stir in the soy sauce and return to a boil. Boil for 1 minute, then turn off the heat.

Ladle the soup into a steamboat, a soup tureen, or individual serving bowls. Tear a sprig or two of cilantro over each serving.

CLEAR-BROTH SOUP WITH GROUND PORK, GARLIC, AND WATER SPINACH

Kaeng Chued Pak Bung Chin Mu Sub

Serves 4 to 6

This wholesome soup is reminiscent of a Mexican *albondigas*, but here the meatballs are light and crumbly. Ground pork is seasoned with fresh garlic, white pepper and fish sauce, then gently spooned, like small dumplings, into the simmering stock. With no eggs or bread to hold them together, the meatballs break up a bit as they cook, creating a wonderful texture.

½ pound ground pork

10 cloves garlic, pounded to a mash or crushed and chopped

½ teaspoon white pepper

1 tablespoon Thai fish sauce (*nam pla*)

½ tablespoon sugar

½ pound water spinach (*pak bung*) or common spinach

4½ cups Chicken Stock (page 72) or canned chicken broth

Sprigs of cilantro

Combine the pork, garlic, pepper, fish sauce, and sugar in a small mixing bowl. Mix by hand until blended. Set aside.

Trim off all but the top third of the long stems from the water spinach. Chop the spinach into 2½- to 3-inch pieces. Set aside.

Pour the stock into a soup pot and set over high heat. Bring to a low boil. Using a tablespoon, gather up scoops of the pork mixture and drop them, one by one, into the broth. The meatballs should be variously sized and shaped—that's part of the soup's charm.

Bring the soup back to a boil so the meatballs have time to release their seasonings into the broth. Stir in the water spinach, return to a boil, and turn off the heat.

Ladle the soup into a steamboat, a soup tureen, or individual serving bowls. Tear a sprig or two of cilantro over each serving.

CLEAR-BROTH SOUP
WITH FLOATING ISLANDS

Kaeng Chued Mara Sod Sai Mu Kap Kung

Serves 4 to 6

For some, bitter melon is an acquired taste. Here, its sharp essence plays against the sweetness of the shrimp and pork. Everyone will agree, though, that this distinctive soup is unusually pretty, with its rounds of melon, each stuffed with minced pork and a whole shrimp, the graceful curve of the shrimp's tail arcing out like a palm tree on its own little island.

3 bitter melons, each 5 to 6 inches long (about ¾ pound total)

4 cups water

2 tablespoons salt

½ pound ground pork

½ teaspoon white pepper

2 teaspoons Thai fish sauce (*nam pla*)

9 medium shrimp, peeled, but with tails left on

4 cups Chicken Stock (page 72) or canned chicken broth

Sprigs of cilantro

Trim off the ends of the bitter melons. Cut each one into thirds, creating rounds about 1½ inches thick. With a small knife or a grapefruit spoon, carve out the seeds and spongy inner membranes, leaving nine hollow rings. Pour the water into a large mixing bowl and stir in the salt. Soak the melon rings in the salted water for 30 minutes.

Mix the pork, pepper, and fish sauce in a small bowl. Drain the melon rings. Stuff each ring with some of the pork mixture. Press a shrimp halfway into the center of each, head first, leaving the tail curving out.

Pour the stock into a soup pot and set over high heat. Bring to a boil and add the stuffed bitter melon rings. Return to a boil, then reduce the heat and simmer for about 15 minutes, or until the bitter melon is tender enough to be cut with a spoon.

Ladle the soup into a steamboat, a soup tureen, or individual serving bowls. Tear a sprig or two of cilantro over each serving.

RAIN FOREST SOUP

Tom Kati Nor Wai On Kap Pla Haeng

Serves 4 to 6

Vast areas of Thailand were once covered by tropical rain forests. Today, unfortunately, only a small percentage of the original rain forests remain, in the far south of Thailand, near Malaysia. Rattan flourishes there, along with coconut palms. (Rattan is actually a kind of palm tree, which is why rattan shoots and hearts of palm are so similar in flavor and texture.)

If anything is edible, you can bet the Thai people will find out about it. Young rattan shoots are highly prized. Here they are the featured ingredient in an unusual soup that's rich in contrasting flavors: pungent dried fish and mild, crunchy rattan shoots lightly seasoned and smoothed with coconut milk and palm sugar.

¼ pound dried herring (about 10 fish, each 5 inches long)

2 cups Chicken Stock (page 72) or canned chicken broth

1 can (19 ounces) unsweetened coconut milk

½ cup fresh lemon juice

2 tablespoons Thai fish sauce (*nam pla*)

2 tablespoons coconut-palm sugar or golden brown sugar

1 jar (15 ounces) rattan shoots (*nor wai on*) or canned hearts of palm, drained, each piece angle-cut into three or four pieces

½ teaspoon white pepper

5 small Thai chilies (*phrik khee nu*), stemmed and lightly crushed

½ cup lightly packed Thai basil (*bai horapha*) or purple or Italian basil

Rinse the herring in a bowl of cold water. Trim off and discard the heads and tails. Rinse again. Remove the stomachs by pinching off the small underside areas near each head. Rinse the herring again in several changes of water until the water runs clear, about four or five times.

Put the stock and coconut milk in a soup pot and set over high heat. Bring to a boil, stirring occasionally. Stir in the herring and the lemon juice. Add the fish sauce and sugar, stirring until the sugar is dissolved. Lower the heat to bring the soup down to a simmer, and simmer gently for 1 minute. Stir in the rattan shoots and white pepper. Return the soup to a boil, float the chilies on top, and turn off the heat.

Ladle the soup into a steamboat, a soup tureen, or individual serving bowls. Tear a small handful of basil leaves over each serving.

N O T E : The crushed chilies give the soup a spicy edge. Eating them is optional.

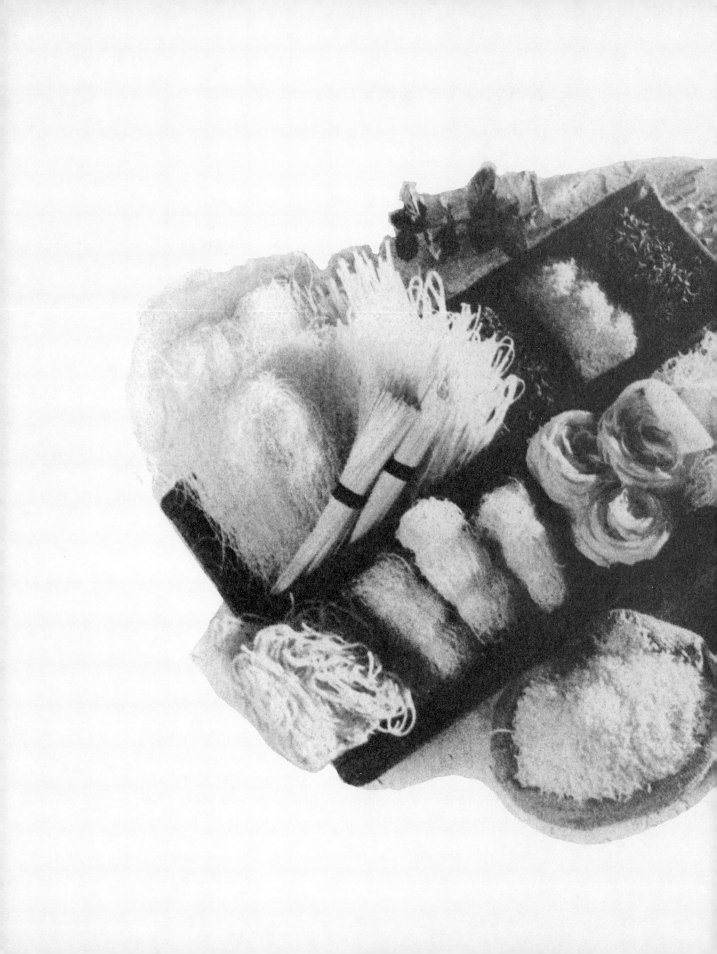

RICE and NOODLES

Khao leh Mee

Our central lands are an enormous river basin blessed with warm weather—perfect for large-scale rice cultivation. According to some scholars, the world's first rice fields were cultivated in Thai locales known as Non Nok Tha and Ban Chien.

Today, five thousand years later, our country is known as "the rice bowl of Asia." More than half of our population works in rice fields. Every year, ceremonies pay tribute to Mae Phosop, the mother and goddess of rice. And rice is the centerpiece of all authentic Thai meals.

In fact, a single word, *khao*, means both "rice" and "food."

The pearl-white color of rice balances the vivid tones of curries and sauces, just as its subtle flavor balances their spiciness and piquancy. Rice is the pale canvas on which a Thai chef paints a feast.

Thai people usually cook more rice than is needed for the meal at hand. Left-over rice can be stir-fried at the next meal, combined in hundreds of variations with vegetables, meats, seafood, herbs, and spices.

Noodles—often made from rice flour—are also very important in Thai cuisine, especially for snacks and quick meals. Noodles may have originally come to us from China, but ancient engravings show Thai people of long-ago times squeezing dough from a cloth sack through a slotted metal disk, as noodles fall into a boiling cauldron of broth.

This chapter will introduce you to a wide variety of rice and noodles, including fragrant jasmine rice, sticky rice, semi-transparent "cellophane" noodles, skinny ver-micelli, broad rice noodles, and wheat-flour noodles.

If you could fly above Thailand during the weeks when grain begins to form on the young rice plants, you would see thousands of colorful little bamboo flags. They remind people to respect the growing shoots. I hope these recipes convince you how much respect rice deserves—not just for being the staff of life of more than half the world's people, but also for being so delicious and versatile.

STEAMED JASMINE RICE

Khao Suoy

Serves 4 to 6

Long-grain white rice, which cooks into fluffy, almost separate, grains, is favored in Southeast Asia. Thai people are most fond of our own jasmine rice, a particularly pleasing long-grain variety with a naturally sweet perfume and a delicate nutty taste.

Jasmine rice is available in Asian markets and specialty stores all over the country and can also be ordered through mail-order catalogs that specialize in Thai ingredients. You may substitute any long-grain white rice except converted rice, because its grains remain distinctly separate no matter how you cook it. Even fluffy-textured jasmine rice has a light clingyness to the grains.

There is no rule for determining how much water to use per quantity of rice. The Chinese add enough water to cover their short-grain rice by the depth of one knuckle—about 1 inch. But a long-grain rice like jasmine requires more water.

The best method I know is as follows: For the first cup of rice, use 2 cups of water. For each added cup of rice, add 1 cup water.

Thai cooks always wash rice before cooking it to remove excess starch and achieve a pure white color. Although washing removes some nutrients, fish sauce and other vitamin-rich ingredients in our cooking more than compensate.

2½ cups (1 pound) jasmine rice (*khao hom mali*) or other long-grain white rice

3½ cups water

Wash the rice in several changes of water, swirling it through your fingers until the water runs almost clear. Drain.

Put the washed rice and water in a heavy-bottomed saucepan and bring to a rolling boil over medium-high heat. Cover tightly and reduce the heat to its lowest setting. Simmer for 18 minutes.

Lift the lid to check for doneness; cook for 1 or 2 minutes longer if necessary. (The rice is done when all the water has been absorbed and the grains are soft enough to crush between your thumb and forefinger.)

Turn off the heat, keep the rice covered, and let it stand, undisturbed, for at least 8 to 10 minutes, or up to 30 minutes, before serving.

Just before serving, fluff the rice with a fork.

THAI SERVING STYLE: Keep the rice fluffy by serving it the Thai way: Instead of scooping it out, which causes it to compress and pack together, use a serving spoon and scrape it across the surface of the rice with soft, gentle motions.

NOTE: Like most Thais, I usually cook a lot more rice than I need for one meal. Cold leftover rice is perfect for the dozens of fried-rice dishes we call *khao phat*—everything from Shrimp-Fried Rice to the elaborate King Rama's Fried Rice. All things are possible when leftover steamed rice is on hand.

COCONUT RICE

Khao Man

Coconut rice is an elegant comfort food—sophisticated yet homey. It's a lush variation of Steamed Jasmine Rice (page 86), enriched with coconut milk, a little sugar, and a pinch of salt. The result is rice with a creamy texture, subtly sweet and fragrant with coconut.

If you're serving hot-chili dishes, such as Green Papaya Salad (page 286), or a fiery curry, coconut rice will soothe the palate between bites. Or blend it with the spicy sauces on your plate, taming them with its sweet, coconutty flavor.

But coconut rice isn't just for spicy meals. It makes a rich, exotic basis for any of your favorite Thai, or even Western, dishes. I especially like it with palace-style cuisine, such as Yellow Peppers Stuffed with Crab and Chicken in Green Curry (page 322).

FOR 4 SERVINGS

1½ cups jasmine rice (*khao hom mali*) or other long-grain white rice

1 can (14 ounces) unsweetened coconut milk

¾ cup water

1 teaspoon sugar

Pinch salt

FOR 6 TO 8 SERVINGS

2½ cups jasmine rice (*khao hom mali*) or other long-grain white rice

1 can (19 ounces) unsweetened coconut milk

1¼ cups water

2 teaspoons sugar

Pinch salt

Wash the rice in several changes of water, swirling it through your fingers until the water runs almost clear. Drain and set aside.

Put the coconut milk, water, sugar, and salt in a heavy-bottomed saucepan. Stir until the sugar is dissolved and the ingredients are well blended.

Add the rice and stir to mix.

Bring to a rolling boil over medium-high heat. Cover tightly and reduce the heat to its lowest setting. Simmer for 18 minutes.

Lift the lid to check for doneness; cook for 1 or 2 minutes longer if necessary. (Some coconut cream may rise to the top, but the rice is done when all the liquid has been absorbed and the grains are soft enough to crush between your thumb and forefinger.)

Turn off the heat, keep the rice covered, and let it stand, undisturbed, for at least 8 to 10 minutes, or up to 30 minutes, before serving.

Just before serving, fluff the rice with a fork, blending in any coconut cream that may have risen to the top.

THAI SERVING STYLE: Keep the rice fluffy by serving it the Thai way: Instead of scooping out the rice, which causes it to compress and pack together, use a serving spoon and scrape it across the surface of the rice with soft, gentle motions.

ISSAN STICKY RICE

Khao Niao Nung

Serves 4 to 6

S ticky rice is a short-grain variety, opaque and very white, with a high gluten content, which gives it its starchy, "sticky" quality. Most Thai people use it only for sweet snacks and desserts, but for millions of Thais in the northern and northeastern provinces, sticky rice is as vital to their way of life as the rains that make it grow.

Because these provincial Thais share the same ethnic heritage as their Laotian brothers and sisters across the Mekong River, there is no real culinary boundary between the nations. In a northern Thai city like Chiang Mai or in the smallest Issan village, sticky rice is eaten at every meal—just as it is in Laos.

Lumps of sticky rice are formed into balls with the fingers of one hand. When pushed or rolled onto bits of meat or vegetables, the sticky little balls pick up everything in their path. They may also mop up a soupy curry sauce, get dunked into dipping sauces, or be drenched with a citrusy salad dressing. Without ever lifting a fork, eaters of sticky rice roll up chewy mouthfuls studded with the flavorful bits and pieces of the whole meal.

Before cooking sticky rice, it's best to soak it overnight, or for at least 6 hours. Presoaking cleans and softens the grains so they can be steamed to just the right texture.

The traditional method of cooking sticky rice is to fill a bamboo steaming basket, or *huad*, with rice and set it over a deep, wide-mouthed pan of water. Halfway through the steaming, the rice must be carefully turned to ensure even cooking.

In testing recipes for this book, we worked out a much easier method. A tiered aluminum steamer can replace the traditional *huad*, and a spritzer bottle filled with water ensures even cooking without the need for turning the rice.

2 cups Thai sticky rice (*khao niao*)	Cheesecloth
2 quarts water	Spray bottle filled with water

Soak the sticky rice in cold water to cover by 2 inches for at least 6 hours, or overnight. Drain, rinse the rice well, and drain again. Pour the 2 quarts of water into the base pot of a tiered aluminum steamer, cover, and bring the water to boil over high heat.

Line a steamer rack with a double thickness of thoroughly dampened cheesecloth. Spread the rice out evenly over the cheesecloth, and when the water reaches a boil, set the rack over the pot. Cover and steam for 15 minutes.

Uncover and spray the surface of the rice with about 15 short blasts of water from the spray bottle. Cover and steam for 5 minutes, then spray the rice a second time. Cover and steam for 5 minutes, then spray the rice a third time. Cover and steam for 5 more minutes, or until the rice is soft and sticky enough to be pressed into little balls.

Turn off the heat, uncover briefly to let the steam dissipate, then cover and let stand until serving time.

Serve warm or at room temperature.

THAI SERVING STYLE: In the more traditional households, or for special occasions, each guest would have his own rice basket, woven in the distinctive geometric patterns of the region. You may stay true to this spirit by serving sticky rice on your prettiest china, then letting your guests eat in the Laotian-Thai style, using their fingers.

SHRIMP-FRIED RICE

Khao Phat Kung

Serves 4 to 6 as a side dish, or 2 as a one-dish meal

F ried-rice dishes are simple, everyday favorites. *Khao phat kung* features shrimp, tomato, and scallions, infused with a fragrant herbal mash of garlic and cilantro. Eggs are optional, but I think they're especially good with fresh shrimp. Bean sprouts are added at the end, so they'll remain just slightly crunchy.

Fried rice can be served as a one-dish meal or a side dish. You can also build a meal around it, instead of steamed rice. To expand the flavors of any fried-rice recipe, especially when it's served as a one-dish meal, Thai people like to offer a small selection of condiments. For shrimp-fried rice, I suggest wedges of fresh lime, chili sauce, cilantro, and crushed peanuts.

SHRIMP-FRIED RICE

4 cups cold cooked jasmine rice (*khao hom mali*) or any long-grain white rice (see Note)

6 cloves garlic

½ cup loosely packed chopped cilantro, including the stems

4 tablespoons vegetable oil

I cup chopped onion

18 medium shrimp (about ½ pound), cleaned and peeled

2 to 3 eggs (optional)

2½ tablespoons Thai fish sauce (*nam pla*)

2 tablespoons golden brown sugar

½ tablespoon white pepper

I tomato, cut in half and sliced into thin wedges

3 scallions, including the green tops, sliced

2 cups bean sprouts

CONDIMENTS

Sprigs of cilantro

¼ cup roasted unsalted peanuts, crushed in a mortar or finely chopped

Lime or lemon wedges

Classic Chili Dipping Sauce (page 49) (optional)

Put the rice in a large mixing bowl and knead it gently through your fingers to separate the grains. Set aside.

Prepare an herbal mash with the garlic and cilantro:

Mortar-and-pestle method: Put the garlic and cilantro in the mortar and pound them to a mash. Set aside.

Alternate method: Crush the garlic with the side of a chef's knife. Mix the chopped cilantro with the crushed garlic and finely chop. Set aside.

Place all of the stir-fry ingredients within easy reach of the cooking area.

Set a wok over medium-high heat. When it is quite hot, add the oil. Rotate the wok a bit so the oil coats the sides. When the oil is hot, add the garlic-cilantro mash and the chopped onion, and stir-fry until the onion is translucent, about 1 minute. Add the shrimp and stir-fry just until they begin to turn pink, about 15 seconds.

If using eggs, break them into the wok and stir-fry for 45 seconds, mixing well.

Add the rice and stir-fry, pressing the rice down into the bottom of the wok. Turn the rice mixture over, press it down into the wok again, and continue to stir-fry for 1 minute. Add the fish sauce, sugar, and pepper and stir-fry for 45 seconds. Add the tomato, scallions, and bean sprouts and stir-fry for 1 minute.

Transfer to a serving platter. Tear a few sprigs of cilantro over the dish and serve with more of the cilantro, crushed peanuts, wedges of fresh lime or lemon, and Classic Chili Dipping sauce, if desired.

NOTE: To give your stir-fried rice perfect texture, always use rice that was cooked a day or more in advance and stored in the refrigerator. Freshly cooked rice would be too soft.

Rice
and
Noodles

PORK-FRIED RICE

Khao Phat Mu

Serves 4 to 6 as a side dish, or 2 as a one-dish meal

This is one of the most basic, and yet most pleasing, versions of stir-fried rice. Featuring medallions of sweet-flavored pork tenderloin, it is mildly seasoned with mushroom soy, white pepper, and garlic.

PORK-FRIED RICE

4 cups cold cooked jasmine rice (*khao hom mali*) or any long-grain white rice (see Note)

4 tablespoons vegetable oil

15 cloves garlic, pounded to a mash or crushed and chopped

½ pound pork tenderloin, cut crosswise into thin medallions

2 to 3 eggs (optional)

2 tablespoons Thai soy sauce with mushroom (*see-eu khao het hom*) or a Chinese brand, such as Pearl River Bridge

½ tablespoon Thai fish sauce (*nam pla*)

½ teaspoon white pepper

6 scallions, including the green tops, sliced

2 tablespoons golden brown sugar

CONDIMENTS

Sprigs of cilantro

1 to 2 small cucumbers, peeled and sliced into spears

Classic Chili Dipping Sauce (page 49) (optional)

Put the rice in a large mixing bowl and knead it gently through your fingers to separate the grains. Set aside.

Place all the stir-fry ingredients within easy reach of the cooking area.

Set a wok over medium-high heat. When it is quite hot, add the oil. Rotate the wok a bit so the oil coats the sides. When the oil is hot, add the garlic and stir-fry briefly, just until golden and aromatic. Add the pork, raise the heat to high, and stir-fry just until the pork turns pink, about 30 seconds.

If using eggs, break them into the wok and stir-fry for 45 seconds, mixing well. Add the rice and stir-fry, pressing the rice down into the bottom of the wok. Turn the rice mixture over, press it down into the wok again, and continue stir-frying for another minute. Add the soy sauce, fish sauce, and pepper and stir-fry for 45 seconds. Add the scallions and sugar and stir-fry for 1 minute.

Transfer to a serving platter. Tear a few sprigs of cilantro over the dish and serve with more of the cilantro, the cucumber spears, and chili sauce, if desired.

NOTE: To give your stir-fried rice perfect texture, always use rice that was cooked a day or more in advance and stored in the refrigerator. Freshly cooked rice would be too soft.

PINEAPPLE WITH FRIED-RICE STUFFING

Khao Phat Supparod

Serves 4 to 6 as a side dish, or 2 as a one-dish meal

B ecause its delicious flavors are matched by such a striking presentation, this classic fried-rice recipe is a favorite at dinner parties all over Bangkok. Fresh Gulf shrimp are tossed with juicy chunks of pineapple, red bell pepper, and aromatic curry powder, creating a sweetly tart and fragrant dish.

A fresh, ripe pineapple is hollowed out, with its topknot of greens left intact, to become the serving dish. The stir-fried rice is mounded within and showered with crushed peanuts and a special Thai condiment known as shrimp powder with chili. Chopped cilantro and minced hot chilies are served alongside.

PINEAPPLE-FRIED RICE

3 cups cold cooked jasmine rice (*khao hom mali*) or any long-grain white rice (see Note)

I large ripe pineapple (about 3¾ to 4 pounds)

1½ tablespoons vegetable oil

10 cloves garlic, pounded to a mash or crushed and chopped

½ pound medium shrimp, cleaned and peeled

1½ teaspoons curry powder

I red bell pepper, diced

3 scallions, including the green tops, sliced

2½ tablespoons sugar

1½ tablespoons Thai fish sauce (*nam pla*)

CONDIMENTS

1½ tablespoons shrimp powder with chili (*kung phrik pon*)

⅓ cup roasted unsalted peanuts, crushed in a mortar or finely chopped

¾ cup loosely packed chopped cilantro, including the stems

6 small Thai chilies (*phrik khee nu*), or 2 serrano chilies, minced

95

Rice

and

Noodles

continued

Put the rice in a large mixing bowl and knead it gently through your fingers to separate the grains. Set aside.

Stand the pineapple up, and, keeping the leaves intact, cut a vertical slice off one side. This slice will become the "lid" for the finished dish of stuffed pineapple.

Lay the pineapple down, cut side up. Carefully hollow it out to remove the fruit, but leave the shell intact for stuffing. Set the shell and lid aside. Core the fruit and chop it into ½-inch cubes. You should have about 2 cups.

Place all of the stir-fry ingredients within easy reach of the cooking area.

Set a wok over medium-high heat. When it is quite hot, add the oil. Rotate the wok a bit so the oil coats the sides. When the oil is hot, add the garlic and stir-fry briefly, just until golden and aromatic. Add the shrimp and stir-fry just until they begin to turn pink, about 15 seconds. Add the pineapple and stir-fry for 2 minutes. Add the rice and stir-fry, pressing the rice down into the bottom of the wok. Turn the rice mixture over, press it down into the wok again, and stir-fry for 1 minute. Add the curry powder and stir-fry for 30 seconds. Add the red bell pepper and scallions and stir-fry for 30 seconds. Add the sugar and stir-fry for 30 seconds. Add the fish sauce and stir-fry for 30 seconds. Turn off the heat.

Put the pineapple shell on a serving platter and lightly pack the fried rice into the hollow. Mound it at the top to create a rounded form. (If the fried rice doesn't all fit in the pineapple shell, keep the remainder warm in the covered wok.)

Dust half the pineapple with some of the shrimp powder and sprinkle the other half with some of the crushed peanuts. Put the remaining shrimp powder and peanuts, and the chopped cilantro and minced chilies, into small individual serving bowls.

Place the reserved pineapple lid alongside the pineapple.

Set out the platter of stuffed pineapple and all the condiments, and serve.

NOTE: To give your stir-fried rice perfect texture, always use rice that was cooked a day or more in advance and stored in the refrigerator. Freshly cooked rice would be too soft.

THAI-STYLE SPANISH RICE

Khao Phat Sauce Makhua Tet

Serves 4 to 6 as a side dish, or 2 as a one-dish meal

Y ou might not expect to find tomato paste as a flavor component in a Thai dish. But fresh tomatoes, catsup, and even tomato paste are used in Thai cooking, especially in the northern provinces near Laos.

I call this Thai-style Spanish rice because it may remind you of many similar dishes that were popular some years ago here in America. These dishes consisted of canned tomatoes, chili powder, sautéed onion and garlic, and a little hot sauce, all simmered together with the rice. My recipe is a mild and sweet stir-fried rice made with pork and seasoned with garlic and Thai spices such as white pepper and thin soy sauce. Tomato paste, in place of canned tomatoes, imparts a richer tomato taste.

Always serve a few condiments with fried-rice dishes. In this instance, scallions, cucumber spears, and a hot chili sauce are the perfect complements.

THAI-STYLE SPANISH RICE

4 cups cold cooked jasmine rice (*khao hom mali*) or any long-grain white rice (see note)

3 tablespoons vegetable oil

12 cloves garlic, pounded to a mash or crushed and chopped

½ pound pork tenderloin, cut into 2-inch pieces about ¼ inch thick

1 tomato, cut in half and sliced into thin wedges

2 to 3 eggs (optional)

4 tablespoons tomato paste

2 tablespoons sugar

½ teaspoon white pepper

2 tablespoons Thai thin soy sauce (*see-eu khao*) or any good light soy sauce

CONDIMENTS

Sprigs of cilantro

1 small bunch scallions

1 to 2 small cucumbers, peeled and sliced into spears

Classic Shrimp Paste and Chili Sauce (page 48) or Classic Chili Dipping Sauce (page 49) (optional)

Put the rice in a large mixing bowl and knead it gently through your fingers to separate the grains. Set aside.

Place all of the stir-fry ingredients within easy reach of the cooking area.

Set a wok over medium-high heat. When it is quite hot, add the oil. Rotate the wok a bit so the oil coats the sides. When the oil is hot, add the garlic and stir-fry just until golden and aromatic. Add the pork, raise the heat to high, and stir-fry just until the pork turns pink, about 30 seconds. Add the sliced tomato and stir-fry for 1 minute.

If using eggs, break them into the wok and stir-fry for 45 seconds, mixing well.

Add the rice and stir-fry, pressing the rice down into the bottom of the wok. Turn the rice mixture over, press it down into the wok again, and stir-fry for another minute.

Add the tomato paste and stir-fry for 1 minute. Add the sugar, pepper, and soy sauce and stir-fry for 1½ minutes.

Transfer to a serving platter. Tear a few sprigs of cilantro over the dish and serve with more of the cilantro, the scallions and cucumber spears, and one of the sauces, if desired.

N O T E : To give your stir-fried rice perfect texture, always use rice that was cooked a day or more in advance and stored in the refrigerator. Freshly cooked rice would be too soft.

BROKEN RICE

Prai Khao Suoy

Broken rice, as the name implies, is simply broken-up bits of long-grain rice. These fractured grains are the perfect basis for a family of specialty soups known as *khao tom*.

Unlike our "dinnertime" soups, which accompany a host of other dishes to make up the evening meal, *khao tom* soups are complete meals in themselves, enjoyed at all hours of the day and night. They are the ultimate Thai "comfort food." A simple breakfast *khao tom* might be made with chicken stock, seasoned ground pork, and perhaps an egg poached in the simmering broth. City people might finish a long evening on the town with an after-hours *khao tom* that is a feast of spices, stir-fried seafood, and specially prepared vegetables. In fact, Bangkok has many shops that serve only *khao tom*, in its several variations, where people capping an evening of nightlife rub shoulders with workers getting an early start on a new day. Customers simply begin with a basic bowl of broth and rice, then add to their heart's delight from a vast menu of condiments.

It's possible to use any kind of rice in a *khao tom* soup, but whenever the waiter asks, "Do you want *khao tom prai khao* (*khao tom* with broken rice)?" I always answer "yes." The broken grains swell with water when cooked, creating a pleasing, porridgelike texture that's essential to a great bowl of *khao tom*.

FOR 4 CUPS COOKED
BROKEN RICE

I cup broken rice (*prai khao*) or any long-grain white rice (see Note)

4 cups water

FOR 6 CUPS COOKED
BROKEN RICE

1½ cups broken rice (*prai khao*) or any long-grain white rice (see Note)

6 cups water

Wash the rice in several changes of water, swirling it through your fingers until the water runs almost clear.

Pour the water into a heavy-bottomed saucepan. Bring it to a boil over medium-high heat. Stir in the broken rice and bring it to a low boil. Cover tightly and reduce the heat to low. Simmer for 20 minutes. The rice is done when all of the water has been absorbed and the grains are soft and plumped with moisture. (A thin film of water may remain in the bottom of the pot.)

Remove from the heat, cover, and set aside. When the rice has cooled to room temperature, refrigerate, covered, until needed.

NOTE: If using long-grain white rice, chop it up slightly after it is cooked and has cooled to room temperature.

LATE-NIGHT SOUP WITH FOUR SPECIAL CONDIMENTS

Kap Khao Khao Tom

Serves 6

"Let's go eat *khao tom*" is a phrase heard frequently in Thai cities, especially late at night. Many exclusive hotels offer a late-night buffet of soups and condiments, but the most lively places are the *khao tom* shops, which serve a basic, healthful broth and a selection of perhaps fifty or one hundred condiments. Most tourists aren't aware of these shops, which are usually open between 11:00 P.M. and 7:00 A.M., but native Thais make their favorite *khao tom* place a second home. They may come in for an invigorating, restorative bowlful after a night of partying, when most regular restaurants are closed. Others skip the soup entirely and just order up platefuls of delicious condiments, sipping from their own bottle of whiskey.

Four of my favorite condiments are included here: Sweet Shrimp, Hot-and-Sour Salty Egg Salad, Sweet Salted Lettuce with Scrambled Eggs, and Dried Shrimp Stir-Fry.

Sweet Shrimp is practically candied in a smooth, savory sauce made with garlic and fish essence. Hot-and-Sour Salty Egg Salad is piquant with fresh ginger, chilies, and lemon juice. It's terrific on its own as well, with just a side dish of steamed rice. Plain salted lettuce right from the can is one of the simpler condiments on a *khao tom* shop's menu. I like to incorporate its sour taste and crunchy character in a quick stir-fry with scrambled eggs with a dash each of white pepper, sugar, and fish sauce. Dried Shrimp Stir-Fry has an earthy flavor, with a wonderful crunchy texture that holds up well in the hot soup.

The soup recipe and some suggested secondary condiments follow on page 103.

True
Thai

SWEET SHRIMP

Kung Wan

16 medium shrimp

1½ tablespoons vegetable oil

12 cloves garlic, pounded to a mash or crushed and chopped

3 tablespoons sugar

1½ tablespoons Thai fish sauce (*nam pla*)

Rinse and peel the shrimp, but leave the tails on. Butterfly and devein. Set aside.

Set a small iron skillet over medium-high heat. When it is quite hot, add the oil. When the oil is hot, add the garlic and stir-fry briefly, just until golden and aromatic. Add the shrimp and stir-fry until they turn pink, about 30 seconds. Add the sugar and stir-fry for 30 seconds. Add the fish sauce and stir-fry for 30 seconds.

Transfer to a small serving bowl, cover to keep warm, if desired, and set aside.

HOT-AND-SOUR SALTY EGG SALAD

Khai Phed Khem

3 hard-boiled salty eggs (*khai khem*)

¼ cup matchstick slices of fresh, peeled ginger

¼ cup loosely packed chopped cilantro, including the stems

2 serrano chilies, finely sliced

5 tablespoons fresh lemon juice

Peel the eggs, cut them in half lengthwise, and slice. Put the sliced eggs and all of the remaining ingredients into a small mixing bowl and stir to blend.

Transfer to a small serving bowl and set aside.

SWEET SALTED LETTUCE WITH SCRAMBLED EGGS

Pak Kad Dong Phat Khai

2 tablespoons vegetable oil

2 cans (5 ounces each) salted lettuce (*pak kad dong*)

2 eggs

1½ tablespoons sugar

1 tablespoon Thai fish sauce (*nam pla*)

½ teaspoon white pepper

Set a large iron skillet over medium heat. When it is quite hot, add the oil. Add the salted lettuce and stir-fry for 1½ minutes. Break the eggs into the skillet and stir briefly to break them up. Add the sugar, fish sauce, and pepper and stir-fry just until the sugar is dissolved and all of the ingredients are well blended, about 30 seconds.

Transfer to a serving bowl, cover to keep warm, if desired, and set aside.

DRIED SHRIMP STIR-FRY

Kung Haeng Phat Phrik Thai

1 package (4 ounces) large dried shrimp (*kung haeng*)

2 tablespoons sugar

½ tablespoon white pepper

2 tablespoons Thai thin soy sauce (*see-eu khao*) or any good light soy sauce

Set a small iron skillet over high heat and dry-fry the shrimp for 1½ minutes, stirring often. Add the sugar, pepper, and soy sauce and stir-fry until the sugar is dissolved and all of the ingredients are well blended, about 1 minute.

Transfer to a small serving bowl, cover to keep warm if desired, and set aside.

SOUP

6 cups cooked Broken Rice (page 98)   9 cups Chicken Stock (page 72) or
                                                 canned chicken broth

Put the cooked broken rice and chicken stock into a soup pot. Set the pot over medium-high heat and bring to a low boil, stirring occasionally.

Turn off the heat, cover, and set aside.

SECONDARY CONDIMENTS

Sprigs of cilantro

3 or 4 sliced scallions, including the
    green tops

4 to 6 tablespoons matchstick slices of
    fresh, peeled ginger

Ground white pepper

4 Tablespoons Golden garlic (page 65)

¼ to ½ cup Chilies-in-Vinegar-Sauce
    (page 52)

Put all the secondary condiments into individual serving bowls and set them on the table, along with the four special condiments.

Ladle the soup into six deep soup bowls. Tear a sprig or two of cilantro over each bowl and serve immediately with a full array of condiments.

THAI SERVING STYLE: Add a spoonful or two of a condiment and sample the result. The condiments can be enjoyed one at a time, or mixed and matched to suit your individual taste. It's wonderful to create different flavor experiences as you go along.

CELLOPHANE NOODLES WITH MIXED SEAFOOD AND CHINESE CELERY

Phat Woon Sen Talay

Serves 4 to 6

A silvery tangle of bean-thread vermicelli holds a catch of mussels, clams, and squid in a garlicky yellow bean sauce with pungent Chinese celery.

Because they are clear and translucent, bean-thread vermicelli are familiarly known as *cellophane noodles.* You might also see them described on a menu as *glass noodles, silver noodles,* or *shining noodles.* These threadlike strands, made from the starch of mung beans, are wonderful for soaking up sauces.

1 package (3½ ounces) dried bean-thread vermicelli (*woon sen*)

¾ pound whole squid

¾ pound New Zealand mussels, placed in a bowl or sink full of cold water

¾ pound littleneck or cherrystone clams, placed in a bowl or sink full of cold water

3 tablespoons vegetable oil

10 cloves garlic, pounded to a mash or crushed and chopped

¼ cup Chicken Stock (page 72) or canned chicken broth

2 tablespoons crushed yellow bean sauce (*tao jiew dam*)

3 tablespoons golden brown sugar

¼ pound Chinese celery (*tang o*), stalks trimmed to 1 inch, leafy stems chopped into 1-inch pieces

½ teaspoon white pepper

Sprigs of cilantro

Classic Chili Dipping Sauce (page 49) (optional)

To soak the noodles: Put the noodles in a large bowl of warm water and soak until soft and translucent, about 12 to 15 minutes. As the noodles become pliable, spread them out with your fingers to ensure quick, even soaking. Put the softened noodles in a colander, drain well, and turn them out onto a cutting board. Using a knife or kitchen shears, cut the mound of noodles into thirds. Set aside.

To clean the seafood: Rinse the squid under cold water. Pull the head from the body. Cut the tentacles off in one piece, just below the eyes, and discard the rest of the head. If the hard little beak is in the center of the set of tentacles, pull it out and discard. Reserve the body sac and tentacles.

Pull out the long, transparent quill from the body sac and discard. Press out the innards by running the body sac between your thumb and fingers, squeezing as you go from the closed to the cut end. Or lay the body sac on a flat work surface and run the dull side of a knife blade along its length, from the closed to the cut end. Rinse out the body sac, making sure to remove any traces of the gelatinous inner matter. Peel off the speckled skin and cut the squid into thirds. Score through one side of each piece with a series of diagonal cuts. Combine them with the tentacles and set aside.

Agitate the water in which the mussels are soaking. Tap the clams against one another. Live mussels and clams open and close to breathe. Any mussels or clams that don't eventually close should be discarded. Scrub and debeard the mussels. Scrub the clams.

Drain the mussels and clams and set aside.

To make the stir-fry: Place all of the ingredients within easy reach of the cooking area.

Set a wok over medium-high heat. When it is quite hot, add the oil. Rotate the wok a bit so the oil coats the sides. When the oil is hot, add the garlic and stir-fry just until golden and aromatic. Add the squid, mussels, and clams, raise the heat to high, and stir-fry until the squid turns opaque and the shellfish begin to open, about 2 minutes. Add the chicken stock, yellow bean sauce, and sugar, and stir just until the sugar is dissolved and blended with the sauce.

Add the noodles and stir-fry for 1 minute, repeatedly pressing them into the sauce at the bottom of the wok so they can drink it up. Add the Chinese celery and pepper and stir-fry briefly, until the celery is cooked through and crisp-tender, about 2 minutes. Check to see if all the shellfish have opened during the cooking. Stir-fry a minute longer, if necessary, then discard any mussels or clams that fail to open.

Transfer to a serving platter, tear sprigs of cilantro over the dish, and serve with classic chili dipping sauce, if desired.

KHANOM CHINE WITH CURRIED TUNA SAUCE AND THAI BASIL

Khanom Chine Nam Ya Pla

Serves 6

*K*hanom chine means "Chinese noodles," but these long white rice-flour noodles have been part of Thai cooking for centuries.

This is a very festive dish. The elongated shape of the noodles symbolizes long life and happiness. Here, they are coiled into bird's-nest shapes, garnished with dark green basil leaves, and set out with a platter of condiments and a tureen of fragrant, ochre-shaded curried tuna sauce that is rich, creamy, and moderately spicy.

There are numerous versions of curried *khanom chine* noodles. They're traditionally served at lunchtime for special occasions, but you can enjoy them any time you'd like to serve an elegant one-dish meal.

In Thailand the noodles are sold freshly made, already coiled into nests. Fresh *khanom chine* noodles aren't available in America yet, so Thai people in this country use Japanese *somen* noodles, which cook to a pure white color reminiscent of true *khanom chine*. Italian angel hair pasta, while not pure white, has all the other attributes—fine flavor and texture and long length for good luck.

CURRIED TUNA SAUCE

2 cans (6½ ounces each) chunk light tuna packed in water (not chunk white or solid albacore)

1 teaspoon white pepper

2 cans (14 ounces each) unsweetened coconut milk

1 cup Classic Red Curry Paste (page 26)

1 cup Chicken Stock (page 72) or canned chicken broth

3 teaspoons rhizome powder (*krachai*), or 1 teaspoon ground ginger

6 tablespoons sugar

3 tablespoons Thai fish sauce (*nam pla*)

1 teaspoon ground turmeric

NOODLES

1 pound Japanese *somen* noodles or angel hair pasta

1½ cups loosely packed Thai basil (*bai horapha*) or purple or Italian basil

CONDIMENTS

½ pound yard-long beans or green beans, angle-cut into ½-inch pieces

¾ pound bean sprouts

3 hard-boiled eggs, sliced

Thai chili powder (*phrik pon*) or other ground red chili to taste, such as New Mexico chili powder or cayenne (optional)

To make the curried tuna sauce: Drain the tuna and put it in the bowl of a food processor fitted with a metal blade. Add the pepper and process until the mixture is puréed, with a somewhat coarse, spreadable texture, about 30 seconds. Transfer to a small bowl and set aside.

Skim the thick cream from the canned coconut milk into a soup pot, reserving the milk. Set the pot over medium-high heat. Stir in the curry paste until blended, and bring to a low boil. Cook, stirring constantly, for 2 minutes. Blend in the tuna purée. Add the reserved coconut milk, chicken stock, and rhizome powder and cook for 1 minute, stirring often to blend. Add the sugar and fish sauce and cook for 1 minute, stirring often. Stir the turmeric into the sauce until blended. Cover and remove from the heat.

To cook the noodles and form them into nests: Fill a large pot with about 3½ quarts of water. Bring the water to a boil, add the *somen* noodles or angel hair pasta, and cook until al dente (1½ to 2 minutes for *somen*, or 2 to 2½ minutes for angel hair), stirring occasionally to keep the noodles from sticking to the bottom of the pot.

Drain immediately in a colander. Rinse well until the noodles are cool, tossing and stirring them with a wooden spoon to remove excess starch. Drain the noodles and transfer them to a mixing bowl.

Place a large serving platter on the counter or work surface, along with the bowl of noodles and the basil.

Take a handful of cooked noodles and coil them around two fingers of your other hand to make a 3- to 4-inch mound shaped like a little bird's nest. Put the nest on the serving platter. Repeat until all of the noodles have been formed into nests.

Arrange a few basil leaves in the hollow of each nest and set the platter aside.

To prepare the condiments: Blanch the beans in plenty of boiling water for 30 seconds. Transfer them with a wire skimmer or slotted spoon to a bowl of cold water, then drain and set aside.

Return the water to a boil. Blanch the bean sprouts for 20 seconds and drain immediately.

Arrange the beans, bean sprouts, and sliced eggs on a serving platter. Put some chili powder in a small serving bowl. Set the platter of bird's-nest noodles and all the condiments on the table.

Slowly reheat the curried tuna sauce over medium-high heat, without letting it come to a boil. Transfer to a serving bowl and serve with the bird's-nest noodles and condiments.

THAI SERVING STYLE: Serve each guest three or four bird's nests with some beans, bean sprouts, and a few slices of egg on the side. Generously ladle the sauce over the noodles. Let each guest combine the eggs and vegetables with the curried noodles to his taste, and season with chili powder, if desired.

RICE-STICK NOODLES WITH CHICKEN AND VEGETABLES

Kwaytiow Sen Lek Lad Na Kai

Serves 2 to 4

*L*ad na is a colorful expression that means, approximately, "I throw it on your face." In culinary terms, it refers to a flavorful topping—in this case a saucy stir-fry "thrown in the face" of rice-stick noodles. *Lad na kai* is a stir-fry of chicken and mixed vegetables that's heaped over a mound of warm noodles dressed with sweet dark soy sauce.

The noodles in this dish are made from rice flour and are readily available in dry form in most Asian markets. They come in a variety of shapes and widths. I like the thin, flat, fettucine-like rice sticks about ⅛ inch wide.

This dish is mild, sweet, and earthy. If any of your guests prefer a spicy alternative, chilies-in-vinegar sauce will fire it up without changing the balance of flavors.

Fresh Ginger Drink (page 347) is a delicious accompaniment to this one-dish meal.

NOODLES

8 ounces dried rice-stick noodles, "chan-taboon" type, or any thin, flat variety about ⅛ inch wide (*sen jahn* or *sen lek*)

2 tablespoons vegetable oil

1 tablespoon sweet black soy sauce (*see-eu wan*)

CHICKEN-AND-VEGETABLE STIR-FRY

2 tablespoons vegetable oil

6 cloves garlic, pounded to a mash or crushed and chopped

¾ pound boneless, skinless chicken breast, cut into 2 × ¼ × ¼-inch strips

¼ pound broccoli, chopped

1 small onion, cut in half and finely sliced

1½ cups chopped eggplant (about ½ medium eggplant)

½ teaspoon white pepper

2 tablespoons Thai fish sauce (*nam pla*)

2 tablespoons crushed yellow bean sauce (*tao jiew dam*)

3 tablespoons golden-brown sugar

¼ cup Chicken Stock (page 72) or canned chicken broth

1 tablespoon cornstarch dissolved in 1 tablespoon water

1 cup bean sprouts

3 large scallions, including the green tops, angle-cut into 1½-inch pieces, bulbs cut in half lengthwise

⅔ cup chopped red bell pepper (about ½ medium pepper)

Chilies-in-Vinegar Sauce (page 52) (optional)

To stir-fry the noodles: Place a heatproof platter in a warm oven while you prepare the noodles.

Soak the rice sticks in a large bowl of warm water until they are soft, about 15 minutes. Drain and set the noodles aside in a colander.

Set a wok over medium-high heat (see Note). When it is quite hot, add the oil. Rotate the wok a bit so the oil coats the sides. When the oil is hot, add the noodles. Stir-fry briskly as you toss the noodles in the hot oil to heat them through, about 45 seconds. Add the soy sauce and stir-fry briskly to coat all the noodles with the sauce, about 1 minute.

Transfer the noodles to the warm serving platter and keep in the oven while you prepare the chicken and vegetables.

To stir-fry the chicken and vegetables: Place all the stir-fry ingredients within easy reach of the cooking area.

Set a clean wok or deep, heavy skillet over medium-high heat. When it is quite hot, add the oil. If using a wok, rotate it a bit so the oil coats the sides. When the oil is hot, add the garlic and stir-fry briefly, just until golden and aromatic. Add the chicken, raise the heat to high, and stir-fry until the chicken begins to lose its raw color and turn opaque, about 30 seconds. Add the broccoli and stir-fry for 30 seconds. Add the sliced onion and eggplant and stir-fry for 2 minutes. Add the pepper, fish sauce, yellow bean sauce, and sugar and stir-fry for 45 seconds. Add the stock, corn-starch-water mixture, bean sprouts, scallions, and red bell pepper and stir-fry just until the vegetables are crisp-tender, about 2 minutes.

Remove the platter of noodles from the oven and ladle the chicken and vegetables over them. Serve with Chilies-in-Vinegar Sauce, if desired.

NOTE: A nonstick wok is handy when cooking rice-stick noodles.

Mahogany Fire Noodles

Kwaytiow Sen Yai Phat Phrik Sod Kap See-Eu Wan

Serves 4 to 6 as a side dish, or 2 to 4 as a one-dish meal

Few chilies are as hot as the tiny Thai chilies we call *phrik khee nu*—and there are thirty of them in this recipe! You could, of course, reduce the number of chilies to a more manageable level, but this dish is traditionally a fire-eater's favorite. When the chili-garlic seasoning paste for this chicken–and–rice noodle stir-fry hits the hot wok, you'll be greeted with a throat-tingling savory smoke indicative of that fiery chili heat. You may even want to have a fan on or a window open while you cook and an ice-cold beer to cool you down in between bites.

30 small Thai chilies (*phrik khee nu*)	I teaspoon white pepper
10 cloves garlic	2 tablespoons sweet black soy sauce (*see-eu wan*)
I pound presliced fresh rice noodles (*sen yai*) or uncut fresh rice noodle sheets (see Note)	I tablespoon oyster sauce
2 tablespoons vegetable oil	I can (8 ounces) bamboo shoot strips, drained
I¼ pounds boneless, skinless chicken breasts, cut into 2 × ¼ × ¼-inch strips	I½ tablespoons sugar
2 tablespoons Thai fish sauce (*nam pla*)	I½ cups loosely packed holy basil (*bai kaprao*) or fresh mint

Make a seasoning paste with the chilies and garlic:

Mortar-and-pestle method: Stem the chilies. Put the garlic and chilies in a mortar and pound until they are thoroughly mashed and pulverized. Set aside.

Alternate method: Stem the chilies. Crush the chilies and garlic with the side of a chef's knife. Mix the chilies and garlic together and mince. Set aside.

Put the sliced noodles in a colander and pour a kettle of hot water over them to remove the protective oil coating and soften them a bit. Unfold and separate the noodles into individual ribbons. (If some break off into short lengths, that's fine—it will create texture. Just be as careful as you can to separate the individual noodles from the folded mass.)

Place all of the ingredients within easy reach of the cooking area.

Set a wok over medium-high heat. When it is quite hot, add the oil. Rotate the wok a bit so the oil coats the sides. When the oil is hot add the chili-garlic paste and stir-fry briefly, about 15 seconds. Raise the heat to high, add the chicken, and stir-fry until it begins to lose its raw color and turn opaque, about 30 seconds. Stir in the fish sauce. Add the noodles and stir-fry briskly for 30 seconds, tossing the noodles to incorporate them with the other ingredients. Stir in the pepper and soy sauce. Add the oyster sauce, bamboo shoots, and sugar and stir-fry for 1 minute.

Turn off the heat. Stir in the basil and cook for a few seconds, just until the basil begins to wilt.

Transfer to a serving platter and serve immediately.

N O T E :   Fresh rice noodles can be stored in the refrigerator, but if you buy them the same day you plan to serve them, keep them at room temperature. They will be easier to unfold.

If buying uncut noodle sheets, slice them lengthwise through the folds into strips about ¾ inch wide.

DRUNKEN SPAGHETTI

Spaghetti Phat Khee Mao Bangkok

Serves 4 to 6

I don't know how this dish got its unusual name. Some people think that chilies are a cure for hangovers. Perhaps a chef decided one day to invent a meal to revive himself. Certainly, the fiery chili pesto that spices the meat sauce will enliven anyone's senses.

Drunken spaghetti is sort of a Thai version of spaghetti Bolognese—tomato-based, with lots of garlic and two kinds of chilies. You can serve it as part of a Thai meal or Italian style—with a tossed green salad and a glass of Chianti.

I pound spaghetti

½ cup Chicken Stock (page 72) or canned chicken broth

8 serrano chilies

24 cloves garlic

I cup loosely packed chopped Italian basil

6 small dried Japanese chilies

2½ tablespoons vegetable oil

I pound ground beef

6 plum tomatoes, cut in half and sliced into thin wedges

I small red onion, cut in half and finely sliced

3 scallions, including the green tops, angle-cut into I-inch pieces, bulbs cut in half lengthwise

3 tablespoons oyster sauce

3 tablespoons Thai fish sauce (*nam pla*)

6 tablespoons sugar

I can (8 ounces) tomato sauce

I tablespoon white pepper

Sprigs of cilantro

Cook the spaghetti in plenty of boiling salted water until it is tender but firm, about 9 to 10 minutes. Drain well and toss with the chicken stock. Set aside.

Make a pesto from the serranos, garlic, basil, and Japanese chilies:

Mortar-and-pestle method: Stem the serranos. Put the serranos and garlic in the mortar and pound them just until they are crushed. Add the basil and Japanese chilies and pound all the ingredients to a mash. Set aside.

Processor method: Stem the serranos. Crush them and the garlic with the side of a chef's knife. Mince the Japanese chilies. Put all the pesto ingredients in the bowl of a food processor fitted with a metal blade. Process until moist and nearly minced. Transfer to a small mixing bowl and set aside.

Place all of the ingredients within easy reach of the cooking area.

Set a large wok over high heat. When it is quite hot, add the oil. Rotate the wok a bit so the oil coats the sides. When the oil is hot, take handfuls of the ground beef and work it through your fingers to break it up a little as you add it to the wok. Stir-fry the beef, pressing it down into the bottom of the wok. Turn the beef over, press it down into the wok again, and continue to stir-fry until the meat begins to brown, about 45 seconds.

Add the chili pesto and stir-fry for 45 seconds. Add the spaghetti–chicken stock mixture and stir-fry for 45 seconds. Add the tomatoes, red onion, and scallions and stir-fry for 45 seconds. Add the oyster sauce and fish sauce and stir-fry for 30 seconds. Add the sugar, tomato sauce, and pepper and stir-fry until the sugar is dissolved and the ingredients are well blended, about 1 minute.

Transfer to a large serving bowl, tear sprigs of cilantro over the spaghetti, and serve.

SPAGHETTI WITH COUNTRY-STYLE TOMATO SAUCE

Spaghetti Nam Phrik Ong

Serves 4 to 6

*N*am phrik ong, the country-style tomato sauce in this recipe, comes from the Chiang Mai region of northern Thailand. It's an earthy, moderately spicy provincial dish traditionally served as a dip, with balls of sticky rice and raw or blanched vegetables. I love to serve this robustly flavored blend of ground pork, tomatoes and curry paste over noodles, especially spaghetti. All my American friends love the cross-cultural combination.

I recipe Country-Style Tomato Sauce with Ground Pork and Red Curry (page 50) (sauce only)

I pound spaghetti

Make the tomato sauce. Cover and set aside.

Cook the spaghetti in plenty of boiling salted water until al dente, about 10 to 12 minutes. When the pasta is nearly cooked, gently reheat the sauce and cover to keep hot.

Drain the cooked spaghetti. Toss with the sauce and serve immediately.

CLASSIC THAI NOODLES

Phat Thai

Serves 4 to 6 as a side dish, or
2 as a one-dish meal

———

E verybody loves *phat Thai*. Many Americans have told me that their first taste of this sweet-and-sour, spicy, peanutty noodle stir-fry is what got them hooked on Thai cuisine. The fettucinelike tangle of rice noodles winds around whole shrimp and bits of chicken or pork, scallions, bean sprouts, and crushed peanuts.

I like to add other traditional ingredients as well—such as pressed bean curd, small dried shrimp, and salted radish—but these are optional. *Phat Thai* is always customized to suit your taste.

Extra peanuts and bean sprouts are always served on the side, along with wedges of fresh lime and sliced chilies or chili sauce.

STIR-FRIED NOODLES

8 ounces dried rice-stick noodles, "chantaboon" type, or any thin, flat variety about ⅛ inch wide (*sen jahn* or *sen lek*)

¼ pound medium shrimp

¼ pound pork tenderloin or boneless chicken, either light meat or dark

4 tablespoons Thai fish sauce (*nam pla*)

6 tablespoons distilled white vinegar

6 tablespoons sugar

1 tablespoon catsup

3 tablespoon vegetable oil

8 cloves garlic, pounded to a mash or crushed and chopped

2 tablespoons small dried shrimp (optional)

¼ cup diced pressed bean curd (optional)

2 tablespoons shredded salted radish (*hua pak kad khem*) (optional)

2 eggs (optional)

½ tablespoon Thai chili powder (*phrik pon*) or other ground red chili to taste, such as New Mexico chili powder or cayenne (optional)

4 scallions, including the green tops, angle-cut into 1½-inch pieces

1½ cups bean sprouts

⅓ cup roasted unsalted peanuts, crushed in a mortar or finely chopped

CONDIMENTS

2 cups bean sprouts

⅓ cup roasted unsalted peanuts, crushed in a mortar or finely chopped

Lime or lemon wedges

6 to 8 small Thai chilies (*phrik khee nu*), finely sliced, or Chilies-in-Vinegar Sauce (page 52) (optional)

Soak the rice sticks in a large bowl of warm water until they are soft, about 15 minutes.

Meanwhile, rinse and peel the fresh shrimp, but leave the tails on. Slice them partway through along the back to butterfly and devein.

Slice the pork or chicken into bite-size strips.

In a small mixing bowl, combine the fish sauce, vinegar, sugar, and catsup. Stir the mixture until the sugar is dissolved.

Drain the noodles and set them aside in a colander.

Place all of the stir-fry ingredients within easy reach of the cooking area. Arrange the condiments on a serving platter, or put them into individual serving bowls, and set them on the table so they will be ready when the noodles are hot out of the wok.

Set a wok over medium-high heat. When it is quite hot, add the oil. Rotate the wok a bit so the oil coats the sides. When the oil is hot, add the garlic and stir-fry for a few seconds before adding the shrimp, pork, or chicken and dried shrimp. Stir-fry until the shrimp and the pork or chicken lose their raw color, about 1 minute.

Stir in the sauce mixture and bring it to a boil. Add the noodles and gently toss them in the sauce. Stir-fry until the noodles absorb the sauce, about 2 minutes.

Mix in the pressed bean curd and salted radish.

Break the eggs into the wok. Break up the yolks a bit, then mix the eggs down under the noodle mixture. Cook without stirring for 15 seconds, then stir-fry until the ingredients are well blended.

Add the Thai chili powder and scallions. Stir-fry until the scallions are cooked through and crisp-tender, about 1 to 2 minutes. Stir in the bean sprouts and peanuts until well mixed.

Transfer to a serving platter and serve immediately.

FAT NOODLE STIR-FRY WITH BOK CHOY, SHRIMP, AND PORK MEATLOAF

Kwaytiow Sen Yai Phat Pak Kwahng Toong, Kung Kap Mu Yoa

Serves 6 to 8 as a side dish, or 4 as a one-dish meal

T his elegant stir-fry highlights two unusual ingredients. Steamed Pork Meatloaf, delicately seasoned and moist, is julienned, then wok-browned and tossed with noodles, shrimp, and pretty, flowering stalks of the Chinese cabbage known as *bok choy sum*.

With its pink shrimp, green leaves, yellow flowers, and its distinctive yet mild, pleasing flavors, this colorful dish would be perfect for a dinner party. If you make the meatloaf in advance, the final preparation is quick and easy. I suggest pairing it with contrasting spicy-sour flavors like those of Green Mango Salad, Chiang Mai Style (page 288).

I Steamed Pork Meatloaf (page 138)

¾ pound large shrimp

I pound flowering bok choy (*pak kwahng toong*)

I½ pounds presliced fresh rice noodles (*sen yai*) or uncut fresh rice noodle sheets (see Note)

3 tablespoons vegetable oil

9 cloves garlic, pounded to a mash or crushed and chopped

2 tablespoons oyster sauce

3 tablespoons Thai soy sauce with mushroom (*see-eu kao het hom*) or a Chinese brand, such as Pearl River Bridge

2 tablespoons sugar

Cut the meatloaf into matchstick slices about 2 by ¼ by ¼ inch. Set aside.

Rinse and peel the shrimp, but leave the tails on. Slice them partway through, along the back to butterfly and devein. Set aside.

Trim the woody stems of the bok choy. Cut the larger stems in half lengthwise, then angle-cut them into thin slices, flowers and all. Set aside.

Put the sliced noodles in a colander and pour a kettle of hot water over them to remove the protective oil coating and soften them a bit. Unfold and separate the noodles into individual ribbons. (If some break off into short lengths, that's fine—it will create texture. Just be as careful as you can to separate the individual noodles from the folded mass.)

Place all of the ingredients within easy reach of the cooking area.

Set a large wok over medium-high heat. When it is quite hot, add the oil. Rotate the wok a bit so the oil coats the sides. When the oil is hot, add the garlic and stir-fry briefly, just until golden and aromatic. Raise the heat to high. Add the shrimp and stir-fry just until they begin to turn pink, about 15 seconds. Add the sliced meatloaf and stir-fry for 30 seconds. Add the noodles and stir-fry briskly for 30 seconds, tossing the noodles to incorporate them with the other ingredients. Stir in the oyster sauce and soy sauce. Stir in the sugar. Add the flowering bok choy (in two batches if necessary) and stir-fry just until the bok choy is cooked through, about 3 minutes.

Transfer to a large serving platter.

N O T E : Fresh rice noodles can be stored in the refrigerator, but if you buy them the same day you plan to serve them, keep them at room temperature. They will be easier to unfold. If buying the uncut noodle sheets, slice them lengthwise through the folds into strips about ¾ inch wide.

Fat Noodles with Sweet Black Bean Sauce and Curried Ground Beef

Kwaytiow Sen Yai Neua Sub

Serves 2 to 4

This is a favorite one-dish lunch throughout Thailand. *Sen yai* means "big path," a poetic description of the fat rice noodles, which are here stir-fried with sweet black soy sauce, then ladled with a fragrant ground-beef topping infused with sweet yellow curry powder and spicy white pepper.

For added spice and savor, serve with a splash of Chilies-in-Vinegar Sauce.

NOODLES

1½ pounds presliced fresh rice noodles (*sen yai*) or uncut fresh rice noodle sheets (see Note)

1½ tablespoons vegetable oil

1½ tablespoons sweet black soy sauce (*see-eu wan*)

CURRIED GROUND BEEF

8 cloves garlic

2 tablespoons chopped cilantro stems

1½ tablespoons vegetable oil

¾ pound ground beef

1 small onion, cut in half and finely sliced

1 tablespoon curry powder

4 tablespoons golden brown sugar

3 tablespoons Thai fish sauce (*nam pla*)

½ tablespoon white pepper

½ cup Chicken Stock (page 72) or canned chicken broth

1 tablespoon cornstarch dissolved in 1 tablespoon water

Sprigs of cilantro

Chilies-in-Vinegar Sauce (page 52) (optional)

Place a heatproof platter in a warm oven while you prepare the noodles.

Put the sliced noodles in a colander and pour a kettle of hot water over them to remove the protective oil coating and soften them a bit. Unfold and separate the noodles into individual ribbons. (If some break off into short lengths, that's fine—it will create texture. Just be as careful as you can to separate the individual noodles from the folded mass.) Set aside.

Set a wok over medium-high heat. When it is quite hot, add the oil. Rotate the wok a bit so the oil coats the sides. When the oil is hot, add the noodles. Stir-fry briskly, tossing the noodles in the hot oil to heat them through, about 1½ minutes. Add the soy sauce and stir-fry briskly to coat all the noodles with the sauce, about 1 minute. Transfer the noodles to the warm serving platter and keep in the warm oven while you prepare the beef topping.

Make a seasoning paste from the garlic and cilantro stems:

Mortar-and-pestle method: Put the garlic and chopped cilantro stems in the mortar and pound them to a mash.

Alternate method: Crush the garlic with the side of a chef's knife. Mix the chopped cilantro stems with the crushed garlic and finely chop.

Place the seasoning paste and all the remaining ingredients, except the chili sauce, within easy reach of the cooking area.

Set a clean wok or a deep, heavy skillet over medium-high heat. When it is quite hot, add the oil. If using a wok, rotate it a bit so the oil coats the sides. When the oil is hot, add the seasoning paste and stir-fry for a few seconds before adding the ground beef. Take handfuls of the beef and work it through your fingers to break it up a little as you add it to the wok. Stir-fry the beef, pressing it down into the bottom of the wok. Turn the beef mixture over, press it down into the wok again, and stir-fry until the meat begins to brown, about 45 seconds.

Add the onion, curry powder, sugar, fish sauce, pepper, and chicken stock and stir-fry for 2 minutes. Add the cornstarch-water mixture and stir-fry until the sauce thickens slightly, about 1 minute.

Remove the platter of noodles from the oven and ladle on the curried ground beef. Tear sprigs of cilantro over the noodles and serve with Chilies-in-Vinegar Sauce, if desired.

N O T E : Fresh rice noodles can be stored in the refrigerator, but if you buy them the same day you plan to serve them, keep them at room temperature. They will be easier to unfold. If buying the uncut noodle sheets, slice them lengthwise through the folds into strips about ¾ inch wide.

POULTRY and MEAT

Kai, Mu leh Neua

People often wonder how Thai cuisine can be so sophisticated and sensual, and yet at the same time so healthful and inexpensive. One clue to that mystery lies in how nature and geography equipped our country. Mile-high mountains in the north and a long mountain range along our western border with Burma direct Thailand's abundant tropical rainfall into a broad network of rivers that crosses our country's enormous central plain.

Our western coast faces the Andaman Sea, while our eastern coastline curves around the Gulf of Siam for hundreds of miles.

Because of its many rivers and long shoreline, Thailand is blessed with an almost unlimited variety of fresh- and saltwater fish and shellfish. They supply a great deal of protein, so Thai people don't raise a great many animals for meat. That's why Thai cuisine naturally conforms with the latest advice of health experts—to serve meat in small amounts. We serve meat in harmony with several other ingredients, not as the mainstay of the meal. Over centuries, Thai cooks have evolved wonderful recipes to make smaller meat portions flavorful and exciting by combining them with aromatic spices, rich curries and sauces, and perfect vegetable and fruit accompaniments.

The recipes in this chapter are closely connected to memories of my childhood. Red Curry with Beef and Green Peppercorns, for example, with its fragrant, spicy sauce and the crunchy texture of fresh peppercorns, reminds me of going out to gather the green pepper berries from vines winding around coconut palms in our neighborhood.

Beef dishes often signal special occasions in my homeland. Our beef comes mostly from water buffalo, which are valued work animals. Whenever my mother bought fresh beef from the vendors whose boats passed our house on the Chao Phraya River, it meant a celebration was likely—perhaps a family birthday dinner or a party in honor of visiting relatives. Whenever my father entertained important clients in our home, my mother would present platters of Sweet Crispy Beef with the predinner drinks.

Pork and chicken usually connote more casual dishes and settings. My mother's Pork and Eggplant Stir-Fry is still the best version of this everyday family favorite that I've ever tasted. And her Sweet-and-Sour Omelet with Chicken and Tomatoes, which she often made when I stayed up late studying, is an easy yet incredibly savory one-dish meal.

Over the years I've acquired other favorite recipes that I've included in this chapter: regional cuisine like the mild, Muslim-influenced Massaman Beef Curry with Potatoes and Pineapple from the south; fiery northern-style Jungle Curry with Grilled Beef, Seasonal Herbs, and Vegetables; Issan-Style Pork-and-Rice Sausages from the northeastern provinces; Thai-Chinese hybrid dishes such as Chicken with Red Chili and Cashews; and the complex, cosmopolitan dishes I discovered as a college student exploring the restaurants of Bangkok.

This selection of recipes will show you the fundamental styles and regional specialties of meat cookery in the Thai tradition, but there is endless variety to discover. For example, three different styles of barbecued chicken—from Bangkok, Chiang Mai, and the Issan provinces—can be found in the "Bangkok Street Cooking" chapter. In the same chapter you'll also find chicken, beef, pork, and lamb versions of Thailand's popular satays, each served with Curried Peanut Sauce.

Recipes developed long ago for the royal court, such as Golden Egg Nets Filled with Stir-Fried Minced Chicken, can be found in the "Royal Thai Cuisine" chapter. Whichever recipes you choose to try, I know you'll find much to be delighted in— especially when you discover how much flavor and sensual appeal you can enjoy while serving a healthfully modest amount of meat.

YELLOW CHICKEN CURRY WITH SPICY CUCUMBER RELISH

Kaeng Kari Kai Kap Nam Thaeng Kwa

Serves 6

This is perhaps the mildest of Thai curries, with a high proportion of herbs and spices, moderate use of chilies, and a generous quantity of coconut milk.

My favorite way to serve *kaeng kari kai* is with a side dish of Spicy Cucumber Relish, as is the custom in southern Thailand. The relish is cool and crisp, with crunchy peanuts and a jolt of chili to contrast with the mellow curry.

4 medium potatoes (about 14 ounces), peeled and cut into 1-inch cubes

2 cans (one 14 ounces, one 19 ounces) unsweetened coconut milk

1 cup Yellow Curry Paste (page 30)

1½ pounds boneless, skinless chicken breast, cut crosswise into ½-inch-thick slices

1¾ cups Chicken Stock (page 72) or canned chicken broth

3 tablespoons Thai fish sauce (*nam pla*)

6 tablespoons sugar

1 large onion, sliced

Spicy Cucumber Relish (page 53)

Parboil the potatoes in boiling water just until they are easily pierced with a fork, about 10 minutes. Drain and set aside.

Skim the thick cream from the top of the canned coconut milk into a soup pot, reserving the milk. Set the pot over medium-high heat. Stir in the curry paste until blended, and bring to a low boil. Cook, stirring constantly, for 2 minutes. Add the chicken and cook for 1 minute, stirring often. Add the reserved coconut milk, chicken stock, fish sauce, and sugar. Stir until the sugar is dissolved and blended. Add the potatoes and onion. Raise the heat to high and bring to a low boil, then reduce the heat, cover, and simmer just until the potatoes and onion are cooked through, about 3 minutes.

Transfer to a serving bowl or covered casserole and serve with Spicy Cucumber Relish and plenty of steamed jasmine rice.

NOTE: I like to make this curry a few hours, or even a full day, before I plan to serve it. Given some time, the flavors will enhance one another and become more pronounced. Keep it covered and refrigerated until ready to use, heat it through without letting it come to a boil, then serve.

CHICKEN WITH RED CHILI AND CASHEWS

Kai Phat Met Ma Muang

Serves 4

This is an easy, everyday dish that shows off some of the best elements of Chinese-style Thai cooking. The deep red chilies and crunchy cashews combine bright color and crisp texture in a manner characteristic of Chinese stir-fries. Thai adaptation comes through with the background note of fish sauce and the subtle, smoky hint of chili-tamarind paste.

The dried chilies are left whole, more for aroma and color than for their heat.

3 tablespoons vegetable oil

10 small dried Japanese chilies

12 cloves garlic, pounded to a mash or crushed and chopped

¾ pound boneless, skinless chicken breast, cut crosswise into ½-inch-thick slices

4 scallions, including the green tops, angle-cut into 2-inch pieces, bulbs cut in half lengthwise

1 small onion, sliced

3 teaspoons Chili-Tamarind Paste (page 46), or 2 teaspoons commercially made chili-tamarind paste (*nam phrik pao*)

¼ cup Chicken Stock (page 72) or canned chicken broth

1 tablespoon oyster sauce

1 tablespoon Thai fish sauce (*nam pla*)

2 tablespoons sugar

¾ cup whole roasted cashews

Sprigs of cilantro (optional)

Place all of the ingredients within easy reach of the cooking area.

Set a wok over medium-high heat. When it is quite hot, add the oil. Rotate the wok a bit so the oil coats the sides. When the oil is hot, add the chilies and stir-fry briefly, just until they deepen in color. Remove the chilies with a slotted spoon and drain on paper towels. Set aside.

Add the garlic and stir-fry briefly, just until golden and aromatic. Add the chicken, raise the heat to high, and stir-fry just until the chicken begins to lose its raw color and turn opaque, about 1 minute. Add the scallions and onion and stir-fry for 30 seconds. Add the chili-tamarind paste, chicken stock, oyster sauce, fish sauce, and sugar and stir-fry for 30 seconds. Add the fried chilies and cashews and stir-fry just until the scallions and onion are tender and cooked through, about 1 minute.

Transfer to a serving platter. Tear sprigs of cilantro over the dish if desired, and serve with plenty of steamed jasmine rice.

CHICKEN IN SOUTHERN-STYLE RED CURRY

Kaeng Phed Kai Meng Dai

Serves 6

This recipe, from the southerly reaches of Thailand, makes a beautiful, sunny orange curry sauce, reminiscent of the saffron-colored robes of Buddhist monks. Its distinctive color comes from the combination of chilies and turmeric, a spice typical of the Muslim traditions that pervade cooking in the south of Thailand.

Just as the color of this curry falls in between pure yellow and pure red, the flavor and fire of the sauce lie somewhere between the very mild, Indian-style yellow curries and the stronger chili heat of the classic red curries.

You can serve this dish confidently to anyone who might be new to Thai cuisine, and those who already love Thai curries will be pleased to find a new favorite.

2 cans (14 ounces each) unsweetened coconut milk

1 cup Red Curry Paste, Southern Style (page 39)

1½ pounds boneless, skinless chicken breast, cut crosswise into ½-inch-thick slices

18 (9 pairs) fresh Kaffir lime leaves (*bai magroot*), or strips of peel from 1 small lime

6 medium serrano chilies, stemmed and sliced in half lengthwise

3 tablespoons coconut-palm sugar or golden brown sugar

¼ cup Thai fish sauce (*nam pla*)

½ cup loosely packed Thai basil (*bai horapha*) or purple or Italian basil

Skim the thick cream from the top of the canned coconut milk into a soup pot, reserving the milk. Set the pot over medium-high heat. Stir in the curry paste until blended, and bring to a low boil. Cook, stirring constantly, for 2 minutes. Add the chicken and cook for 1 minute, stirring often. Add the reserved coconut milk and stir until blended. If using Kaffir lime leaves, tear each leaf in half and add to the pot. If using lime peel, add it to the pot. Add the chilies. Bring to a low boil, stirring occasionally. Add the sugar and stir until dissolved and blended. Stir in the fish sauce. Stir in the basil and cook for a few seconds, just until the basil begins to wilt.

Transfer to a serving bowl or covered casserole and serve with plenty of steamed jasmine rice.

NOTE: I like to make this curry a few hours, or even a full day, before I plan to serve it. Given some time, the flavors will enhance one another and become more pronounced. Keep it covered and refrigerated until ready to use, heat it through without letting it come to a boil, then serve.

Like the fresh lime leaves or peel, the sliced chilies impart flavor and fragrance to the curry but are not meant to be eaten themselves.

GINGER CHICKEN

Kai Phat Khing

Serves 4 to 6

G inger is used here as a primary ingredient, like a vegetable. Sweet black soy sauce gives an added rich note of flavor.

Even though *kai phat khing* is heady with ginger, it isn't spicy-hot. If you want to give it some chili heat and added savor, do what Thai people frequently do: Add a spoonful of Classic Chili Dipping Sauce.

3 tablespoons vegetable oil

8 cloves garlic, pounded to a mash or crushed and chopped

¾ pound boneless, skinless chicken breast, cut crosswise into ½-inch-thick slices

½ pound mushrooms, sliced

1 small onion, sliced

4 scallions, including the green tops, angle-cut into 1-inch pieces, bulbs cut in half lengthwise

1 red jalapeño pepper or red serrano chili

1 tablespoon sweet black soy sauce (*see-eu wan*)

2 tablespoons Thai fish sauce (*nam pla*)

2 tablespoons rice vinegar

2 tablespoons sugar

⅓ cup finely chopped, peeled fresh ginger

Classic Chili Dipping Sauce (page 49) (optional)

Place all of the ingredients except the dipping sauce within easy reach of the cooking area.

Set a wok over medium-high heat. When it is quite hot, add the oil. Rotate the wok a bit so the oil coats the sides. When the oil is hot, add the garlic and stir-fry briefly, just until it is golden and aromatic. Raise the heat to high. Add the chicken and stir-fry for 1 minute. Add the mushrooms and stir-fry for 1 minute. Add all of the remaining ingredients and stir-fry just until the chicken and vegetables are cooked through, about 4 to 5 minutes.

Transfer to a serving platter. Serve with steamed jasmine rice and Classic Chili Dipping Sauce, if desired.

CHICKEN IN RED CURRY WITH BAMBOO SHOOTS

Kaeng Phed Kai Kap Normai On

Serves 4 to 6

Late summer, when the rains begin, is also the start of Buddhist Lent. The monks stay in the temples for three months. They leave behind earthly things to meditate and teach.

Thai people support the monks with gifts of food. We call the practice *tum boon*, which means "making merit."

The rainy season brings new growth everywhere. Young, fresh bamboo shoots soon become plentiful, and the people are eager to eat them. This curry, in which crunchy bamboo shoots are featured, is typical of the dishes offered to "make merit."

I can (19 ounces) unsweetened coconut milk

I cup Classic Red Curry Paste (page 26)

¾ pound boneless, skinless chicken breast, cut crosswise into ½-inch-thick slices

10 (5 pairs) fresh Kaffir lime leaves (*bai magroot*), or strips of peel from I small lime

I can (15 ounces) bamboo shoots, drained and sliced lengthwise into strips

3 tablespoons coconut-palm sugar or golden brown sugar

2 tablespoons Thai fish sauce (*nam pla*)

I cup loosely packed Thai basil (*bai horapha*) or purple or Italian basil

Skim the thick cream from the top of the canned coconut milk into a soup pot, reserving the milk. Set the pot over medium-high heat. Stir in the curry paste until blended, and bring to a low boil. Cook, stirring constantly, for 2 minutes.

Add the chicken and cook for 1 minute, stirring occasionally. Add the reserved coconut milk and cook for 1 minute, stirring often. If using Kaffir lime leaves, tear each leaf in half and add to the pot. If using lime peel, add it to the pot. Cook for 1 minute, stirring occasionally. Stir in the bamboo shoots. Add the sugar and fish sauce and stir until the sugar is dissolved and blended. Simmer, covered, for 3 minutes. Turn off the heat. Stir in the basil and cook for a few seconds, just until the basil begins to wilt.

Transfer to a serving bowl or covered casserole and serve with plenty of steamed jasmine rice.

NOTE: I like to make this curry a few hours, or even a full day, before I plan to serve it. Given some time, the flavors will enhance one another and become more pronounced. Keep it covered and refrigerated until ready to use, heat it through without letting it come to a boil, then serve.

CHICKEN WITH LEEKS

Kai Phat Tom Hom Yai

Serves 4 to 6

F resh leeks and yellow bean sauce give this simple stir-fry an earthy yet mellow quality. The overlapping of Thai and Chinese cooking styles is apparent in this dish. Flour is added to thicken the sauce slightly, in the Chinese manner, but the fish sauce and garlic are sure signs that this is a Thai recipe.

2 leeks (about 1 pound)

½ tablespoon quick-mixing flour

⅓ cup Chicken Stock (page 72) or canned chicken broth

2 tablespoons vegetable oil

6 cloves garlic, pounded to a mash or crushed and chopped

1 pound boneless, skinless chicken breasts, cut crosswise into ½-inch-thick slices

5 tablespoons sugar

3 tablespoons Thai fish sauce (*nam pla*)

3 tablespoons whole yellow bean sauce (*tao jiew khao*)

Trim off the root ends of the leeks and all but about 3 inches of the green tops. Angle-cut the green tops into thin slices. Cut the white bulbs in half lengthwise, then angle-cut them into thin slices. Put the sliced leeks in a colander and wash them well. Drain and set aside. (You should have about 5 cups.)

Stir the quick-mixing flour into the chicken stock until blended.

Place all of the ingredients within easy reach of the cooking area.

Set a wok over medium-high heat. When it is quite hot, add the oil. Rotate the wok a bit so the oil coats the sides. When the oil is hot, add the garlic and stir-fry briefly, just until golden and aromatic. Add the chicken, raise the heat to high, and stir-fry for 1 minute. Stir in the sugar, fish sauce, and leeks and stir-fry for 1 minute. Add the yellow bean sauce and the chicken stock–flour mixture. Cook, stirring occasionally, just until the meat and vegetables are tender and cooked though, and the sauce reduces slightly, about 1 to 1½ minutes.

Transfer to a serving platter and serve with plenty of steamed jasmine rice.

Sweet-and-Sour Omelets with Chicken and Tomatoes

Khai Yat Sai Kap Kai, Makhua Tet

Makes 3 large omelets

Omelets, made with either chicken or duck eggs, are popular throughout Thailand—but are seldom found in Thai restaurants in America.

We love omelets for lunch, fresh from the wok of our favorite street vendor, or at home, as a predinner appetizer or one-dish meal. Thai omelets are often quite simple—ground pork, chicken, or shrimp and vegetables make up the filling, with chili sauce served on the side. My mother's recipe, given here, is really something special. It's already savory and saucy; nothing needs to be added to enhance it.

Try this omelet at lunch or brunch, or as a late supper. Serve steamed jasmine rice on the side, to absorb the delicious sauce, and you have a great one-dish meal. The omelets are large enough to be cut in half and shared, if you wish.

FILLING

3 tablespoons vegetable oil

10 cloves garlic, pounded to a mash or crushed and chopped

¾ pound boneless, skinless chicken breast, cut into ¼-inch cubes

1 tablespoon oyster sauce

2 tablespoons Thai fish sauce (*nam pla*)

1 can (5½ ounces) stewed tomatoes

½ cup golden brown sugar

1 large tomato, cut in half and thinly sliced

1 medium onion, cut in half and thinly sliced

1 large red bell pepper, finely chopped

1 teaspoon quick-mixing flour, dissolved in 1 tablespoon water

OMELETS

6 tablespoons vegetable oil

8 large eggs, lightly beaten

Sprigs of cilantro

To make the filling: Place all of the filling ingredients within easy reach of the cooking area.

Set a wok over medium-high heat. When it is quite hot, add the oil. Tilt the wok a bit so the oil coats the sides. Add the garlic and stir-fry briefly, just until golden and aromatic. Add the chicken and stir-fry for 30 seconds. Add the oyster sauce, fish sauce, and stewed tomatoes and stir-fry for 1 minute. Add the sugar and stir-fry for

1 minute. Add the tomato, onion, and red pepper and stir-fry for 1 minute. Cover and cook for 1½ to 2 minutes, or until the vegetables are tender. Add the flour-water mixture and stir until blended. The sauce should be rather liquid. Turn off the heat, cover, and set aside.

To make the omelet: Set a nonstick wok or heavy nonstick skillet over medium-high heat. When the wok or skillet is quite hot, add 2 tablespoons of the oil. If using a wok, rotate it a bit so the oil coats the sides. Add a third of the beaten eggs. Let the eggs set for about 10 seconds, then slowly rotate the wok or skillet to distribute the eggs into a large circle, using a spatula if necessary. Cook just until the omelet is set but not completely dry, about 1½ minutes. Spoon a third of the filling into the center. Fold two opposite sides of the omelet over the filling, leaving some of the filling exposed. Cook briefly, about 15 to 30 seconds. Using a spatula, slide the finished omelet onto an ovenproof platter and keep warm in a low oven.

Repeat the procedure with the remaining ingredients to make two more omelets. Transfer the omelets to a serving platter. Tear sprigs of cilantro over the omelets and serve with plenty of steamed jasmine rice.

CHICKEN IN PANDANUS LEAVES WITH SWEET BLACK BEAN SAUCE

Kai Hoh Bai Toey

Makes about 24 bundles

———————

Pandanus is an aromatic tropical plant with long, tapering green leaves. Thai cooks prize pandanus leaves for their distinctive sweet-and-smoky, vanilla-like taste.

Here, pandanus leaves wrap around bite-size pieces of marinated chicken, making small bundles that are then deep-fried. The leaves not only impart their own delicate flavor, they also seal in the flavors of the chicken and its marinade.

There is no suitable substitute for pandanus leaves, and for years I was homesick for their unique flavor. Now, however, more and more authentic Thai ingredients are available at Asian groceries in America, including fresh-frozen pandanus leaves direct from Thailand.

Kai hoh bai toey is terrific as an appetizer or as part of a dinner menu. Sweet Black Bean Sauce is the traditional accompaniment.

¼ cup white sesame seeds, crushed or ground

1 pound boneless, skinless chicken breast or thigh, cut into 1-inch cubes

2 tablespoons whiskey

2 tablespoons Thai thin soy sauce (*see-eu kao*) or any good light soy sauce

1 tablespoon white pepper

2 tablespoons sugar

2 packages (4 ounces each) frozen pandanus leaves (*bai toey*), defrosted

Toothpicks to secure bundles

1½ cups vegetable or peanut oil for shallow-frying

Sweet Black Bean Sauce (page 60)

Put the ground sesame seeds, chicken, whiskey, soy sauce, pepper, and sugar in a large mixing bowl. Mix the ingredients well, cover, and marinate for at least 1 hour, or up to 24 hours in the refrigerator.

Select a pandanus leaf at least 1 inch wide (or overlap two thin leaves lengthwise). Place a piece of chicken coated with the marinade about 2 inches from one end. Fold the leaf over the chicken and roll down to the end of the leaf. Hold in one hand as you take another leaf to wrap over the exposed sides. Secure with a toothpick. Repeat until each chicken piece is wrapped in its own bundle.

Pour the oil into a large, heavy skillet. Heat the oil over medium-high heat. When sizzling hot (about 360°F), shallow-fry the bundles in batches of six, turning them two or three times as they cook, for a total of 1½ to 2 minutes.

Drain on paper towels. Adjust the heat, if necessary, to maintain an even cooking temperature. Continue frying until all of the bundles are cooked.

Transfer to a serving platter and serve immediately.

THAI SERVING STYLE: Set out the platter of chicken in pandanus along with another platter to collect the leaves as the bundles are unwrapped by your guests. Serve with Sweet Black Bean Sauce.

NOTE: The leaves impart flavor to the chicken, but they are discarded before eating. You can assemble the bundles up to one day beforehand, then cook them just before serving.

CHICKEN WITH GREEN CHILI AND HOLY BASIL

Kai Phat Bai Kaprao

Serves 4 to 6

This fiery, delicious stir-fry is very typically Thai. Tradition dictates an abundance of fresh chili and holy basil. Neither ingredient is subtle—the slivers of serrano chili are sizzling hot, and holy basil is quite vibrant itself—yet these two key ingredients do not fight each other. Instead they make a great marriage, in which each individual is proud and strong.

3 tablespoons vegetable oil

6 cloves garlic, pounded to a mash or crushed and chopped

8 medium serrano chilies, stemmed and cut lengthwise into slivers (about ½ cup)

1 pound boneless, skinless chicken breasts, cut crosswise into ½-inch-thick slices

1 large onion, thinly sliced

2 tablespoons Thai fish sauce (*nam pla*)

1 tablespoon sugar

1 tablespoon distilled white vinegar

1 tablespoon sweet black soy sauce (*see-eu wan*)

1½ cups loosely packed holy basil (*bai kaprao*) or fresh mint

Place all of the ingredients within easy reach of the cooking area.

Set a wok over medium-high heat. When it is quite hot, add the oil. Rotate the wok a bit so the oil coats the sides. Add the garlic and chilies and stir-fry briefly, just until the garlic is golden and aromatic. Raise the heat to high. Add the chicken and onion and stir-fry for 3 minutes, separating the onion slices into rings as you stir. Add the fish sauce, sugar, vinegar, and soy sauce. Stir-fry just until the chicken is tender and cooked through, about 2 to 3 minutes. Turn off the heat. Stir in the basil and cook for a few seconds, just until the basil begins to wilt.

Transfer to a serving platter and serve with plenty of steamed jasmine rice.

SWEET PORK

Mu Wan

Serves 4

This dish is easy and addictively delicious, yielding a nice sauce from the meat juices and seasonings. It can be a side dish to a larger meal or a comforting treat by itself when served over a big bowl of jasmine rice, ladled with pan juices, and topped with a generous handful of Crispy Shallots (page 67).

3 tablespoons vegetable oil

6 cloves garlic, pounded to a mash or crushed and chopped

¾ pound pork tenderloin, cut crosswise into thin medallions

2 tablespoons Thai fish sauce (*nam pla*)

4 tablespoons golden brown sugar

½ teaspoon white pepper

Place all of the ingredients within easy reach of the cooking area.

Set a wok over medium-high heat. When it is quite hot, add the oil. Rotate the wok a bit so the oil coats the sides. When the oil is hot, add the garlic and stir-fry for a few seconds, then add the pork. Stir-fry for 1 minute. Add the remaining ingredients and stir-fry for 1½ minutes.

Serve hot or warm.

PORK AND
EGGPLANT STIR-FRY

Mu Phat Makhua Yao

Serves 4 to 6

T his is an everyday dish, delicious yet simple, as likely to be found in someone's home kitchen as it would be in a neighborhood café.

3 tablespoons vegetable oil

10 cloves garlic, pounded to a mash or crushed and chopped

½ pound ground pork

½ teaspoon white pepper

I tablespoon oyster sauce

I tablespoon crushed yellow bean sauce (*tao jiew dam*)

I pound Japanese eggplant, angle-cut into ¼-inch-thick slices

¼ cup Chicken Stock (page 72) or canned chicken broth

2 tablespoons sugar

Place all of the ingredients within easy reach of the cooking area.

Set a wok over medium-high heat. When it is quite hot, add the oil. Rotate the wok a bit so the oil coats the sides. When the oil is hot, add the garlic and stir-fry briefly, just until golden and aromatic. Raise the heat to high. Add the pork and white pepper and stir-fry for 30 seconds. Stir in the oyster sauce, yellow bean sauce, and eggplant. Stir-fry for 1 minute. Add the chicken stock and stir-fry for 1½ minutes. Add the sugar and stir-fry just until the eggplant is tender and cooked through, about 2½ minutes.

Transfer to a serving platter and serve with steamed jasmine rice.

PORK WITH PINEAPPLE AND YELLOW BEAN SAUCE

Mu Phat Supparod Kap Tao Jiew Leing

Serves 4 to 6

This vividly colored stir-fry combines juicy, golden pineapple, bright red bell pepper, and the green tops of scallions.

Thai people love to put the sweet-and-sour tang of fresh pineapple into savory dishes. It's a taste we call *raad chat*, and it goes beautifully with the mild sweetness of pork.

3 tablespoons vegetable oil

14 cloves garlic, pounded to a mash or crushed and chopped

¾ pound pork tenderloin, cut crosswise into thin medallions

3 tablespoons crushed yellow bean sauce (*tao jiew dam*)

2 tablespoons golden brown sugar

I red bell pepper, chopped

1⅔ cups chopped fresh pineapple (about half of a medium pineapple)

½ tablespoon white pepper

6 scallions, including the green tops, angle-cut into 1-inch pieces, bulbs cut in half lengthwise

Place all of the ingredients within easy reach of the cooking area.

Set a wok over medium-high heat. When it is quite hot, add the oil. Rotate the wok a bit so the oil coats the sides. Add the garlic and stir-fry briefly, just until golden and aromatic. Raise the heat to high. Add the pork and stir-fry just until the pork turns pink, about 30 seconds. Stir in the yellow bean sauce. Add the sugar, red pepper, and pineapple and stir-fry for 1 minute. Add the white pepper and scallions and stir-fry for 1 minute. Reduce the heat, cover, and simmer just until the meat and vegetables are tender and cooked through, about 1 minute.

Transfer to a serving platter and serve with steamed jasmine rice.

STEAMED PORK MEATLOAF

Mu Yoa

Serves 4 to 6

Issan people, who live in the northeastern provinces of Thailand, are famous for their sausages. A less well-known but equally wonderful Issan specialty is *mu yoa*—steamed pork meatloaf.

I haven't seen *mu yoa* featured in cookbooks or restaurants here in America, yet it's well worth knowing about. Because it is precooked, it will keep nicely, allowing you to use a bit here and there, in combination with other ingredients. *Mu yoa* goes well in many dishes, as you will see in the following two recipes. The first is a healthful, vegetable-rich everyday stir-fry, the next, a wonderfully savory curried omelet suitable for an elegant brunch. In the "Thai Salads" chapter, you'll also find Green Mango Salad with Steamed Pork Meatloaf (page 216), in which I julienne the *mu yoa* and toss it with tangy green mango, lemon grass, and fresh mint.

Mu yoa is very satisfying on its own as well. Sometimes I'm happiest just taking a few slices to eat with my rice for a simple lunch break or easy dinner.

¾ pound boneless pork

6 cloves garlic

1 tablespoon white pepper

½ tablespoon Thai soy sauce with mushroom (*see-eu khao het hom*) or a Chinese brand, such as Pearl River Bridge

1½ teaspoons all-purpose flour

1 small egg

Trim the pork of any excess fat and cut it into 1-inch cubes. Put the pork and the remaining ingredients in the bowl of a food processor fitted with a metal blade. Process to a fine, almost pastelike consistency, about 1½ minutes. (The mixture should be more finely ground than hamburger meat.)

Transfer the ground pork mixture to a flat work surface and mold it into a loaf about 7 by 3 by 2 inches. Roll up the loaf in a double thickness of aluminum foil, folding the sides of the foil in as you roll to make a tight seal. Set aside.

Fill the base pot of a tiered aluminum steamer with 10 cups of water. Cover and bring the water to a boil over medium-high heat. (If using a small steamer, fill the base pot half full and check the water level occasionally. When it is necessary to replenish the base pot, add hot water.)

Put the foil-wrapped meatloaf on a steaming rack. When the water reaches a boil, set the rack over the pot, cover, and steam for 1 hour.

Remove the meatloaf from the steamer and let it cool to room temperature before unwrapping.

Slice the meatloaf and serve with steamed jasmine rice, or use as an ingredient in stir-frys, omelets, or salads.

STEAMED PORK MEATLOAF
WITH STIR-FRIED VEGETABLES

Mu Yoa Phat Pak Ruam Mit

Serves 4 to 6

To the master recipe for Steamed Pork Meatloaf (page 138), you need add only fresh seasonal vegetables to create a unique and satisfying stir-fry.

This recipe features baby Shanghai bok choy, a type of cabbage that is popular throughout Asia. The stalk is mild in flavor, the spoon-shaped leaves just a little stronger.

The vegetables create a good deal of liquid that blends with chicken stock, a splash of fish sauce, and some sugar to create a mildly seasoned, healthy sauce.

1 Steamed Pork Meatloaf (page 138)

½ pound broccoli

3 tablespoons vegetable oil

12 cloves garlic, pounded to a mash or crushed and chopped

6 scallions, including the green tops, angle-cut into 2-inch pieces, bulbs cut in half lengthwise

1 red bell pepper, chopped

2 tablespoons Thai fish sauce (*nam pla*)

3 tablespoons golden brown sugar

½ pound mushrooms, sliced

¼ pound baby Shanghai bok choy (about 2 heads), cut in half lengthwise, then angle-cut into thin slices (see Note)

3 tablespoons Chicken Stock (page 72), canned chicken broth, or water

Place all of the ingredients within easy reach of the cooking area.

Slice the meatloaf in half lengthwise, then cut each half crosswise into ¼-inch slices. Set aside.

Trim the woody stem of the broccoli. Slice the florets off the stem. Peel the stem and angle-cut into thin slices. Set aside.

Set a wok over high heat. When it is quite hot, add the oil. Rotate the wok a bit so the oil coats the sides. When the oil is hot, add the garlic and stir-fry briefly, just until golden and aromatic. Add the broccoli and scallions and stir-fry for 1 minute. Stir in the red pepper, fish sauce, and sugar. Add the mushrooms and stir-fry for 1 minute. Add the bok choy and stir-fry for 1 minute. Add the chicken stock and stir-fry for 30 seconds. Add the meatloaf and stir-fry just until the vegetables are tender and cooked through, about 1½ minutes.

Transfer to a serving platter and serve with steamed jasmine rice.

NOTE: If baby bok choy is unavailable, you can substitute regular bok choy, but be aware that since an average head weighs about 2 pounds, you'll have a lot left over.

PANANG CURRY OMELET

Khai Yat Sai Mu Yoa Lad Na Panang

Makes 2 large omelets

I n Thailand we often serve a simple omelet with a sophisticated, spicy curry. But in this dish I combine the best of both to create an elegant one-dish meal. Creamy eggs, so homey and pleasing, are perfect with the tangy Kaffir lime, fragrant Siamese ginger, and hot red chili of Panang curry.

This omelet is a stand-out at brunch. Serve it with plenty of steamed jasmine rice, a carved pineapple (page 390), and hot jasmine tea.

FILLING

1¼ cups unsweetened coconut milk

½ cup Panang Curry Paste (page 32), or 1 can (4 ounces) commercially made Panang curry paste

12 (6 pairs) fresh Kaffir lime leaves (*bai magroot*), finely sliced into slivers, or ½ teaspoon grated lime zest

10 Thai red pickled chilies (*phrik daeng dong*), sliced

3 tablespoons golden brown sugar

3 tablespoons Thai fish sauce (*nam pla*)

1 Steamed Pork Meatloaf (page 138), cut into small dice

OMELETS

4 tablespoons vegetable oil

8 large eggs, lightly beaten

Sprigs of cilantro

To make the filling: Pour the coconut milk into a medium saucepan set over medium-high heat. Stir in the curry paste until blended. Bring to a low boil, stirring occasionally. Add the lime leaves or zest, pickled chilies, sugar, and fish sauce and cook for 30 seconds, stirring constantly. Add the meatloaf and cook for 1 minute, stirring constantly. Turn off the heat, cover, and set aside.

To make the omelets: Set a nonstick wok or heavy nonstick skillet over medium-high heat. When the wok or skillet is hot, add 2 tablespoons of the oil. If using a wok, rotate it a bit so the oil coats the sides. Add half of the beaten eggs. Let the eggs set in the bottom of the wok or skillet for about 10 seconds, then slowly rotate the wok or skillet to distribute the eggs into a large circle, using a spatula if necessary. Cook just until the omelet is set but not completely dry, about 1½ minutes. Spoon half of the filling into the center. Fold two opposite sides of the omelet over the filling, leaving some of the filling exposed. Cook briefly, about 15 to 30 seconds. Using a spatula, slide the finished omelet onto an ovenproof platter and keep warm in a low oven.

Repeat the procedure with the remaining ingredients to make one more omelet. Transfer the omelets to a serving platter. Tear sprigs of cilantro over the omelets and serve with steamed jasmine rice.

PORK WITH GARLIC AND CRUSHED BLACK PEPPER

Mu Kratiem Phrik Thai

Serves 4

Chilies were brought to Thailand by Portuguese traders in the sixteenth century. Before that time, black and white pepper were our fundamental spices. Freshly ground pepper, and plenty of it, is the keynote of this centuries-old favorite. The quantity of garlic may seem large, but it is well balanced with the other ingredients and not overstated at all.

Serve *mu kratiem phrik Thai* with lots of steamed rice, as a counterpoint to its assertive flavors.

20 cloves garlic	¼ cup sweet black soy sauce (*see-eu wan*)
2½ teaspoons black peppercorns	
4 tablespoons vegetable oil	2 tablespoons coconut-palm sugar or golden brown sugar
¾ pound pork tenderloin, cut crosswise into thin medallions	2 tablespoons Thai fish sauce (*nam pla*)

Make a seasoning paste with the garlic and black peppercorns:

Mortar-and-pestle method: Place the garlic in the mortar and pound to a mash with the pestle. Add the peppercorns and pound until they are finely crushed and well ground into the mashed garlic.

Alternate method: Crush the garlic with the side of a chef's knife and finely chop. Coarsely grind the peppercorns in a pepper mill or spice mill. Mix the chopped garlic with the ground pepper.

Place all of the ingredients within easy reach of the cooking area.

Set a wok over medium-high heat. When it is quite hot, add the oil. Rotate the wok a bit so the oil coats the sides. Add the seasoning paste and stir-fry just until the garlic is golden and aromatic. Raise the heat to high. Add the pork and stir-fry for 30 seconds. Stir in the soy sauce. Add the sugar and stir-fry until it is dissolved and blended. Add the fish sauce and stir-fry just until the pork is tender and cooked through, about 1 to 1½ minutes.

Transfer to a serving platter and serve with plenty of steamed jasmine rice.

SPICY CHIANG MAI SAUSAGES

Sai Klok Chiang Mai

Serves 6 to 8

These terra-cotta–colored, leaf-green–flecked sausages derive much of their character from red curry paste and Kaffir lime leaves. They will be fresher, leaner, and far more flavorful than any sausages you buy in the market, and they freeze beautifully.

Don't be afraid to make sausages at home. You don't need special equipment, just a food processor and an inexpensive pastry bag and tip purchased from your local cookware store. It takes only one session to become capable and confident, especially if someone is handy to squeeze the pastry bag as you help the sausage mixture ease its way into the casing.

Serve *sai klok Chiang Mai* at your next barbecue or buffet the way we do in Bangkok—with assorted condiments like lemon, ginger, and peanuts, all rolled up in lettuce leaves.

SAUSAGES

¾ pound pork tenderloin, trimmed and cut into 1-inch cubes

12 (6 pairs) fresh Kaffir lime leaves (*bai magroot*), finely sliced into slivers, or ½ teaspoon grated lime zest

1 tablespoon Thai fish sauce (*nam pla*)

½ cup chopped garlic

1 tablespoon white pepper

½ tablespoon whole coriander seed, crushed or ground

¼ cup finely chopped cilantro stems

3 tablespoons Classic Red Curry Paste (page 26), or ½ to 1 tablespoon canned red curry paste

Sausage casings (see Note)

Kitchen string

12-inch pastry bag

#6 plain round pastry tip

CONDIMENTS

A few small heads of salad greens (Boston lettuce, romaine, cabbage, and radicchio are all good choices)

1 small cucumber

Sprigs of cilantro

1 small knob ginger

5 small Thai chilies (*phrik khee nu*)

⅓ cup roasted unsalted peanuts

1 small lemon

To make the sausages: Put the pork, lime leaves or zest, fish sauce, garlic, pepper, coriander seed, cilantro stems, and curry paste in the bowl of a food processor fitted with a metal blade. Process to a hamburger-like consistency, about 1½ minutes. The mixture should have a uniform texture and a pale terra-cotta color. Transfer to a large mixing bowl.

Fit the pastry tip into the pastry bag. Spoon about half of the sausage mixture into the bag. Slip one end of a sausage casing over the pastry tip. Twist the top of the pastry bag to create a firm, uniform pressure as you force the sausage mixture slowly into the casing. Knead the casing occasionally, using a slight downward pressure, to help the mixture along. Try to keep a uniform diameter of about 1 to 1½ inches. (Be patient to make sure the casing doesn't split. But if it does, don't worry. Just tie the broken end with a piece of string and begin again.)

When you have forced the first pastry bag full of sausage mixture into the casing, gently tie off the sausage every 4 inches with kitchen string to make four links.

Refill the pastry bag and repeat the procedure to make four more links.

Coil the links into a covered container and let them cure overnight in the refrigerator.

To prepare the condiments: Select small, cup-shaped leaves from your choice of salad greens and arrange them on a serving platter. Set aside.

Peel, seed, and finely slice the cucumber. Chop the cilantro. Peel and finely slice the ginger. Chop the chilies and the peanuts. Trim the ends of the lemon, but do not peel. Slice it into ½-inch rounds, then stack the rounds and chop them into small dice.

Arrange all of the condiments on a large serving platter. Set aside.

To grill or sauté the sausages:

Grilling method: Cut the sausage into separate links. Prick each sausage lightly with a fork. Grill slowly over medium coals until evenly browned. Cut the sausages into 1-inch slices and arrange them on a serving platter.

Sautéing method: Cut the sausage into separate links. Prick each sausage lightly with a fork. Set a large, heavy skillet over medium-high heat. When it is quite hot, add just enough vegetable oil to coat the surface, about 2 tablespoons. Sauté the sausages, turning them often to brown evenly, about 8 minutes. Cut the sausages into 1-inch slices and arrange them on a serving platter.

THAI SERVING STYLE: Set out the platters of lettuce cups, condiments, and sausages. Put a slice of sausage and your choice of condiments into a lettuce cup. Fold up and eat out of hand. Vary the selection of condiments to find your favorite flavor accents, between sips of cold Thai beer or whiskey, if desired.

NOTE: Call local butchers to find the sausage casings. They should be wide enough for sausages about 1½ inches in diameter. Store the casings in a container filled with fresh salted water. Cover and refrigerate until ready to use.

ISSAN-STYLE PORK-AND-RICE SAUSAGES

Sai Klok Issan

Serves 6 to 8

T hese sausages are seasoned with the age-old Thai flavors of garlic, cilantro, and pepper, with cooked rice added to make them tender and mellow.

In the Thai countryside, *sai klok Issan* are wrapped in banana leaves and heaped onto a barbecue grill. Sometimes a handful or two of squeezed-dry coconut meat, left over from making coconut milk, is thrown onto the fire to sweeten the smoke. But you don't need anything more exotic than a backyard barbecue or a hot skillet to cook these sausages. Pull one right off the grill to enjoy with a cold beer, or serve them Bangkok-style, with a full range of condiments, as I do for friends.

SAUSAGES

¾ pound pork tenderloin, trimmed and cut into 1-inch cubes

½ cup chopped garlic

1 tablespoon white pepper

½ tablespoon whole coriander seed, crushed or ground

¼ cup finely chopped cilantro stems

½ teaspoon salt

½ cup cold cooked rice

Sausage casings (see Note)

Kitchen string

12-inch pastry bag

#6 plain round pastry tip

CONDIMENTS

A few small heads of salad greens (Boston lettuce, romaine, cabbage, and radicchio are all good choices)

A few scallions

Sprigs of cilantro

1 small knob ginger

8 small Thai chilies *(phrik khee nu)*

⅓ cup roasted unsalted peanuts

1 small lemon

To make the sausages: Put all of the sausage ingredients except the rice in the bowl of a food processor fitted with a metal blade. Process to a hamburger-like consistency, about 1½ minutes. The mixture should have a uniform texture. Transfer to a large mixing bowl. Mix in the rice by hand until blended.

Fit the pastry tip into the pastry bag. Put about half of the sausage mixture into the bag. Slip one end of a sausage casing over the pastry tip. Twist the top of the pastry bag to create a firm, uniform pressure as you force the sausage mixture slowly into the casing. Knead the casing occasionally, using a slight downward pressure, to help the mixture along. Try to keep a uniform diameter of about 1 to 1½ inches.

(Be patient to make sure the casing doesn't split. But if it does, don't worry. Just tie the broken end with a piece of string and begin again.)

When you have forced the first pastry bag full of sausage mixture into the casing, gently tie off the sausage every 4 inches with kitchen string to make four links.

Refill the pastry bag and repeat the procedure to make four more links.

Coil the links into a covered container and let them cure overnight in the refrigerator.

To prepare the condiments: Select small, cup-shaped leaves from your choice of salad greens and arrange them on a serving platter. Set aside.

Trim and slice the scallions, including some of the green tops. Chop the cilantro. Peel and finely slice the ginger. Chop the chilies and the peanuts. Trim the ends of the lemon, but do not peel. Slice it into ½-inch rounds, then stack and chop them into small dice.

Arrange all of the condiments on a large serving platter. Set aside.

To grill or sauté the sausages:

Grilling method: Cut the sausage into separate links. Prick each sausage lightly with a fork. Grill slowly over medium coals until evenly browned. Cut the sausages into 1-inch slices and arrange them on a serving platter.

Sautéing method: Cut the sausage into separate links. Prick each sausage lightly with a fork. Set a large, heavy skillet over medium-high heat. When it is quite hot, add just enough vegetable oil to coat the surface, about 2 tablespoons. Sauté the sausages, turning them often to brown evenly, about 8 minutes. Cut the sausages into 1-inch slices and arrange them on a serving platter.

THAI SERVING STYLE: Set out the platters of lettuce cups, condiments, and sausages. Put a slice of sausage and your choice of condiments into a lettuce cup. Fold up and eat out of hand. Vary the selection of condiments to find your favorite flavor accents, between sips of cold Thai beer or whiskey, if desired.

NOTE: Call local butchers to find the sausage casings. They should be wide enough for sausages about 1½ inches in diameter. Store the casings in a container filled with fresh salted water. Cover and refrigerate until ready to use.

Poultry
and
Meat

RED CURRY WITH BEEF
AND GREEN PEPPERCORNS

Kaeng Phed Neua Phrik Thai On

Serves 6 to 8

Three chili flavors merge in this spicy classic dish from central Thailand: dried red chilies in the curry paste, fresh green serranos and braised bamboo shoots spiced with crushed red chilies in the sauce. When you combine chilies, their flavors build on one another. Every mouthful is subtly different from the one before.

The creamy red sauce gets an added flavor, as well as contrasting color and crunchy texture, from green peppercorns. In Thailand we would use fresh-picked peppercorns, but brine-cured peppercorns, packed in cans and jars, are a good substitute. They still have the crunchy exterior and tender insides of fresh-picked pepper berries.

This is a particularly spicy curry. If you'd prefer a milder version, omit the serranos. In Thailand, however, even a spicy curry such as this is often accompanied by Classic Chili Dipping Sauce.

2 cans (19 ounces each) unsweetened coconut milk

1 cup Classic Red Curry Paste (page 26)

1 pound beef top round, cut into thin 1 × 2½-inch slices

½ cup (scant) drained, brine-cured green peppercorns (*phrik Thai on*)

1 cup braised bamboo-shoot tips with chili (see Note 1)

3 tablespoons Thai fish sauce (*nam pla*)

5 tablespoons coconut-palm sugar or golden brown sugar

5 small serrano chilies, stemmed and cut lengthwise into slivers (optional)

1⅔ cups loosely packed Thai basil (*bai horapha*) or purple or Italian basil

Classic Chili Dipping Sauce (page 49) (optional)

Skim the thick cream from the top of the canned coconut milk into a soup pot, reserving the milk. Set the pot over medium-high heat. Stir in the curry paste until blended and bring to a low boil. Cook, stirring constantly, for 2 minutes. Stir in the beef. Stir in the peppercorns and bamboo-shoot tips. Stir in the reserved coconut milk. Add the fish sauce and sugar and stir until the sugar is dissolved and blended. Raise the heat to high. Cover and bring to a boil, about 1 minute. Uncover and add the chilies, if desired. Turn off the heat. Stir in the basil and cook for a few seconds, just until the basil begins to wilt.

Transfer to a serving bowl or covered casserole. Serve with plenty of steamed jasmine rice and Classic Chili Dipping Sauce, if desired.

N O T E 1 : Braised bamboo shoots with chilies can be found in the canned-goods section of your nearest Thai market. Omit them if they're unavailable, or substitute plain bamboo shoots.

N O T E 2 : I like to make this curry a few hours, or even a full day, before I plan to serve it. Given some time, the flavors will enhance one another and become more pronounced. Keep it covered and refrigerated until ready to use, heat it through without letting it come to a boil, then serve.

BEEF WITH BROCCOFLOWER

Kap Phat Neua Pak Broccoflower

Serves 4 to 6

My mother always made this dish with cauliflower. I've recently begun using broccoflower, which is a cross between broccoli and cauliflower. It has the shape of a cauliflower, with a lively spring-green color and a flavor that's sweet and mild.

This is an easy-to-prepare stir-fry that goes nicely with a spicy soup or salad.

3 tablespoons vegetable oil

8 cloves garlic, pounded to a mash or crushed and chopped

½ pound beef tenderloin (preferably filet mignon), trimmed and cut crosswise into ¼-inch-thick slices

1 tablespoon oyster sauce

2 tablespoons crushed yellow bean sauce (*tao jiew dam*)

3 tablespoons golden brown sugar

1 head broccoflower or cauliflower, florets only, broken into bite-size pieces

2 tablespoons Chicken Stock (page 72), canned chicken broth, or water

Chilies-in-Vinegar Sauce (page 52) (optional)

Place all of the ingredients except the chili sauce within easy reach of the cooking area.

Set a wok over medium-high heat. When it is quite hot, add the oil. Rotate the wok a bit so the oil coats the sides. Add the garlic and stir-fry briefly, just until golden and aromatic. Raise the heat to high. Add the beef and stir-fry for 30 seconds. Stir in the oyster sauce, yellow bean sauce, and sugar and stir-fry for 30 seconds. Add the broccoflower and stir-fry for 1 minute. Add the chicken stock and stir-fry for about 1½ minutes. Reduce the heat to low, cover, and simmer just until the broccoflower is tender and cooked through, about 1½ to 2 minutes.

Transfer to a serving platter and serve with steamed jasmine rice and Chilies-in-Vinegar Sauce, if desired.

CRISPY SWEET BEEF

Neua Wan

Serves 4 to 6

I 've loved this sweet, chewy snack all my life. Deep-fried beef slices coated with a sweet-and-savory sauce may not qualify as health food, but just a little bit of this appetizer can be very satisfying—especially when served in the traditional Thai style, on social occasions, accompanied by a cold beer or a small glass of whiskey.

3 cups plus 1 tablespoon vegetable or peanut oil

1 pound beef bottom round, cut along the grain into long slabs about 1½ inches wide, then thinly sliced across the grain

3 tablespoons coconut-palm sugar

1 tablespoon Thai fish sauce (*nam pla*)

1 tablespoon white pepper

Pour 3 cups of oil into a wok or a large, heavy saucepan. Set it over medium-high heat until the oil is sizzling hot, about 360°F. (To test the oil temperature, dip a wooden spoon in the hot oil. The oil should bubble and sizzle gently around the bowl of the spoon.)

Fry the beef about eight slices at a time, turning occasionally, until it is richly browned, about 1½ to 2 minutes.

Drain on paper towels. Adjust the heat, if necessary, to maintain an even cooking temperature. Continue frying until all the beef is cooked.

Put the remaining tablespoon of oil into a clean wok or a large, heavy saucepan and set it over high heat. Add the sugar, fish sauce, and pepper. Stir until the sugar is dissolved and blended. Bring to a boil and add the beef. Stir briefly, just until all the beef slices are coated with sauce.

Transfer to a serving platter and serve at room temperature.

NOTE: You can make this a day in advance. Store it covered in the refrigerator, then bring it back to room temperature before serving.

GREEN CURRY WITH BEEF, EGGPLANT, AND GREEN CHILI

Kaeng Khiew Wan Neua

Serves 6 to 8

This beautiful jade-green curry is smooth, elegant, and lively. The chili heat is in perfect balance with the sensual herbal ingredients.

In this recipe, the earthy qualities of beef and eggplant perfectly complement the curry. The beef should be nicely trimmed, with just a little fat remaining for the sake of flavor.

In Thailand we have a dozen or more varieties of eggplant. For this curry I've chosen slender, dark purple Japanese eggplant for flavor and *makhua khun*, a small, pale, egg-shaped variety, for texture.

2 cans (one 14 ounces and one 19 ounces) unsweetened coconut milk

1 cup Fresh Green Chili Curry Paste (page 28)

1½ pounds sirloin, sliced across the grain into ¼-inch-thick slices, about 1 × 2 inches

¼ cup coconut-palm sugar or golden brown sugar

¼ cup Thai fish sauce (*nam pla*)

¼ pound round Thai eggplant (*makhua khun*), stemmed, cut in half, and sliced (optional)

½ pound Japanese eggplant, angle-cut into ¼-inch-thick slices

1 large green bell pepper, sliced

6 medium serrano chilies, stemmed and sliced in half lengthwise (see Note 1)

1 cup loosely packed Thai basil (*bai horapha*) or purple or Italian basil

Skim the thick cream from the top of the canned coconut milk into a soup pot, reserving the milk. Set the pot over medium-high heat. Stir in the curry paste until blended, and bring to a low boil. Cook, stirring constantly, for 2 minutes.

Stir in the beef and the reserved coconut milk and bring to a low boil, stirring occasionally. Add the sugar and fish sauce and stir until the sugar is dissolved and blended. Stir in the eggplant and green bell pepper and cook for 1 minute. Add the chilies and return to a low boil, stirring occasionally. Cook for 1 minute. Turn off the heat. Stir in the basil and cook for a few seconds, just until the basil begins to wilt.

Transfer to a serving bowl or covered casserole and serve with plenty of steamed jasmine rice.

NOTE 1: The serrano chilies are meant to flavor the curry sauce. Don't eat them unless you crave intense chili heat.

NOTE 2: I like to make this curry a few hours, or even a full day, before I plan to serve it. Given some time, the flavors will enhance one another and become more pronounced. Keep it covered and refrigerated until ready to use, heat it through without letting it come to a boil, then serve.

MASSAMAN BEEF CURRY WITH POTATOES AND PINEAPPLE

Kaeng Massaman Neua

Serves 6

This is one of the mildest and loveliest of Thai curries. It appeals to kids as much as it does to grown-ups. You first notice the subtle but lingering perfumes of cardamom and cloves, spices that Muslim immigrants brought to Thailand long ago.

In fact, *Massaman* is the Thai transliteration of "Muslim." Many of Thailand's Muslims live far to the south, along the Malaysian border. Settlers from these regions operate dozens of Massaman curry restaurants in and around Bangkok.

2½ tablespoons vegetable oil

1½ pounds boneless stew beef, cut into 1½-inch cubes

1 large onion, chopped

1 large potato (about ¾ pound), peeled and cut into 1-inch cubes

2 cans (one 14 ounces and one 19 ounces) unsweetened coconut milk

1 cup Massaman Curry Paste (page 36)

½ cup roasted unsalted peanuts

½ cup coconut-palm sugar or golden brown sugar

7 tablespoons Thai fish sauce (*nam pla*)

¼ cup Tamarind Sauce (page 61) or liquid tamarind concentrate

1 cup chopped fresh pineapple

Set a soup pot over high heat and add the oil. When the oil is sizzling hot, sear the meat, turning until it is browned on all sides. Add the onions and stir-fry just until tender, about 1½ minutes. Add just enough water to cover. Bring to a boil. Reduce the heat, cover, and simmer for 15 minutes. Add the potatoes, cover, and simmer just until the potatoes are tender and partially cooked, about 15 minutes.

Strain out the meat and vegetables and reserve the broth. (You should have at least 2 cups of broth.) Set the meat and vegetables aside. Set the reserved broth aside.

Skim the thick cream from the top of the canned coconut milk into a soup pot, reserving the milk. Set the pot over medium-high heat. Stir in the curry paste until blended, and bring to a low boil. Cook, stirring constantly, for 2 minutes. Mix in the meat, potatoes, and peanuts. Stir in the reserved coconut milk. Add the sugar, fish sauce, and tamarind sauce. Stir until the sugar is dissolved and blended. Add the pineapple and stir in about ½ cup or more of the reserved broth to thin the sauce to your taste. Cook, stirring occasionally, for 2 to 3 minutes, or just until the potatoes are cooked through.

Transfer to a serving bowl or covered casserole and serve with plenty of steamed jasmine rice.

N O T E : I like to make this curry a few hours, or even a full day, before I plan to serve it. Given some time, the flavors will enhance one another and become more pronounced. Keep it covered and refrigerated until ready to use, heat it through without letting it come to a boil, then serve.

FIERY JUNGLE CURRY WITH GRILLED BEEF, HERBS, AND VEGETABLES

Kaeng Pha Neua Kap Pak Ruam Mit

Serves 6 to 8

Before this century, northern Thailand was isolated by dense forests, white-water rivers, hilly ranges, and small, fertile valleys. Much of the country is still wild, with patches of cultivation and a wonderful variety of nutritious edible plants, many of which have no English names at all.

Jungle curry represents the best of northern-style country cooking. It isn't just a recipe, it's a way to take advantage of the bounty of the Thai countryside. As rural people walk along roadsides or jungle trails after a day's work in the fields, they keep their eyes on the wild, uncultivated growth along the way, looking for vines, young shoots, herbs, leaves, and blossoms, selecting edible treasures from what the season has to offer. They may also take young corn, wild mushrooms, cherry tomatoes, garlic, or other cultivated crops growing on the fringes of the jungle. Once they reach home, their harvest immediately becomes a curry dinner. Since coconut palms do not thrive in the north, they use no coconut milk to tame its chili fire. This is traditionally one of the spiciest of all Thai curries.

In America, the best way to make jungle curry is to take a walk through a farmers' market or supermarket, selecting seasonal herbs and vegetables, gathering a mixture of the sweet and the slightly bitter. Vary the selection according to the flavors of the season and you will be true to the spirit of jungle curry.

1¼ pounds choice boneless beef round rump roast, cut into sixteen pieces about ½ inch thick and 2 to 2½ inches square

¼ cup vegetable oil

⅓ cup garlic cloves, pounded to a mash or crushed and chopped

1⅓ cups Jungle Curry Paste (page 40)

18 (9 pairs) fresh Kaffir lime leaves (*bai magroot*), or strips of peel from 1 small lime

6 ounces Japanese eggplant, sliced

2 cups mixed fresh herbs:
    ½ cup roughly torn Italian basil

    ½ cup roughly torn Thai basil (*bai horapha*) or purple or Italian basil

    ½ cup chopped tarragon

    ¼ cup chopped chives

    ¼ cup roughly torn arugula

1 leek (about ½ pound), including some of the green top, sliced

6 scallions, including the green tops, finely sliced

½ pound mushrooms, sliced

¼ pound okra, stemmed

6 tablespoons coconut-palm sugar or golden brown sugar

7 tablespoons Thai fish sauce (*nam pla*)

1 cup Chicken Stock (page 72) or canned chicken broth

Over hot barbecue coals, or on a stovetop grill, sear the beef on one side for 2 minutes. Turn and sear on the second side for about 2 minutes. Turn and cook about 1 minute more on each side, just until medium-rare. (If using a stovetop grill, you may need to grill the meat in two or more batches.)

Holding your knife at a 45-degree angle, slice the beef into ¼-inch-thick slices. Set aside.

Set a soup pot over medium-high heat and add the oil. When the oil is sizzling hot, add the garlic and stir-fry briefly, just until golden and aromatic. Add the curry paste and stir-fry for 2 minutes. If using Kaffir lime leaves, tear each leaf in half and add to the pot. If using lime peel, add to the pot. Add the eggplant, herbs, leek, scallions, mushrooms, and okra. Stir-fry for 30 seconds. Add the grilled beef and sugar and stir-fry for 2 minutes. Stir in the fish sauce and chicken stock and cook just until the vegetables are tender, about 2½ minutes, stirring occasionally.

Transfer to a serving bowl or covered casserole and serve with plenty of steamed jasmine rice.

FISH *and* SEAFOOD

Pla leh Ahan Talay

I grew up alongside the banks of the Chao Phraya River in a two-story Victorian-style teakwood house that had Thai adornments mixed into its gingerbread trim. We had no refrigerator, but our food was always perfectly fresh—thanks to the river. A little pavilion stood at the water's edge, and merchants in long, slender boats would row up every day to sell fresh fish, produce, spiced coffee, and other wonderful things to eat.

It was quite a romantic way to grow up, and it's a style of life that still exists. Many Thai people live beside a lively waterway. Our rivers and canals are the arteries and veins of the country. They bring the water that floods our millions of acres of rice paddies. They transport most of our commerce, from little marketplace crafts to massive oceangoing freighters that sail up the Chao Phraya to reach Bangkok.

Fish and seafood recipes hold a vital connection to Thai custom and traditions. Alongside rice, the sea is the greatest supporter of life in our country. Some of our most highly skilled traditional fishermen can tell, just by listening to the ocean's sounds, what kind of fish is near, how big the school, and how close.

When our New Year celebration rolls around, during a mid-April festival called Songkran, children splash water on everyone walking by, especially in the streets of Phra Pradaeng, the city where the Chao Phraya River meets the ocean. No one gets angry at the children, because water washes away the old year and cleanses everything for the new. Even the statues of Buddha are sprinkled with water and perfume.

Six months later, during the Loy Krathong festival, we send floating offerings— banana leaves folded into the shapes of birds and boats, decorated with lotus blossoms, coins, and lighted candles—down all the rivers, streams, and canals. They carry everyone's prayers for forgiveness and good fortune, and all of our thanks to the water for giving us life.

There's a taste of the ocean in practically every Thai meal, even when no fish is on the table. *Nam pla,* Thai fish sauce, is our most widespread cooking ingredient and condiment. Very few meals are served without it—a good thing, as *nam pla* is very rich in nutrients.

In fact, the abundance of fish is one reason that the Thai diet is so healthful. Researchers now say that one or two fish dishes per week may cut your risk of heart disease in half. This comes as no surprise to Thai mothers, who have told their children for thousands of years—as mine always told me—that good food is always good medicine.

You'll find numerous types of seafood in this chapter, reflecting the wealth available to the Thai people: lobsters, mussels, crabs, shrimp, various salt- and freshwater fish, squid, even frog legs. There are ocean-dwelling and freshwater fish, cooked whole, cut into steaks or fillets, even minced into dumplings. Some are steamed, others fried, grilled, or stir-fried. Some are in rich coconut curries and some in savory, pungent dry curries.

You will learn ways of preparing fish that you may never have tried before. For example, Thai recipes often call for serving bone-in steaks of fish, rather than fillets, to enrich the flavors of curries and sauces. You will also find new ideas for foods to accompany seafood, as in Curried Mussels with Pumpkin and Thai Basil.

There are also variations on old favorites. If you enjoy French or Italian steamed mussels, try the very healthy Thai version: Steamed Mussels with Lemon Grass and Thai Basil has no butter, cream, or wine—just an aromatic broth infused with herbs and spices.

Some of these recipes reflect home-style cooking. Seafood Dumplings, and Shrimp and Baby Corn in Chili-Tamarind Sauce, for example, will put you in touch with everyday Thai life. Other recipes are sophisticated enough for fine restaurants, such as Whole Lobster in a Sea of Curry, Dear Blue Crab, and the simple yet elegant Steamed Salmon with Pink Pickled Ginger, Red Onion, and Lemon Grass.

Since fish and seafood are so central to Thai existence, they will emerge again and again in other chapters. I hope the flavors and textures of Thai-style seafood will become almost as familiar to you as they are to the people who live along the Chao Phraya.

Steamed Swordfish with Sour Curry and Yard-Long Beans

Kaeng Som Pla Kap Thua Fak Yao

Serves 4 to 6

Kaeng som pla is a steamed fish curry with the seductive flavors of red chili and tamarind. Small whole fish, or, in this case, fish fillets, are steamed in a bath of sour-curry sauce. The sauce itself is somewhat thin, almost a gravy, yet the flavor is round and rich.

I recipe (about ¾ cup) Sour Curry Paste (page 38)

1½ cups Chicken Stock (page 72) or canned chicken broth

3 tablespoons golden brown sugar

I tablespoon Thai fish sauce (*nam pla*)

¼ cup Tamarind Sauce (page 61) or liquid tamarind concentrate

1½ pounds swordfish fillets

¾ pound yard-long beans or green beans, angle-cut into 2-inch pieces

Sprigs of cilantro

Set a wok over medium-high heat. (Use a nonstick wok if you have one.) When it is quite hot, add the curry paste and cook for 2 minutes, stir-frying briskly to keep it from burning. Add the chicken stock and sugar and cook, stirring often, for 1 minute. Stir in the fish sauce and tamarind sauce and bring the mixture to a boil, stirring often. Boil for 1 minute, stirring occasionally. Turn off the heat.

Pour the curry sauce into a heatproof bowl deep enough to hold the sauce, the fish, and the beans. The bowl should fit inside a steamer rack with at least 1 inch of clearance all around.

Put the swordfish fillets in the bowl with the curry sauce. As much as possible, avoid overlapping them. (The fillets don't have to lie flat; they can conform to the shape of the bowl.) Put the beans on top.

Fill the base pot of a tiered aluminum steamer about one-third full of water. Cover, and bring the water to a boil over medium-high heat.

Set the bowl with all of the ingredients in the middle of a steaming rack. When the water reaches a boil, set the rack over the pot, cover, and steam until the beans are tender and the fish is cooked through, about 15 minutes. Remove the bowl of curried fish from the steamer.

Transfer to a deep serving platter or large covered casserole. Tear sprigs of cilantro over the curry and serve with plenty of steamed jasmine rice.

FRIED RED SNAPPER WITH PHRIK KHING CURRY

Phrik Khing Pla Daeng Tod

Serves 4 to 6

I n Thailand we love the "dry" curries like *phrik khing* for their unique texture and pungent spice. The moist curry paste, heady with chilies, black pepper, and Siamese ginger, is briskly stir-fried with chicken stock, oyster sauce, and palm sugar, creating a smooth, puréelike sauce.

Red snapper fillets are cut into squares and fried to a golden crisp so they can be sauced with the curry and still retain a pleasing shape and texture.

FISH

1½ pounds red snapper fillets

½ teaspoon salt

¼ cup all-purpose flour

3 cups vegetable or peanut oil for frying

CURRY

2 tablespoons vegetable oil

I cup Phrik Khing Curry Paste (page 34)

3 tablespoons plus I teaspoon coconut-palm sugar or golden brown sugar

5 tablespoons Chicken Stock (page 72) or canned chicken broth

I tablespoon oyster sauce

4 (2 pairs) fresh Kaffir lime leaves (*bai magroot*), finely sliced into slivers, or a pinch or two of grated lime zest

Sprigs of cilantro

To fry the fish: Cut the fillets into pieces about 2 inches square. Mix the salt with the flour. Lightly dredge the fish pieces in the seasoned flour.

Pour the oil into a large wok or heavy saucepan set over medium-high heat and bring the oil to 360°F. Carefully add enough fish pieces to fill the pan without crowding, about eight per batch. Fry, turning two or three times, until crispy and deep golden brown, about 5 minutes total. Adjust the heat if necessary to maintain a consistent frying temperature. Lift out the fish pieces with a wire skimmer or slotted spoon and drain on paper towels.

Return the oil to 360°F and fry the rest of the fish as above.

Keep the fish warm in a low oven while you prepare the curry.

To make the curry: Set a wok over medium-high heat. When it is quite hot, add the oil. Rotate the wok a bit so the oil coats the sides. When the oil is hot, reduce the heat to low and add the curry paste. Cook for 2 minutes, stir-frying briskly to keep it from burning. Add the sugar and stir-fry until it is dissolved and blended. Stir in the chicken stock and oyster sauce. Add the lime leaves or zest. Turn off the heat.

Spoon some of the curry sauce onto a large serving platter. Arrange the fried fish on the platter, then spoon the remaining curry sauce over the fish.

Tear sprigs of cilantro over the curry and serve with steamed jasmine rice.

CRISPY CATFISH CURRY

Pla Duk Tod Krob Phat Phed

Serves 4 to 6

In this Bangkok-style fish curry, freshly cut catfish steaks are fried a rich golden brown and sauced with red curry and Thai basil. Instead of coconut milk, chicken stock is the main liquid ingredient in this dry-style curry.

I've given methods for frying fish fillets as well as bone-in steaks. Many Americans prefer fillets, but I urge you to try serving this classic dish in authentic Thai style—in a casual setting with family or friends, where everyone feels free to pick up a fish steak and nibble the meat right off the bone.

FISH

1 whole catfish (about 2½ pounds), cleaned, head and tail removed, or 1½ pounds catfish fillets

½ teaspoon salt

¼ cup all-purpose flour

2 cups vegetable or peanut oil for frying

CURRY

3 tablespoons vegetable oil

10 cloves garlic, pounded to a mash or crushed and chopped

¾ cup Classic Red Curry Paste (page 26)

3 tablespoons golden brown sugar

5 tablespoons Chicken Stock (page 72) or canned chicken broth

1½ bell peppers (any color), chopped

½ cup canned, drained bamboo-shoot strips

2 tablespoons Thai soy sauce with mushroom (*see-eu kao het hom*) or a Chinese brand, such as Pearl River Bridge

1½ cups loosely packed Thai basil (*bai horapha*) or purple or Italian basil

Sprigs of cilantro

To fry the fish: If using whole fish: Using kitchen shears, a cleaver, or a sharp knife, trim and discard the fins. Cut the fish crosswise, creating bone-in steaks about ½ inch thick, using a heavy cleaver and a mallet or hammer. Cut until the cleaver meets the bone, then use the mallet or hammer to pound the cleaver clear through. Rinse the fish steaks under cold water and dry them thoroughly with a kitchen towel.

Mix the salt with the flour. Lightly dredge the fish steaks in the seasoned flour.

Pour the oil into a large wok or deep heavy skillet set over medium-high heat, and bring the oil to 360°F. Carefully add enough fish steaks to fill the pan without crowding, about four to six per batch. Fry, turning two or three times, until crispy and deep golden brown, about 10 minutes total. Adjust the heat if necessary to maintain a consistent frying temperature. Lift the fish steaks out with a wire skimmer or slotted spoon and drain on paper towels.

Return the oil to 360°F and fry the rest of the fish as above.

Keep the fish warm in a low oven while you prepare the curry.

If using fillets: Cut the fillets into pieces about 2 inches square. Mix the salt with the flour. Lightly dredge the fish pieces in the seasoned flour.

Pour the oil into a wok or a deep heavy skillet set over medium-high heat and bring the oil to 360°F. Carefully add enough fish pieces to fill the pan without crowding, about eight per batch. Fry, turning two or three times, until crispy and deep golden brown, about 5 minutes total. Adjust the heat if necessary to maintain a consistent frying temperature. Lift the fish pieces out with a wire skimmer or slotted spoon and drain on paper towels.

Return the oil to 360°F and fry the rest of the fish as above.

Keep the fish warm in a low oven while you prepare the curry.

To make the curry: Set a wok over medium-high heat. When it is quite hot, add the oil. Rotate the wok a bit so the oil coats the sides. When the oil is hot, add the garlic and stir-fry briefly, just until golden and aromatic.

Reduce the heat to low and add the curry paste. Stir-fry briskly for 45 seconds. Add the sugar and chicken stock and stir until the sugar is dissolved and blended.

Raise the heat to medium-high. Add the bell pepper, bamboo-shoot strips, and soy sauce and stir-fry briskly until the pepper is crisp-tender, about 2 minutes.

Add the fried fish and stir-fry until the vegetables are cooked and the fish is heated through, about 1 minute.

Turn off the heat. Stir in the basil and cook for a few seconds, just until the basil begins to wilt.

Transfer to a large serving platter or covered casserole. Tear sprigs of cilantro over the curry and serve with plenty of steamed jasmine rice.

THAI SERVING STYLE: In Thailand it is perfectly acceptable to use your fingers when eating fish that has bones in it. Take a spoonful of rice and curry, then pick up a fish steak and nibble the fish from the bone.

CURRIED MUSSELS WITH KABOCHA AND THAI BASIL

Kaeng Kua Hoy Meng Phu Kap Fak Thong

Serves 4 to 6

Kabocha, or Japanese squash, as it's sometimes called, is a New World vegetable that probably came to Siam with Portuguese traders. We love its sweet, rich taste, creamy texture, and bright color. It has become a favorite ingredient not only in sweet snacks and desserts but in our classic savory cooking, too. Recently, many American supermarkets have begun carrying kabocha. If your grocer doesn't have it yet, substitute a winter squash, such as butternut or acorn.

Here the kabocha's smooth orange flesh is a sweet and colorful accent to green-tipped, briny mussels and a *kua* curry, a mild yet earthy red curry that has been turned golden with coconut milk.

1 pound kabocha (see Note)

2 pounds New Zealand mussels, placed in a bowl or sink full of cold water

1 can (19 ounces) unsweetened coconut milk

½ cup Kua Curry Paste (page 45)

12 (6 pairs) fresh Kaffir lime leaves (*bai magroot*), or strips of peel from 1 small lime

3 tablespoons coconut-palm sugar or golden brown sugar

3 tablespoons Thai fish sauce (*nam pla*)

1 cup loosely packed Thai basil (*bai horapha*) or purple or Italian basil

Scoop out and discard the seeds and fibers from the kabocha. With a sharp heavy knife or cleaver, chop it into quarters. Cut off most of the peel and slice the kabocha into thin, bite-size pieces.

Agitate the water in which the mussels are soaking. Live mussels open and close to breathe. Any mussels that don't eventually close should be discarded. Scrub and debeard the mussels. Drain and set aside.

Skim the thick cream from the top of the canned coconut milk into a soup pot, reserving the milk. Set the pot over medium-high heat. Stir in the curry paste until blended and bring to a low boil. Cook, stirring constantly, for 2 minutes. Add the kabocha and cook for 2 minutes, stirring occasionally. Add the mussels and reserved coconut milk and cook for 1 minute, stirring occasionally. If using Kaffir lime leaves, tear each leaf in half and add to the pot. If using lime peel, add it to the pot. Add the sugar and stir until dissolved and blended. Stir in the fish sauce and cook at a low boil, stirring occasionally, for 4 to 5 minutes, or until the mussels have opened and the curry is perfumed with the lime leaves. (Discard any mussels that fail to open.)

Turn off the heat. Stir in the basil and cook for a few seconds, just until the basil begins to wilt.

Transfer to a serving bowl or covered casserole and serve with plenty of steamed jasmine rice.

N O T E : You need a 1-pound piece of kabocha for this recipe. Most Asian markets sell kabocha whole and by the piece. If your market sells them only whole, buy a small one, about 2 pounds, and reserve half for another recipe, such as Pumpkin in Sweet Coconut Milk (page 334) or Curried Pumpkin-Fried Rice (page 250).

Frog Legs in Yellow Curry with Green Chili

Kop Phat Kari Phrik Sod

Serves 4 to 6

Frogs are quite plentiful in Thailand. After every rainfall, our flooded rice paddies are full of their song. It's a sound that pleases the ears of good cooks from the villages to the cities.

In Bangkok we often prepare frog legs as I have in this recipe, in a simple stir-fry with curry and basil. Almost any curry will do, but I particularly like to use the mild, Indian-style yellow curry, which enhances but doesn't overwhelm the sweet flavor of the frog legs. Slivers of fresh green chili and spicy, anise-flavored Thai basil accentuate this dish, which is wonderfully different from the French-style frog leg recipes you may be familiar with.

6 pairs of frog legs (about 1 pound), split in two at the joint

2 tablespoons vegetable oil

16 cloves garlic, pounded to a mash or crushed and chopped

2 tablespoons Yellow Curry Paste (page 30)

¼ cup sugar

3 tablespoons Thai fish sauce (*nam pla*)

½ cup Chicken Stock (page 72) or canned chicken broth

4 serrano chilies, stemmed and cut lengthwise into slivers

1 cup loosely packed Thai basil (*bai horapha*) or purple or Italian basil

Rinse the frog legs under cold water and dry with paper towels. Score each leg five or six times on each side, down to the bone.

Set a wok over medium-high heat. When it is quite hot, add the oil. Rotate the wok a bit so the oil coats the sides. When the oil is hot, add the garlic and stir-fry briefly, just until golden and aromatic. Add the frog legs and stir-fry for 1 minute. Add the curry paste and stir-fry for 1 minute. Add the sugar and fish sauce and stir until the sugar is dissolved and blended. Add the chicken stock and chilies and stir-fry for 1 minute.

Turn off the heat. Stir in the basil and cook for a few seconds, just until the basil begins to wilt.

Transfer to a serving platter and serve with plenty of steamed jasmine rice.

CHU CHEE SCALLOPS

Kaeng Chu Chee Hoy Shell

Serves 4 to 6

Although we have fine deep-water scallops in Southeast Asia, they've only recently become popular in Thailand. We must thank European and American visitors for bringing our attention to one of the few sea creatures we overlooked. Perhaps that's why we've taken to calling scallops *hoy shell,* after the scallop-like Shell gas-station signs that can be seen all over Thailand.

I've paired *chu chee,* a traditional curry used only with seafood, with the newly popular scallops. This moderately hot red curry is tamed with coconut milk and perfumed with Kaffir lime leaves and the bright sea flavor of the scallops. For those who want a spicier curry, the optional fresh green chili will intensify the heat.

I can (19 ounces) unsweetened coconut milk

I cup Chu Chee Curry Paste (page 42)

1½ pounds sea scallops, each sliced horizontally into two to three rounds

4 tablespoons Thai fish sauce (*nam pla*)

4 tablespoons coconut-palm sugar or golden brown sugar

12 (6 pairs) fresh Kaffir lime leaves (*bai magroot*), finely sliced into slivers, or ½ teaspoon grated lime zest

4 medium serrano chilies, stemmed and cut lengthwise into slivers (optional)

I cup loosely packed Thai basil (*bai horapha*) or purple or Italian basil

Skim the thick cream from the top of the canned coconut milk into a soup pot, reserving the milk. Set the pot over medium-high heat. Stir in the curry paste until blended, and bring to a low boil. Cook, stirring constantly, for 2 minutes. Stir in the reserved coconut milk and add the scallops. Cook at a low boil for 2 minutes, stirring occasionally. Stir in the fish sauce. Add the sugar and stir until it is dissolved and blended. Add the lime leaves or zest, and the chilies, if desired, and cook for 1 minute, stirring often.

Transfer to a deep serving platter or covered casserole and shower the scallops with the Thai basil. Serve with plenty of steamed jasmine rice.

169

Fish

and

Seafood

SEAFOOD DUMPLINGS WITH CHU CHEE CURRY

Kaeng Chu Chee Luk Chin Pla

Serves 4 to 6

*L*uk chin pla are bite-size seafood dumplings, or fish balls, as we often call them. Roadside stands, elegant restaurants, and everyday cooks all make *luk chin pla.*

The most basic type is made from white-fish fillets, ground to a paste and lightly seasoned, then dropped by the teaspoonful into boiling water or stock. To keep these dumplings from being overpowered by a complex, earthy curry like *chu chee,* fresh chopped shrimp are added for more body and richer flavor.

DUMPLINGS

1 pound fish fillets (any mild white-fleshed variety, such as catfish, cod, red snapper, or flounder)

¼ pound medium shrimp, cleaned and peeled

6 cloves garlic, pounded to a mash or crushed and chopped

1 teaspoon white pepper

½ tablespoon chopped cilantro

CURRY

1 can (19 ounces) unsweetened coconut milk

1 cup Chu Chee Curry Paste (page 42)

4 tablespoons Thai fish sauce (*nam pla*)

4 tablespoons coconut-palm sugar or golden brown sugar

12 (6 pairs) fresh Kaffir lime leaves (*bai magroot*), finely sliced into slivers, or ½ teaspoon grated lime zest

4 medium serrano chilies, stemmed and cut lengthwise into slivers (optional)

1 cup loosely packed Thai basil (*bai horapha*) or purple or Italian basil

To make the dumplings: Chop the fish fillets into 1-inch pieces. Chop the shrimp. Put the chopped fish, shrimp, and all of the other dumpling ingredients into the bowl of a food processor fitted with a metal blade. Process to a smooth paste, about 2 to 3 minutes, stopping once or twice to scrape down the sides of the work bowl. Transfer the seafood paste to a small bowl.

Bring a medium saucepan of lightly salted water to a boil. Meanwhile, fill a mixing bowl with ice water and have it standing by. You will need this to collect the cooked dumplings so they'll stop cooking and become firm.

Drop the dumpling mixture by rounded teaspoonfuls into the boiling water, about eight to ten at a time. They will cook quickly, in less than a minute, and float to the surface. Lift them out with a wire skimmer or slotted spoon and quickly place them in the ice water.

Continue making the dumplings as above. After the last ones go into the ice water, drain and set aside.

To make the curry: Skim the thick cream from the top of the canned coconut milk into a soup pot, reserving the milk. Set the pot over medium-high heat. Stir in the curry paste until blended, and bring to a low boil. Cook, stirring constantly, for 2 minutes. Stir in the fish sauce. Add the sugar and stir until it is dissolved and blended. Stir in the reserved coconut milk and bring to a low boil. Add the seafood dumplings, lime leaves or zest, and the chilies, if desired, and cook for 1 minute, stirring often.

Turn off the heat. Stir in the basil and cook for a few seconds, just until the basil begins to wilt.

Transfer to a deep serving platter or covered casserole and serve with plenty of steamed jasmine rice.

WHOLE LOBSTER IN A SEA OF CURRY

Kaeng Panang Kung Mongkong

Serves 6

S weet lobster meat, fresh out of its shell, is matched here with a superlative Panang curry. Smoky dried red chilies and fragrant herbs and spices are carefully blended so that no one flavor predominates. The result is deeply flavorful yet subtle, perfect with the rich lobster. Smoothed with coconut milk, sprinkled with crushed peanuts, and spiked with shards of fresh hot chili, the curry is carefully spooned back into the sections of bright red lobster shell, set in a deep platter, then ladled with more curry sauce. When placed before your guests, the lobster seems to be swimming in a sea of curry.

I love the large lobsters found here in America. For this dish, always select the biggest, liveliest one you can find. Lobster is one of the costliest kinds of seafood you can buy, so search out an Asian seafood market for the freshest seafood at the lowest prices. Buy a female lobster if possible, so you can blend into the curry any coral, or roe, it may hold.

Cooking and shelling a whole lobster may seem daunting, but I'll take you through it step by step. Although it's a challenge to keep the shells intact when removing the meat, you don't have to do it perfectly for this dish to be successful. We have a saying in Thailand: *Mai pen rai*—"It will work out."

I large live lobster (4½ to 5 pounds), preferably female

I can (19 ounces) unsweetened coconut milk

I cup Panang Curry Paste (page 32)

5 tablespoons coconut-palm sugar or golden-brown sugar

½ cup roasted unsalted peanuts, crushed in a mortar or finely chopped

4 tablespoons Thai fish sauce (*nam pla*)

5 serrano chilies, stemmed and cut lengthwise into slivers

I cup loosely packed Thai basil (*bai horapha*) or purple or Italian basil

To cook the lobster: Select a heavy pot with a tight-closing lid, big enough to hold the lobster. Fill with enough water to cover the lobster (but don't put the lobster in yet). Lightly salt the water and bring it to a boil over high heat. Carefully plunge the lobster in head first. Cover and simmer for 10 minutes. Lift the lobster out and rinse under cold water.

To shell the lobster: Chop or twist off the large front claws and set aside.

Break off the walking legs along each side so the body is easier to handle, but leave the antennae intact for presentation. Set aside the walking legs.

Holding the lobster over a large bowl to catch its juices, twist the tail apart from the rest of the body. Set aside the head and body portion.

To remove the meat from the tail, first break off and discard the small flippers. Place the tail, shell side down, on a flat work surface. Using kitchen shears or a sharp knife, cut away the undershell along both edges, exposing the tail meat. Pull out the tail meat, leaving the hard shell intact. Set aside the shell and add the tail meat to the bowl of lobster juices.

Holding the head and body portion over the bowl to catch any juices, pry the shell away from the meat. To do this, insert a thumb in the crack between the shell and the meat. Holding the hard shell with your other hand, pull it away from the meat. Set the shell aside.

Put the body meat on a work surface, curved side down. Split it in half lengthwise with a cleaver or kitchen shears. Scoop out the tomalley, the soft yellow-green strip in the body, and add it to the bowl of juices. Scoop out the roe, if any, and add to the bowl. Remove and discard all nonmeat matter, including the feathery lungs near the sides, the stomach sac, and the gray intestinal tract. Pick out any lobster meat in the body and add it to the bowl.

Use a cracking tool, such as a nutcracker, to remove the meat from the walking legs. Crack them at each knuckle and pull out the meat with a metal pick or toothpick. Add the meat to the bowl and discard the shells of the walking legs.

Crack the claws with a nutcracker, cleaver, or small hammer at the ends where they joined the body, being careful to keep the claw shells as intact as possible for presentation. Hold the claws over the bowl and pour out the juices. Pull out the meat. Set aside the claw shells and add the meat to the bowl.

Remove the sections of lobster meat from the bowl and cut them into bite-size pieces. Return the pieces to the bowl and mix together with the juices, tomalley, and roe, if any. Set aside.

To make the curry: Skim the thick cream from the top of the canned coconut milk into a wok, reserving the milk. Set the wok over medium-high heat. Stir in the curry paste until blended and bring to a low boil. Cook, stirring constantly, for 2 minutes.

Add the lobster, with the juices, tomalley, and roe, if any, and stir-fry for 30 seconds. Add the sugar and stir until it is dissolved and blended. Mix in the crushed peanuts. Add the reserved coconut milk and stir-fry for 1 minute. Add the fish sauce and chilies and stir-fry for 1 minute.

continued

Turn off the heat. Stir in the basil and cook for a few seconds, just until the basil begins to wilt.

To assemble the dish: Select a serving platter large enough to hold the whole stuffed lobster and the sea of curry.

Take the back shell with the lobster head and place it about one-third of the way back on the platter. Using a slotted spoon, mound some of the lobster curry in the space created under the shell. Next, mound some of the lobster curry into the tail shell and carefully invert it onto the platter behind the head. Then ladle the remaining curry all around the stuffed lobster. Finally, take the claws and arrange them naturalistically at each side of the head with the pincers extending well out in front of the head.

Serve with plenty of steamed jasmine rice.

FRIED SQUID WITH THREE DIPPING SAUCES

Pla Muek Tod Krob

Serves 6 to 8

F ried squid is an appetizer that's loved all over the world. This Thai version features a delicate, crispy texture and a startlingly white appearance. The batter is very light, almost like a tempura batter, but with a unique consistency that comes from combining rice flour and the Thai arrowroot we call *tao yai mom*.

I like to set out a variety of dipping sauces, such as the sweet-tart Thai Plum Sauce, chili-flecked Sweet-and-Spicy Dipping Sauce, and Vietnamese-Style Dipping Sauce, so my guests can enjoy a small feast of contrasting flavors and colors with the lacy white squid.

2¾ pounds whole squid (about 4 large)

2 cups arrowroot (*tao yai mom*)

2 cups rice flour

2 cups water

2 egg yolks

4 cups vegetable or peanut oil for deep-frying

Thai Plum Sauce (page 57) (optional)

Sweet-and-Spicy Dipping Sauce (page 54) (optional)

Vietnamese-Style Dipping Sauce (page 59) (optional)

To clean the squid: Rinse the squid under cold water. Pull the head from the body. Cut the tentacles off in one piece, just below the eyes, and discard the rest of the head. If the hard little beak is in the center of the set of tentacles, pull it out and discard. Reserve the body sac and tentacles.

Pull out the long, transparent quill from the body sac and discard. Press out the innards by running the body sac between your thumb and fingers, squeezing as you go from the closed to the cut end. Or lay the body sac on a flat work surface and run the dull side of a knife blade along its length, from the closed to the cut end. Rinse out the body sac so you're sure to remove any traces of the gelatinous inner matter.

Slice the squid bodies into rings about ¼ inch wide, combine them with the tentacles, and set aside.

To fry the squid: In a large mixing bowl, whisk together the flours, water, and egg yolks, blending until smooth. Mix the squid rings and tentacles into the batter.

Pour the oil into a large wok or heavy saucepan. Set over medium-high heat and bring the oil to 375°F. Carefully add enough squid rings and tentacles to fill the pan without crowding, about twelve pieces per batch. Fry, turning once or twice, until crispy, about 3 to 4 minutes total. Adjust the heat if necessary to maintain a consistent frying temperature. Lift out the squid with a wire skimmer or slotted spoon and drain on a tray or plate lined with paper towels.

Return the oil to 375°F and fry the rest of the squid as above.

Transfer immediately to a serving platter and serve with one or more of the dipping sauces.

DEEP-FRIED POMFRET WITH HOT CHILI AND SWEET BELL PEPPER SAUCE

Pla Jaramet Tod Lad Na Phrik Sod

Serves 4 to 6

Beautiful, silvery pomfret is among the most sought-after sea creatures in all Southeast Asia. Throughout Thailand, Burma, Vietnam, Malaysia, and Java, gourmet cooks prize its delicate, sweet flavor and pearly-white flesh.

Pomfret looks similar to butterfish and pompano, but unlike these somewhat fatty fish, it is decidedly lean. The flesh comes away easily from the bones, making it a pleasure to serve whole, as in this recipe.

The fish is fried whole until crisp and deep golden brown, then topped with an eye-catching sauce of sweet red pepper and hot green chili. In Thailand, the sauce would be a fearsome mix of assorted hot chilies, without the sweet bell peppers to cool it down. Here I've blended the hot with the sweet, creating a moderately spicy sauce full of the rich flavors of chicken stock, garlic, and yellow bean sauce. If you crave that fiery authenticity, you can always add more hot chilies. For a milder dish, replace some of the serrano chilies with a chopped green bell pepper.

The sauce is also delicious on steamed fish, particularly with a whole steamed red snapper. The recipe for this variation follows on page 178.

FISH

1 whole pomfret, cleaned (about 1½ pounds), head and tail intact

Vegetable or peanut oil for frying

SAUCE

8 to 10 serrano chilies (or 2 to 3 serrano chilies and 1 green bell pepper), chopped

1 large red bell pepper, chopped

2 tablespoons vegetable oil

5 cloves garlic, pounded to a mash or crushed and chopped

3 tablespoons golden brown sugar

2 tablespoons crushed yellow bean sauce (*tao jiew dam*)

2 tablespoons Thai fish sauce (*nam pla*)

½ cup Chicken Stock (page 72), canned chicken stock, or water

1½ cups loosely packed Thai basil (*bai horapha*) or purple or Italian basil

Sprigs of cilantro

To fry the fish: Place a heatproof platter in a warm oven while you prepare the fish.

Rinse the pomfret under cold water and dry thoroughly with a kitchen towel. Score both sides of the fish with diagonal cuts almost to the bone, about every inch or so.

Pour the oil into a large wok or deep, heavy skillet to a depth of 2 inches. Bring the oil to 375°F over medium-high heat. Carefully slide the fish into the hot oil and ladle some oil over any parts left exposed. Fry, turning once, until crispy and deep golden brown on both sides, about 8 to 10 minutes total.

Lift out the fried fish and drain briefly on a tray or plate lined with paper towels. Transfer the fish to the warm serving platter and set aside.

To make the sauce: Put the chopped chilies and bell pepper in the bowl of a food processor fitted with a metal blade. Process until finely chopped.

Set a wok over medium-high heat. When it is quite hot, add the oil. Rotate the wok a bit so the oil coats the sides. When the oil is hot, add the garlic and stir-fry briefly, just until golden and aromatic. Add the chili–bell pepper mixture and cook for 1 minute, stirring occasionally. Add the sugar and yellow bean sauce and stir-fry for 1 minute. Stir in the fish sauce and chicken stock. Turn off the heat. Stir in the basil and cook for a few seconds, just until the basil begins to wilt.

Pour the sauce over the fried fish. Tear sprigs of cilantro over the dish and serve with steamed jasmine rice.

THAI SERVING STYLE: Cut the fish down to the bone along the full length of the spine, from head to tail. Pushing away from the center cut with a serving spoon, nudge the fish meat slightly away from the spine on both sides. You will now have two portions. Slide a knife blade or spatula under each portion, lift off the bone, and serve. The backbone will be exposed and easy to remove. Grasp the tail end of the bone, lift it up, pull it away from the meat, and discard. Cut the remaining fillet into two portions and serve. Pick up and chew the small, crispy, calcium-rich bones of the tail and lower fin. They are considered a delicacy.

Fish
and
Seafood

STEAMED RED SNAPPER WITH
HOT CHILI AND SWEET BELL PEPPER SAUCE

Pla Daeng Nung Lad Na Phrik Sod

Serves 4

FISH

1 whole red snapper (about 2 pounds),
cleaned, head and tail intact

Vegetable or peanut oil for the
steaming rack

To steam the fish: Place a heatproof platter in a warm oven while you prepare the fish.

Rinse the snapper under cold water and dry it thoroughly with a kitchen towel. Score each side of the fish with three diagonal cuts almost to the bone.

Fill the base pot of a tiered aluminum steamer about one-third full of water. Cover and bring the water to a boil over medium-high heat. Lightly oil a steamer rack. Put the fish on the rack. (If it is too large, bend up or cut off the tail so it fits comfortably.) When the water reaches a boil, set the rack over the pot, cover, and steam until the fish is cooked through, about 10 to 12 minutes. The fish is done when a knife tip easily penetrates the thickest part and the flesh is opaque.

Transfer the fish to the warm serving platter.

Prepare the sauce and serve the fish following the instructions on page 176.

THAI SERVING STYLE: Follow the serving instructions on page 177, but do not eat the bones.

SHRIMP AND BABY CORN IN CHILI-TAMARIND SAUCE

Kung Phat Nam Phrik Pao Khao Phod On

Serves 4 to 6

This is a delicious yet simple stir-fry that's perfect for a casual dinner for family and friends. The rich, earthy flavor of chili-tamarind paste is blended with a splash of chicken stock and a little sugar for balance, making a wonderfully savory sauce that's a bit smoky, sweet, and spicy—a delicious counterpoint to the fresh shrimp and crunchy baby corn.

Fresh baby corn is becoming easier to find in markets and gardens across the country. Use it when available for the ultimate in sweet corn flavor and texture. Otherwise, canned baby corn is just fine.

1 pound medium shrimp

1½ tablespoons vegetable oil

10 cloves garlic, pounded to a mash or crushed and chopped

5½ teaspoons Chili-Tamarind Paste (page 46), or 4 teaspoons commercially made chili-tamarind paste (*nam phrik pao*)

2 teaspoons Thai fish sauce (*nam pla*)

2 tablespoons sugar

¾ pound fresh baby corn, husked and broken into 2-inch pieces, or 1 can (15 ounces) baby corn, drained

2 tablespoons Chicken Stock (page 72), canned chicken broth, or water

Sprigs of cilantro

Rinse and peel the shrimp, but leave the tails on. Slice them partway through along the back to butterfly and devein.

Place all of the ingredients within easy reach of the cooking area.

Set a wok over medium-high heat. When it is quite hot, add the oil. Rotate the wok a bit so the oil coats the sides. When the oil is hot, add the garlic and stir-fry briefly, just until golden and aromatic. Raise the heat to high, add the shrimp, and stir-fry just until they begin to turn pink, about 15 seconds. Add the chili-tamarind paste, fish sauce, and sugar and stir-fry until the sugar is dissolved and blended. Add the baby corn and chicken stock and stir-fry just until the corn is cooked through, about 2½ minutes for fresh or 1 to 1½ minutes for canned.

Transfer to a serving platter and tear sprigs of cilantro over the dish. Serve with steamed jasmine rice.

FRIED STRIPED BASS WITH CHILI-TAMARIND SAUCE

Pla Kaphong Tod Lad Na Nam Phrik Pao

Serves 4

The chili-tamarind sauce in this dish is a *lad na*-style sauce, or topping, for the fried striped bass: It is prepared separately, and includes fresh chopped vegetables, creating a sort of cooked salsa that you spoon over the top of the crisp-fried fish.

FISH

1 whole striped bass (about 1¾ pounds), cleaned, head and tail intact

Vegetable or peanut oil for frying

SAUCE

3 tablespoons vegetable oil

10 cloves garlic, pounded to a mash or crushed and chopped

3 tablespoons Chili-Tamarind Paste (page 46), or 2 tablespoons commercially made chili-tamarind paste (*nam phrik pao*)

5 tablespoons Chicken Stock (page 72) or canned chicken broth

4 tablespoons sugar

5 scallions, including the green tops, angle-cut into ¾-inch pieces

1 red bell pepper, finely chopped

1 tablespoon Thai fish sauce (*nam pla*)

Sprigs of cilantro

To fry the fish: Place a heatproof platter in a warm oven while you prepare the fish.

Rinse the fish under cold water and dry thoroughly with a kitchen towel. Score both sides with diagonal cuts almost to the bone, about every inch or so.

Pour the oil into a large wok or deep, heavy skillet to a depth of 2 inches. Bring the oil to 375°F over medium-high heat. Carefully slide the fish into the hot oil and ladle some oil over any parts left exposed. Fry, turning once, until crispy and deep golden brown on both sides, about 8 to 10 minutes total.

Lift out the fried fish and drain briefly on a tray or plate lined with paper towels. Transfer the fish to the warm serving platter and set aside.

To make the sauce: Set a wok over medium-high heat. When it is quite hot, add the oil. Rotate the wok a bit so the oil coats the sides. When the oil is hot, add the garlic and stir-fry briefly, just until golden and aromatic. Add the chili-tamarind paste and stir-fry for 45 seconds. Add the chicken stock and sugar and stir-fry until the sugar is dissolved and blended. Add the scallions and red bell pepper and stir-fry for

30 seconds. Add the fish sauce and stir occasionally until the mixture comes to a low boil, about 2 minutes. Turn off the heat.

Pour the sauce over the fried fish. Tear sprigs of cilantro over the dish and serve with steamed jasmine rice.

THAI SERVING STYLE: Cut the fish down to the bone along the full length of the spine, from head to tail. Pushing away from the center cut with a serving spoon, nudge the fish meat away from the spine on both sides. You will now have two portions. Slide a knife blade or spatula under each portion, lift off the bone, and serve. The backbone will be exposed and easy to remove. Grasp the tail end of the bone, lift it up, pull it away from the meat, and discard. Cut the remaining fillet into two portions and serve.

Fried Garlic Chips

(page 66)

Sprinkle some over a Caesar salad or a platter of steamed or sautéed vegetables—steamed asparagus with grated Parmesan and fried garlic chips is a delicious example. Or sprinkle them over lobster tails served with Savory Tamarind Sauce (page 269) in place of drawn butter.

181

Fish

and

Seafood

SPICY STIR-FRIED SQUID WITH RED CHILI AND HOLY BASIL

Phat Phed Pla Muek Phrik Sod Bai Kaprao

Serves 4 to 6

This fiery stir-fry achieves richness of taste with only a few simple ingredients. Garlic, hot chili, and the spicy, mint-like bite of holy basil make sparks fly, while the tender squid provides a sea-fresh flavor.

In Thailand, we use finger-sized hot red chilies called *phrik chee fa* for this dish. Red jalapeños are a wonderful substitute. I don't seed the chilies because the seeds hold much of their heat and because my mother always taught me that the seeds of the chili are where the plant's healing powers are concentrated. "They're good for you," she often says, "they're medicine."

1½ pounds whole squid

2 tablespoons vegetable oil

13 cloves garlic, pounded to a mash or crushed and chopped

3 ounces red jalapeño peppers (about 10), stemmed and cut lengthwise into slivers

2 tablespoons Golden Mountain sauce (*poo kow thong*) or Maggi seasoning

2 tablespoons golden brown sugar

2 cups loosely packed holy basil (*bai kaprao*) or fresh mint

To clean the squid: Rinse the squid under cold water. Pull the head from the body. Discard the head with its tentacles, reserving only the body sac.

Pull out the long transparent quill and discard. Press out the innards by running the body sac between your thumb and fingers, squeezing as you go from the closed to the cut end. Or lay the body sac on a flat work surface and run the dull side of a knife blade along its length, from the closed to the cut end. Rinse out the body sac so you're sure to remove any traces of the gelatinous inner matter. Peel off the speckled outer skin and cut the squid into thirds. Score through one side of each piece with a series of diagonal cuts. Set aside.

To make the stir-fry: Set a wok over medium-high heat. When it is quite hot, add the oil. Rotate the wok a bit so the oil coats the sides. When the oil is hot, add the garlic and stir-fry briefly, just until golden and aromatic.

Raise the heat to high, add the squid, and stir-fry for 30 seconds. Add the jalapeños and stir-fry for 1 minute. Add the Golden Mountain sauce and the sugar and stir-fry until the sugar is dissolved and blended.

Turn off the heat. Stir in the basil and cook for a few seconds, just until the basil begins to wilt.

Transfer to a serving platter and serve with steamed jasmine rice.

STIR-FRIED SHRIMP WITH CHINESE BROCCOLI

Kung Phat Pak Ka Na

Serves 4 to 6

In Thailand, Chinese broccoli is called *pak ka na.* It has a bright flavor with a delicious edge of bitterness to it—perfect with the sweet, rich shrimp. Unlike the broccoli American shoppers are used to, *pak ka na* has long slender stems, large broad leaves, and small white buds and flowers.

Sometimes I make this stir-fry with seafood dumplings, like those on page 170, for a subtly different flavor and texture.

2 tablespoons vegetable oil

4 cloves garlic, pounded to a mash or crushed and chopped

I pound medium shrimp, cleaned and peeled, or I recipe Seafood Dumplings (page 170)

¼ cup crushed yellow bean sauce (*tao jiew dam*)

¼ cup Chicken Stock (page 72) or canned chicken broth

3 tablespoons dark brown sugar

I pound Chinese broccoli, stalks angle-cut into I-inch pieces, leafy stems angle-cut into 3-inch pieces

Sprigs of cilantro

Bottled Thai chili sauce (*sriracha*) or any good Mexican or Louisiana-style hot sauce (optional)

Place all of the ingredients except the hot sauce within easy reach of the cooking area.

Set a wok over medium-high heat. When it is quite hot, add the oil. Rotate the wok a bit so the oil coats the sides. When the oil is hot, add the garlic and stir-fry briefly, just until golden and aromatic. Add the shrimp or seafood dumplings and stir-fry for 30 seconds. Add the yellow bean sauce, chicken stock, and sugar and stir-fry until the sugar is dissolved and blended. Add the Chinese broccoli and stir-fry until cooked through, about 2 to 3 minutes.

Transfer to a serving platter. Tear sprigs of cilantro over the stir-fry and serve with steamed jasmine rice and Thai chili sauce, if desired.

Shrimp with Garlic, Cucumber, and Scrambled Eggs

Kung Phat Thaeng Kwa Kap Khai

Serves 4 to 6

This home-style stir-fry is a year-round favorite in small cafés all over Bangkok. You can serve it alone with steamed rice for a simple lunch or dinner, or match its mellow tastes with a spicy curry or barbecued chicken.

For sweet, juicy shrimp, keep the stir-fry tempo brisk and the cooking time short. The eggs are broken right into the wok and cooked until creamy, then folded in with the shrimp and cucumber.

¾ pound medium shrimp

2 medium cucumbers

2 tablespoons vegetable oil

13 cloves garlic, pounded to a mash or crushed and chopped

1 tablespoon oyster sauce

1 tablespoon Thai fish sauce (*nam pla*)

1 tablespoon golden brown sugar

½ tablespoon white pepper

2 eggs

Sprigs of cilantro

Place all of the ingredients within easy reach of the cooking area.

Rinse and peel the shrimp, but leave the tails on. Slice them partway through along the back to butterfly and devein. Set aside.

Peel the cucumbers. Cut them in half lengthwise and slice them into pieces ¼ inch thick.

Set a wok over medium-high heat. When it is quite hot, add the oil. Rotate the wok a bit so the oil coats the sides. When the oil is hot, add the garlic and stir-fry briefly, just until golden and aromatic. Add the shrimp and stir-fry just until they begin to turn pink, about 15 seconds. Add the oyster sauce, fish sauce, and sugar and stir-fry until the sugar is dissolved and blended. Mix in the cucumbers and white pepper.

Break the eggs into the wok. Stir just enough to break up the yolks, then let them cook until partially set, about 15 seconds. Gently fold the mixture over and cook for 10 seconds. Cover and cook for 1 minute. Turn off the heat.

Transfer to a serving platter. Tear sprigs of cilantro over the dish and serve with steamed jasmine rice.

STIR-FRIED MUSSELS WITH FLOWERING CHIVES

Hoy Meng Phu Phat Dok Kun Chai

Serves 4 to 6

Plump New Zealand mussels, with their iridescent, green-tipped shells, are similar to one of Thailand's favorite varieties, *hoy meng phu*. I always use them in this dish, in which the mussels are served on the half shell, to show off the lovely yellow-orange meat.

The mussels are strewn with handfuls of Chinese flowering chives, which add dark-green brushstrokes of color and an earthy flavor that is sharper than that of common chives. Chinese flowering chives are allowed to grow to maturity. They are picked in spring and summer, when teardrop-shaped buds appear on the stems.

If you grow chives in your garden, pick them after their lavender flowers have blossomed. They will have deeper flavor. You can use them, blossoms and all, as a substitute for Chinese flowering chives.

2 pounds New Zealand mussels, placed in a bowl or sink full of cold water

2 tablespoons vegetable oil

14 cloves garlic, pounded to a mash or crushed and chopped

2 teaspoons white pepper

2 tablespoons coconut-palm sugar or golden brown sugar

2 tablespoons oyster sauce

1 tablespoon Thai soy sauce with mushroom (*see-eu khao het hom*) or a Chinese brand, such as Pearl River Bridge

½ pound Chinese flowering chives, or 1 large bunch common chives with blossoms, angle-cut into 1½-inch pieces, flowers and all

Agitate the water in which the mussels are soaking. Live mussels open and close to breathe. Any mussels that don't eventually close should be discarded. Scrub and debeard the mussels, then drain. Gently pry the mussels open, breaking them apart at the hinge end. Discard the upper shells, reserving the mussels on their half shells.

Place all of the ingredients within easy reach of the cooking area.

Set a wok over medium-high heat. When it is quite hot, add the oil. Rotate the wok a bit so the oil coats the sides. When the oil is hot, add the garlic and stir-fry briefly, just until golden and aromatic. Stir in the pepper, add the mussels, shell sides down, and gently stir-fry, keeping the mussels upright, for 30 seconds. Turn the mussels over and cook for 1 minute, stirring occasionally. Add the sugar, oyster sauce, and soy sauce and stir-fry just until the sugar is dissolved and blended. Add the chives and stir-fry just until they are cooked through yet retain their bright color, about 1 to 1½ minutes.

Transfer to a serving platter and serve with steamed jasmine rice.

STIR-FRIED SHRIMP WITH ANGLED LOOFA

Kung Phat Buab Sod

Serves 4 to 6

*B*uab is the Thai name for a vegetable commonly called "angled loofa" in the English-speaking world. A staple in markets and country gardens throughout Thailand, it is a long, tapered squash that grows on a tangle of leafy vines. Its pale green skin is marked by ten deep ridges. *Buab* can grow up to 8 or 9 feet long in the tropical Thai climate, but the best ones for cooking are young and small, no longer than a foot or so. The flesh has a spongy, fibrous texture and bland flavor, with a pleasing hint of bitterness. It has a marvelous way of soaking up a sauce, mellowing it in the process.

In this recipe I've combined *buab* with shrimp, garlic, and a mild yellow bean sauce for a dish that exemplifies Thai home-style cooking. Since the sauce is mild, Thai people like to add a splash or two of a spicy condiment such as Classic Chili Dipping Sauce.

2 pounds angled loofa (3 or 4)

12 large shrimp

2 tablespoons vegetable oil

9 cloves garlic, pounded to a mash or crushed and chopped

2 tablespoons plus ½ teaspoon crushed yellow bean sauce (*tao jiew dam*)

2 tablespoons sugar

4 tablespoons Chicken Stock (page 72) or canned chicken broth

Classic Chili Dipping Sauce (page 49) (optional)

Trim off the edges and most of the peel from the loofa with a sharp paring knife. Trim off the ends, slice the loofa in half lengthwise, and cut crosswise into pieces about ½ inch thick. Set aside.

continued

187

Fish
and
Seafood

Rinse and peel the shrimp, but leave the tails on. Slice them partway through along the back to butterfly and devein.

Place all of the ingredients except the dipping sauce within easy reach of the cooking area.

Set a wok over medium-high heat. When it is quite hot, add the oil. Rotate the wok a bit so the oil coats the sides. When the oil is hot, add the garlic and stir-fry briefly, just until golden and aromatic.

Raise the heat to high. Add the shrimp and stir-fry just until they begin to turn pink, about 15 seconds. Add the loofa and stir-fry for 30 seconds. Add the yellow bean sauce, sugar, and chicken stock and stir-fry for 2 minutes.

Transfer to a serving platter and serve with steamed jasmine rice and Classic Chili Dipping Sauce, if desired.

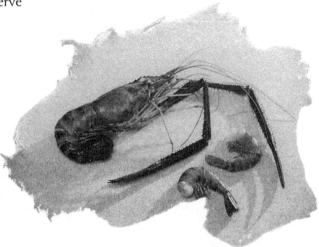

Mixed Seafood Stir-Fry, Gulf Port Style

Ahan Klai Talay Phat Bai Kaprao

Serves 4 to 6

D otted along the coast of the great Gulf of Thailand and the opposite shores of the Andaman Sea are seaside resorts and gulf ports like Pattaya and Hua Hin. Their fishing fleets supply seafood to all corners of Thailand. There is no fresher seafood anywhere in the world than at the dockside cafés and markets of these towns.

Restaurant patrons make their selections from neon-lit stalls heaped with fat Gulf shrimp, glistening clams and mussels, speckled squid, and all manner of freshly caught fish. It will all be cooked to order and brought to tables out on the pier, overlooking the fishing boats at anchor.

This recipe was inspired by a wonderful platter of seafood with an irresistible sauce that I had one night. It's a stir-fry of mussels, clams, squid, and shrimp with three seasoning sauces, a few small hot chilies, and a shower of pungent holy basil. The mixed seafood liquors are released in the cooking to permeate a smoky, sweet gravy of oyster, sweet black soy, and Golden Mountain sauces.

½ pound New Zealand mussels, placed in a bowl or sink full of cold water

½ pound littleneck or cherrystone clams, placed in a bowl or sink full of cold water

¾ pound whole squid

½ pound medium shrimp

3 to 6 small Thai chilies (*phrik khee nu*)

9 cloves garlic

2 tablespoons vegetable oil

I tablespoon sweet black soy sauce (*see-eu wan*)

I tablespoon Golden Mountain sauce (*poo kow thong*) or Maggi seasoning

1½ tablespoons golden brown sugar

I tablespoon oyster sauce

I red bell pepper, chopped

2 cups loosely packed holy basil (*bai kaprao*) or fresh mint

continued

To clean the seafood: Agitate the water in which the mussels are soaking. Tap the clams against one another. Live mussels and clams open and close to breathe. Any mussels or clams that don't eventually close should be discarded. Scrub and debeard the mussels. Scrub the clams. Let the mussels and clams soak while you prepare the squid.

Rinse the squid under cold water. Pull the head from the body. Cut the tentacles off in one piece, just below the eyes, and discard the rest of the head. If the hard little beak is in the center of the set of tentacles, pull it out and discard. Reserve the body sac and tentacles.

Pull out the long, transparent quill from the body sac and discard. Press out the innards by running the body sac between your thumb and fingers, squeezing as you go from the closed to the cut end. Or lay the body sac on a flat work surface and run the dull side of a knife blade along its length, from the closed to the cut end. Rinse out the body sac so you're sure to remove any traces of the gelatinous inner matter. Peel off the speckled skin and cut the squid into thirds. Score through one side of each piece with a series of diagonal cuts. Combine them with the tentacles and set aside.

Rinse and peel the shrimp, but leave the tails on. Slice them partway through along the back to butterfly and devein. Set aside.

Drain the mussels and clams and set aside.

To make a seasoning paste with the chilies and garlic:

Mortar-and-pestle method: Stem the chilies. Put the garlic and chilies in the mortar and pound until they are thoroughly mashed and pulverized. Set aside.

Alternate method: Stem the chilies. Crush the garlic and chilies with the side of a chef's knife. Mix the chilies and garlic together and mince.

To make the stir-fry: Place all of the ingredients within easy reach of the cooking area.

Set a wok over medium-high heat. When it is quite hot, add the oil. Rotate the wok a bit so the oil coats the sides. When the oil is hot, add the chili-garlic seasoning paste and stir-fry briefly, just until the garlic is golden and aromatic. Add all the seafood, raise the heat to high, and stir-fry for 30 seconds.

Add the soy sauce, Golden Mountain sauce, sugar, and oyster sauce and stir-fry until the sugar is dissolved and blended. Bring the sauce to a boil, add the bell pepper, and stir-fry for 1 minute. Cover and cook until the bell pepper is tender and cooked through, about 45 seconds.

Discard any mussels or clams that have failed to open.

Turn off the heat. Stir in the basil and cook for a few seconds, just until the basil begins to wilt.

Transfer to a serving platter and serve with plenty of steamed jasmine rice.

STEAMED SALMON WITH PINK PICKLED GINGER, RED ONION, AND LEMON GRASS

Pla Nung Manao

Serves 4 to 6

This exquisite yet simple dish embodies the principles of Thai cooking. It's light and healthy, yet rich with sensual pleasures.

Soft, beautiful colors are the first things your guests will notice as this dish arrives at the table: bright rose-colored pickled ginger, the creamy coral-pink fillets of salmon, and diced red onion turned pale lavender in the citrusy broth.

The refreshing tartness of freshly squeezed lemon juice is balanced by the sweetness of sugar and the pungency of garlic and chilies. Infused with the rich taste of the salmon itself, this is an exceptionally memorable broth. Spoon it generously over your rice for a pleasing side dish.

1¾ to 2 pounds salmon fillets

12 cloves garlic, pounded to a mash or crushed and chopped

½ cup chopped red onion

3 medium serrano chilies, minced

½ cup pink pickled ginger slices

2 stalks lemon grass, tough outer leaves discarded, lower stalks trimmed to 4 inches and sliced on a sharp diagonal, or strips of peel from 1 small lemon

½ teaspoon salt

1 tablespoon white sugar

1 cup fresh lemon juice

Fill the base pot of a tiered aluminum steamer about one-third full of water. Cover and bring the water to a boil over medium-high heat.

Put the salmon in a heatproof bowl deep enough to hold it and the rest of the ingredients. The bowl should fit in a steamer rack with at least 1 inch of clearance all around.

Set the bowl with all of the ingredients in the middle of the steaming rack. When the water reaches a boil, set the rack over the pot. Cover and steam until the salmon is cooked through and the herbs have infused the broth, about 18 to 20 minutes.

Transfer the fish with all the aromatic broth to a deep serving platter or covered casserole. Serve with plenty of steamed jasmine rice.

STEAMED MUSSELS WITH LEMON GRASS AND THAI BASIL

Hoy Meng Phu Op Mo Din

Serves 4

Many French recipes for steamed mussels, such as *moules marinière* and *moules à la crème*, are made with wine, butter, or cream. In contrast, this Thai preparation is a bit lighter. Its flavors come from fresh aromatic herbs: Kaffir lime leaves, Siamese ginger, lemon grass, and our anise-scented basil. Cloves of garlic and hot little chilies also infuse the steaming liquid with a hint of spice. The result is a lively, healthful broth.

Although this recipe calls for some exotic ingredients, you can easily substitute more familiar ones, such as lemon peel in place of lemon grass. Other alternate ingredients are listed below.

When you make these Thai-style mussels, it's fun to eat them the French way: Use a hinged pair of shells like tongs. Pluck the mussels out of their shells, then dip them in the broth and hot sauce.

2 pounds New Zealand mussels, placed in a bowl or sink full of cold water

3 cups water

2 stalks lemon grass, tough outer leaves discarded, angle-cut into 4-inch pieces, or strips of peel from 1 small lemon

10 (5 pairs) fresh Kaffir lime leaves (*bai magroot*), or strips of peel from 1 small lime

5 cloves garlic, lightly crushed

3 large slices (about 2 ounces) unpeeled Siamese ginger (galanga or *kha*), or 3 pieces dried or common ginger

⅛ teaspoon white pepper

4 to 6 small Thai chilies (*phrik khee nu*), or 1 serrano chili, lightly crushed

1 cup loosely packed Thai basil (*bai horapha*) or purple or Italian basil

Bottled Thai chili sauce (*sriracha*) or any good Mexican or Louisiana-style hot sauce

Agitate the water in which the mussels are soaking. Live mussels open and close to breathe. Any mussels that don't eventually close should be discarded. Scrub and debeard the mussels. Drain and set aside.

Pour the water into a large soup pot or kettle and add the lemon grass, lime leaves, garlic, ginger, and white pepper. Bring to a boil over medium-high heat. Reduce the heat and simmer for 3 minutes. Raise the heat to high and bring back to a boil. Add the cleaned mussels, cover, and cook for 4 to 6 minutes, shaking the pot after a minute or two to allow room for all the mussels to open. Discard any that fail to open. Using a slotted spoon, transfer the mussels to a serving bowl or platter.

Reduce the heat, add the crushed chilies and ¾ cup of the basil to the broth, and simmer for 2 minutes. Strain the broth through a fine mesh strainer. Reserve the broth and discard the solids.

Pour the broth into a serving bowl or gravy boat.

Chop the remaining ¼ cup basil leaves and shower them over the mussels.

Serve the mussels with the broth and hot sauce on the side. Set out small individual serving bowls so your guests can mix the broth with a few drops of hot sauce to their own taste.

CURRIED SEAFOOD MOUSSE GRILLED IN BANANA LEAVES

Ayuthaya Haw Mok Talay

Serves 6 to 8

This wonderfully elegant yet rustic dish is perfect for a casual backyard barbecue or a formal sit-down dinner. It's seldom found in restaurants, just in the homes of very good cooks—like my mother.

The seafood mousse is a sophisticated blend of shrimp, fish, and crab, flavored with homemade red curry paste, eggs, herbs, spices, and creamy coconut milk. It is cooked on the stove until it begins to thicken, then wrapped in banana leaves. The leafy packages are grilled over a charcoal fire, suffusing the seafood-and-curry mixture with a smoky herbal flavor.

You can buy I-pound packages of frozen banana leaves in Thai or Vietnamese markets. When defrosted, the leaves become pliable, and they retain their fresh green color as well. You can substitute aluminum foil, but the authentic item makes an unforgettable impression. Just looking at these handsome green bundles and savoring their aroma as it rises from the grill will make you feel as if the tropics have come to your backyard.

SEAFOOD MOUSSE

¾ pound fish fillets (any mild, white-fleshed variety, such as catfish, cod, red snapper, or flounder)

¾ pound medium shrimp, cleaned and peeled

½ pound fresh crabmeat, or I can (6 ounces) crabmeat, drained well

16 (8 pairs) fresh Kaffir lime leaves (*bai magroot*), finely sliced into slivers, or ½ teaspoon grated lime zest

5 serrano chilies, stemmed and finely sliced

I can (I9 ounces) unsweetened coconut milk

I cup Classic Red Curry Paste (page 26)

3 large eggs

4 tablespoons coconut-palm sugar

4 tablespoons Thai fish sauce (*nam pla*)

BANANA-LEAF PACKAGES

I package (I pound) frozen banana leaves, defrosted

2 cups loosely packed Thai basil (*bai horapha*) or purple or Italian basil

16 bamboo skewers, soaked in a tray of cold water for at least ½ hour

To make the seafood mousse: Chop the fish fillets into 1-inch pieces. Put the fish pieces into the bowl of a food processor fitted with a metal blade. Process to a smooth paste, about 2 minutes, stopping once or twice to scrape down the sides of the bowl.

Transfer the fish paste to a large mixing bowl. Stir in the remaining seafood mousse ingredients and mix until thoroughly blended.

Transfer the mousse mixture to a large saucepan and cook over medium-high heat, stirring occasionally, until the mixture begins to thicken, about 6 to 8 minutes. Remove from the heat and set aside.

To assemble the banana-leaf packages: Carefully unfold a banana leaf and spread it out horizontally on an uncluttered work surface. Fold it in half, or thirds, to create a rectangle about 14 inches wide and 16 inches long. You will need about seven or eight large leaves. (If some leaves are less than 14 inches wide, overlap two narrow ones to a 14-inch width, then trim to a length of 16 inches.)

Reserve one good leaf to line a serving platter for presentation, if desired.

Put about ¼ cup basil leaves in the center of the banana leaf. Mound 1 cup of the seafood mousse on top of the basil. Fold the left and right sides of the leaf over the mousse, forming a tube shape. Fold the bottom and top ends toward the center and secure with two bamboo skewers. Create an X pattern by inserting the skewers diagonally, one from the lower right corner through to the upper left, the other from the lower left to the upper right corner.

Repeat the above steps until all the basil and mousse are wrapped in banana-leaf packages and secured with skewers.

(*If using foil:* Overlap two double-thick lengths of foil to make a rectangle 14 inches wide by 16 inches long. Mound the basil and mousse ingredients as above. Fold the left and right sides of the foil over the mousse, forming a tube shape. Roll the bottom and top ends toward the center, pressing down as you go to create a tight seal. Repeat the above steps until all the basil and mousse are wrapped in foil.)

To grill the banana-leaf packages: Grill the packages over a medium-hot fire on a charcoal barbecue or gas grill. Use the bamboo skewers as handles to turn as they brown, about 4 to 6 minutes per side. They should be evenly browned on both sides. A little bit of scorching is fine, but be careful not to burn holes in them.

Serve with plenty of steamed jasmine rice.

THAI SERVING STYLE: For an informal gathering, such as an outdoor barbecue, simply heap the grilled packages onto a serving platter and pass them around to your guests. Each person can unwrap a package and slide the mousse directly onto a plate of steamed rice. For a more formal meal, unwrap the packages in the kitchen and transfer the mousse to a large serving platter lined with the reserved banana leaf.

SOUTHERN-STYLE
SEAFOOD BARBECUE

Ahan Talay Dai

Serves 4

April, May, and June are Thailand's hottest months. Schoolchildren are on vacation, so many families make their holiday pilgrimage to one of dozens of beach resorts along our double-sided southern coastline.

On vacations, simple cooking is best. I love to throw a beach-house barbecue and serve skewers of grilled fresh seafood and shellfish, with tempting dipping sauces on the side. Later in the evening I pass around a platter of fresh tropical fruits—our Thai watermelon and mangoes are heavenly—or, if I'm a little more ambitious, I serve homemade Coconut Ice Cream (page 340) with chopped roasted peanuts.

You can serve *talay dai* as an appetizer or a main course. Sweet Gulf shrimp and tender squid are my favorites, but use whatever seafood you like best—as long as it's impeccably fresh and lightly grilled. The dipping sauces, one sweet and one tart, will complement any choice.

1 pound whole squid

½ pound medium shrimp

14 to 16 short (8-inch) bamboo skewers, soaked in a tray of cold water for at least ½ hour

Sweet-and-Spicy Dipping Sauce with Peanuts (page 54)

Fresh Lemon-Chili Sauce (page 60)

To clean the seafood: Rinse the squid under cold water. Pull the head from the body. Cut the tentacles off in one piece, just below the eyes, and discard the rest of the head. If the hard little beak is in the center of the set of tentacles, pull it out and discard. Reserve the body sac and tentacles.

Pull out the long, transparent quill from the body sac and discard. Press out the innards by running the body sac between your thumb and fingers, squeezing as you go from the closed to the cut end. Or lay the body sac on a flat work surface and run the dull side of a knife blade along its length, from the closed to the cut end. Rinse out the body sac so you're sure to remove any traces of the gelatinous inner matter. Peel off and discard the speckled outer skin. Score through one side of each squid body with a series of diagonal cuts. Combine the scored squid bodies with the tentacles and set aside.

Rinse and peel the shrimp, but leave the tails on. Set aside.

To grill the seafood: Thread a squid body onto a skewer. Keep it fully extended so it lies somewhat flat. Add one set of tentacles to the skewer. Proceed with the rest of the squid bodies and tentacles, using just one of each per skewer. Skewer the shrimp, using two or three per skewer. The skewer should pass through each shrimp twice: Pierce the shrimp through the tail, then bring the skewer out through the top of the curve.

Grill the squid and shrimp over a medium-hot fire on a charcoal barbecue or gas grill. Cook the squid, turning once, for about 5 minutes total. They should be opaque and firm, but still tender. Cook the shrimp, turning once, for about 3 minutes total, or just until pink.

Arrange the skewers of barbecued seafood on a large serving platter and serve with the sweet and tart dipping sauces.

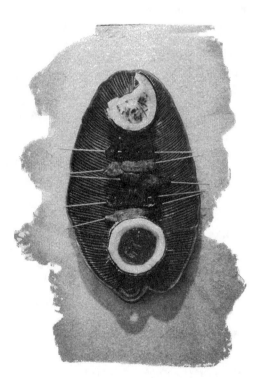

Fish
and
Seafood

GRILLED CATFISH WITH SWEET AND BITTER HERBS AND SAVORY TAMARIND SAUCE

Sadow Nam Pla Wan

Serves 4 to 6

T hai meals are often composed of a generous bowl of steamed rice with many side dishes surrounding it. But we also have main courses that coordinate two, three, or more components into a symphony of flavors and textures and can stand alone as a complete meal.

Sadow nam pla wan is a wonderful example. Savory tamarind sauce—with its bracing sweet-and-sour flavor and saucy texture, topped with crisp-fried garlic chips, shallot rings, and red chilies—is the meal's central theme.

The sauce unifies three other components: grilled catfish, steamed jasmine rice, blended with the heady flavors of the sauce and its crunchy toppings, and the contrasting flavors of fresh garden herbs—cilantro for sweetness and arugula for its pleasingly bitter tang. Serve each guest a portion of grilled fish, a handful of herbs, and some steamed jasmine rice, then set out individual bowls of sauce. They will spoon sauce over their fish and rice, then tear a few sprigs of herbs and dip them into the sauce.

2 whole catfish (about 1¾ pounds each), cleaned, heads removed, or 1½ pounds thickly cut catfish fillets

Vegetable oil (if using fillets)

7½ tablespoons coconut-palm sugar

9 tablespoons Tamarind Sauce (page 61) or liquid tamarind concentrate

6 tablespoons Thai fish sauce (*nam pla*)

4½ tablespoons water

1¾ cups vegetable or peanut oil for frying

10 small dried Japanese chilies

⅓ cup thinly sliced garlic (about 18 cloves)

⅔ cup thinly sliced shallots (5 or 6)

1 large bunch arugula

1 large bunch cilantro

To prepare the fish for grilling:

If using whole fish: Rinse the fish under cold water. Score both sides with diagonal cuts almost to the bone, about every inch or so. Set aside.

If using fillets: Brush the fillets lightly with vegetable oil on both sides and set aside.

To make the sauce: Put the sugar, tamarind sauce, fish sauce, and water in a saucepan and set over medium-high heat. Stir until the sugar is dissolved and blended and bring the mixture to a boil. Boil gently, stirring occasionally, until slightly thickened, about 3 to 4 minutes. Set the sauce aside while you fry the chilies, garlic, and shallots.

Pour the oil into a large wok or heavy saucepan, set over medium-high heat, and bring the oil to 360°F. (To test the oil temperature, dip a wooden spoon in the hot oil. The oil should bubble and sizzle gently around the bowl of the spoon.) Add the chilies and cook, stirring occasionally, just until they deepen in color, about 30 seconds. Remove with a wire skimmer or slotted spoon and drain on paper towels.

Return the oil temperature to 360°F. Add the garlic and cook until golden brown, stirring occasionally, about 1 minute. Remove with a wire skimmer or slotted spoon and drain on paper towels.

Return the oil temperature to 360°F and fry the shallots, stirring frequently, about 2 minutes. Remove with a wire skimmer or slotted spoon and drain on paper towels.

Transfer the sauce to a serving bowl. Top with the fried chilies, garlic, and shallots. Set the bowl of sauce in the center of a large serving platter and arrange the sprigs of arugula and cilantro on either side. Set aside while you grill the fish.

To grill the fish:

If using whole fish: Grill them over a medium-hot fire on a charcoal barbecue or gas grill. Cook, turning once, until the outside is lightly browned and the flesh turns opaque, about 15 to 18 minutes total.

If using fillets: Grill them over a medium-hot fire. Cook, turning once, until the fillets turn opaque and the grill marks them a light brown, about 8 to 10 minutes total.

Transfer the grilled fish to a large serving platter. Set the fish out along with the platter of fresh herbs and Savory Tamarind Sauce.

Serve with plenty of steamed jasmine rice.

THAI SERVING STYLE: If using whole fish, cut each fish down to the bone along the full length of the spine, from head to tail. Pushing away from the center cut with a serving spoon, nudge the fish meat slightly away from the spine on both sides. You will now have two portions. Cut into smaller serving pieces if desired, then slide a knife blade or spatula under each portion, lift off the bone, and serve. The backbone will be exposed and easy to remove. Grasp the tail end of the bone, lift it up, pull it away from the meat, and discard. Cut the remaining fillet into serving-size portions and serve.

DUNGENESS CRAB IN GREEN CURRY

Pu Yai Sod Sai Lad Na Kaeng Khiew Wan

Serves 4 to 6

Thai cooking appeals to all of the senses. In this dish, for example, the meat of a whole steamed crab is extracted and mixed with additional crabmeat, ground pork, and spices, then stuffed back into the upper and lower halves of the crab's shell. A few crabmeat dumplings made from the stuffing surround the stuffed whole crab. The result, presented in a pool of green curry sauce, is beautiful to look at, deeply fragrant, and full of flavor.

Sweet, meaty Dungeness crabs from the Pacific Coast remind me of the Siamese crabs we call *pu talay*, so I've specified them in this recipe. One good-sized Dungeness can make a meal for four people, so there's only one crab to be cleaned and picked.

It's best, whenever possible, to select a female crab: You can blend the flavorful roe into the stuffing.

1 live Dungeness crab (1 to 1½ pounds), preferably female

STUFFING

14 cloves garlic

1 cup loosely packed chopped cilantro, including the stems

1 teaspoon white pepper

2 teaspoons Thai fish sauce (*nam pla*)

3 teaspoons sugar

¼ pound ground pork

½ pound fresh crabmeat or frozen crabmeat, defrosted and drained

CURRY

1 can (19 ounces) unsweetened coconut milk

¾ cup Fresh Green Chili Curry Paste (page 28)

3 tablespoons Thai fish sauce (*nam pla*)

3 tablespoons golden brown sugar

1 cup loosely packed chopped Thai basil (*bai horapha*) or purple or Italian basil

To prepare the crab for stuffing: Fill the base pot of a tiered aluminum steamer about one-third full of water. Cover and bring the water to a boil over medium-high heat. Set a steamer rack over the boiling water and put the crab on the rack. Cover and steam until the shell turns red, about 4 minutes. Remove the crab and rinse under cold water.

Put the crab on its back. With the tip of a knife, pry up the apron, the triangular flap on the underside of the body. Pull off the apron and discard.

Turn the crab over. Starting at the rear, using a firm tug, pry off the top shell in one piece.

Spoon out the creamy yellow tomalley, or crab butter, from the bottom shell and reserve. Hold the crab body in one hand and, with a knife in the other, trim off and discard the spongy gills at each side. Scrape out and discard any greenish matter running through the center of the crab body. Using your finger, work out the roe, if any, from both the top and bottom shells and reserve. Scoop out any brown meat from the top shell and reserve. Pick out and reserve as much crabmeat as possible from the body without breaking the shell. Remove any bits of shell or cartilage. Leave the legs and claws intact on the shell.

Turn the top shell over so the cavity is exposed, and trim away some of the shell with kitchen shears to open out the cavity for stuffing. Set aside both the top and bottom shells.

Put the reserved tomalley, the roe, if any, and the steamed crabmeat in a bowl and set aside.

To make the stuffing and the crab-ball dumplings: Prepare an herbal mash from the garlic and cilantro:

Mortar-and-pestle method: Put the garlic and cilantro in the mortar and pound to a mash.

Alternate method: Crush the garlic with the side of a chef's knife. Mix the chopped cilantro with the crushed garlic and finely chop.

Put the herbal mash in a large mixing bowl. Add the remaining stuffing ingredients, the reserved crabmeat, the tomalley, and any roe.

Mix the ingredients together by hand until well blended. Take enough of the stuffing to form eight balls about 1½ inches in diameter. Set the crab balls aside.

To stuff and steam the crab: Mound the remaining stuffing mixture into the reserved crab shells.

Refill the base pot of the steamer about one-third full with fresh water. Cover and bring the water to a boil over medium-high heat. Put the stuffed shells, stuffing side up, on a steaming rack. When the water reaches a boil, set the rack over the pot, cover, and steam for 15 minutes.

Transfer the stuffed crab shells to a large serving platter. The bottom shell with legs attached should sit in the center of the platter with its stuffing exposed. Place the stuffed upper shell directly behind the bottom shell, stuffing side down, to expose the bright red shell. Set aside.

continued

To make the curry: Skim the thick cream from the top of the canned coconut milk into a medium saucepan, reserving the milk. Set the pan over medium-high heat. Stir in the curry paste until blended, and bring to a low boil. Cook, stirring constantly, for 2 minutes. Add the reserved coconut milk and cook for 45 seconds, stirring often. Add the fish sauce and sugar and stir until the sugar is dissolved and blended. Add the crab balls, raise the heat to high, and bring to a boil. Boil for 2 minutes, stirring occasionally. Spoon out the crab balls and arrange them around the platter of stuffed crab shells. Spoon some of the curry sauce over the mound of stuffing in the bottom shell, but leave the bright red top shell free of sauce for color and textural contrast. Ladle the rest of the curry sauce all around the platter. Shower the dish with the chopped basil and serve with plenty of steamed jasmine rice.

VARIATION: For a simpler version, you can make Crab Ball Curry. Omit the live crab. Add ¾ pound more crabmeat to the stuffing ingredients, for a total of 1¼ pounds of crabmeat. Form all of the stuffing mixture into little dumplings. Cook them in the curry sauce, as directed, and serve with steamed jasmine rice.

DEAR BLUE CRAB

Pu Jaa

Serves 6

In Thai cuisine, subtle variations on a theme can create distinctively different results. This recipe uses the same stuffing and the same steaming method used in the previous recipe, Dungeness Crab in Green Curry. But here three small blue crabs are stuffed and steamed, then fried until golden brown and caught in a lacy, edible net made from beaten egg. And, instead of a curry, *pu jaa* is accompanied by three contrasting dipping sauces—one hot, one sweet and spicy, and one sharp and herbal.

Dear blue crab is one of Thailand's most-loved dishes, whether served as a snack or as part of a complete meal.

3 live blue crabs (about 1¼ pounds total)

14 cloves garlic

1 cup loosely packed chopped cilantro, including the stems

1 teaspoon white pepper

2 teaspoons Thai fish sauce (*nam pla*)

3 teaspoons sugar

¼ pound ground pork

½ pound fresh crabmeat or frozen crabmeat, defrosted and drained

2 large eggs, lightly beaten

3 cups peanut or vegetable oil for frying

Sprigs of cilantro

Bottled Thai chili sauce (*sriracha*) or any good Mexican or Louisiana-style hot sauce

Sweet-and-Spicy Dipping Sauce (page 54)

Spicy Cucumber Relish (page 53)

To prepare the crabs for stuffing: Fill the base pot of a tiered aluminum steamer about one-third full of water. Cover and bring the water to a boil over medium-high heat. Set a steamer rack over the boiling water and put the crabs on the rack. Cover and steam until the shells turn red, about 4 minutes. Remove the crabs and rinse under cold water.

Put each crab on its back. With the tip of a knife, pry up the apron, the triangular flap on the underside of the body. Pull off the apron and discard.

Turn the crabs over. Starting at the rear, using a firm tug, pry off each top shell in one piece. Pour any crab juices collected in the top shells into a bowl and reserve.

Spoon out the creamy yellow tomalley, or crab butter, from the bottom shells and reserve. Hold each crab body in one hand and, with a knife in the other, trim off and discard the spongy gills at each side. Scrape out and discard any greenish matter running through the center of each crab body. Using your finger, work out the roe, if any, from both the top and bottom shells and reserve. Leave the legs and claws intact on the bottom shells.

Turn each top shell over so the cavity is exposed, and trim away some of the shell with kitchen shears to open out the cavity for stuffing. Set aside both the top and bottom shells.

Combine the reserved crab juices, tomalley, and roe, if any, and set aside.

To make the stuffing: Prepare an herbal mash from the garlic and cilantro:

Mortar-and-pestle method: Put the garlic and cilantro in the mortar and pound to a mash.

Alternate method: Crush the garlic with the side of a chef's knife. Mix the chopped cilantro with the crushed garlic and finely chop.

Put the herbal mash in a large mixing bowl. Add the reserved crab juice, the tomalley and any roe, the white pepper, fish sauce, sugar, ground pork, and crabmeat.

Mix the ingredients together by hand until well blended.

To stuff and steam the crabs: Mound the stuffing mixture into the reserved crab shells.

Refill the base pot of the tiered aluminum steamer about one-third full with fresh water. Cover and bring the water to a boil over medium-high heat. Put the stuffed shells, stuffing side up, on two steaming racks. When the water reaches a boil, set the racks over the pot, cover, and steam until the stuffing is cooked through, about 10 minutes.

To fry the stuffed crabs and egg net: Pour the lightly beaten eggs onto a plate. Dip each stuffed crab in the beaten egg to coat both sides. (Don't worry if it doesn't adhere perfectly to the hard top shells.) Reserve the leftover beaten egg to make the egg net.

Pour the oil into a large wok or deep, wide pot, set over medium-high heat, and bring the oil to 360°F. Carefully add enough crabs, stuffing side down, to fill the pan without crowding, about two to three per batch. (Moisture in the stuffing may cause the oil to pop. Take a step or two away from the pot as you lower the stuffed crabs into the hot oil.) Fry, turning once or twice, until golden brown, about 1½ to 2 minutes total. Adjust the heat if necessary to maintain a consistent frying temperature.

Lift out the crabs with a wire skimmer or slotted spoon and drain them, shell sides down, on paper towels. Return the oil to 360°F and fry the rest of the crabs as above.

Arrange the stuffed crabs on a large serving platter, shell sides down, with the stuffing exposed. Set aside.

Return the oil to 360°F and have the reserved beaten egg standing by. Dip your fingers and palm into the beaten egg and wave your hand back and forth about 12 inches above the surface of the hot oil with unhurried, even strokes. The beaten egg will trail off your fingers in fine, liquid threads. Dip your hand back into the eggs, this time trailing the egg at right angles to the first threads, making a crosshatch pattern. Repeat until you've used up all the beaten egg.

Cook until the egg net is light golden on the bottom and thoroughly set, about 30 seconds. Carefully turn it over with a wire skimmer and cook until the other side is also light golden, about 30 seconds. Lift the net from the oil and briefly drain on paper towels.

Drape the egg net over the platter of stuffed crabs. Tear sprigs of cilantro over the crabs caught in the net and serve with the three dipping sauces.

N O T E : These little crabs yield only a small amount of meat, so I simply clean them before adding the stuffing. Then, as my guests finish their meal, they can pick out the bits of crabmeat hiding in the shells, legs, and claws. You can save the hard top shells for reuse. Wash and dry them well before storing in Ziploc plastic bags or an airtight container.

THAI SALADS

Yam

A Thai salad is a quintessential Thai dish—full of variety and appetizing contrast, artfully composed, and made from the freshest ingredients. Thai people eat salads at almost every meal, right alongside the other dishes, never as a side dish or an afterthought, and their salads always feature a tantalizing variety of colors, textures, and tastes.

There's a big difference between the American and Thai concepts of "salad." But the dishes in this chapter are so healthy (there is no oil in the dressings), satisfying, and visually attractive—that I think you'll agree the time has come to introduce Americans to an expanded range of authentic Thai salads.

When we began planning this book, I sketched a list of all the Thai salads I wanted to include. It soon extended beyond sixty, so I had to make difficult choices.

The sixteen recipes in this chapter were selected because they're individually terrific and because they represent the whole spectrum of Thai salad types: spicy salads, salads with noodles, salads that fold into lettuce leaves, to be eaten out of hand, salads combining meat and seafood.

If you were to peek into the back room of a typical Thai restaurant at break time, you'd see the kitchen workers relaxing over Coconut, Lemon, and Ginger Salad with Sweet Shrimp Sauce—or, as they would call it, *miang kam*. This is one of the great homeland favorites, a "roll-your-own" salad that allows each person to compose the flavor balance he likes best. It's one of many Thai salads using lettuce leaves as cups. Another is Issan-Style Chopped Meat Salad with Toasted Rice Powder, known in Thailand as *laab*. Yet another leaf-wrapped favorite is Chiang Mai Grilled Fish Salad.

Those who like the exciting, pleasant fire of fresh chilies on the tongue will want to try Fiery Grilled Beef Salad.

Other salads highlight familiar ingredients in unusual settings, such as Fresh Oyster Salad on the Half Shell, and Grilled Steak and Crunchy Vegetables with Chili Dipping Sauce.

By the way, even more Thai salad recipes (including the very popular regional favorite, Green Papaya Salad with Thai Chili and Lime) can be found within the "Bangkok Street Cooking," "Thai Vegetarian Cuisine," and "Royal Thai Cuisine" chapters.

Crispy Shallots
(page 67)

Shower crispy shallots and torn Thai basil leaves over a bowl of tomato soup. Or combine them with Fried Garlic Chips (page 66) over a bowl of steamed jasmine rice for a healthy, low-calorie side dish.

WINGED BEAN SALAD WITH TOASTED COCONUT AND CRISPY SHALLOTS

Yam Tua Poo

Serves 4

The squarish, frilly-edged winged bean was brought to Thailand from Europe many years ago, and it thrived in our climate. The pale green beans have a delicate, asparagus-like flavor. Although string beans are not as eye-catching, they make an excellent substitute.

An important aspect of Thai religious life is known as *tum boon*, which means "merit making." One way of making merit is to offer food to monks. During July, August, and September, the time of Buddhist Lent, monks devote themselves to study and teaching. Since this is when winged beans are at their peak, this refreshing summer salad is a favorite *tum boon* offering.

To make *yam tua poo* a main course or a light lunch, just cook half a dozen large shrimp and add them to the salad.

I pound winged beans (*tua poo*), thinly sliced, or green beans, trimmed and stringed, left whole or cut into long diagonal slices

I tablespoon Chili-Tamarind Paste (page 46) or commercially made chili-tamarind paste (*nam phrik pao*)

½ cup fresh lemon juice

1½ tablespoons coconut-palm sugar or golden brown sugar

1½ tablespoons Thai fish sauce (*nam pla*)

I stalk lemon grass, tough outer leaves discarded, lower stalk trimmed to 4 inches and finely sliced

I to 3 small Thai chilies (*phrik khee nu*) or serrano chilies, minced

Toasted Coconut (page 62)

Crispy Shallots (page 67)

Sprigs of cilantro

Bring a large pot of water to a boil. Blanch the beans until tender, about 30 to 45 seconds. (Green beans may take a little longer.) Drain in a colander and refresh under cold running water. Set aside.

To make the dressing, combine the chili-tamarind paste, lemon juice, sugar, and fish sauce in a blender or mixing bowl. Blend well to dissolve the paste and sugar.

Put the winged beans, lemon grass, and chilies in a large mixing bowl. Add the dressing and toss gently to mix.

Transfer the salad to a large serving platter and shower it with Toasted Coconut and Crsipy Shallots. Tear sprigs of cilantro over the salad and serve.

ISSAN-STYLE CHOPPED MEAT SALAD WITH TOASTED RICE POWDER

Laab

Serves 6

This salad originated in northeastern Thailand but has become popular throughout the country, particularly at parties and celebrations. It has many variants, and all of them are delicious. *Laab neua,* made with beef, is best when the meat is cooked medium-rare. If you substitute pork in the recipe, you will make *laab mu.* I've also made this dish with ground turkey, with excellent results.

Thai people like to accompany their *laab* with sips of beer or whiskey.

1 pound boneless, skinless chicken breast, cut into 1-inch cubes (see Note)

1½ cups water

½ cup fresh lemon juice

1 cup loosely packed fresh mint

1 cup loosely packed cilantro

2 stalks lemon grass, tough outer leaves discarded, lower stalks trimmed to 3 inches and finely sliced

1 tablespoon golden brown sugar

2 tablespoons Thai fish sauce (*nam pla*)

3 scallions, including the green tops, finely sliced

½ tablespoon Thai chili powder (*phrik pon*) or other ground red chili to taste, such as New Mexico chili powder or cayenne

Toasted Rice Powder (page 63)

A few small heads of salad greens (Boston lettuce, romaine, cabbage, and radicchio are all good choices)

Put the cubed chicken in the bowl of a food processor fitted with a metal blade. Process, using the pulse setting, until the chicken reaches the consistency of hamburger.

In a medium saucepan set over high heat, bring the water to a boil. Add the ground chicken, stirring often to break up the meat, and cook it through, about 1 minute. Remove the pan from the heat. Use a slotted spoon to transfer the meat to a large bowl, leaving any excess liquid behind. Stir in the remaining ingredients except the salad greens. Mix gently.

Select small, cup-shaped leaves from your choice of salad greens and arrange them on a serving tray. Spoon some salad into each lettuce leaf until you've portioned out all the salad. Serve at once.

Fold up and eat out of hand with a cold Thai beer, if desired.

N O T E : If you wish to substitute pork in this recipe, use 1 pound boneless pork loin. If you want to use beef, you can use ground beef from the market, but I recommend buying 1 pound of boneless sirloin and grinding it yourself.

GRILLED STEAK AND CRUNCHY VEGETABLES WITH CHILI DIPPING SAUCE

Seua Rong Hai

Serves 6

B ecause it is a rural, mountainous, somewhat isolated region, northeastern Thailand—Issan—has kept its distinctive local cooking traditions alive.

The people there like to say of their spicy invigorating food, *"Seua rong hai,"* which translates as "It makes a tiger cry." That's the name given this dish, which is characteristically Issan—robust and uncomplicated.

This dish is popular as an appetizer, accompanied by beer or other drinks. With everyone busily adding meat and crunchy raw vegetables to his plate, dipping them in the fiery sauce, and taking sips in between, this is a wonderful dish for making conversation come alive at the table.

1½ pounds beef steak (round eye, top sirloin, or flank steak)

Sprigs of cilantro

Assorted fresh vegetables, such as I small cucumber, sliced into rounds, a wedge or two of green cabbage, and a few handfuls of carrot sticks, broccoli or cauliflower florets, green beans, or baby corn

Classic Chili Dipping Sauce (page 49)

Build a hot charcoal fire or preheat a gas grill or broiler. Grill or broil the meat slowly, several inches from the fire, to keep it juicy. Cook until medium-rare, turning occasionally, about 5 to 8 minutes total. Transfer to a cutting board. Holding your knife at a 45-degree angle, cut the steak crosswise into very thin slices.

Transfer the meat, with its juices, to a large serving platter. Fan the slices attractively on the platter and tear sprigs of cilantro over them. Surround the grilled steak with your choice of fresh vegetables, and serve hot or warm with the dipping sauce.

FIERY GRILLED BEEF SALAD

Yam Neua

Serves 4 to 6

Yam neua is a Bangkok classic, served in homes as well as in cafés and restaurants all over the city. Sliced charcoal-grilled strips of beef are tossed with fresh vegetables, lemon grass, and mint. The fire is in the dressing, made with fresh serrano chilies, balanced with lemon and cilantro.

DRESSING

¼ cup loosely packed chopped cilantro stems

2 tablespoons chopped serrano chilies (about 4)

3 cloves garlic, roughly chopped

2 tablespoons coconut-palm sugar or golden brown sugar

1½ tablespoons Thai fish sauce (*nam pla*)

¼ teaspoon white pepper

½ cup fresh lemon juice

SALAD

1 pound beef steak (round eye, top sirloin, or flank steak)

1 large stalk lemon grass, tough outer leaves discarded, lower stalk trimmed to 4 inches and finely sliced

1 small red onion, cut in half and finely sliced

½ pound small pickling cucumbers, peeled and finely sliced

1 tomato, cut in half and sliced into thin wedges

½ cup loosely packed fresh mint

A few leaves of romaine or other leaf lettuce to line the platter (optional)

Combine all of the dressing ingredients in a blender or mixing bowl. Blend well to dissolve the sugar. Set aside.

Build a hot charcoal fire or preheat a gas grill or broiler. Grill or broil the meat slowly, several inches from the fire, to keep it juicy. Cook until medium-rare, turning occasionally, about 5 to 8 minutes total. Transfer to a cutting board. Holding your knife at a 45-degree angle, cut the steak crosswise into very thin slices.

Transfer the meat, with its juices, to a mixing bowl and toss with the remaining salad ingredients. Add the dressing and toss to mix well.

Arrange the lettuce leaves on a serving platter, if desired, and transfer the salad to the platter. Serve warm, for best flavor, or at room temperature.

FRESH OYSTER SALAD ON THE HALF SHELL

Yam Hoy Sod

Serves 4

Near the southern tip of Thailand, on the side of the Andaman Sea, exist tribes of people whom we call *chao lay*. Westerners call them "sea gypsies." Though they've lived among us for generations, they're not really Thai. The sea gypsies probably migrated to our mainland from the Andaman Islands, nearly four hundred miles offshore in the direction of India.

By the age of three, a sea gypsy boy is trained to stay underwater as long as human lungs will permit, searching out lobsters and oyster beds. When this salad is served in Thailand, there's a good chance that a sea gypsy brought the oysters to land.

One of the tastiest ways to enjoy fresh oysters is on the half shell. In this salad, which can be served as either an appetizer or a first course, fresh-shucked oysters are returned to their half shells, dressed in aromatic herbs and a tangy, moderately spicy Thai dressing. They should be eaten within minutes of opening, so keep them chilled in their shells until the dressing is ready, and make a bed of crushed ice for the serving platter.

DRESSING

3 tablespoons fresh lemon juice

1 tablespoon Thai fish sauce (*nam pla*)

1 tablespoon coconut-palm sugar or golden brown sugar

1 tablespoon Chili-Tamarind Paste (page 46) or commercially made chili-tamarind paste (*nam phrik pao*)

1 large stalk lemon grass, tough outer leaves discarded, lower stalk trimmed to 2½ inches and finely sliced

4 cloves garlic, pounded to a mash or crushed and finely chopped

4 scallions, including the green tops, finely sliced

3 small Thai chilies (*phrik khee nu*), minced

SALAD

2¾ pounds large Louisiana oysters in the shell (8 large, about 5 to 6 inches long; see Note)

1 cup loosely packed fresh mint leaves, plus a few whole sprigs

Crushed ice

To make the dressing: Combine the lemon juice, fish sauce, sugar, and chili-tamarind paste in a large mixing bowl. Stir well to dissolve the sugar and chili paste. Add the lemon grass, garlic, scallions, and chilies. Mix well and set aside.

To make the salad: Wash the oysters well, scrubbing them with a stiff brush if necessary. To shuck: Hold an oyster with the rounder, more cup-shaped, shell down and insert the pointed end of a beer-can opener between the shells at the hinge end. Pry up with the opener—the shells should snap open. Slide a knife blade against the flat upper shell to sever the muscle. Break off and discard the upper shell and slide the knife under the oyster to release it from the bottom shell. Keep the freed oyster on the half shell until you've shucked all the oysters. Clean them of any bits or fragments of shell and transfer them to the mixing bowl with the dressing. Add the mint leaves and mix gently.

Rinse off the half shells. Line a large serving platter with a bed of crushed ice. Return the oysters, with some of the dressing, to their half shells.

Arrange the dressed oysters on the platter of crushed ice and garnish with a few whole sprigs of mint. Serve at once.

N O T E : Buy a few extra oysters, in case one or two have to be discarded.

GREEN MANGO SALAD WITH STEAMED PORK MEATLOAF

Yam Mamuang Kap Mu Yoa

Serves 6 to 8

The delicate taste and texture of steamed pork meatloaf are quite different from those of the hearty ground-beef meatloaf typical of home-style American cuisine. The light, sweet pork plays well against the tart green mango. Both are julienned and tossed in a tangy-sweet citrus dressing with slivered lemon grass, crushed peanuts, and coconut-palm sugar.

1 Steamed Pork Meatloaf (page 138)

2 large green mangoes (about ½ pound each)

3 to 5 small Thai chilies (*phrik khee nu*), finely sliced

3 scallions, including the green tops, finely sliced

6 tablespoons thinly sliced shallots

1 stalk lemon grass, tough outer leaves discarded, lower stalk trimmed to 6 inches and finely sliced

½ cup fresh lime juice

3 tablespoons Thai fish sauce (*nam pla*)

2 tablespoons coconut-palm sugar or golden brown sugar

3 tablespoons roasted unsalted peanuts, crushed in a mortar or finely chopped

Slice the meatloaf in half lengthwise, then cut each half crosswise into ¼-inch slices. Stack and cut the slices to make julienned strips about 3 inches long. Put the pork in a large mixing bowl and set aside.

Meanwhile, julienne the mangoes: Slice the stem end off a mango. With a sharp knife, score the skin lengthwise in quarters first on one side then the other. Pull off the skin, using the scored sections as a guide. Hold the peeled mango in the palm of one hand, exposing half the fruit, and make a series of quick parallel cuts, slicing almost to the seed. When the surface is fully scored, slice crosswise to release the fruit, creating julienne strips. Repeat, scoring the mango down to the seed and slicing off the remaining fruit. Turn the mango over and repeat the tap-cut technique to julienne the rest of the fruit. Then julienne the other mango.

Add the mango to the mixing bowl with the pork. Add the chilies, scallions, shallots, and lemon grass and mix gently.

To make the dressing, combine the lime juice, fish sauce, and sugar in a blender or small mixing bowl. Blend well to dissolve the sugar. Pour the dressing into the bowl of salad ingredients and mix gently.

Transfer the salad to a large serving platter. Sprinkle with crushed peanuts and serve.

SPICY SHRIMP SALAD WITH CUCUMBER, HOT CHILI, AND MINT

Yam Kung

Serves 4 to 6

Yam kung is another simple way to give a lively accent to the sweet, smoky flavors of grilled shrimp. Flecks of minced chilies provide heat, which is relieved by fresh mint and cool, crisp cucumber slices.

1¼ pounds medium shrimp

6 to 8 short (8-inch) bamboo skewers, soaked in a tray of cold water for at least ½ hour

Leaves from 1 small head leaf lettuce, and assorted salad greens (romaine, green-leaf lettuce, and butter lettuce are good choices)

1 medium cucumber (about ½ pound), peeled, cut in half lengthwise, seeded, and finely sliced

½ small red onion, finely sliced

½ cup fresh lemon juice

3 tablespoons finely sliced shallots

2 tablespoons Thai fish sauce (*nam pla*)

2 tablespoons golden brown sugar

2 tablespoons minced garlic

1 stalk lemon grass, tough outer leaves discarded, lower stalk trimmed to 4 inches and finely sliced

½ to 1 tablespoon minced serrano chilies or small Thai chilies (*phrik khee nu*)

½ cup loosely packed fresh mint

Skewer the shrimp in their shells, using two or three per skewer. The skewer should pass through each shrimp twice: Pierce the shrimp through the tail, then bring the skewer out through the top of the curve.

Build a medium-hot charcoal fire or preheat a gas grill or stovetop grill accessory. Grill the shrimp, turning once, just until pink, about 3 minutes total. Set aside to cool slightly.

Make a bed of salad greens on a serving platter. Arrange the cucumber slices and red onion on top. Peel the shrimp and arrange them on top of the salad ingredients.

To make the dressing, combine the lemon juice, shallots, fish sauce, sugar, and garlic in a blender. Process until the sugar is dissolved and blended. Pour the mixture into a bowl and stir in the lemon grass and chilies. Mix well.

Pour the dressing over the platter of shrimp salad, top with the fresh mint leaves, and serve.

CELLOPHANE-NOODLE SALAD WITH SHRIMP, CHICKEN, AND PORK

Yam Woon Sen

Serves 4

Thai chefs love to combine meat and seafood in a single dish. In this recipe, a favorite at Bangkok dinner parties, shrimp, chicken, and pork are caught in a thread-like tangle of bean thread, or "cellophane," noodles, which readily soak up the sweet-and-spicy lemon dressing.

1 package (1.8 ounces) dried bean-thread vermicelli (*woon sen*)

8 medium shrimp, peeled and cleaned

¼ pound boneless, skinless chicken breast, cut into bite-size pieces

¼ pound pork tenderloin, cut into bite-size pieces

2 stalks lemon grass, tough outer leaves discarded, lower stalks trimmed to 4 inches and finely sliced

3 scallions, including the green tops, finely chopped

½ tablespoon minced small Thai chilies (*phrik khee nu*) or serrano chilies

1 cup loosely packed fresh mint, chopped

5 tablespoons fresh lemon juice

1 tablespoon Thai fish sauce (*nam pla*)

1 tablespoon Chili-Tamarind Paste (page 46) or commercially made chili-tamarind paste (*nam phrik pao*)

1 tablespoon coconut-palm sugar or golden brown sugar

6 large leaves romaine

1 tablespoon roasted unsalted peanuts, crushed in a mortar or finely chopped

Sprigs of cilantro

Put the noodles in a large bowl of warm water and soak them until they begin to soften, about 10 minutes. As the noodles become pliable, spread them out with your fingers. Put the softened noodles in a colander, drain well, and turn out onto a cutting board. Using a knife or kitchen shears, cut the mound of noodles into thirds.

Cook the noodles in a pot of boiling water until tender, about 30 seconds. Lift out the cooked noodles with a wire skimmer or slotted spoon and set aside in a colander to drain.

Plunge the shrimp into the pot of boiling water and cook just until they turn pink, about 45 to 60 seconds. Remove with a wire skimmer or slotted spoon.

Cook the chicken and pork in the boiling water just until cooked through, about 1 minute, and drain.

Combine the noodles, shrimp, chicken, and pork in a large mixing bowl. Add the lemon grass, scallions, chilies, and mint and toss until well mixed.

To make the dressing, combine the lemon juice, fish sauce, chili-tamarind paste, and sugar in a blender or small mixing bowl. Blend well to dissolve the chili paste and sugar. Pour the dressing over the salad and toss until well blended.

Line a serving platter with the lettuce leaves and mound the salad on top. Sprinkle on the crushed peanuts, tear a few sprigs of cilantro over the salad, and serve.

GRILLED LOBSTER SALAD WITH GREEN MANGO

Yam Kung Mongkong Kap Mamuang

Serves 6 to 8

Sweet, delicate medallions of grilled lobster meat are tossed with tart shreds of green mango, bits of hot chili, crushed peanuts, and fresh mint. Like changing, multicolored images inside a kaleidoscope, the various flavors shift and rebalance beautifully with each bite.

The use of lobster makes this a special-occasion dish, one I'd recommend for a grand summer celebration.

You can save time by purchasing a precooked lobster tail, but grilling the lobster in its shell will infuse the meat with a subtle, smoky flavor.

3 pounds green mangoes

6 tablespoons thinly sliced shallots

1 to 1½ tablespoons minced small Thai chilies (*phrik khee nu*) or serrano chilies

½ cup roasted unsalted peanuts, crushed in a mortar or finely chopped

1 cup loosely packed fresh mint

1 scant cup fresh lemon juice

3 tablespoons coconut-palm sugar or golden brown sugar

6 tablespoons Thai fish sauce (*nam pla*)

2½ pounds lobster tails, thawed if frozen

Slice the stem end off a mango. With a sharp knife, score the skin lengthwise into quarters first on one side then the other. Pull the skin off, using the scored sections

continued

as a guide. Hold the peeled mango in the palm of one hand, exposing half the fruit, and make a series of quick parallel cuts, slicing almost to the seed. When the surface is fully scored, slice crosswise to release the fruit, creating julienne strips. Repeat, scoring the mango down to the seed and slicing off the remaining fruit. Turn the mango over and repeat the tap-cut technique to julienne the rest of the fruit. Julienne the remaining mango in the same manner.

Put the mango in a large mixing bowl and add the shallots, chilies, peanuts, and mint. Stir gently to mix and set aside.

To make the dressing, combine the lemon juice, sugar, and fish sauce in a blender or small mixing bowl. Blend well to dissolve the sugar.

Pour the dressing over the mango mixture and stir gently until the shredded mango is coated with dressing. Set aside while you grill the lobster.

Build a medium-hot charcoal fire or preheat a gas grill.

Holding each lobster tail with its shell side down, cut off and discard the ribbed membrane with kitchen shears, trimming as close to the shell as possible. Grill the lobster tails, shell sides down, over glowing coals, for 10 minutes, turning them occasionally from side to side. Cover the grill and cook just until they're cooked through, about 5 to 10 minutes.

Remove the lobster meat in one piece from each shell. Slice the meat in half lengthwise, then cut crosswise into ultra-thin medallions. (Don't worry if some of the slices crumble.) Reserve a few choice medallions for garnishing the platter, and gently mix the rest in with the mango salad.

Transfer to a serving platter. Arrange the reserved lobster medallions on top of the salad and serve at once.

Salads

Try a favorite Thai salad dressing such as Thai Emeralds Dressing (page 221), over a platter of sliced tomatoes or grilled vegetables. Or use it in a Thai-style coleslaw, topped with crushed peanuts.

GRILLED SHRIMP SALAD WITH GREEN MANGO AND THAI EMERALDS DRESSING

Yam Kung Pao Kap Mamuang

Serves 4 to 6

For a quicker, less costly version of the previous lobster-salad recipe, you can combine shredded green mango with grilled shrimp. For this combination I make Thai Emeralds Dressing, which gets its color from lime juice and cilantro stems whirled in a blender with other Thai seasonings.

SALAD

1 large green mango (about ½ pound)

½ pound large shrimp

3 to 4 short (8-inch) bamboo skewers, soaked in a tray of cold water for at least ½ hour

Leaves from 1 small head leaf lettuce, or assorted salad greens (romaine, green-leaf, and butter lettuce are good choices)

5 tablespoons finely sliced shallots

1 cup loosely packed fresh mint

THAI EMERALDS DRESSING

¼ cup plus 1 tablespoon fresh lime juice

2½ tablespoons loosely packed chopped cilantro stems

1 tablespoon Thai fish sauce (*nam pla*)

6 cloves garlic, roughly chopped

2 to 3 small Thai chilies (*phrik khee nu*), finely sliced

1 tablespoon coconut-palm sugar or golden brown sugar

Sprigs of cilantro

To make the salad: Slice the stem end off the mango. With a sharp knife, score the skin lengthwise into quarters first on one side then the other. Pull the skin off, using the scored sections as a guide. Hold the peeled mango in the palm of one hand, exposing half the fruit, and make a series of quick parallel cuts, slicing almost to the seed. When the surface is fully scored, slice crosswise to release the fruit, creating julienne strips. Repeat, scoring the mango down to the seed and slicing off the remaining fruit. Turn the mango over and repeat the tap-cut technique to julienne the rest of the fruit. Put the mango in a large mixing bowl and set aside.

Skewer the shrimp, using two or three per skewer. The skewer should pass through each shrimp twice: Pierce the shrimp through the tail, then bring the skewer out through the top of the curve.

Build a medium-hot charcoal fire or preheat a gas grill or stovetop grill accessory. Grill the shrimp, turning once, just until pink, about 3 minutes total. Set aside to cool slightly.

continued

Make a bed of salad greens on a serving platter. Set aside.

Peel the shrimp and put them in the bowl with the mango. Mix in the shallots and mint.

To make the dressing: Combine the lime juice, cilantro stems, fish sauce, garlic, chilies, and sugar in a blender. Process until the sugar is dissolved and blended. Pour the dressing into the bowl of shrimp salad and stir well to mix.

Transfer the salad to the prepared platter. Tear sprigs of cilantro over the top and serve at once.

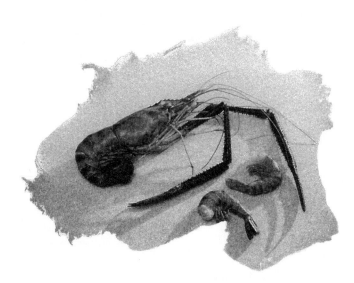

THAI-STYLE DUCK EGG SALAD WITH BABY GINGER

Yam Khai Yeow Ma Kap Khing On

Serves 6 to 8

Yam khai yeow ma is served in restaurants throughout Thailand. The "thousand-year-old" duck eggs used in the recipe are a Chinese tradition, but the sharp, salty mix of flavors is decidedly Thai.

Because the baby ginger is pleasantly spicy and the eggs creamy, this salad is rich-tasting yet light and piquant.

4 Chinese preserved duck eggs

I medium head romaine

¼ pound baby ginger or mature ginger, peeled and julienned (about I cup)

3 small Thai chilies (*phrik khee nu*), or I serrano chili, finely sliced (optional)

I cup chopped scallions, including the green tops

½ small onion, finely sliced

1⅓ cups fresh lemon juice

⅓ cup coconut-palm sugar or golden brown sugar

1½ tablespoons Thai fish sauce (*nam pla*)

Sprigs of cilantro

Clean the eggs under cold running water. Scrape off the thick coating and rinse thoroughly. Put the eggs in a saucepan of cold water and slowly bring to a boil. Reduce the heat and simmer the eggs for 10 minutes. Transfer with a wire skimmer or slotted spoon to a small bowl of cold water and set aside.

Stem and core the romaine. Set aside the large outer leaves and chop the heart. Place the chopped leaves in the bottom of a wide, somewhat shallow, serving bowl. Arrange the larger leaves, stem ends down, in a fan shape going halfway around the bowl. Set aside.

Peel the hard-boiled eggs and cut each in half lengthwise. Cut each half crosswise into five or six pieces. Place the sliced eggs in a mixing bowl. Add the ginger, chilies, scallions, and onion.

To make the dressing, combine the lemon juice, sugar, and fish sauce in a blender or small mixing bowl. Blend well to dissolve the sugar. Pour the dressing over the egg salad and mix gently until well blended.

Transfer the salad to the bowl of romaine. Tear sprigs of cilantro over the salad and serve.

MUSSEL, SHRIMP, AND LEMON GRASS SALAD WITH THAI BASIL

Pla Hoy Meng Phu Pla Kung

Serves 4 to 6

I like to serve this salad on a bed of mixed baby salad greens. Here in California we can buy all kinds of fancy field greens and baby lettuces direct from the growers at local farmers' markets. And many upscale supermarkets now carry a prepackaged fancy greens mix that's cleaned and ready to use. Any favorite lettuce in season from your own market or garden will be fine.

½ pound medium shrimp

1 pound New Zealand mussels, placed in a bowl or sink full of cold water

2 cups water

1 cup fresh lemon juice

1½ tablespoons coconut-palm sugar or golden brown sugar

3 tablespoons Thai fish sauce (*nam pla*)

1¾ tablespoons Chili-Tamarind Paste (page 46), or 1 tablespoon plus 1 teaspoon commercially made chili-tamarind paste (*nam phrik pao*)

½ cup loosely packed chopped cilantro stems

8 cloves garlic, roughly chopped

1 large stalk lemon grass, tough outer leaves discarded, lower stalk trimmed to 6 inches and finely sliced

¾ cup loosely packed Thai basil (*bai horapha*) or purple or Italian basil

3 small Thai chilies (*phrik khee nu*), finely sliced

2 to 4 ounces mixed baby lettuce leaves or any favorite salad greens

1 large tomato, cut in half and sliced into thin wedges

½ small red onion, finely sliced

½ medium cucumber, finely sliced

Sprigs of cilantro

Rinse and peel the shrimp, but leave the tails on. Slice them partway through along the back to butterfly and devein.

Agitate the water in which the mussels are soaking. Live mussels open and close to breathe. Any mussels that don't eventually close should be discarded. Scrub and debeard the mussels. Drain and set aside.

Bring the water to a boil in a medium saucepan. Add the mussels. Cover and steam until the mussels open, about 2 minutes. (Discard any mussels that fail to open.) Remove with a wire skimmer or slotted spoon and set aside. Return the water to a boil and add the shrimp. Cook just until they turn pink, about 45 to 60 seconds. Drain immediately.

Peel the shrimp and put them in a large mixing bowl. Remove the mussels from their shells and add them to the bowl.

To make the dressing, combine the lemon juice, sugar, fish sauce, chili-tamarind paste, cilantro stems, and garlic in a blender. Blend well to dissolve the sugar and chili paste. Pour the mixture into a bowl and stir in the lemon grass, basil, and chilies. Mix well.

Add the lettuce, tomato, onion, and cucumber to the bowl of seafood. Pour the dressing over the salad and toss gently until well mixed.

Transfer the salad to a serving platter. Tear sprigs of cilantro over the dish and serve.

CHIANG MAI GRILLED FISH SALAD

Miang Pla Tu

Serves 6 to 8

In Thailand we make this salad with a small native mackerel called *pla tu.* Flounder, Chilean sea bass, and red snapper make excellent stand-ins. The important thing is to have tasty, moist flakes of charcoal-grilled fish to toss with the lime-chili-tamarind dressing.

A scattering of crunchy peanuts and licorice-scented Thai basil completes this elegant salad, which is served in crisp lettuce cups and goes great with a cold beer on a hot summer day.

3 pounds fillet of flounder, Chilean sea bass, red snapper, or halibut, preferably with skin intact (see Note)

Vegetable oil for brushing the fish

1 cup fresh lime juice

2 tablespoons coconut-palm sugar or golden brown sugar

4 tablespoons Thai fish sauce (*nam pla*)

4 tablespoons Chili-Tamarind Paste (page 46), or 3 tablespoons commercially made chili-tamarind paste (*nam phrik pao*)

1½ teaspoons minced small Thai chilies (*phrik khee nu*) or serrano chilies

2½ tablespoons matchstick slices of peeled fresh ginger

5 tablespoons roasted unsalted peanuts, crushed in a mortar or finely chopped

1 cup loosely packed cilantro leaves

1 cup loosely packed Thai basil (*bai horapha*) or purple or Italian basil

A few small heads of salad greens (Boston lettuce, romaine, cabbage, and radicchio are all good choices)

Build a moderately low charcoal fire or preheat a gas grill. Let the coals burn down to a light coating of gray ash over red-hot coals. Position the grill rack several inches above the fire. Brush the fish with a little oil and place it on the grill, skin side down. The fish will cook quickly, so don't leave it untended. Grill just until cooked through but still tender and succulent, no more than 10 minutes per inch of thickness.

When the fish is cooked, remove the skin and put the meat in a mixing bowl. Flake the meat into small chunks with a fork.

To make the dressing, combine the lime juice, sugar, fish sauce, and chili-tamarind paste in a blender or small mixing bowl. Blend well to dissolve the sugar and chili paste. Stir in the chilies and ginger. Pour the dressing into the bowl of grilled fish chunks. Add the peanuts, cilantro, and basil and mix gently but thoroughly.

Select small, cup-shaped leaves from your choice of salad greens and arrange them on a serving tray. Spoon some salad into each lettuce leaf until you've portioned out all the salad. Serve at once.

Fold up and eat out of hand.

N O T E : If you can, buy a large whole fish (about 4½ pounds) and have it filleted, keeping the fish in one piece and leaving the skin intact. It can then be grilled skin side down, without turning. Otherwise, grill the fish on an oiled, perforated sheet of aluminum foil. Make plenty of holes in the foil so the smoke can penetrate and flavor the fish.

ROASTED RED AND YELLOW PEPPER SALAD WITH CHICKEN, PORK, AND SHRIMP

Yam Phrik Yang Kap Kai, Mu Leh Kung

Serves 4 to 6

B right flavors, rich colors, and a crunchy texture are all at play in this sumptuous roasted-pepper salad. Balance—the highest ideal of Thai cooking—is exemplified by the contrast of the red and yellow smoky-flavored peppers with the peanuts, the shrimp, and two different meats, the whole dressed in a rich lemon-coconut reduction and showered with crushed peanuts, chilies, and cilantro.

2 red bell peppers

2 yellow bell peppers

½ pound medium shrimp, peeled and cleaned

½ pound boneless, skinless chicken breast, cut into bite-size pieces

½ pound pork tenderloin, cut into bite-size pieces

½ cup unsweetened coconut milk

2 tablespoons Thai fish sauce (*nam pla*)

2 tablespoons coconut-palm sugar or golden brown sugar

4 tablespoons fresh lemon juice

2 tablespoons finely sliced shallots

½ to I tablespoon minced serrano chilies

2 tablespoons roasted unsalted peanuts, crushed in a mortar or finely chopped

½ cup loosely packed chopped cilantro, including the stems

Prick the peppers a few times with a fork. Roast them under a preheated broiler about 2 inches from the heat, turning them every few minutes, until the skins are blistered and charred, about 15 to 25 minutes total. Transfer them to a brown paper bag and roll the top down to let the peppers steam. When the peppers are cool enough to handle, the charred skins will be easy to peel. Remove the skins, starting at the blossom end, then cut off the tops and discard the seeds and ribs. Slice the peppers into strips about ½ inch wide. Put them in a bowl and set aside.

Plunge the shrimp into a saucepan of boiling water and cook just until they turn pink, about 45 to 60 seconds. Remove them with a wire skimmer or slotted spoon. Cook the chicken and pork in the boiling water just until cooked through, about 1 minute, and drain. Put the shrimp, chicken, and pork in the bowl with the peppers.

To make the dressing, pour the coconut milk into a medium saucepan set over high heat. Cook for 2 minutes, stirring occasionally as it boils. Stir in the fish sauce, sugar, and lemon juice. Lower the heat to medium and cook for 2 minutes, stirring well to dissolve the sugar.

Remove the pan from the heat. Add the peppers, shrimp, chicken, and pork and mix gently but thoroughly.

Transfer the salad with all the dressing to a serving platter. Sprinkle on the shallots, chilies, peanuts, and cilantro and serve.

COCONUT, LEMON, AND GINGER SALAD WITH SWEET SHRIMP SAUCE

Miang Kam

Serves 4 to 6

A great introduction to the uninhibited country flavors of northern Thailand, *miang kam* is frequently found in Thai restaurants—but never on the menu, only in the back room!

This salad is a favorite of our kitchen staff at the Siamese Princess. It's a poignant reminder of life back in Thailand—very home-style, eaten in a highly sociable environment. Diced lemon and ginger, toasted coconut, peanuts, chilies, and other condiments are set out on a platter. Fresh leafy greens make bite-size wrappers, and a sweet, rich sauce is set alongside. In Thailand, the greens would likely be from the Thai leaf lily, or *bai cha plu*, a relative of the betel nut. Its dark green and glossy, somewhat heart-shaped leaves are perfect for wrapping into a delicate mouthful. Here in America I often use Chinese broccoli, spinach, or butter-lettuce leaves, cutting them to a similar size.

Although it's traditionally served as a late-afternoon or evening snack, *miang kam* would also be a great dish to take to a party.

SWEET SHRIMP SAUCE

2½ tablespoons shrimp paste (*kapi*), wrapped neatly in a double layer of aluminum foil

I cup dried shrimp (*kung haeng*)

1½ cups water

I cup coconut-palm sugar or golden brown sugar

CONDIMENTS

Toasted Coconut (page 62)

I small lemon

I small knob of ginger (½ inch or smaller)

3 medium shallots, roughly chopped

4 small Thai chilies (*phrik khee nu*) or serrano chilies, finely chopped

⅓ cup roasted unsalted peanuts

⅓ cup dried shrimp (*kung haeng*)

LEAF LILIES

12 large leaves of Chinese broccoli, spinach, or butter lettuce

To make the Sweet Shrimp Sauce: Set a small skillet over medium heat. Place the foil-wrapped shrimp paste in the skillet and roast it for about 5 minutes, until aromatic, turning the packet over once or twice. Remove the packet from the skillet and set it aside to cool.

Grind the dried shrimp in a mortar or food processor fitted with a metal blade. Process thoroughly, until they become a flaky powder.

Bring the water to a boil in a medium saucepan. Add the sugar and stir constantly until it is dissolved. Lower the heat slightly. Reduce the liquid at a gentle boil, stirring often, to three fourths of its original volume, about 10 minutes. Add the roasted shrimp. paste. Mix thoroughly to dissolve all of the paste. Add the ground shrimp. Stir well to mix. Remove the pan from the heat and let cool to room temperature.

To prepare the condiments:

Make the Toasted Coconut.

Trim the ends off the lemon, but do not peel it. Slice it into ½-inch rounds; stack them and chop them into small dice.

Peel the ginger and cut it into thin slices. Stack them and chop them into small dice.

In the center of a large serving platter, place a serving bowl of the Sweet Shrimp Sauce. Arrange all the condiments in neat little heaps around the platter.

To make the leaf lilies: Stack the Chinese broccoli leaves and cut them into 4-inch circles with kitchen shears. (Or make heart shapes to resemble *bai cha plu.*) Arrange the shaped leaves on a serving platter and serve with the Sweet Shrimp Sauce and condiments.

THAI SERVING STYLE: Place your choice of condiments on a leaf lily and spoon on a little Sweet Shrimp Sauce. Fold the lily into a little bundle and eat out of hand.

GRILLED EGGPLANT-AND-SHRIMP SALAD WITH HOT CHILI–LEMON DRESSING

Yam Makhua Yao Pao Kap Kung

Serves 4 to 6

Japanese eggplant and shrimp, treats fresh from the garden and the sea, are brought together over a charcoal fire to enrich their individual flavors in a smoky perfume. Fresh mint enlivens both the sweet shrimp and the creamy grilled eggplant. This is a salad that's as pretty and colorful as it is beautifully flavored. Shrimp powder with chili, a Thai condiment you may find wonderfully addicting, is sprinkled over the top for a light infusion of crunchiness and chili heat.

DRESSING

¼ cup loosely packed chopped cilantro stems

2 tablespoons chopped serrano chilies (about 4)

3 cloves garlic, roughly chopped

2 tablespoons coconut-palm sugar or golden brown sugar

1½ tablespoons Thai fish sauce (*nam pla*)

¼ teaspoon white pepper

½ cup fresh lemon juice

SALAD

4 Japanese eggplants (about ¾ pound)

½ pound medium shrimp

3 to 4 short (8-inch) bamboo skewers, soaked in a tray of cold water for at least ½ hour

½ small red onion, finely sliced

1 medium cucumber (about ½ pound), peeled, cut in half lengthwise, seeded, and finely sliced

1 tomato, cut in half and sliced into thin wedges

½ cup loosely packed fresh mint

4 tablespoons shrimp powder with chili (*kung phrik pon*)

Sprigs of cilantro

To make the dressing: Combine all of the dressing ingredients in a blender or mixing bowl. Blend well to dissolve the sugar. Set aside.

To make the salad: Build a medium-hot charcoal fire or preheat a gas grill. Wrap the eggplants in a double layer of aluminum foil. Grill them in the packet, turning once, about 5 minutes on each side, or just until the eggplants are soft and their skins are wrinkled. Unwrap and set aside to cool slightly.

Skewer the shrimp in their shells, using two or three per skewer. The skewer should pass through each shrimp twice: Pierce the shrimp through the tail, then bring the skewer out through the top of the curve. Grill the shrimp, turning them once, for about 3 minutes total, or just until they turn pink. Set aside to cool slightly.

Angle-cut the eggplant into ½-inch ovals and put them in a mixing bowl. Peel the shrimp and add them to the bowl. Add the onion, cucumber, tomato, and mint. Toss gently to mix. Pour in the salad dressing and mix well.

Transfer the salad to a serving platter and sprinkle the shrimp powder with chili on top. Tear a few sprigs of cilantro over the salad and serve warm or at room temperature.

THAI VEGETARIAN CUISINE

Ahan Pak

Although some 93 percent of our population practices Buddhism, in Thailand even the monks eat meat. Historically, we have not been strict vegetarians. ("Strict" is an out-of-place word in any discussion of Thai cuisine. "Pleasurable" is an aspect we usually find far more important.) The genius of Thai food, really, is in taking plain-flavored staples such as rice and presenting them in intriguing, nicely harmonized, richly flavored curries, seasonings, and sauces. But more and more nowadays, both Thais and Americans are saying that this genius should be applied to dishes that are free of all animal products.

Fortunately, Thai cuisine is very well equipped to supply this growing demand for vegetarian cookery. Tofu and other vegetarian ingredients get just as much of a flavor lift from Thai seasonings as do animal-derived foods.

I've always included a large number of vegetarian dishes on the menu of my restaurant here in Los Angeles. A vegetarian version of jungle curry, for example, is ordered by both Steve Martin and Madonna nearly every time they visit. L.A. food enthusiasts, who were the first to embrace Thai food on a big scale in this country, have always been concerned about healthfulness, freshness, and savor. As more and more of my customers requested vegetarian meals, I eventually created a whole menu for them. Many of those recipes found their way into this chapter.

Vegetarian cooking can be a great creative outlet for anyone who loves to cook and eat well. That's why I've made this chapter something of a self-contained book, encompassing soups, salads, one-dish meals, and entrées—all of them entirely without meat, fish, or any animal products whatsoever.

Even some of the "building blocks" of Thai cuisine, including four different curry pastes and the essential condiment known as *nam phrik pao*, are presented here in vegetarian form.

I know all of you, vegetarians *and* nonvegetarians, will love the delicious recipes in this chapter, such as Vegetarian-Style Pumpkin-Coconut Soup, Sweet Corn Fritters, and Home-Fried Tofu Squares with Savory Tamarind Sauce.

Even my nonvegetarian customers, seeing a waiter walk by with a fragrant, appealing dish and learning that it is a meatless recipe, will sometimes ask to see the vegetarian menu—just because it has wonderful new flavors that they want to experience.

RED CURRY PASTE, VEGETARIAN STYLE

Krung Kaeng Phed, Mangsawirat

Makes about 1½ cups

For a vegetarian version of this essential Thai seasoning paste, follow the instructions for making Classic Red Curry Paste (page 26) EXCEPT: Omit the shrimp paste and substitute 3 tablespoons creamy peanut butter, adding it to the food processor with the soaked chilies.

FRESH GREEN CHILI CURRY PASTE, VEGETARIAN STYLE

Krung Kaeng Khiew Wan, Mangsawirat

Makes about 2 cups

For a vegetarian version of this essential Thai seasoning paste, follow the instructions for making Fresh Green Chili Curry Paste (page 28) EXCEPT: Omit the shrimp paste and substitute 3 tablespoons creamy peanut butter, adding it to the food processor with the soaked chilies.

MASSAMAN CURRY PASTE, VEGETARIAN STYLE

Krung Kaeng Massaman, Mangsawirat

Makes about 1½ cups

For a vegetarian version of this essential Thai seasoning paste, follow the instructions for making Massaman Curry Paste (page 36) EXCEPT: Omit the shrimp paste and substitute 3 tablespoons creamy peanut butter, adding it to the food processor with the soaked chilies.

JUNGLE CURRY PASTE, VEGETARIAN STYLE

Krung Kaeng Pha, Mangsawirat

Makes about 1⅓ cups

For a vegetarian version of this wilderness-inspired Thai seasoning paste, follow the instructions for making Jungle Curry Paste (page 40) EXCEPT: Omit the shrimp paste and use ½ cup chopped sage leaves instead of the chives and arugula.

CHILI-TAMARIND PASTE, VEGETARIAN STYLE

Nam Phrik Pao, Mangsawirat

Makes about 1 cup

I often use this in my restaurant instead of the conventional, nonvegetarian version. Although mellow, it's a smoky, concentrated seasoning agent that can also be spread on toast points or crisp rice cakes. Among the recipes that call for it in this chapter are Sweet-and-Sour Grilled Eggplant Salad and Mixed Vegetable Stir-Fry with Chili-Tamarind Sauce.

Follow the instructions for making Chili-Tamarind Paste (page 46) EXCEPT: Omit the dried shrimp. Add ½ cup whole yellow bean sauce (*tao jiew khao*) to the blender or food processor with the other chili paste ingredients. Substitute Thai soy sauce with mushroom (*see-eu khao het hom*) for the fish sauce. When cooked, this chili paste will turn brown.

VEGETABLE STOCK

Soup Pak

Makes about 8 cups

The vegetables you select for making this stock are what will build its flavor. Cilantro lends a Thai accent.

Use vegetable stock wherever chicken stock is called for—in curries and stir-fries, as the basis for soups, and to give definition to sauces.

I large potato, thickly sliced

2 medium carrots, cut in half

I medium onion, cut in half

4 ribs celery, cut in thirds

1½ pounds additional mixed vegetables, such as green beans, leeks, zucchini, crookneck and pattypan squash, mushrooms, bean sprouts, lettuce, and Japanese eggplant (larger vegetables should be thickly sliced)

6 cloves garlic, lightly crushed

½ teaspoon whole black peppercorns

I small bunch cilantro

2 large, leafy stems of basil

1½ teaspoons Thai soy sauce with mushroom (*see-eu khao het hom*) or a Chinese brand, such as Pearl River Bridge

10 cups water

Put all of the ingredients in a large stockpot. Gradually bring to a boil over medium-high heat, then lower the heat and simmer for 40 minutes.

Strain the stock through a fine-mesh sieve into a medium saucepan or heatproof bowl. Discard the solids. Cool the stock to room temperature before storing in the refrigerator.

Covered and refrigerated, it will keep for about 1 week. You can also freeze it for several months.

VEGETARIAN-STYLE PUMPKIN-COCONUT SOUP

Tom Kati Fak Thong Kap Tao Hoo Leh Maengluk

Serves 2 to 4

This is a great vegetarian version of an elegant palace-style soup. The vegetable stock and coconut milk combine for a creamy broth, while two different citrus ingredients add complexity. The mellowness of the kabocha is offset by the deeper flavor of Thai basil. Savory baked tofu makes it especially nourishing and substantial.

½ pound kabocha (see Note)

1¾ cups Vegetable Stock (page 239) or canned vegetable broth

1 can (14 ounces) unsweetened coconut milk

10 (5 pairs) fresh Kaffir lime leaves (*bai magroot*), or strips of peel from 1 small lime

3 ounces savory baked tofu, cut into ½-inch cubes

2 tablespoons coconut-palm sugar or golden brown sugar

2 tablespoons Thai thin soy sauce (*see-eu khao*) or any good light soy sauce

3 tablespoons fresh lemon juice

½ teaspoon white pepper

2 cups loosely packed Thai lemon basil (*bai maengluk*) or the more commonly available Thai basil (*bai horapha*) or Italian basil

4 small Thai chilies (*phrik khee nu*), or 2 serrano chilies, lightly crushed (optional)

Scoop out and discard the seeds and strings from the kabocha. With a sharp, heavy knife or cleaver, chop it into quarters. Cut off most of the peel and slice the kabocha into thin bite-size pieces.

Put the stock and coconut milk in a soup pot and set it over medium-high heat. Bring the mixture to a boil, stirring occasionally. If using Kaffir lime leaves, tear each leaf in half and add to the pot. If using lime peel, add to the pot.

Return the stock to a boil, stirring occasionally. Add the kabocha and tofu. Stir until mixed and cook for 2 minutes. Add the sugar, soy sauce, lemon juice, and white pepper. Cook, stirring occasionally, until the kabocha is tender, about 1½ to 2 minutes. Turn off the heat. Stir in the basil and cook for a few seconds, just until the basil begins to wilt.

Float the chilies on top, if desired, and ladle the soup into a steamboat, a soup tureen, or individual serving bowls.

NOTE: You need a ½-pound piece of kabocha for this recipe. Most Asian markets sell kabocha whole and by the piece. If your market sells only whole kabocha, buy a small one and reserve the rest for a stir-fry or dessert. You may also substitute butternut or acorn squash.

The crushed chilies give the soup a spicy edge. Eating them is optional.

PINEAPPLE-GINGER SOUP

Kaeng Chued Supparod Kap Khing On

Serves 4 to 6

Y ou'll find this sweet, peppery soup delicious and intriguing but essentially mild. Make it with baby ginger whenever possible.

6 ounces baby ginger or mature ginger, peeled and finely sliced

2 large shallots, chopped

10 cloves garlic, chopped

6 cups Vegetable Stock (page 239)

1 tablespoon vegetable oil

1 can (20 ounces) pineapple rings, drained and roughly chopped

1 box (10½ ounces) soft tofu, cut into ½-inch cubes

4 scallions, including the green tops, angle-cut into 1-inch pieces

⅓ cup sugar

4 tablespoons Thai thin soy sauce (*see-eu khao*) or any good light soy sauce

1 teaspoon white pepper

Sprigs of cilantro

Arrange some of the sliced ginger in a small stack and julienne. Measure out ¼ cup of the julienned ginger and set it aside.

Put the remaining ginger slices, shallots, and garlic in the bowl of a food processor fitted with a metal blade. Process until minced. Transfer to a small bowl and set aside.

Begin warming the stock in a soup pot set over medium-high heat. Meanwhile, set a wok or skillet over medium-high heat. When it is quite hot, add the oil. If using a wok, rotate it a bit so the oil coats the sides. When the oil is hot, add the minced ginger mixture and stir-fry for 2 minutes, until the mixture is fully fragrant. Transfer the stir-fry to the soup pot. Stir to mix well and bring the stock to a boil. Add the pineapple, tofu, and scallions and stir. Add the sugar, soy sauce, and white pepper and return the soup to a boil, stirring occasionally. Turn off the heat and sprinkle in the reserved julienned ginger.

Ladle the soup into a steamboat, a soup tureen, or individual serving bowls. Tear a sprig or two of cilantro over each serving.

THAI CITRUS VINAIGRETTE

Nam Manao

Makes about ½ cup

This oil-free dressing gets its pretty green color from lime juice and cilantro stems. The juice also contributes to the tang and spice provided by the chilies and garlic. While most Thai-style salad dressings have a few splashes of fish sauce, this has mushroom soy sauce instead. Use it to dress mixed salad greens, or pour it over a platter of grilled vegetables or sliced mushrooms and avocados.

½ tablespoon chopped garlic

1 small Thai chili (*phrik khee nu*), finely sliced

⅓ cup fresh lime juice

2 tablespoons chopped cilantro stems

2 teaspoons Thai soy sauce with mushroom (*see-eu khao het hom*) or a Chinese brand, such as Pearl River Bridge

2 teaspoons coconut-palm sugar or golden brown sugar

Put all of the ingredients in a blender and liquefy, making sure the sugar is completely dissolved and blended into the dressing.

CURRIED PEANUT SALAD DRESSING AND DIPPING SAUCE

Nam Jeem Tua Lisong

Makes about 4½ cups

This moderately spicy concoction, though vegetarian, comes very close to the hearty character of a satay sauce. The recipe as given makes enough to dress a large salad of mixed greens, with enough left over to use as a dip for raw vegetables.

This dressing is thick enough to hold up even when tossed with moist salad greens.

1 can (19 ounces) unsweetened coconut milk

1 cup Red Curry Paste, Vegetarian Style (page 237)

1 cup Vegetable Stock (page 239) or canned vegetable broth

1 cup chunky peanut butter

5 tablespoons coconut-palm sugar

Skim the thick cream from the top of the canned coconut milk into a medium saucepan, reserving the milk. Set the pan over medium-high heat. Cook, stirring often, until the cream liquefies. Stir in the curry paste until blended and bring to a low boil. Cook, stirring constantly, for 2 minutes. Add the reserved coconut milk and vegetable stock and cook for 2 minutes, stirring often.

Reduce the heat to low and add the peanut butter. Cook, stirring constantly, for 1½ minutes. Add the sugar and cook, stirring often, until the sugar is dissolved and the sauce is well blended, about 1 minute.

Cool to room temperature before tossing with salad greens or serving as a dip.

This will keep for at least 2 weeks if refrigerated in a covered container.

VEGETARIAN-STYLE GREEN MANGO SALAD

Som Tum Mamuang, Mangsawirat

Serves 2 to 4

This is a lively, refreshing salad that is uniquely Thai. Though green, the mango still has a pleasing, savory sweetness to it. This isn't simply a set of vegetarian substitutions to the usual green mango salad. I've slimmed the recipe down to a very simple and tasty dish in which the green mangoes predominate, with background accents of shallots, mint, crushed peanuts, and the citrusy vinaigrette.

1½ pounds green mangoes (about 2 large)

2 tablespoons finely sliced shallots

½ cup loosely packed fresh mint

¼ cup Thai Citrus Vinaigrette (page 242)

3½ tablespoons roasted unsalted peanuts, crushed or finely chopped

Sprigs of cilantro (optional)

Slice the stem end off a mango. With a sharp knife, score the skin lengthwise into quarters, first on one side then the other. Pull the skin off, using the scored sections as a guide. Hold the peeled mango in the palm of one hand, exposing half the fruit, and make a series of quick, parallel cuts, slicing into the flesh almost to the seed. When the surface is fully scored, slice crosswise to release the fruit, creating julienne strips. Repeat, scoring the mango down to the seed and slicing off the remaining fruit. Turn the mango over and repeat the tap-cut technique to julienne the rest of the fruit. When all the mangoes are julienned, you should have about 3 cups.

Put the sliced mango in a mixing bowl along with the shallots and mint. Pour the vinaigrette over the salad and mix in the crushed peanuts.

Transfer the salad to a serving platter. Tear a few sprigs of cilantro over the salad, if desired, and serve.

VEGETARIAN-STYLE GREEN PAPAYA SALAD

Som Tum Ma Muang, Mangsawirat

Serves 4 to 6

I 've kept this vegetarian version of the Issan classic sweet, hot, juicy, and full of peanuts. Thin soy sauce replaces the fish sauce, and an extra-generous helping of peanuts supplies protein and rich flavor.

1½ pounds green papayas (about 2 medium)

8 cloves garlic

8 small Thai chilies (*phrik khee nu*), stemmed

3 rounded tablespoons coconut-palm sugar or golden brown sugar

3 tablespoons Thai thin soy sauce (*see-eu khao*) or any good light soy sauce

½ cup sliced green beans (2-inch lengths)

6 large cherry tomatoes, quartered

½ cup fresh lime juice

½ cup roasted unsalted peanuts, crushed in a mortar or finely chopped

1 head Boston lettuce or green cabbage (optional)

Peel the papayas, cut them in half lengthwise, then scoop out and discard the seeds. Cut the papayas into long, thin shreds, or use a food processor fitted with a shredding disk. You should have about 4 cups. Set aside.

Put the garlic and chilies in a large heavy mortar and pound them to bits. Blend in the sugar and soy sauce with the pestle. Use a large spoon to scrape down the sides of the mortar and turn up any bits of undissolved sugar. Gradually add the shredded papaya and green beans and pound gently to crush them slightly. Use the spoon to scrape down the mortar and turn the mixture over as you work.

Add the tomatoes and crush them lightly to release some of their juice. Add the lime juice and crushed peanuts and mix well.

Transfer the salad to a platter and serve.

If using salad greens, select small, cup-shaped leaves from the head of lettuce or cut the cabbage into thick wedges. Set out the lettuce cups or cabbage wedges on a serving tray and place next to the salad. To serve, spoon some of the salad into a lettuce cup or cabbage leaf. Fold up and eat out of hand.

VIETNAMESE-STYLE
VEGETARIAN SALAD ROLLS

Poh Pia Sod Mangsawirat

Makes about 8 salad rolls, or 16 appetizer-sized bundles

———

The cuisines of Thailand, Cambodia, and Vietnam have all borrowed liberally from one another. One trick we've adopted from the Vietnamese is their way of rolling leafy herbs and vegetables in a delicate rice-paper wrapper. It makes for a wonderful appetizer or snack that's very refreshing on a hot day.

The amounts given would make a light lunch for two or an appetizer or snack for four, but the recipe doubles easily for a larger group.

I bunch scallions

I package (7 ounces) Vietnamese rice sheets (see Note)

1⅓ cups shredded cabbage (any kind)

I carrot, grated

I red bell pepper, cut into matchsticks

¼ cup loosely packed chopped cilantro, including the stems

¼ cup loosely packed Thai basil (*bai horapha*) or purple or Italian basil

2 serrano chilies, finely sliced (optional)

Vietnamese-Style Plum Sauce (page 58)

Bring a saucepan of water to a boil. Meanwhile, cut the tops off the scallions. Set the tops aside. Choose two of the fattest bulbs and reserve the rest for another use. Slice the two bulbs in half lengthwise, then cut each piece into lengthwise shreds. Set aside.

Plunge the scallion tops into the boiling water until limp, then refresh in cold water. Drain and set aside.

Fill a lasagna pan or large skillet with warm water and set it on a clear work space with all of the ingredients and a cutting board.

Dip a sheet of rice paper into the warm water. Press down gently to keep it fully submerged, about 10 to 12 seconds. Carefully transfer the rice sheet to the cutting board.

Arrange some of the shredded cabbage in a horizontal line across the center of the wrapper. Place some grated carrot on top, then some scallion shreds, bell pepper, cilantro, and basil. Finish with some sliced chilies, if desired. Fold the bottom of the wrapper up and over the filling, tucking it under the filling ingredients to form a cylinder. Roll it up to the top, leaving the sides open.

To secure the roll, use some softened scallion tops as ties: Tear a scallion top in half lengthwise, then tie the two ends together. Lift up one end of the salad roll and slip the tie underneath, about 2 inches from the open end. Tie the ends around the roll and secure with a simple knot. Tear another scallion top, tie it together, and secure the opposite end of the roll as before. Trim off and discard the open ends with kitchen shears or a sharp knife, then cut the roll in half to make two bundles. Set the bundles aside on a tray or cookie sheet.

Continue filling and rolling the moistened rice papers until you've used up all the filling. (Store any leftover wrappers in an airtight container.)

When all of the salad rolls are tied, cut, and trimmed, place them on a serving tray and serve with the Vietnamese-style plum sauce.

N O T E : The rice sheets require moistening and are sometimes hard to find in stores. For a simplified version, use the more readily available spring roll pastry sheets, which do not need soaking.

SWEET-AND-SOUR ROASTED EGGPLANT SALAD

Yam Makhua Pao

Serves 4 to 6

Roasted eggplant is earthy and substantial, a perfect foil to the sweet-and-smoky tang of a dressing based on chili-tamarind paste. Lemon juice and palm sugar round out the flavors.

2¼ pounds firm, glossy Japanese eggplants (about 6 to 8 large)

½ cup fresh lemon juice

1 tablespoon Chili-Tamarind Paste, Vegetarian Style (page 238)

½ tablespoon coconut-palm sugar

1 stalk lemon grass, tough outer leaves discarded, lower stalk trimmed to 4 inches and finely sliced

1½ tablespoons finely sliced shallots

½ cup loosely packed chopped cilantro, including the stems

½ cup loosely packed fresh mint

Preheat the oven to 400°F. Prick the eggplants in several places and bake them until they are soft and their skins are wrinkled, about 20 minutes. Turn them over after 10 minutes to roast evenly.

When the eggplants are cool enough to handle, slice them in half lengthwise and peel the skins away from the flesh. (Don't worry if some of the skin doesn't peel away easily; leave it on, it will lend character to the dish. It's more important that all the creamy flesh be left for the salad and not pulled away with the skin.) Roughly chop the eggplant and set it aside in a mixing bowl.

To make the dressing, place the lemon juice, chili paste, and sugar in a blender and liquefy or place them in a bowl and stir with a wooden spoon. The sugar and chili paste should be thoroughly dissolved and blended into the lemon juice.

Add the dressing to the bowl of roasted eggplant. Add the lemon grass and shallots and mix gently.

Transfer to a serving platter, shower the salad with the cilantro and mint, and serve.

TOFU SALAD WITH TOASTED RICE POWDER AND MINT, SERVED IN LETTUCE CUPS

Laab Tao Hoo Mangsawirat

Serves 6

---

*L*aab is a favorite salad from northern Thailand that's usually highlighted by spiced, minced meat. Preparing this easy-to-make vegetarian version amounts to assembling a wonderful tofu salad to eat out of hand in lettuce cups. The toasted rice powder, the only part of the recipe that requires any cooking at all, lends crunchiness and a light, nutlike flavor.

6 ounces pressed tofu or savory baked tofu, finely diced

6 scallions, including the green tops, finely sliced

¾ cup finely sliced shallots

1¼ cups loosely packed fresh mint

¼ cup Thai thin soy sauce (*see-eu khao*) or any good light soy sauce

½ cup fresh lime juice

¼ cup golden brown sugar

Toasted Rice Powder (page 63; double the recipe to make ½ cup)

Thai chili powder (*phrik pon*) or other ground red chili to taste, such as New Mexico chili powder or cayenne

A few small heads of salad greens (Boston lettuce, romaine, cabbage, and radicchio are all good choices)

Put the tofu, scallions, shallots, and mint in a large bowl. Add the soy sauce, lime juice, and sugar and toss to mix. Stir in the toasted rice powder. Season to taste with the chili powder and mix well.

Select small cup-shaped leaves from your choice of salad greens and arrange them on a serving tray. Spoon some tofu salad into the lettuce cups until you've portioned out all the salad. Serve at once.

CURRIED PUMPKIN-FRIED RICE

Khao Phat Kamin

Serves 2 to 4

You might call this delicious dish a sort of Thai comfort food. The spicing is subtle—yellow curry powder, a little golden-brown sugar, and white pepper. The kabocha, which has a flavor midway between that of common pumpkin and acorn squash, has a creamy texture. The fried rice itself is as nourishing and comforting as mashed potatoes.

You can serve this as a main course or a side dish.

2½ cups cold cooked jasmine rice (*khao hom mali*) or other long-grain white rice (see Note 1)

½ pound kabocha (see Note 2)

2 tablespoons vegetable oil

5 cloves garlic, pounded to a mash or a crushed and chopped

½ cup sliced shallots

1½ tablespoons golden brown sugar

2 tablespoons Thai soy sauce with mushroom (*see-eu khao het hom*) or a Chinese brand, such as Pearl River Bridge

½ teaspoon curry powder

½ teaspoon ground turmeric

1 teaspoon white pepper

Sprigs of cilantro

Put the rice in a large mixing bowl and knead it gently through your fingers to separate the grains. Set aside.

Scoop out and discard the seeds and fibers from the kabocha. With a sharp, heavy knife or cleaver, chop it into quarters. Cut off most of the peel and cut the kabocha into ½-inch dice. You should have about 1 cup.

Place all of the ingredients within easy reach of the cooking area.

Set a wok over medium-high heat. When it is quite hot, add the oil. Rotate the wok a bit so the oil coats the sides. When the oil is hot, add the garlic and shallots and stir-fry briefly, just until golden and aromatic. Add the kabocha and stir-fry for 3 minutes. Add the rice, sugar, and soy sauce and stir-fry, pressing the rice down into the bottom of the wok. Turn the rice mixture over, press it down into the wok again, and continue to stir-fry for 2 minutes. Add the curry powder, turmeric, and white pepper and mix well.

Transfer to a serving platter. Tear sprigs of cilantro over the fried rice and serve.

NOTE 1: To give your stir-fried rice perfect texture, always use rice that was cooked a day or more in advance and stored in the refrigerator. Freshly cooked rice would be too soft.

NOTE 2: You need a ½-pound piece of kabocha for this recipe. Most Asian markets sell kabocha whole and by the piece. If your market sells only whole kabocha, buy a small one, about 2 pounds, and reserve the rest for another recipe, such as Pumpkin in Sweet Coconut Milk (page 334). You may also substitute butternut or acorn squash.

FRIED RICE WITH WALNUTS AND RAISINS

Khao Phat Tua Kap Lukked

Serves 2 to 4

This vegetarian fried rice is quite full flavored but also carries subtle touches—chewy, sweet golden raisins made savory with mushroom soy sauce, balanced against the crunchiness and dry heat of walnuts and white pepper.

2½ cups cold cooked jasmine rice (*khao hom mali*) or other long-grain white rice (see Note)

2 tablespoons vegetable oil

5 cloves garlic, pounded to a mash or a crushed and chopped

2½ tablespoons golden raisins

2 scallions, including the green tops, angle-cut into 1½-inch pieces, bulbs cut in half lengthwise

1 small tomato, cut in half and sliced into thin wedges

2 tablespoons Thai soy sauce with mushroom (*see-eu khao het hom*) or a Chinese brand, such as Pearl River Bridge

1½ tablespoons golden brown sugar

½ teaspoon white pepper

¼ cup walnut halves

Sprigs of cilantro

Put the rice in a large bowl and knead it gently through your fingers to separate the grains.

Place all of the ingredients within easy reach of the cooking area.

Set a wok over medium-high heat. When it is quite hot, add the oil. Rotate the wok a bit so the oil coats the sides. When the oil is hot, add the garlic and stir-fry briefly, just until golden and aromatic. Add the rice and the raisins and press the rice down into the bottom of the wok. Turn the rice mixture over, press it down into the wok again, and continue to stir-fry for 1 minute.

Add the scallions and tomato and stir-fry for 30 seconds. Add the soy sauce and stir-fry for 30 seconds. Add the sugar and white pepper and stir-fry for 30 seconds. Add the walnuts and stir-fry for 30 seconds.

Transfer to a serving platter. Tear sprigs of cilantro over the fried rice and serve.

NOTE: To give your stir-fried rice perfect texture, always use rice that was cooked a day or more in advance and stored in the refrigerator. Freshly cooked rice would be too soft.

TANGY RICE-STICK NOODLES WITH VEGETABLES AND BLACK-EYED PEAS

Phat Kwaytiow Sen Lek Kap Tua Dam

Serves 6

A lively, light, and tangy stir-fry of rice noodles, this dish gets its subtle sweet-and-sour flavor from vinegar, mushroom soy sauce, vegetable stock, and a little sugar. Black-eyed peas and pressed tofu give it substantial vitamins and protein, along with the flavorful scallions and tomatoes.

8 ounces dried rice-stick noodles, "chantaboon" type, or any thin, flat variety about ⅛ inch wide (*sen jahn* or *sen lek*)

3 tablespoons vegetable oil

9 tablespoons garlic, pounded to a mash or crushed and chopped

⅓ cup Vegetable Stock (page 239) or canned vegetable broth

6 scallions, including the green tops, angle-cut into 1½-inch pieces, bulbs cut in half lengthwise

1 large tomato, cut in half and sliced into thin wedges

3 ounces pressed tofu, cut into ¼-inch dice

¾ cup cooked or canned black-eyed peas

4 tablespoons golden brown sugar

3 tablespoons Thai soy sauce with mushroom (*see-eu khao het hom*) or a Chinese brand, such as Pearl River Bridge

1 teaspoon white pepper

1 tablespoon plus 1 teaspoon distilled white vinegar

½ pound bean sprouts

Sprigs of cilantro

Soak the rice-stick noodles in a large bowl of warm water until they are soft, about 15 minutes. Drain and set the noodles aside in a colander.

Place all of the ingredients within easy reach of the cooking area.

Set a wok over medium-high heat. When it is quite hot, add the oil. Rotate the wok a bit so the oil coats the sides. When the oil is hot, add the garlic and stir-fry briefly, just until golden and aromatic. Add the noodles and stir-fry for 1 minute. Add the vegetable stock and stir to mix. Add the scallions, tomatoes, tofu, and black-eyed peas and stir-fry for 1 minute. Add the sugar and soy sauce and stir-fry for 1 minute. Add the white pepper, vinegar, and bean sprouts and stir-fry for 1 minute, mixing well.

Transfer to a serving platter. Tear sprigs of cilantro over the noodles and serve.

CLASSIC THAI NOODLES, VEGETARIAN STYLE

Phat Thai Mangsawirat

Serves 4 to 6 as a side dish, or 2 as a one-dish meal

This is the vegetarian version of *phat Thai*, a dish that's as basic to Thai cooking as spaghetti marinara is to Italian. It's a dish that lends itself to infinite variations. Here, protein-rich garbanzo beans and tofu more than compensate for the absence of the usual shrimp and bits of pork.

STIR-FRIED NOODLES

8 ounces dried rice-stick noodles, "chantaboon" type, or any thin, flat variety about ⅛ inch wide (*sen jahn* or *sen lek*)

2 tablespoons vegetable oil

3 cloves garlic, pounded to a mash or crushed and chopped

8 ounces firm tofu, cut into fat matchstick-size pieces

5 tablespoons Vegetable Stock (page 239) or canned vegetable broth

3 tablespoons distilled white vinegar

4 tablespoons sugar

½ teaspoon white pepper

4 scallions, including the green tops, finely sliced

3 tablespoons Thai soy sauce with mushroom (*see-eu khao het hom*) or a Chinese brand, such as Pearl River Bridge

1 tablespoon paprika, Thai chili powder (*phrik pon*), or other ground red chili to taste, such as New Mexico chili powder or cayenne

½ cup cooked or canned garbanzo beans

1 cup bean sprouts

⅓ cup roasted unsalted peanuts, crushed in a mortar or finely chopped

CONDIMENTS

2 cups bean sprouts

⅓ cup roasted unsalted peanuts, crushed in a mortar or finely chopped

Lime or lemon wedges

Sprigs of cilantro

6 to 8 small Thai chilies (*phrik khee nu*), finely sliced, or Chilies-in-Vinegar Sauce (page 52) (optional)

Soak the rice-stick noodles in a large bowl of warm water until they are soft, about 15 minutes. Drain and set the noodles aside in a colander.

Place all of the stir-fry ingredients within easy reach of the cooking area.

Arrange the condiments on a serving platter or put them into individual serving bowls, and set them on the table so they will be ready when the noodles are hot out of the wok.

Set a wok over medium-high heat. When it is quite hot, add the oil. Rotate the wok a bit so the oil coats the sides. When the oil is hot, add the garlic and stir-fry for a few seconds. Add the tofu and stir-fry for 1 minute. Add the vegetable stock and the noodles and stir-fry briskly for about 1 minute, tossing the noodles to mix well. Add the vinegar and stir-fry for 1 minute. Add the sugar, white pepper, and scallions and mix well. Add the soy sauce and stir-fry for 1 minute. Add the paprika and stir-fry briskly for ½ to 2 minutes. Stir in the garbanzo beans, bean sprouts, and peanuts until well mixed.

Transfer to a serving platter and serve immediately.

KHANOM CHINE WITH VEGETARIAN CURRY SAUCE AND THAI BASIL

Khanom Chine Nam Ya Mangsawirat

Serves 4 to 6

*K*hanom chine dishes, which involve ladling a tasty curry sauce over palm-of-the-hand-sized noodle nests, make for a very sociable meal. Each person takes what he wants from a central platter, including crisp and spicy condiments, to personalize his own dish. For all its varied and complex flavors, a *khanom chine* lunch is a surprisingly light one-dish meal.

The delicious, medium-spicy curry sauce for this vegetarian version is based on garbanzos, red curry paste, and coconut milk.

VEGETARIAN CURRY SAUCE

I cup cooked or canned garbanzo beans

I can (19 ounces) unsweetened coconut milk

I cup Red Curry Paste, Vegetarian Style (page 237)

I teaspoon rhizome powder *(krachai)*, or ¼ teaspoon ground ginger

½ cup Vegetable Stock (page 239) or canned vegetable broth

5 tablespoons golden brown sugar

¼ cup Thai thin soy sauce *(see-eu khao)* or any good light soy sauce

NOODLE NESTS

12 ounces Japanese *somen* noodles or angel hair pasta

1½ cups loosely packed Thai basil *(bai horapha)* or purple or Italian basil

CONDIMENTS

¼ pound baby winged beans *(tua poo)*, finely sliced, or snow peas, stems and strings removed

¾ pound bean sprouts

Thai chili powder *(phrik pon)* or other ground red chili to taste, such as New Mexico chili powder or cayenne (optional)

To make the curry sauce: Put the garbanzos in the bowl of a food processor fitted with a metal blade. Process until the beans are roughly ground and crumbly. Transfer to a small bowl and set aside.

Skim the thick cream from the canned coconut milk into a soup pot, reserving the milk. Set the pot over medium-high heat. Add the ground garbanzos and cook for 2 minutes, stirring frequently. Add the curry paste and rhizome powder and stir-fry until well blended, about 1 minute. Stir in the reserved coconut milk, mixing well.

Add the vegetable stock and cook for 1 minute, stirring often. Add the sugar and soy sauce and cook for 1 minute, stirring often.

Cover and remove from the heat.

To cook the noodles and form them into nests: Fill a large pot with about 3 quarts of water. Bring the water to a boil, add the *somen* noodles or angel hair pasta, and cook until al dente (1½ to 2 minutes for *somen*; 2 to 2½ minutes for angel hair), stirring occasionally to keep the noodles from sticking to the bottom of the pan.

Drain immediately in a colander. Rinse well until the noodles have cooled, tossing and stirring them with a wooden spoon to remove excess starch. Drain the noodles and transfer them to a mixing bowl.

Set a large serving platter before you on the counter or work surface, along with the bowl of noodles and the basil.

Take a handful of cooked noodles and coil them around two fingers of your other hand to make a 3- to 4-inch mound shaped like a little bird's nest. Put the nest on the serving platter. Repeat until all the noodles have been formed into nests.

Arrange a few basil leaves in the hollow of each nest and set the platter aside.

To prepare the condiments: Blanch the winged beans in plenty of boiling water for 30 seconds. Transfer them with a wire skimmer or slotted spoon to a bowl of ice water; drain and set aside.

Return the water to a boil. Blanch the bean sprouts for 20 seconds and drain them immediately.

Arrange the blanched vegetables on a serving platter. Put some chili powder in a small saucer, if desired.

Set the platter of bird's-nest noodles and all the condiments on the table.

Slowly reheat the curry sauce over medium-high heat. Transfer to a serving bowl and set alongside the bird's-nest noodles and condiments.

THAI SERVING STYLE: Serve each guest three or four bird's nests with some winged beans and bean sprouts on the side. Generously ladle the sauce over the noodles. Let each guest combine the vegetables with the curried noodles to his taste and season with chili powder, if desired.

FAT NOODLES WITH BROCCOFLOWER AND SWEET BLACK BEAN SAUCE

Kwaytiow Sen Yai Phat Pak Broccoflower Kap See-eu Wan

Serves 4 to 6

Numerous Thai dishes marry sweet black soy sauce with fat, slippery rice noodles in a hot wok. It's a combination that always works: The sugar in the soy sauce starts to caramelize, creating a wonderful smoky sweetness that sticks to the bland noodles and turns them an appealing earthy-brown shade. White pepper and Chilies-in-Vinegar Sauce can turn up the spice level as much—or as little—as you want.

1 pound presliced fresh rice noodles (*sen yai*) or uncut fresh rice noodle sheets (see Note)

2 tablespoons vegetable oil

8 cloves garlic, pounded to a mash or crushed and chopped

1 head broccoflower or cauliflower, florets only, broken into bite-size pieces

3 tablespoons Vegetable Stock (page 239) or canned vegetable broth

1 tablespoon sweet black soy sauce (*see-eu wan*)

2 tablespoons Thai soy sauce with mushroom (*see-eu khao het hom*) or a Chinese brand, such as Pearl River Bridge

3 tablespoons golden brown sugar

¾ cup cooked or canned black beans

CONDIMENTS

Sprigs of cilantro

Ground white pepper

Chilies-in-Vinegar Sauce (page 52)

Put the sliced noodles in a colander and pour a kettle of hot water over them to remove the protective oil coating and soften them a bit. Unfold and separate the noodles into individual ribbons. (If some break off into short lengths, that's fine—it will create texture. Just be as careful as you can to separate the individual noodles from the folded mass.)

Place all of the stir-fry ingredients within easy reach of the cooking area.

Set a wok over medium-high heat. When it is quite hot, add the oil. Rotate the wok a bit so the oil coats the sides. When the oil is hot, add the garlic and stir-fry briefly, just until golden and aromatic. Add the broccoflower and vegetable stock and stir-fry for 1 minute. Add the noodles and stir-fry briskly for 30 seconds, tossing the noodles to incorporate them with the other ingredients.

Add the sweet black soy sauce and stir-fry until well blended, about 30 seconds. Add the mushroom soy sauce and sugar and stir-fry until the sugar is dissolved into the sauce. Add the black beans and stir-fry just until the broccoflower is cooked through and crisp-tender, about 1 to 2 minutes.

Transfer to a serving platter. Tear sprigs of cilantro over the noodles and serve with the white pepper and Chilies-in-Vinegar Sauce on the side.

NOTE: Fresh rice noodles can be stored in the refrigerator, but if you buy them the same day you plan to serve them, keep them at room temperature. They will be easier to unfold. If using uncut noodle sheets, slice them lengthwise through the folds into strips about ¾ inch wide.

TROPICAL-FRUIT WONTONS WITH GREEN PEPPERCORNS

Polamai Khanom Jeeb Phrik Thai Sod

Makes about 46 wontons

No matter how many times you've had wontons, you've never had any quite like these. It may seem strange to use fruit instead of the usual pork, chicken, or other traditional wonton fillings, but the results are lyrical. The green peppercorns dotted among the puréed fruit add a peppery, herbal note that seems to expand the fruit flavors.

Assorted canned tropical fruits (drained weight 12 ounces):

    4 ounces (about ⅔ cup) rambutan stuffed with pineapple

    4 ounces (about ⅔ cup) mango slices

    4 ounces (about ⅔ cup) whole longan

or

1 can (20 ounces) tropical fruit salad, drained

1 cup loosely packed chopped cilantro, including the stems

⅓ cup drained, brine-cured green peppercorns (*phrik Thai on*)

2 tablespoons all-purpose flour

1 package (12 ounces) wonton wrappers (3½ inches square)

Vegetable or peanut oil for deep-frying

Thai Plum Sauce (page 57) or bottled plum sauce

To make the filling: Put the tropical fruits and cilantro into the bowl of a food processor fitted with a metal blade. Process until the mixture becomes a pulpy purée. Transfer to a mixing bowl. Stir in the peppercorns. Add the flour and mix until blended.

continued

To make the wontons: Line a tray or cookie sheet with waxed paper and set it on a flat work surface, with the filling and wonton wrappers alongside. Take one wrapper and set it down with a pointed edge toward you. Place 1 teaspoon of filling in the center of the wrapper. Fold the wrapper in half to form a triangle by bringing the bottom half up and over the filling. (The points shouldn't meet each other exactly.) Roll the wonton once to form a cylinder with the side points open. Seal the wonton by bringing the two side points together and pinching them closed. (The moisture in the filling should make the wrapper adhere as you form the wontons; if not, moisten the edges with a little water before sealing.)

Set the wonton aside on the waxed paper. Continue making wontons until you've used up all the filling. Any leftover wrappers can be rewrapped and frozen. Space the wontons out on the waxed paper to keep them from sticking together.

Pour the oil in a wok or saucepan to a depth of 1 inch. Set over medium heat until the oil is sizzling hot, about 360 to 375°F. (To test the oil temperature, drop in a little piece of wrapper; if it sizzles immediately, the oil is ready.) Add about eight wontons to the oil and fry, turning once or twice, until golden brown, about 1 minute.

Remove the wontons with a wire skimmer or slotted spoon and drain on paper towels. Return the oil to its original temperature and fry the rest of the wontons as above.

Place the wontons on a serving platter and serve with plum sauce.

SWEET CORN FRITTERS

Tod Mun Khao Pod

Makes about 2 dozen fritters

———————

Enjoy these fritters as an appetizer or a side dish. No eggs are needed to hold the fresh corn kernels in their light potato-starch batter, which is formed into round patties and shallow-fried.

Red curry paste and mushroom soy sauce infuse the recipe with subtle flavor and spice. The crispness and sweet-and-sour edge of Spicy Cucumber Relish is just the right counterpoint to the savory fritters.

4 cups corn kernels (about 6 large ears)

1 box (12 ounces) potato starch

2 tablespoons Red Curry Paste, Vegetarian Style (page 237)

15 cloves garlic, pounded to a mash or crushed and chopped

½ cup finely chopped cilantro, including the stems

2 tablespoons Thai soy sauce with mushroom (*see-eu khao het hom*) or a Chinese brand, such as Pearl River Bridge

1 teaspoon white pepper

½ cup water

Vegetable or peanut oil for frying

Spicy Cucumber Relish (page 53)

Put the corn in a large mixing bowl. Lightly crush the kernels with the back of a wooden spoon to release some of their liquid. Add the potato starch, curry paste, garlic, cilantro, soy sauce, and white pepper. Mix with your hands until the ingredients are well blended. Add the water and blend thoroughly until the mixture begins to adhere and can be formed into patties.

Take a small handful of batter and press it into a patty about 3 inches in diameter. Set the patty aside on a tray or cookie sheet. Continue making patties until you've used up all the batter.

Pour the oil into a wok or a deep, wide skillet to a depth of ½ inch. Set over medium heat until the oil is sizzling hot, about 360 to 375°F. (To test the oil temperature, drop in a little piece of fritter mix; if it sizzles immediately, the oil is ready.) Add about four patties to the hot oil and fry, turning once or twice, until golden brown, about 3 minutes. Remove the fritters with a wire skimmer or slotted spoon and drain on paper towels. Return the oil to its original temperature and fry the rest of the fritters as above.

Place the fritters on a serving platter and serve with Spicy Cucumber Relish.

VEGETARIAN SPRING ROLLS

Poh Pia Tod Mangsawirat

Makes about 12 large spring rolls

I 've filled these spring rolls with cellophane noodles, carrots, bamboo shoots, and scallions, but you can improvise with whatever combinations of vegetables you find pleasing. Do try the trick of using two spring-roll wrappers per roll. It allows you to make nice, fat spring rolls that can later be sliced into halves or thirds for serving-sized pieces.

I package (3½ ounces) dried bean-thread vermicelli (*woon sen*)

I large shallot, finely sliced

2 carrots, grated

4 scallions, including the green tops, finely sliced

16 cloves garlic, finely sliced

2 cups loosely packed chopped cilantro, including the stems

I cup sliced canned bamboo shoots

4 tablespoons Thai soy sauce with mushroom (*see-eu khao het hom*) or a Chinese brand, such as Pearl River Bridge

5 tablespoons sugar

1½ teaspoons white pepper

I package (12 ounces) spring-roll wrappers

Vegetable or peanut oil for deep-frying

Sweet-and-Spicy Dipping Sauce (page 54)

Put the noodles in a large bowl of warm water and soak them until they are soft and translucent, about 12 to 15 minutes. As the noodles become pliable, spread them out with your fingers to ensure quick, even soaking. Put the softened noodles in a colander, drain well, and turn out onto a cutting board. Using a knife or kitchen shears, cut the mound of noodles roughly into quarters so the noodle-filling mixture will be easier to handle.

Put the noodles, shallots, carrots, scallions, garlic, cilantro, and bamboo shoots in a large mixing bowl. Mix with your hands until the ingredients are well blended. Add the soy sauce, sugar, and white pepper and mix well.

Set a dry wok over medium-high heat. Add the noodle-filling mixture and stir-fry until the vegetables release their moisture and become tender and the noodles are soft and clear, about 4 minutes.

Transfer the filling to a large bowl and let it cool to room temperature.

Gently separate the spring-roll wrappers from the pack. Keep the wrappers covered with a dampened paper towel as you make the spring rolls. Place two wrappers, one on top of the other, on a flat work surface with a pointed edge toward you.

Place about 3 tablespoons of filling in the center of the diamond. Fold the bottom of the wrapper up and over the filling, tucking it under the filling to form a fat cylinder. Fold the right and left sides in toward the middle, then roll it tightly right up to the top. Moisten the edges with water to seal the finished roll. Set the roll aside on a platter or cookie sheet with the seam side down.

Continue making spring rolls, using two wrappers at a time, until you've used up all the filling.

Pour the oil into a large wok or deep, wide saucepan to a depth of 2 inches. Set over medium heat until the oil is sizzling hot, about 360 to 375°F. (To test the oil temperature, drop in a little piece of wrapper; if it sizzles immediately, the oil is ready.) Carefully slide a spring roll into the hot oil; it should begin sizzling at once. Add two or three more and fry the rolls, turning them occasionally, until golden brown, about 3 minutes. Remove the spring rolls with a wire skimmer or slotted spoon and drain them on a tray or plate lined with paper towels.

Return the oil to its original temperature and fry the rest of the spring rolls as above.

Angle-cut the spring rolls into thirds and place them on a serving platter. Serve with Sweet-and-Spicy Dipping Sauce on the side.

PICKLED CHINESE MUSTARD WITH GARBANZO BEANS AND SWEET PICKLED GINGER

Hua Pak Kad Dong Kap Tua Luang Leh Khing Dong

Serves 4 to 6

P ickled mustard greens are very popular all over Thailand. Their sour note is paired in this vegetarian stir-fry with garbanzo beans and sweet pickled ginger for an example of a very homey, everyday-cooking sort of Thai dish.

2 tablespoons vegetable oil

18 cloves garlic, pounded to a mash or crushed and chopped

1 jar (24 ounces) pickled Chinese mustard (*hua pak kad dong*), drained and sliced

¾ cup cooked or canned garbanzo beans

¾ cup drained, finely cut shreds of pickled ginger (*khing dong*)

4 tablespoons golden brown sugar

2 tablespoons Thai soy sauce with mushroom (*see-eu khao het hom*) or a Chinese brand, such as Pearl River Bridge

8 scallions, including the green tops, angle-cut into 1½-inch pieces, bulbs cut in half lengthwise

Sprigs of cilantro

Place all of the ingredients within easy reach of the cooking area.

Set a wok over medium-high heat. When it is quite hot, add the oil. Rotate the wok a bit so the oil coats the sides. When the oil is hot, add the garlic and stir-fry briefly, just until golden and aromatic. Add the Chinese mustard and stir-fry for 30 seconds. Add the garbanzo beans and stir-fry for 30 seconds. Add the pickled ginger, sugar, and soy sauce and stir-fry for 1 minute. Add the scallions and stir-fry until they are cooked through and crisp-tender, about 1 to 2 minutes.

Transfer to a serving platter. Tear sprigs of cilantro over the dish and serve with steamed jasmine rice.

STIR-FRIED NAPA CABBAGE WITH GARLIC AND YELLOW BEAN SAUCE

Pak Kad Kap Kratiem Leh Tao Jiew Leing

Serves 4

This tasty, home-style dish is easy to prepare. And while it's made from a comparatively short list of very humble ingredients, it goes with just about everything and is richly satisfying.

3 tablespoons vegetable oil

8 cloves garlic, pounded to a mash or crushed and chopped

1 large head Napa cabbage, quartered lengthwise and roughly chopped

3 tablespoons Vegetable Stock (page 239) or canned vegetable broth

2 tablespoons crushed yellow bean sauce (*tao jiew dam*)

2 tablespoons golden brown sugar

Place all of the ingredients within easy reach of the cooking area.

Set a wok over medium-high heat. When it is quite hot, add the oil. Rotate the wok a bit so the oil coats the sides. Add the garlic and stir-fry briefly, just until golden and aromatic. Add the cabbage and stir-fry for 1 minute. Add the vegetable stock and stir-fry for 1 minute. Add the yellow bean sauce and sugar and stir-fry briskly to mix well, about 1½ to 2 minutes.

Transfer to a serving platter and serve with steamed jasmine rice.

STIR-FRIED PUMPKIN WITH TOFU AND THAI BASIL

Fak Thong Phat Tao Hoo Kap Horapha

Serves 4 to 6

Kabocha, pumpkin found in many Thai recipes, is always delicious. Anise-scented *horapha* and a light vegetable stock–based sauce make it stand out even more.

1 pound kabocha (see Note)

3 tablespoons vegetable oil

10 cloves garlic, pounded to a mash or crushed and chopped

2 tablespoons crushed yellow bean sauce (*tao jiew dam*)

2½ tablespoons golden brown sugar

1 teaspoon white pepper

3 tablespoons Vegetable Stock (page 239) or canned vegetable broth

19 ounces firm tofu, cut into bite-size pieces

¾ cup loosely packed Thai basil (*bai horapha*) or purple or Italian basil

Classic Chili Dipping Sauce (page 49) (optional)

Scoop out and discard the seeds and fibers from the kabocha. With a sharp, heavy knife or cleaver, chop it into quarters. Cut off most of the peel and slice the kabocha into thin, bite-size pieces.

Place all of the stir-fry ingredients within easy reach of the cooking area.

Set a wok over medium-high heat. When it is quite hot, add the oil. Rotate the wok a bit so the oil coats the sides. When the oil is hot, add the garlic and stir-fry briefly, just until golden and aromatic. Add the kabocha and stir-fry for 3 minutes. Add the yellow bean sauce and sugar and stir-fry until blended, about 1 minute. Add the white pepper and vegetable stock and stir-fry for 30 seconds. Add the tofu and stir-fry until it is heated through, about 1½ minutes. Turn off the heat. Stir in the basil and cook for a few seconds, just until the basil begins to wilt.

Transfer to a serving platter and serve with steamed jasmine rice and Classic Chili Dipping Sauce, if desired.

NOTE: You need a 1-pound piece of kabocha for this recipe. Most Asian markets sell kabocha whole and by the piece. If your market sells only whole kabocha, buy a small one, about 2 pounds, and reserve half for another recipe, such as Pumpkin in Sweet Coconut Milk (page 334) or Curried Pumpkin-Fried Rice (page 250).

STIR-FRIED OYSTER MUSHROOMS WITH TOFU AND BABY CORN

Het Hoy Naengrong Phat Tao Hoo Leh Khao Phod On

Serves 4 to 6

The subtle, earthy flavors of the oyster mushrooms predominate in this lightly seasoned stir-fry.

3 tablespoons vegetable oil

10 cloves garlic, pounded to a mash or crushed and chopped

12 ounces firm tofu, cut into bite-size cubes

2 tablespoons crushed yellow bean sauce (*tao jiew dam*)

2 tablespoons golden brown sugar

½ pound oyster mushrooms, wiped clean and left whole

12 ears canned baby corn (about half a 15-ounce can)

6 scallions, including the green tops, angle-cut into 1½-inch pieces, bulbs cut in half lengthwise

Place all of the ingredients within easy reach of the cooking area.

Set a wok over medium-high heat. When it is quite hot, add the oil. Rotate the wok a bit so the oil coats the sides. When the oil is hot, add the garlic and stir-fry briefly, just until golden and aromatic. Add the tofu and stir-fry for 30 seconds. Add the yellow bean sauce and sugar and stir-fry for 30 seconds. Add the mushrooms, baby corn, and scallions and stir-fry until the vegetables are cooked through, about 2 minutes.

Transfer to a serving platter and serve with steamed jasmine rice.

MIXED VEGETABLE
STIR-FRY WITH
CHILI-TAMARIND SAUCE

Pak Ruam Mit Phat Nam Phrik Pao Mangsawirat

Serves 4

Ruam mit translates loosely as "Everybody get together." The heart and soul of this dish is its big, friendly jumble of vegetables—including baby corn, baby ginger, plum tomatoes, and napa cabbage—all united by the superb, haunting tang of chili-tamarind paste.

3 tablespoons vegetable oil

12 cloves garlic, pounded to a mash or crushed and chopped

1 cup Vegetable Stock (page 239) or canned vegetable broth

4 tablespoons Chili-Tamarind Paste, Vegetarian Style (page 238)

12 ears canned baby corn (about half a 15-ounce can)

6 scallions, including the green tops, angle-cut into 1½-inch pieces, bulbs cut in half lengthwise

1 red bell pepper, chopped

2 plum tomatoes, cut in half and sliced into thin wedges

½ pound Napa cabbage, roughly chopped

2 ounces baby ginger or mature ginger, peeled and thinly julienned

5 tablespoons sugar

2 tablespoons Thai thin soy sauce (*see-eu khao*) or any good light soy sauce

1 cup loosely packed Thai basil (*bai horapha*) or purple or Italian basil

Place all of the ingredients within easy reach of the cooking area.

Set a large wok over medium-high heat. When it is quite hot, add the oil. Rotate the wok a bit so the oil coats the sides. When the oil is hot, add the garlic and stir-fry briefly, just until golden and aromatic. Add the vegetable stock and vegetarian chili-tamarind paste and cook for 1 minute, stirring well to blend the paste into the liquid. Add all of the vegetables and the baby ginger and stir-fry for 1 minute. Add the sugar and soy sauce, mixing well. Stir-fry until the vegetables are cooked through and crisp-tender, about 3 to 4 minutes. Turn off the heat. Stir in the basil and cook for a few seconds, just until the basil begins to wilt.

Transfer to a serving platter and serve with steamed jasmine rice.

NOTE: Use a large (14-inch) wok if you have one. Otherwise, add the vegetables in two batches.

HOME-FRIED TOFU SQUARES WITH SAVORY TAMARIND SAUCE

Tao Hoo Tod Kap Nam Makham

Serves 4

This dish is proof that Thai-style vegetarian dishes aren't just recipes that omit meat. They're wonderfully developed, tasty, rich, and satisfying meals that are right up there with anything else the cuisine has to offer.

The homemade fried tofu squares are pretty simple to make from scratch. Puffy and crispy on the outside, soft and mellow on the inside, their consistency is a perfect foil for the piquant tamarind sauce and the crispy fried garlic slices and shallot rings. Store-bought fried tofu squares, with their spongier texture, are better used in stir-fries and soups.

4½ tablespoons Vegetable Stock (page 239) or canned vegetable broth

5 tablespoons coconut-palm sugar

2 tablespoons Tamarind Sauce (page 61) or liquid tamarind concentrate

1 tablespoon Thai soy sauce with mushroom (*see-eu khao het hom*) or a Chinese brand, such as Pearl River Bridge

½ teaspoon white pepper

2½ cups vegetable or peanut oil for frying

¼ cup thinly sliced garlic (about 12 cloves)

⅔ cup thinly sliced shallots (about 5 or 6)

12 ounces firm Chinese-style tofu, cut into 10 cubes about 1¾ inches square

2 plump scallions, including the green tops, finely sliced

Sprigs of cilantro

To make the sauce: Combine the vegetable stock and sugar in a small saucepan and set over medium-high heat. Stir until the sugar is dissolved and blended and bring the mixture to a boil. Add the tamarind sauce, soy sauce, and white pepper, stirring after each addition. Boil gently, stirring occasionally, until slightly thickened, about 3 to 4 minutes. Cover and set aside.

To fry the garlic, shallots, and tofu squares: Pour the oil into a large, deep skillet set over medium-high heat and bring the oil to 360°F. (To test the oil temperature, dip a wooden spoon in the hot oil. The oil should bubble and sizzle gently around the bowl of the spoon.)

Add the garlic and cook until golden brown, stirring occasionally, about 1 minute. Remove with a wire skimmer or slotted spoon and drain on paper towels.

Return the oil temperature to 360°F and fry the shallots, stirring frequently, until crisp and brown, about 2 minutes. Remove with a wire skimmer or slotted spoon and drain on paper towels.

Return the oil temperature to 360°F. Shallow-fry the tofu squares, turning them after about 1 minute on each side, until the cubes are puffy and golden brown on all sides, about 6 minutes total.

To assemble the dish: Transfer the fried tofu squares to a serving platter. Quickly rewarm the sauce, if necessary, and pour it over the tofu. Sprinkle the scallions, fried garlic, and crispy shallot rings over the tofu. Tear sprigs of cilantro over the dish and serve at once.

GREEN CURRY WITH MIXED VEGETABLES, TOFU, AND THAI BASIL

Kaeng Khiew Wan Kap Pak, Tao Hoo Leh Horapha

Serves 4

This is an elegant, earthy curry with a light and airy quality. Because they're so sensuous and herbal, green curries are often used in palace cooking. This one is highlighted by vegetables such as bell peppers, winged beans, and baby corn, and a generous hand with the anise-flavored Thai basil called *horapha*.

The counterpoint to all Thai curries, of course, is generous helpings of steamed jasmine rice. Owing to the Indian influence in their region, however, many southern Thais prefer folding their curries—especially green ones—into an Indian flatbread called *roti*. Here in America you can substitute store-bought chapatis. Another alternative is to ladle the curry over *khanom chine* noodles or their close cousin, angel hair pasta.

I can (19 ounces) unsweetened coconut milk

I cup Fresh Green Chili Curry Paste, Vegetarian Style (page 237)

3 cups roughly chopped mixed vegetables, such as broccoli florets, baby corn, red, yellow, or green bell peppers, winged beans, and Japanese eggplant

⅓ cup Vegetable Stock (page 239) or water

5 tablespoons golden brown sugar

⅓ cup Thai thin soy sauce (*see-eu khao*) or any good light soy sauce

6 ounces firm tofu, cut into bite-size cubes

I cup loosely packed Thai basil (*bai horapha*) or purple or Italian basil

12 warm chapatis, or 1 pound cooked angel hair pasta (optional)

Skim the thick cream from the top of the canned coconut milk into a soup pot, reserving the milk. Set the pot over medium-high heat. Stir in the curry paste until blended and bring to a low boil. Cook, stirring constantly, for 2 minutes.

Stir in the reserved coconut milk and add the mixed vegetables. Simmer, stirring occasionally, for 2 minutes. Stir in the vegetable stock and cook for 1 minute. Add the sugar and soy sauce and stir until the sugar is dissolved and blended. Cook, stirring occasionally, until the vegetables are cooked through and crisp-tender, about 1 minute, depending on the vegetables chosen. Add the tofu and stir to mix well. Turn off the heat. Stir in the basil and cook for a few seconds, just until the basil begins to wilt.

Transfer to a serving bowl or covered casserole. Serve with plenty of steamed jasmine rice, or the chapatis or pasta, if desired.

Thai

Vegetarian

Cuisine

Massaman Curry with Sweet Potato, Fried Tofu Squares, and Peanuts

Kaeng Massaman Kap Manwan, Tao Hoo Tod Leh Tua Lisong

Serves 6

Massaman curry is usually served with beef, but many of my friends swear that their favorite Massaman is this vegetarian version. One thing that makes it enjoyable is the rich, mild sauce soaks right into the squares of fried tofu. The result is mellow and delicious, with a lightly spicy aftertaste.

I large sweet potato (about 8 to 10 ounces)

6 ounces deep-fried tofu (in cube form)

I can (19 ounces) unsweetened coconut milk

I cup Massaman Curry Paste, Vegetarian Style (page 237)

I cup Vegetable Stock (page 239) or canned vegetable broth

½ cup roasted unsalted peanuts

3 tablespoons coconut-palm sugar or golden brown sugar

3 tablespoons Thai thin soy sauce (*see-eu khao*) or any good light soy sauce

Peel the potato and chop it into ½-inch cubes. Steam the potato over boiling water just until tender, about 5 to 6 minutes. Set aside.

Cut the fried tofu squares into quarters. Set aside with the potato.

Skim the thick cream from the top of the canned coconut milk into a soup pot, reserving the milk. Set the pot over medium-high heat. Stir in the curry paste until blended and bring to a low boil. Cook, stirring constantly, for 2 minutes. Add the steamed sweet potato, fried tofu, reserved coconut milk, and vegetable stock. Cook for 2 minutes, stirring often. Add the peanuts and sugar and stir until the sugar is dissolved and blended. Add the soy sauce and cook for 30 seconds.

Transfer to a serving bowl or covered casserole and serve with plenty of steamed jasmine rice.

NOTE: I like to make this curry a few hours, or even a full day, before I plan to serve it. Given some time, the flavors will enhance one another and become more pronounced. Keep it covered and refrigerated until ready to use. Heat it through without letting it come to a boil, then serve.

272

True

Thai

FIERY JUNGLE CURRY, VEGETARIAN STYLE

Kaeng Pha Mangsawirat

Serves 4 to 6

This is one of the spiciest Thai dishes. In Thailand it would be made with young shoots and leafy greens gathered from roadsides and riverbanks, but the herbs available in America also make a wonderful dish. The curry turns out nice and saucy, even though it contains no coconut milk.

3 tablespoons vegetable oil

1⅓ cups Jungle Curry Paste, Vegetarian Style (page 238)

4 cups Vegetable Stock (page 239) or canned vegetable broth

I cup fresh corn kernels or canned baby corn

I cup sliced yard-long beans or green beans (3-inch lengths)

I cup halved cherry tomatoes

1½ cups halved mushrooms

5 tablespoons golden brown sugar

6 tablespoons Thai thin soy sauce (*see-eu khao*) or any good light soy sauce

2 cups mixed fresh herbs:

½ cup roughly torn Italian basil

½ cup roughly torn Thai basil (*bai horapha*)

½ cup chopped tarragon

½ cup chopped sage

Pour the oil into a soup pot set over medium-high heat. When the oil is hot, add the curry paste and stir-fry for 2 minutes. Stir in the vegetable stock until it is blended and bring the mixture to a low boil. Cook for 5 minutes, stirring occasionally. Lower the heat to medium. Add the corn, beans, tomatoes, and mushrooms and stir to mix well. Add the sugar and soy sauce and simmer for 2 to 3 minutes, or until the vegetables are cooked through. Turn off the heat. Stir in the mixed herbs and cook for a few seconds, or just until they begin to wilt.

Transfer to a large serving platter. Serve with plenty of steamed jasmine rice.

BANGKOK STREET COOKING

Ahan Rim Tanon

Mention "street cooking" to most Americans and they'll think of hot-dog carts on the streets of New York, or Philadelphia's soft pretzels squirted with yellow mustard. Those are probably the only images that will come to mind. But in Bangkok, people eat extremely well without ever setting foot into a restaurant, café, or home kitchen, enjoying all kinds of wonderful food from street vendors—everything from simple treats such as sliced fresh sugar cane to complex dishes such as Chiang Mai Noodle Curry with stewed beef, crunchy noodle topping, and a host of Thai condiments.

In a way, the streets of our capital city are really just one big open-air café.

Thai people love being out in a crowd. We have an expression for it—*pai tio*—the practice of simply walking around neighborhoods to see what, and whom, you can see. Of course, that usually includes seeing what's cooking and enjoying a bite to eat.

We have a belief that the right time to eat is any time you're hungry. And going *pai tio* is a surefire way to build up your appetite.

Fortunately, there is always lively, deliciously prepared food available right out on the streets—or just off the streets, at special counters in supermarkets and department stores. The offerings may be tender little coconut pancakes, several varieties of fried rice, grilled meat satays, soupy noodle curries, green papaya salad, fresh fish cakes, spiced teas and coffees, or dozens of other little snacks and desserts.

Although many of the foods sold by street vendors are simply prepared, quite a number are complex dishes that Thai people often prefer to leave to specialists. That's why some street vendors produce dishes that rival those in the best restaurants. It's a bit like the "gourmet take-out" trend that we've seen lately in America.

Because there's a great deal of appreciation in Bangkok for artistry in cooking, people come to be famous in their neighborhoods for the dishes they do best. My mother, who is still my greatest inspiration in cooking, makes banana fritters that are so tasty, she has sold them for many years both to neighbors and to supermarkets. (You'll find her recipe on page 303.) Other people become "community cooks," bringing inexpensive home-cooked meals to their neighbors' doorsteps throughout the week. You just study their menus and, if you like what you see, "subscribe" to the service. With all these options, busy people don't really have to cook anything more at home than a pot of steamed rice.

Great ready-cooked food is also sold along rivers and canals by entrepreneurs in long, narrow boats, hawked from the platforms of railway stations, and even found in the clearings where trails to jungle outposts converge.

Having this abundance of terrific, ready-made food within easy reach at all times is one of the great aspects of daily life in Thailand. When you try out these street-vendor recipes, you'll understand why each one is a great popular favorite.

STEAMED DUMPLINGS WITH MINCED CHICKEN AND SHRIMP

Khanom Jeeb

Makes about 32 dumplings

A favorite streetside snack, these dumplings become a wonderful appetizer when you prepare them at home. They are made of wonton wrappers gathered around chicken, shrimp, and crunchy water-chestnut slivers and accented with three great condiments—Golden Garlic, Sweet Black Bean Sauce, and spicy Thai hot sauce.

I like to serve these tasty dumplings in the afternoon, with beer, but they're elegant enough to be served at evening with cocktails or fine wine.

Any leftover dumplings can be made tender again by resteaming them for 5 minutes.

FILLING

¾ pound medium shrimp, peeled and roughly chopped

½ pound ground chicken

3 scallions, including the green tops, finely sliced

1 can (8 ounces) water chestnuts, finely chopped

2 tablespoons minced garlic

2 egg yolks

3 tablespoons Golden Mountain sauce (*poo kow thong*) or Maggi seasoning

1 tablespoon white pepper

1 tablespoon golden brown sugar

WONTONS

1 package (1 pound) wonton wrappers (round or 3½-inch square)

1 egg, lightly beaten

CONDIMENTS

Golden Garlic (page 65)

Sweet Black Bean Sauce (page 60)

Bottled Thai chili sauce (*sriracha*) or Quick Street-Vendor's Hot Sauce (page 56)

Put the chopped shrimp in the bowl of a food processor fitted with a metal blade. Process until the shrimp is ground into small pieces. Transfer the ground shrimp to a large mixing bowl. Add the remaining filling ingredients, and, using your hands, knead and mix until blended. Let the mixture stand for 10 minutes at room temperature before filling the wontons.

continued

Place the bowl of filling, the wonton wrappers, and a saucer of the beaten egg on a clear work space. Have a lightly oiled cookie sheet nearby to hold the dumplings.

Place 1 tablespoon of the filling in the center of a wonton wrapper. Moisten the four corners with a little of the beaten egg, then gather up the sides and pinch them around the top to resemble a little drawstring pouch. Set the dumpling aside on the cookie sheet. Continue making dumplings until you've used up all the filling. (Any leftover wrappers can be rewrapped and frozen.) Space the dumplings out on the cookie sheet enough to keep them from touching, so they won't stick together.

Fill the base pot of a tiered aluminum steamer about one-third full of water. Cover and bring the water to a boil over medium-high heat. Lightly oil a steamer rack (or two racks) and space the dumplings on the rack (or racks) so that they don't touch each other. When the water reaches a boil, set the rack(s) over the pot, cover, and steam until firm yet tender, about 10 to 15 minutes.

Transfer the steamed dumplings to a large serving platter and serve at once with the Golden Garlic, warm Sweet Black Bean Sauce, and Thai chili sauce.

THAI SERVING STYLE: Spoon a little Golden Garlic, with its oil, over a serving of the steamed dumplings, then spoon on some Sweet Black Bean Sauce, and finally, a little chili sauce to taste.

FRESH SALMON TOAST WITH SPICY CUCUMBER RELISH

Khanom Pang Na Pla

Serves 6 to 8

You'll find this treat sold from bicycle-wheeled pushcarts on Bangkok street corners. Usually made from chicken, pork, or shrimp, it's essentially a minced, seasoned topping spread on bread slices, which are then deep-fried and served with a dipping sauce.

My version is topped with fresh ground salmon, seasoned with garlic, white pepper, chopped cilantro stems, and an aromatic dash of *krachai*, a member of the ginger family. I prefer to use sliced French bread rather than the thin sandwich bread a Bangkok street vendor might employ. It makes lighter and puffier toasts.

For special occasions, try cutting the bread slices into special shapes—a school of toasted, salmon-topped fish shapes would be terrific. Or you could scallop the bread to make simple flowers.

An alternate version of this recipe, substituting chicken, is given below.

¾ pound fresh salmon fillets

½ tablespoon dried rhizome powder (*krachai*)

6 cloves garlic, roughly chopped

2 tablespoons chopped cilantro stems

3 scallions, including the green tops, finely sliced

½ tablespoon white pepper

2 teaspoons golden brown sugar

½ tablespoon Thai fish sauce (*nam pla*)

1 egg, beaten

1 loaf day-old French bread, cut into ½-inch slices, crusts trimmed

Vegetable or peanut oil for frying

Sprigs of cilantro

Spicy Cucumber Relish (page 53)

Remove any skin or fine bones from the salmon and cut it into 1-inch pieces. Combine the salmon, rhizome powder, garlic, cilantro stems, scallions, pepper, sugar, fish sauce, and beaten egg in the bowl of a food processor fitted with a metal blade. Process until the mixture becomes a smooth paste. Transfer the salmon paste to a bowl.

Spread the salmon paste on the bread slices about ½ inch thick, right up to the edges of the bread. Cut the salmon-topped slices into quarters to make pie-shaped pieces, or into novelty shapes if you want to be fancy.

Place a heatproof platter in a warm oven while you fry the toasts.

Pour the oil into a large wok or a heavy 12-inch skillet to a depth of ½ inch. Set over medium heat until the oil is sizzling hot, about 360 to 375°F. (To test the oil temperature, dip a wooden spoon in the hot oil. The oil should bubble and sizzle gently around the bowl of the spoon.) Place a few bread pieces into the hot oil without crowding, salmon side down. Fry them on both sides until crisp and golden brown, about 1 minute on each side. Remove with a wire skimmer or slotted spoon, shaking and holding them over the skillet to drain them for a few moments before transferring them to a tray or cookie sheet lined with paper towels. When well drained, transfer the fried salmon toasts to the warm oven.

Continue frying the salmon toasts, taking care to return the oil to the original frying temperature each time and to keep the toasts as grease-free as possible by blotting them dry on plenty of paper towels before placing them in the warm oven.

Transfer the salmon toasts to a serving platter and tear sprigs of cilantro over them. Serve hot, with Spicy Cucumber Relish on the side.

CHICKEN TOAST WITH SPICY CUCUMBER RELISH

Khanom Pang Na Kai

Substitute ½ pound boneless, skinless chicken for the salmon. Cut the chicken into ½-inch cubes. Omit the rhizome powder and proceed as directed for Fresh Salmon Toast.

GRILLED BEEF OR LAMB SATAY WITH CURRIED PEANUT SAUCE

Satay Neua

Serves 6

Satay migrated north from Indonesia a long time ago to become Thailand's ultimate street food. But it's so well loved that it can also be found everywhere from the humblest backstreet café to the most upscale restaurant. Fortunately, it also translates perfectly to your own backyard.

Satay is a captivating snack/appetizer, usually made from lean, narrow strips of beef, chicken, or pork that are threaded on skewers, marinated in spices and coconut milk, and quick-grilled over charcoal. I've found that my customers also love lamb satay, which can be prepared from the same recipe given for beef.

Serve your satays with toast points to catch their drippings and to mop up the delicious peanut sauce. The toast can easily be made on the grill while you tend the meat.

Recipes for chicken and pork satay, which follow, feature different spices and slightly different cooking times.

MARINADE

1 cup unsweetened coconut milk

4 tablespoons Classic Red Curry Paste (page 26) or 2 tablespoons canned red curry paste

2 tablespoons dark-brown sugar

2 tablespoons Thai fish sauce (*nam pla*)

1 tablespoon whole coriander seed, ground

SATAY

1 pound beef steak, such as sirloin, round, or flank steak; or lean, boneless lamb (preferably leg of lamb)

18 long (12-inch) bamboo skewers, soaked in a tray of cold water for at least ½ hour

6 slices sandwich bread for toast points (optional)

Curried Peanut Satay Sauce (page 55)

Spicy Cucumber Relish (page 53)

Combine the marinade ingredients in a bowl and mix well to dissolve the sugar and blend the curry paste.

Slice the meat into strips about 3 inches long and 1 inch wide. Add the meat to the marinade and stir to coat all the pieces. Cover and refrigerate for at least 3 to 4 hours, or as long as 24 hours.

Build a medium-hot charcoal fire or preheat a gas grill or a broiler. Meanwhile, thread the marinated meat onto the soaked bamboo skewers, about two pieces per skewer.

Grill or broil the sticks of satay until cooked, turning once or twice, about 3 to 5 minutes total. If making toast points, grill the bread as you tend the satay, then stack and cut the grilled bread into toast points before serving.

Transfer the satay to a large serving platter. Serve at once with the Curried Peanut Satay Sauce, Spicy Cucumber Relish, and toast points, if desired.

GRILLED CHICKEN SATAY WITH CURRIED PEANUT SAUCE

Satay Kai

Serves 6

The marinade for chicken satay is flavored by Panang curry paste, a milder seasoning mix than Red Curry Paste, because chicken is lighter in flavor than either beef or lamb. Chicken also grills a bit faster.

MARINADE

1 cup unsweetened coconut milk

4 tablespoons Panang Curry Paste (page 32), or 2 tablespoons canned Panang curry paste

2 tablespoons dark-brown sugar

2 tablespoons Thai fish sauce (*nam pla*)

1 tablespoon whole coriander seed, ground

SATAY

1 pound boneless, skinless chicken breast

18 long (12-inch) bamboo skewers, soaked in a tray of cold water for at least ½ hour

6 slices sandwich bread for toast points (optional)

Curried Peanut Satay Sauce (page 55)

Spicy Cucumber Relish (page 53)

Combine the marinade ingredients in a bowl and mix well to dissolve the sugar and blend the curry paste.

Slice the chicken breasts in half horizontally to make thin, flat slabs, then cut them into strips 3 inches long by 1 inch wide. Add the chicken to the marinade and stir to coat all the pieces. Cover and refrigerate for at least 3 to 4 hours or as long as 24 hours.

Build a medium-hot charcoal fire or preheat a gas grill or a broiler. Meanwhile, thread the marinated chicken onto the soaked bamboo skewers, about two pieces per skewer.

Grill or broil the sticks of satay until cooked, turning once or twice, about 3 to 4 minutes total. If making toast points, grill the bread as you tend the satay, then stack and cut the grilled bread into toast points before serving.

Transfer the satay to a large serving platter. Serve at once with the Curried Peanut Satay Sauce, Spicy Cucumber Relish, and toast points, if desired.

GRILLED PORK SATAY WITH CURRIED PEANUT SAUCE

Satay Mu

Serves 6

Yellow curry paste, the perfect foil for pork satay, is full of aromatics that complement the meat's sweet flavor.

MARINADE

1 cup unsweetened coconut milk

4 tablespoons Yellow Curry Paste (page 30), or 2 tablespoons canned yellow curry paste

2 tablespoons dark brown sugar

2 tablespoons Thai fish sauce (*nam pla*)

1 tablespoon whole coriander seed, ground

SATAY

1 pound lean, boneless pork

18 long (12-inch) bamboo skewers, soaked in a tray of cold water for at least ½ hour

6 slices sandwich bread for toast points (optional)

Curried Peanut Satay Sauce (page 55)

Spicy Cucumber Relish (page 53)

Combine the marinade ingredients in a bowl and mix well to dissolve the sugar and blend the curry paste.

Slice the pork into strips about 3 inches long by 1 inch wide. Add the pork to the marinade and stir to coat all the pieces. Cover and refrigerate for at least 3 to 4 hours or as long as 24 hours.

Build a medium-hot charcoal fire or preheat a gas grill or a broiler. Meanwhile, thread the marinated pork onto the soaked bamboo skewers, about two pieces per skewer.

Grill or broil the sticks of satay until cooked, turning once or twice, about 4 to 6 minutes total. If making toasts points, grill the bread as you tend the satay, then stack and cut the grilled bread into toast points before serving.

Transfer the satay to a large serving platter. Serve at once with the Curried Peanut Satay Sauce, Spicy Cucumber Relish, and toast points, if desired.

Vietnamese-Style Salad Rolls with Chicken and Vegetables

Poh Pia Sod

Makes about 8 salad rolls, or 16 appetizer-sized bundles

Salad rolls are healthful, delicate bundles of fresh vegetables, and perhaps some chicken or shrimp, spiced with a light, sweet sauce. The Vietnamese wrap their salad rolls in thin rice sheets. This recipe borrows that technique to make a light, refreshing appetizer or snack. And since they're prettily tied up with blanched strips of scallion, they also make lovely party fare.

These rolls are usually made with chicken, but I'd also recommend them as a great way to serve leftover roast turkey after the holidays—rolled up with fresh vegetables and dipped in a piquant plum sauce.

I bunch scallions

I package (7 ounces) Vietnamese rice sheets (see Note)

1⅓ cups shredded green cabbage

I cup shredded cooked chicken or turkey

I carrot, grated

I ounce savory baked tofu, cut into matchsticks

¼ cup loosely packed chopped cilantro, including the stems

2 serrano chilies, finely sliced (optional)

Vietnamese-Style Plum Sauce (page 58)

Bring a saucepan of water to a boil. Meanwhile, cut the tops off the scallions. Set the tops aside. Choose two of the fattest bulbs and reserve the rest for another use. Slice the two bulbs in half lengthwise, then cut each piece into lengthwise shreds. Set aside.

Plunge the scallion tops into the boiling water until limp, then refresh them in cold water. Drain and set aside.

Fill a lasagna pan or large skillet with warm water and set it on a clear work space with all the ingredients and a cutting board.

Dip a sheet of rice paper into the warm water. Press down gently to keep it fully submerged, about 10 to 12 seconds. Carefully transfer the rice sheet to the cutting board.

Arrange some of the shredded cabbage in a horizontal line across the center of the wrapper. Place some shredded chicken on top, then some grated carrot, tofu, scallion shreds, and cilantro. Finish with some sliced chilies, if desired. Fold the bottom of the wrapper up and over the filling, tucking it under the filling to form a cylinder. Roll it up to the top, leaving the sides open.

To secure the roll, use some softened scallion tops as ties: Hold up a scallion top and tear it in half lengthwise, then tie the two ends together. Lift up one end of the salad roll and slip the tie underneath, about 2 inches from the open end. Tie the ends around the roll and secure them with a simple knot. Tear another scallion top, tie it together, and secure the opposite end of the roll as before. Trim off and discard the open ends with kitchen shears or a sharp knife, then cut the roll in half to make two bundles. Set the bundles aside on a tray or cookie sheet.

Continue filling and rolling the moistened sheets until you've used up all the filling. (Store any leftover wrappers in an airtight container.) When all the salad rolls are tied, cut, and trimmed, place the bundles on a serving tray and serve with the Vietnamese-style plum sauce.

NOTE: The rice sheets require moistening and are sometimes hard to find in stores. For a simplified version, use the more readily available spring roll pastry sheets, which do not need soaking.

GREEN PAPAYA SALAD
WITH THAI CHILI AND LIME

Som Tum Issan

Serves 4 to 6

O n my restaurant's menu, this northern Thai classic is known as "heat-wave salad." The nickname is apt for two reasons: First, with its refreshing lime juice and crispy, white shreds of green papaya, this salad is a great hot-weather treat. Second, the salad's spiciness generates a heat wave of its own.

You don't yet find *som tum Issan* on many Thai menus in America, but I predict that you soon will. It's often served at ethnic festivals, such as the annual Lotus Festival in Los Angeles, and from the lines of non-Thai people I've seen waiting patiently at *som tum* booths, I'd say that folks are quickly catching on to how delicious this salad is.

This is a great dish to introduce to a big group. The variation that follows is a modern adaptation, perfect for picnics, pot lucks, buffets, or any time you need to make a dish for sixteen or more. You can make it ahead of time, then quickly assemble it at the desired location.

1½ pounds green papaya (about 2 medium)

8 cloves garlic

8 small Thai chilies (*phrik khee nu*), stemmed

1½ tablespoons coconut-palm sugar or golden brown sugar

3 tablespoons Thai fish sauce (*nam pla*)

½ cup sliced green beans (2-inch lengths)

6 large cherry tomatoes, quartered

6 tablespoons fresh lime juice

½ cup roasted unsalted peanuts, crushed in a mortar or finely chopped

1 head Boston lettuce or green cabbage (optional)

Peel the papayas, cut them in half lengthwise, then scoop out and discard the seeds. Cut the papayas into long thin shreds, or use a food processor fitted with a shredding disc. You should have about 4 cups. Set aside.

Put the garlic and chilies in a large heavy mortar and pound them to bits. Blend in the sugar and fish sauce with the pestle. Use a large spoon to scrape down the sides of the mortar and turn up any bits of undissolved sugar. Gradually add the shredded papaya and green beans and pound gently to crush them slightly. Use the spoon to scoop down into the mortar and turn the mixture over as you work. Add the cherry tomatoes and crush them lightly to release some of their juice. Add the lime juice and crushed peanuts and mix well.

Transfer the salad to a platter and serve.

If using salad greens, select small cup-shaped leaves from the head of lettuce, or cut the cabbage into thick wedges.

Set out the lettuce cups or cabbage wedges on a serving tray and place it by the green-papaya salad. To serve, spoon some of the salad into a lettuce cup or cabbage leaf. Fold it up and eat out of hand.

GREEN PAPAYA SALAD FOR A CROWD

Som Tum Kann Leng

Serves 16 to 20 as a side dish

Having served this at many pot lucks and picnics, I can attest that it's a real crowd-pleaser.

You can shred the papaya a day in advance and store it in the refrigerator in a large Ziploc bag. Use a blender to mix the dressing. Transport the dressing and the peanuts in their own separate containers. Just before serving, toss the papaya with the dressing and then mix in the peanuts.

3½ pounds green papayas (about 2 large)

14 small Thai chilies (phrik khee nu), finely chopped

16 cloves garlic, roughly chopped

6 tablespoons coconut-palm sugar or golden brown sugar

6 tablespoons Thai fish sauce (*nam pla*)

1 cup fresh lime juice

1½ cups roasted unsalted peanuts, crushed in a mortar or finely chopped

Peel the papayas, cut them in half lengthwise, then scoop out and discard the seeds. Cut the papayas into long, thin shreds, or use a food processor fitted with a shredding disk. You should have about 12 cups. Transfer to a large mixing bowl and set aside.

To make the dressing, put all the remaining ingredients, except the peanuts, in a blender. Blend until the chilies and garlic are finely ground and the sugar is dissolved and blended into the liquid.

Pour the dressing into the bowl of green papaya and mix well. Just before serving, mix in the crushed peanuts.

Transfer the salad to a large serving bowl or platter and serve.

287

Bangkok
Street
Cooking

GREEN MANGO SALAD, CHIANG MAI STYLE

Som Tum Mamuang

Serves 6

This northern salad features the tart fruitiness of green mangoes. When unripe, mangoes taste slightly more like a vegetable, but with a definite hint of the mature fruit's flavor. That sweet-tartness is great alongside grilled meats and sticky rice.

½ cup large dried shrimp (*kung haeng*)

2½ pounds green mangoes (about 5 medium)

16 cloves garlic

8 medium serrano chilies, sliced

4 small tomatoes, cut in half and sliced into thin wedges

½ cup fresh lemon juice

4 tablespoons Thai fish sauce (*nam pla*)

5 tablespoons coconut-palm sugar or golden brown sugar

½ cup roasted unsalted peanuts, crushed in a mortar or finely chopped

Put the dried shrimp in a small bowl of water to cover. Soak for 15 minutes.

Meanwhile, julienne the green mangoes: Slice the stem end off a mango. With a sharp knife, score the skin lengthwise into quarters, first on one side then the other. Pull the skin off, using the scored sections as a guide. Hold the peeled mango in the palm of one hand, exposing half the fruit, and make a series of quick parallel cuts, slicing into the flesh almost to the seed. When the surface is fully scored, slice crosswise to release the fruit, creating julienne strips. Repeat, scoring the mango down to the seed and slicing off the remaining fruit. Turn the mango over and repeat the tap-cut technique to julienne the rest of the fruit. Julienne the remaining mangoes in the same manner. When all the mangoes are julienned, you should have about 4 cups. Put the sliced mango in a mixing bowl and set aside.

Drain the dried shrimp and put them in a large, heavy mortar. Add the garlic and chilies and pound them to bits. Transfer them to the bowl of sliced mango. Put the tomato wedges in the mortar and lightly crush them with the pestle. Add a few handfuls of sliced mango and mix with your hands so the tomato juices get absorbed by the mango. Transfer the mixture back to the mixing bowl.

To make the dressing, put the lemon juice, fish sauce, and sugar in a blender, or mix them by hand with a wooden spoon. The sugar should be completely dissolved and blended into the liquid.

Pour the dressing into the bowl of salad and mix well. Mix in the crushed peanuts.

Transfer to a serving platter and serve.

CHIANG MAI NOODLE CURRY

Khao Soi

Serves 8 to 10

Khao soi may have originated in the Shan states of nearby Burma. It is a very showy and even grand dish that's a favorite lunch in Chiang Mai and other northern towns. Whether you buy it on the street or in an upscale restaurant, it's always served with a wonderful range of condiments.

Khao soi has its own curry paste, full of the citrus tang of Kaffir lime leaves, plus fragrant star anise, turmeric, and curry powder. It's a dish that requires some time to prepare. Though it's well worth the effort, you'll certainly appreciate what a resource we enjoy in having vendors throughout Thailand who make this complex, wonderful dish.

continued

KHAO SOI CURRY PASTE

1 package (3 ounces) dried red California chili

1 teaspoon shrimp paste (*kapi*), neatly wrapped in a double layer of aluminum foil

4 whole star anise

½ teaspoon ground turmeric

1 teaspoon curry powder

1½ tablespoons minced fresh Kaffir lime peel or domestic lime peel

2 stalks lemon grass, tough outer leaves discarded, lower stalks trimmed to 3 inches and finely sliced

2 tablespoons chopped garlic

1 can (14 ounces) unsweetened coconut milk

CURRIED NOODLES

6 cups water

1 pound boneless stew beef, cut into 1-inch cubes

1 can (14 ounces) unsweetened coconut milk

7 tablespoons sugar

4 tablespoons Thai fish sauce (*nam pla*)

1½ pounds fresh Chinese-style egg noodles (*ba mee*)

Vegetable or peanut oil for frying

CONDIMENTS

Thai chili powder (*phrik pon*) or other ground red chili to taste, such as New Mexico chili powder or cayenne

Fried Garlic Chips (page 66)

1 large red onion, chopped

¾ cup chopped pickled Chinese mustard (*hua pak kad dong*)

Lime wedges

To make the curry paste: With kitchen shears or a chef's knife, stem the chilies and shake out most of the seeds. Cut the chilies in half lengthwise and remove any tough, dried ribs. Cut them crosswise into ¾-inch pieces and put them in a bowl. Add water to cover and soak for 30 minutes.

Meanwhile, set a small skillet over medium heat. Place the foil-wrapped shrimp paste in the skillet and roast it for about 5 minutes, until aromatic, turning the packet once or twice. Remove the packet from the skillet and set it aside to cool.

Put the star anise in a large heavy mortar and grind to a powder. Transfer the ground star anise to the bowl of a food processor fitted with a metal blade. Add the turmeric and curry powder.

Combine the minced lime peel and lemon grass in the mortar and pound for a minute or so to break down the fibers. Transfer the crushed mixture to the food processor.

Pound the garlic in the mortar just until crushed and transfer it to the food processor.

Unwrap the shrimp paste and add it to the food processor.

Drain the chilies and add them to the food processor. Add the coconut milk.

Process the ingredients until a smooth, sauce-like paste forms, stopping occasionally to scrape down the sides of the work bowl.

Transfer the paste to an airtight container and store it in the refrigerator (up to 24 hours) or freezer until ready to use.

To make the noodle curry: Bring the water to a boil in a medium saucepan. Add the beef and boil gently for 10 to 15 minutes. With a wire skimmer or slotted spoon, remove the beef to a small bowl and set it aside. Reserve the beef broth.

Skim the thick cream from the top of the canned coconut milk into a soup pot, reserving the milk. Set the pot over medium-high heat. Stir in the reserved *khao soi* curry paste until blended, and bring to a low boil. Cook, stirring constantly, for 2 minutes. Add the stewed beef and stir-fry to coat it evenly with the curry. Add the reserved coconut milk, reserved beef broth, sugar, and fish sauce. Bring the mixture to a boil. Lower the heat, cover, and simmer while you prepare the noodles.

Separate the egg noodles into ½-pound and 1-pound portions.

Pour the oil into a large wok or deep, heavy saucepan to a depth of 3 inches. Set over medium heat until the oil is sizzling hot, about 360°F. (To test the oil temperature, drop in a couple of strands of noodles; if they sizzle and immediately begin to puff and crisp, the oil is ready.) Add a handful of the egg noodles to the hot oil. When puffed and crisped on one side, turn them to fry on the other side, about 8 to 10 seconds total. Transfer the fried noodles to a bowl lined with paper towels and drain them well. Continue frying the noodles in batches until the ½-pound of egg noodles is all cooked. Set aside.

Bring a large pot of water to a boil and cook the remaining 1-pound batch of egg noodles until tender, about 4 to 6 minutes. Drain, then run under cold water to stop the cooking, and drain again.

Place a handful of cooked noodles into eight to ten large individual serving bowls. Ladle some beef curry into each bowl and top with handfuls of the crunchy fried noodles.

Serve at once with the full array of condiments.

FISH MAW SOUP WITH BLACK MUSHROOMS AND BAMBOO SHOOTS

Ka Pohpa Kap Khai Nok Ka Ta

Serves 4 to 6

F or the adventurous, this is an example of Thai soul food. What is called the "maw" is actually the fish's swim bladder, an inflatable organ for adapting to changes in pressure at different depths in the ocean. After being removed and cleaned, the maw is deep-fried, which expands the walls of the organ and makes them crunchy. When you put a presoaked maw into a soup or sauce, it absorbs the flavors like a sponge.

The texture might be an acquired taste, but it's certainly one of my favorites. While many Thai soups feature clear broths, fish maw soup is typically thicker, more like a gravy, which makes it more homey.

1 tablespoon vegetable oil

5 cloves garlic, pounded to a mash or crushed and chopped

4 cups Chicken Stock (page 72) or canned chicken broth

1 tablespoon golden-brown sugar

½ tablespoon Thai fish sauce (*nam pla*)

½ tablespoon Thai soy sauce with mushroom (*see-eu khao het hom*) or a Chinese brand, such as Pearl River Bridge

1 package (2 ounces) fried fish maw, soaked in hot water until soft

6 to 8 quail eggs, hard-boiled and peeled (optional)

½ cup bamboo-shoot strips

3 fresh shiitake mushrooms or canned Chinese black mushrooms, cut crosswise into ¼-inch slices

½ tablespoon white pepper plus more for the table

¼ cup quick-mixing flour, dissolved in ¾ cup water

2 scallions, including the green tops, finely sliced

Sprigs of cilantro

Chilies-in-Vinegar Sauce (page 52)

Pour the oil into a soup pot and set the pot over medium-high heat. When the oil is hot, add the garlic and stir-fry briefly, just until golden and aromatic. Add the chicken stock, cover, and bring to a low boil. Stir in the sugar, fish sauce, and soy sauce and let simmer, uncovered.

Drain the fish maw, rinse it under cold water, and drain again. Chop into 1-inch pieces and add to the soup. Add the quail eggs and the bamboo shoots. Stir and return to a low boil. Add the mushrooms and white pepper. Stir in the flour-water mixture. Bring the soup to a boil, then turn off the heat.

Ladle the soup into individual serving bowls. Top each serving with some scallions and torn sprigs of cilantro.

Serve at once with some ground white pepper and Chilies-in-Vinegar Sauce, and season to taste.

PINK SOUP NOODLES WITH SEAFOOD

Yen Ta Fo

Serves 8 to 10

———

This is another example of a street dish that's surprisingly sophisticated. Vendors who specialize in *yen ta fo* try to distinguish themselves by the quality and variety of their condiments.

The unusual hue of this soup comes from pickled red bean curd. My version of *yen ta fo* uses rice-stick noodles, but any kind of cooked noodles will work.

The seafood is a mélange of homemade fish dumplings (called "fish balls"), fresh shrimp, and dried, reconstituted squid, which we prize for its chewy yet tender texture. You could, of course, substitute fresh squid or another type of seafood.

You'll see ready-made sauces for this soup on the shelves of Asian markets, but avoid them. They'll never compare to this nicely balanced homemade sauce based on the pungent pickled red bean curd, rice vinegar, and garlic.

6 ounces fish fillets (any mild white-fleshed variety, such as catfish, cod, red snapper, or flounder)

1 jar (8 ounces) pickled red bean curd

1⅓ cups rice vinegar

26 cloves garlic, pounded to a mash or crushed and chopped

8 cups Chicken Stock (page 72) or canned chicken broth

1 cup water

2 cups sugar

½ pound water spinach (*pak bung*) or common spinach

¼ pound medium shrimp, cleaned and peeled

6 ounces dried, reconstituted squid, sliced crosswise into bite-size strips, or fresh squid, cleaned and sliced

8 ounces dried rice-stick noodles

4 ounces deep-fried tofu (in cake form), diced

3 scallions, including the green tops, finely sliced

Golden Garlic (page 65)

Chilies-in-Vinegar Sauce (page 52), Thai chili powder (*phrik pon*), or other ground red chili to taste, such as New Mexico chili powder or cayenne

3 tablespoons roasted unsalted peanuts, crushed in a mortar or finely chopped

Chop the fish into 1-inch pieces. Put the fish in the bowl of a food processor fitted with a metal blade. Process to a smooth paste, stopping once or twice to scrape down the sides of the work bowl. Transfer the fish paste to a small bowl and set aside.

Combine the red bean curd with its sauce, rice vinegar, and garlic in a blender. Process until smooth. Transfer the red sauce to a soup pot. Add the chicken stock, water, and sugar and set the pot over medium-high heat. Stir well to blend and bring the soup to a boil. Lower the heat and simmer gently while you prepare the water spinach, seafood, and rice sticks.

Trim off all but the top third of the long stems from the water spinach. Chop the spinach into 2½- to 3-inch lengths. Set aside.

Bring a large saucepan of water to a boil. Place the water spinach, shrimp, reserved fish paste, squid, and rice-stick noodles within easy reach of the cooking area. Fill a bowl with ice water and have it standing by to collect the cooked fish balls so they stop cooking and become firm. Set out a few more empty bowls to collect the cooked water spinach and seafood.

Blanch the water spinach in the boiling water until bright green, about 20 to 30 seconds. Lift out with a wire skimmer or slotted spoon, shaking and holding the spinach over the pot to drain, then set aside. Add the shrimp to the boiling water and cook just until they begin to turn pink but are not fully cooked, about 30 to 40 seconds. Lift them out to drain and set aside. Cook the squid in the boiling water for 1 minute. Lift out to drain and set aside.

Drop teaspoonfuls of the fish paste one by one into the boiling water. They will cook quickly (in less than a minute) and float to the surface. Lift them out with a wire skimmer or slotted spoon and quickly place them in the ice water. After the last ones go into the ice water, drain and set aside.

Cook the rice-stick noodles in the boiling water until tender, about 1½ minutes. Drain in a colander, rinse under cold water, and drain again.

Put servings of noodles, water spinach, fish balls, squid, and shrimp into large individual serving bowls. Top with some fried tofu and scallions. Ladle some of the hot soup into each bowl, and serve at once with the Golden Garlic, chili sauce or chili powder, and crushed peanuts.

CHICKEN AND RICE WITH GINGER SAUCE AND THAI BROTH

Khao Man Ok Kai

Serves 4 to 6

This is an intoxicatingly flavorful one-dish meal that's so popular in Thailand, many cafés specialize in it. For some reason, however, it is practically never found in Thai restaurants in America. That's too bad, because it's one of the most sure-to-please Thai dishes.

Khao man ok kai is eaten both at lunch and dinner. It's typically made with a whole chicken; I prefer using only chicken breasts.

The thick Ginger Sauce is heady, aromatic, and peppery—just the right balance of flavors. Slices of poached chicken, laid atop a mound of glistening stock-cooked rice, are bathed in the fragrant sauce. Cucumber slices act as a crisp, cooling counterpoint to the vivid flavors. A special Thai Broth set alongside for sipping is the final accompaniment. It's an elegant-looking presentation, even though the dish is quite easy to prepare.

For a special touch, carve the cucumbers into pinwheels.

GINGER SAUCE

1 cup peeled, finely sliced rounds of baby ginger or mature ginger (6 to 8 ounces)

¼ cup sweet black soy sauce (*see-eu wan*)

½ cup whole yellow bean sauce (*tao jiew khao*)

½ cup distilled white vinegar

2½ tablespoons sugar

1 tablespoon Chinese-style chili-garlic sauce, preferably Lee Kum Kee brand

2 tablespoons sliced Pickled Garlic (page 64) or commercially made pickled garlic (about 1½ small bulbs)

CHICKEN AND RICE

3½ pounds chicken breast (with skin and bones), split

6 cups water

2½ cups (1 pound) jasmine rice (*khao hom mali*) or other long-grain white rice

THAI BROTH

6 cups Chicken Stock (page 72)

2 tablespoons shredded salted radish (*hua pak kad khem*)

2 scallions, including the green tops, finely sliced

CONDIMENTS

2 small pickling cucumbers, peeled and
    cut crosswise into very thin slices, or
    carved into Cucumber Pinwheels
    (page 389)

Ground white pepper

Sprigs of cilantro

Stack ¼ cup of the sliced ginger and julienne. Reserve the julienned ginger until serving time.

Combine the remaining ¾ cup sliced ginger and the remaining Ginger Sauce ingredients in a blender. Blend to a liquid purée; set aside.

Put the chicken breasts and water in a soup pot. Bring to a boil over medium-high heat. Skim off any froth that collects on the surface. Reduce the heat and simmer, uncovered, until tender, about 15 to 20 minutes. When the chicken is done, transfer it to a platter and set aside.

Measure out 3½ cups of stock from the pot and pour it into a heavy-bottomed saucepan. (Any leftover stock can be chilled, then defatted and used another time.) Add the rice and bring to a rolling boil over medium-high heat. Cover tightly and reduce the heat to its lowest setting. Simmer for 18 minutes. Lift the lid to check for doneness; cook 1 or 2 minutes longer if necessary. (The rice is done when all the stock has been absorbed and the grains are soft enough to crush between your thumb and forefinger.) Turn off the heat, keep the rice covered, and let it stand, undisturbed, for 15 minutes.

Meanwhile, remove the skin and bones from the chicken. Cut the meat at a 45-degree angle to make flat 2 by 1-inch slices.

Heat the 6 cups of ready-made chicken stock in a large saucepan set over medium heat. Add the salted radish and bring to a boil. Sprinkle the broth with the scallions and remove the pan from the heat.

Mound the cooked rice on a large serving platter. Arrange the chicken slices on top. Garnish the platter with the cucumber slices at one end and the reserved julienned ginger at the other. Ladle some Ginger Sauce over the chicken and rice. Sprinkle some white pepper on top and tear a few sprigs of cilantro over the dish.

Serve at once with individual serving bowls of the broth to sip between bites.

BARBECUED CHICKEN, BANGKOK STYLE

Kai Yang Bangkok

Serves 4 to 6

From midday until late at night, in every city and town the length of Thailand, a person out for a walk will find large outdoor stalls where butterflied chickens cook on blackened steel grates, clamped securely between thin slats of bamboo, giving off light and fragrant smoke as they barbecue. The birds are drenched in special marinades, which vary from region to region, and they're served with spiced dipping sauces. They're one of the meatiest, most satisfying treats that Thailand's street cuisine has to offer. All Thai cooks have a number of favorite recipes for barbecued chicken.

I've pared my personal list down to three, representing key regions and different styles. Bangkok style features a creamy/saucy marinade. A liquid marinade flavors the Chiang Mai version. Issan style is based on a pungent seasoning paste.

Thai chickens are much smaller than those sold in American markets. We normally split two of these small chickens in half before marinating and grilling them. To approximate this, these recipes call for two frying chickens. You could use one large roasting hen, but by grilling two smaller chickens, you get double the pieces for your guests. Apart from their varying seasonings, all the barbecued chicken recipes are similarly grilled, and all are served with Sweet-and-Spicy Dipping Sauce.

2 frying chickens (about 3½ pounds each), split in half

I can (14 ounces) unsweetened coconut milk

2 tablespoons Yellow Curry Paste (page 30), or I tablespoon curry powder

2 tablespoons Thai fish sauce (*nam pla*)

6 cloves garlic, roughly chopped

⅓ cup loosely packed chopped cilantro, including the stems

2½ tablespoons golden brown sugar

½ tablespoon white pepper

Sweet-and-Spicy Dipping Sauce (page 54)

Place the chicken halves, skin-side up, in a shallow roasting pan. Lightly score the chicken to allow the marinade to penetrate. Set aside.

Combine the coconut milk, curry paste, fish sauce, garlic, cilantro, sugar, and pepper in a blender. Blend until smooth.

Pour the marinade over the chicken halves, then turn them skin-side down. Spoon some of the marinade into the cavities. Marinate in the refrigerator for at least 3 hours, or up to 24 hours, turning occasionally to coat each half.

Grill or roast the chicken:

Grilling method: Build a hot charcoal fire or preheat a gas grill. Arrange the chicken halves on the grill and cook for about 30 minutes, or until the juices run clear when you pierce the leg joint with a fork. Turn the chicken now and then and baste frequently with the marinade.

Roasting method: Roast the chicken, meat-side up, in a 425°F oven for about 40 minutes, or until the juices run clear when you pierce the leg joint with a fork. Baste once or twice during the roasting. When the chicken is done, place it under the broiler for a few minutes to crisp the skin and give it a bit of char.

Transfer the chicken to a cutting board and chop into serving pieces with a Chinese cleaver or heavy chef's knife. Each chicken half can yield five pieces: one drumstick, wing, and thigh, and two pieces of breast meat, made by chopping the single breast in half lengthwise.

Arrange the chicken pieces on a large serving platter and serve hot, warm, or at room temperature with the dipping sauce.

BARBECUED CHICKEN, CHIANG MAI STYLE

Kai Yang Chiang Mai

Serves 4 to 6

C hiang Mai chicken is flavored with a peppery citrus marinade made from fresh oranges, black peppercorns, and lots of garlic. A bottle of beer gives additional flavor and makes the marinade quite liquid.

2 frying chickens (about 3½ pounds each), split in half	½ tablespoon salt
1 small bunch cilantro	1 bottle (12 ounces) beer, allowed to go flat
1 large orange	Sweet-and-Spicy Dipping Sauce (page 54)
3½ tablespoons roughly chopped garlic	
2 tablespoons whole black peppercorns, ground	

Place the chicken halves, skin-side up, in a shallow roasting pan. Lightly score the chicken to allow the marinade to penetrate. Set aside.

Chop the cilantro stems and reserve the leaves for another use. You should have about ¾ cup loosely packed chopped stems. Trim off the ends of the orange and discard. Cut the orange into ½-inch slices and remove any seeds. Stack and cut the slices into small cubes. You should have about ¾ cup. Combine the cilantro stems, orange cubes, garlic, pepper, and salt in the bowl of a food processor fitted with a metal blade. Process until the mixture is ground to a rough-textured paste. With the motor running, pour the beer through the feed tube. Process until the mixture is well blended.

Pour the marinade over the chicken halves, then turn them skin-side down. Spoon some of the marinade into the cavities. Marinate in the refrigerator for at least 3 hours, or up to 24 hours, turning occasionally to coat each half well.

Grill or roast the chicken:

Grilling method: Build a hot charcoal fire or preheat a gas grill. Arrange the chicken halves on the grill and cook for about 30 minutes, or until the juices run clear when you pierce the leg joint with a fork. Turn the chicken now and then and baste frequently with the marinade.

Roasting method: Roast the chicken, meat side up, in a 425°F oven for about 40 minutes, or until the juices run clear when you pierce the leg joint with a fork. Baste once or twice during the roasting. When the chicken is done, place it under a broiler for a few minutes to crisp the skin and give it a bit of char.

Transfer the chicken to a cutting board and chop into serving pieces with a Chinese cleaver or heavy chef's knife. Each chicken half can yield five pieces: one drumstick, wing, and thigh, and two pieces of breast meat, made by chopping the single breast in half lengthwise.

Arrange the chicken on a large serving platter and serve hot, warm, or at room temperature with the dipping sauce.

BARBECUED CHICKEN, ISSAN STYLE

Kai Yang Issan

Serves 4 to 6

F or Issan-style barbecued chicken, the marinade ingredients—which include fresh ginger, garlic, cilantro, and black pepper—are pulverized, creating a seasoning paste that is spread over the chickens.

2 frying chickens (about 3½ pounds each), split in half

1 cup loosely packed cilantro, including the stems

3 tablespoons coarsely chopped garlic

1½ tablespoons whole black peppercorns, ground

2 tablespoons plus 1 teaspoon minced, peeled fresh ginger

2 tablespoons coconut-palm sugar or golden brown sugar

2 tablespoons vegetable or peanut oil

Sweet-and-Spicy Dipping Sauce (page 54)

Place the chicken halves, skin side up, in a shallow roasting pan. Lightly score the chicken to allow the marinade to penetrate. Set aside.

Combine the cilantro, garlic, pepper, ginger, sugar, and oil in the bowl of a food processor fitted with a metal blade. Process until the mixture is puréed.

Spread the marinade over the chicken halves, then turn them skin-side down. Spoon some of the marinade into the cavities. Marinate in the refrigerator for at least 3 hours, or up to 24 hours, turning occasionally to coat each half well.

Grill or roast the chicken:

Grilling method: Build a hot charcoal fire or preheat a gas grill. Arrange the chicken halves on the grill and cook for about 30 minutes, or until the juices run clear when you pierce the leg joint with a fork. Turn the chicken now and then to cook evenly.

Roasting method: Roast the chicken, meat-side up, in a 425°F oven for about 40 minutes, or until the juices run clear when you pierce the leg joint with a fork. Baste once or twice with the pan drippings.

When the chicken is done, transfer it to a cutting board and chop it into serving pieces with a Chinese cleaver or heavy chef's knife. Each chicken half can yield five pieces: one drumstick, wing, and thigh, and two pieces of breast meat, made by chopping the single breast in half lengthwise.

Arrange the chicken on a large serving platter and serve hot, warm, or at room temperature with the dipping sauce.

MOM'S BANANA FRITTERS WITH COCONUT AND SESAME

Kluay Kaeg Tod

Makes 24 fritters

M y mother has made and sold these delicate banana fritters for many years. They're a great favorite, as a between-meal snack or dessert. I think the neighborhood will be crushed if she ever retires.

Though they can be made in advance, they're best when served warm. The coconut should be very finely grated, almost minced and powdery. A food processor with a metal blade does the job quickly and neatly.

I cup rice flour

⅓ cup all-purpose flour

1⅓ cups finely grated fresh coconut or dried shredded coconut, preferably unsweetened

3 tablespoons sesame seeds

I teaspoon baking powder

I cup water

Vegetable oil for deep-frying

6 medium bananas (about 2¼ pounds), ripe but firm

Confectioners' sugar (optional)

Combine the flours, coconut, sesame seeds, and baking powder in a mixing bowl. Stir until mixed, then whisk in the water until blended. Let the batter stand for 5 minutes.

Pour the oil into a wok or heavy saucepan to a depth of 1¾ inches. Heat the oil to 375°F over medium heat. Meanwhile, peel the bananas, cut each one in half crosswise, then slice each half lengthwise to make four pieces.

Dip each piece of banana into the batter and coat evenly. Deep-fry the bananas, a few pieces at a time, until they are golden brown and crispy, about 2 to 3 minutes. Turn the bananas occasionally to cook and brown them evenly. Remove with a wire skimmer or slotted spoon and drain on paper towels. When the bananas are all cooked, sprinkle some drops of the batter with your fingertips into the hot oil. Fry until golden brown and drain on paper towels.

Transfer the banana fritters to a serving platter. Sprinkle the golden crisps of fried batter over the fritters, dust with confectioners' sugar, if desired, and serve immediately.

ROYAL THAI CUISINE

Khong Saweoy

We Thai people hold our royal family in an esteem that can only
be called adoration. This has been true down through the
ages, but especially during the last two centuries, while the Rama dynasty
has occupied Thailand's royal palace. Of all the countries in Southeast
Asia, ours is the only one that never became a foreign nation's colony—

thanks to the cleverness and strength of our kings throughout the peak years of European imperialism.

The current royal couple, King Bhumibol Adulyadej (Rama IX) and Queen Sirikit, are just as well loved as any of their predecessors. He rose to the throne at the age of nineteen and has reigned since 1946, longer than any other living monarch on earth. They're a great example of a monarchy that is a gift to the people. They've secured their place in the popular heart through exceptional devotion to public service—traveling to the most remote villages and initiating land reforms, rural water projects, and many other forms of economic development.

One example of the king's work is *pla nin*, a freshwater fish he introduced to our waterways almost thirty years ago. It has become an important source of protein, especially for people living in the interior of the country, and everyone calls it "the king's fish."

Combine this love of royalty with the natural Thai inclination to love every aspect of cooking, and you understand why the food prepared for royal feasts is especially fascinating. In fact, in the early 1800s, King Rama II wrote whole cycles of poetry about Thai food, and those poems are still cherished today.

Anyone who can cook simple Thai food can also cook the royal dishes. Some are actually quite simple to prepare—such as Curried Mussels with Sweet Pineapple and Thai Basil, Stir-Fried Chicken with Sweet-and-Savory Coconut Cream, and Royal Thai Crab Cakes with Piquant Dipping Sauce. Others are more labor-intensive, perhaps best prepared with help by your side, yet are still within any good cook's scope. These include Royal Ladies' Lunch and King Rama V's Fried Rice.

Royal Thai cuisine may have originated as an ancient tradition that was practiced when our kings had many wives. Every New Year, a culinary competition would take place. Each wife had her own kitchen and apartments in the palace, and each set out to invent the most lavish and irresistible dish of the year. The royal awards ranged from fine clothing to large tracts of land.

From that tradition, and from kingly challenges issued down through the years to the best chefs, royal Thai cuisine emerged. Its hallmarks are subtle layering of flavors, contrasting textures, and beautiful appearance.

Royal Thai Crab Cakes with Piquant Dipping Sauce is an example. The crabmeat is blended with fluffy cooked rice instead of bread crumbs, resulting in a crab cake that's exceptionally fine, light, and moist.

I hope that your knowing something of regal Thai traditions will add to your enjoyment of these recipes. Hundreds of years went into developing these time-honored classics. I'm proud to interpret them for modern cooks.

CURRIED PUMPKIN-COCONUT SOUP WITH THAI BASIL

Kaeng Liang Fak Thong

Serves 4 to 6

This tasty soup, rather like an exotic and delicate shrimp bisque, is an example of "new royal cuisine." The curry paste, *kaeng liang*, is of ancient origin, but the recipe for the soup is a more recent invention. It's the kind of dish you'll find served in the houses of Bangkok's noble families.

Kaeng liang balances the light muskiness of dried shrimp with the dry spiciness of white peppercorns and the herbal notes of fresh green chilies, shallots, and garlic.

¾ cup large dried shrimp (*kung haeng*)

I pound kabocha (see Note)

½ cup Liang Curry Paste (page 44)

I can (19 ounces) unsweetened coconut milk

1¾ cups Chicken Stock (page 72) or canned chicken broth

¾ cup loosely packed Thai lemon basil (*bai mangluk*) or the more commonly available Thai basil (*bai horapha*) or Italian basil

4 small Thai chilies (*phrik khee nu*), or 2 serrano chilies, lightly crushed (optional)

Soak the dried shrimp in cold water to cover for about 10 minutes while you prepare the kabocha.

Scoop out and discard the seeds and fibers from the piece of kabocha. With a sharp heavy knife or cleaver, chop it into quarters. Cut off most of the peel and slice the flesh into thin, bite-size pieces. You should have about 3 cups. Set aside.

Drain the dried shrimp. Grind the shrimp and curry paste together in a large mortar or blend in a food processor to a fine, smooth paste. If using a food processor, you can add a few tablespoons of water to ease the grinding. Small, coarse bits of the shrimp are all right in an otherwise smooth paste. Set aside.

Put the kabocha and coconut milk in a soup pot and set the pot over medium-high heat. Bring the mixture to a boil, stirring occasionally. Cook at a gentle boil, just until the kabocha is cooked through, about 5 to 6 minutes. Stir in the curry paste mixture. Add the chicken stock and stir well to blend. Lower the heat and simmer for 3 to 4 minutes, stirring occasionally.

Turn off the heat. Stir in the basil and cook for a few seconds, just until the basil begins to wilt.

continued

Float the chilies on top, if desired, and ladle the soup into a steamboat, a soup tureen, or individual serving bowls.

N O T E :   You need a 1-pound piece of kabocha for this recipe. Most Asian markets sell kabocha whole and by the piece. If your market sells only whole kabocha, buy a small one and reserve the rest for a stir-fry or dessert. You may also substitute butternut or acorn squash.

The crushed chilies give the soup a spicy edge. Eating them is optional.

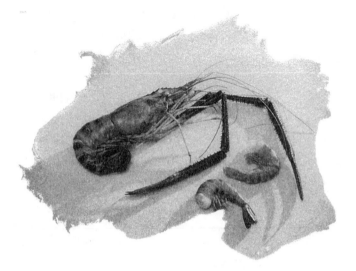

PINK POMELO AND GRILLED SHRIMP SALAD

Yam Som-O

Serves 4 to 6

Pomelo, which originated in Thailand, is the ancestor of grapefruit. It tastes so much sweeter and more pleasant than grapefruit, however, you'll wonder why it hasn't become more available in America.

The pink-fleshed variety of pomelo looks especially pretty in contrast with the coral color of the shrimp, but the paler-colored fruits will be just as delicious. If you have to substitute pink grapefruit, increase the sugar in the dressing by ½ tablespoon or so.

This is a very sophisticated salad, found only in the finest restaurants, where it's sometimes served in a hollowed-out pomelo half intricately carved with a flower pattern.

SALAD

1 large pomelo (about 1½ pounds)

½ pound medium shrimp, in the shell

6 to 8 long (12-inch) bamboo skewers, soaked in a tray of cold water for at least ½ hour

Half a medium cucumber

1 small tomato, cut in half and sliced into thin wedges

1 cup loosely packed fresh mint

⅓ cup roasted unsalted peanuts, crushed in a mortar or finely chopped

3 tablespoons shrimp powder with chili (*kung phrik pon*)

DRESSING

3 tablespoons fresh lime juice

1 teaspoon salt

½ teaspoon white pepper

2 tablespoons plus 1 teaspoon coconut-palm sugar or golden brown sugar

TOPPINGS

Fried Garlic Chips (page 66)

Crispy Shallots (page 67)

Sprigs of cilantro

Cut off the ends of the pomelo. With a sharp knife, score the skin lengthwise into eighths. Pull off the rind with all the pith, using the scored sections as a guide. Separate the fruit into segments and completely remove the tough, thin membrane enclosing each one: Snip the membrane with a pair of kitchen shears and peel it away from the juice sac. It's an easy job because the sacs are firm, neat bundles that easily roll out intact. Break the fruit into bite-size pieces and remove any seeds. Put the pomelo in a large bowl and set aside.

Build a medium-hot charcoal fire or preheat a gas grill or a broiler. Meanwhile, thread the unshelled shrimp onto the soaked bamboo skewers, about four or five shrimp per skewer. Grill or broil the shrimp, turning once or twice, just until they turn pink, about 3 to 4 minutes total. Remove the shrimp from the skewers, peel, and add them to the bowl with the pomelo.

Peel the cucumber half. Slice it in half lengthwise and scoop out the seeds with a spoon. Cut the halves crosswise into thin slices and add them to the bowl. Add the remaining salad ingredients to the bowl and toss gently to mix. Set aside.

Combine the dressing ingredients in a blender and blend until smooth and liquid. Pour the dressing over the salad and toss until well mixed.

Transfer the salad to a large serving bowl or platter and sprinkle the Fried Garlic Chips and Crispy Shallots on top. Tear sprigs of cilantro over the salad and serve.

GOLDEN MONEY BAGS

Tung Thong

Makes 32 "money bags"

When I was a college student, my greatest indulgence was an occasional exploration, with friends, of some of Bangkok's more elegant restaurants. After these sojourns, I would return home and experiment, trying to duplicate whatever I had discovered at those sophisticated tables.

This recipe, one of the ones I strove to copy, originated more than a century and a half ago, during the reign of King Rama IV. It is an elegant and sensual finger food: wrappers made of dried bean-curd skin enclosing a filling of minced pork and shrimp, tied with scallion tops, deep-fried until light and crispy, and served with one or more dipping sauces.

8 to 12 scallions

1 pound boneless pork tenderloin, trimmed of fat and cut into 1-inch cubes

½ pound medium shrimp, peeled and roughly chopped

12 cloves garlic, roughly chopped

1 tablespoon coarsely ground black pepper

4 tablespoons Thai soy sauce with mushroom (*see-eu khao het hom*) or a Chinese brand, such as Pearl River Bridge

2 packages (1.5 ounces each) bean-curd skins

Vegetable or peanut oil for frying

Sweet-and-Spicy Dipping Sauce (page 54) and/or Vietnamese-Style Plum Sauce (page 58)

Select two of the fattest scallions from the bunch. Finely slice them, including the green tops. Reserve the sliced scallions for the filling and set aside. Cut the tops off the remaining scallions for use as ties. (Reserve the bulbs for another dish.) Bring a saucepan of water to a boil. Plunge the green tops into the boiling water until limp, then refresh them in cold water. Drain them on paper towels. Hold up a scallion top and tear or cut it lengthwise into four or more slender strands. Continue tearing the tops into strands until you've used all the tops. Set aside.

Combine the pork, shrimp, garlic, pepper, and soy sauce in the bowl of a food processor fitted with a metal blade. (Depending on the size of your food processor, you may need to grind the mixture in two batches.) Process until the mixture is well ground but not smooth; it should have some texture. Transfer the mixture to a large bowl and mix in the reserved sliced scallions.

Place the bowl of filling, the packaged bean-curd skins, and the scallion strands on a clear work space. Have a lightly oiled cookie sheet nearby to hold the money bags.

Soak the bean-curd skins in a large bowl of warm water until soft, about 1 or 2 minutes, then drain immediately.

Carefully unfold the bean-curd sheets, but don't open them up all the way; the goal is to have each sheet folded in half lengthwise, creating a double thickness for wrapping the money bags. Cut the doubled sheets into 4-inch squares. You should have thirty-two double-thick squares.

Place a tablespoon of the filling in the center of a square of bean-curd skin. Gather up the sides and pinch them together around the top to resemble a little drawstring pouch; tie it with a scallion strand. Set the money bag aside on the cookie sheet. Continue making money bags until you've used up all the filling. Space them out on the cookie sheet enough to keep them from touching, so they won't stick together.

Pour the oil into a wok or wide, deep skillet to a depth of 1 inch. Set over medium heat until the oil is sizzling hot, 360 to 375°F. Fry the money bags a few at a time until golden brown and crisp, about 2 minutes, turning once or twice so they cook and brown evenly. Remove with a wire skimmer or slotted spoon and drain on paper towels. Return the oil to its original temperature and fry the rest of the money bags as above.

Place the money bags on a serving platter and serve at once with one or both of the dipping sauces.

GOLDEN EGG NETS
FILLED WITH STIR-FRIED
MINCED CHICKEN

Rum

Makes about 30 golden egg nets

Try these for a buffet, or as an appetizer. A lacy net is formed by lightly drizzling beaten egg across a hot skillet. It's then used to wrap up seasoned, minced chicken into bite-sized bundles, with the savory filling visible between the strands of the net.

9 cloves garlic, roughly chopped

¾ cup loosely packed chopped cilantro, including the stems

½ teaspoon white pepper

¾ pound ground chicken

3 scallions, including the green tops, chopped

I tablespoon Thai fish sauce (*nam pla*)

I tablespoon coconut-palm sugar or golden brown sugar

Vegetable oil or cooking-oil spray

9 eggs, beaten

I small head Pickled Garlic (page 64) or commercially made pickled garlic (optional)

Sweet-and-Spicy Dipping Sauce with Peanuts (page 54), bottled Thai chili sauce (*sriracha*), or any good Mexican or Louisiana-style hot sauce

Combine the garlic, cilantro, pepper, ground chicken, scallions, fish sauce, and sugar in the bowl of a food processor fitted with a metal blade. Process until the mixture forms a fairly smooth paste, stopping occasionally to scrape down the sides of the work bowl.

Set a nonstick wok or 8-inch nonstick skillet over medium-high heat. When the pan is hot, give it a light coating of oil: Drizzle a small amount of oil into the pan, spread it throughout the pan with some rolled-up paper towels, and wipe off any excess. (Or use a spray can of cooking oil.)

Transfer the chicken paste to the hot pan. Raise the heat to high and stir-fry the mixture, pressing it down into the bottom of the pan. Turn the mixture over, press it down into the pan again, and stir-fry until the chicken is cooked through, about 2 minutes. Transfer the mixture to a bowl and set aside.

Wipe the wok or skillet clean and set it over medium-low heat. Give it a light coating of oil, as before. Put a bowl with the beaten eggs nearby, along with a cookie sheet and some waxed paper. Make your first egg net simply to test the heat of the pan and to practice the technique: Dip your fingers and palm into the beaten egg, and wave your hand back and forth across the width of the pan with unhurried, even strokes. The beaten egg will trail off your fingers in fine, liquid threads. Dip your hand back into the eggs, this time trailing the egg at right angles to the first threads, making a crosshatch pattern. Repeat this technique until you have three or four layers that form a fine netting. Cook until the egg is firmly set and light yellow. It should be just cooked through, with no browning. Use a spatula to loosen the net carefully around the edges, then lift it out of the pan and set it aside on the cookie sheet.

Continue making egg nets until you've used up all the beaten eggs. Stop to reoil the pan now and then, if needed, and stack the finished nets on the cookie sheet between layers of waxed paper.

If using pickled garlic, trim away any stem and cut the garlic crosswise into paper-thin slices. Put the sliced garlic in a saucer and set it on a clear work space with the egg nets and the stir-fried chicken.

Place about 1 tablespoon of the chicken mixture in the center of an egg net. (You may use a little more or less, depending on the size of the circle of netting.) Top the filling with a slice of pickled garlic, if desired. Fold the bottom of the net over the filling, turn in the sides, and roll it into a neat bundle. Set the bundle, seam-side down, on a large serving platter. Continue making the bundles until you've used up all the filling.

Serve at room temperature with the dipping sauce or Thai chili sauce.

ROYAL SON-IN-LAW EGGS

Khai Look Koey Saweoy

Serves 8 to 10

In an everyday setting, people would enjoy this dish by putting one of the eggs on a mound of rice, then spooning a simple tamarind sauce over the top.

For this royal version, the sauce is enhanced with minced chicken, and crisp-fried garlic chips and shallots are showered over the eggs. As a result, many flavors balance and dance on your tongue with every bite.

I also like to serve this appetizer-style, cutting the eggs in half and serving the sauce on the side. The pretty, bright-yellow color of the yolks then contrasts with the crispy-golden exterior of the deep-fried eggs.

SAUCE

3 tablespoons vegetable oil

¾ pound ground chicken

1 cup Tamarind Sauce (page 61) or liquid tamarind concentrate

4 tablespoons Chicken Stock (page 72) or canned chicken broth

7 tablespoons golden brown sugar

2 tablespoons Thai fish sauce (*nam pla*)

1 scallion, including the green top, finely sliced

EGGS

Vegetable or peanut oil for deep-frying

¼ cup thinly sliced garlic (about 12 cloves)

¾ cup thinly sliced shallots (about 6 or 7)

8 eggs, hard-boiled and shelled

6 small Thai chilies (*phrik khee nu*), finely sliced

Sprigs of cilantro

To make the sauce: Set a wok over medium-high heat. When it is quite hot, add the oil. Rotate the wok a bit so the oil coats the sides. When the oil is hot, add the ground chicken and press it down into the bottom of the wok. Turn the chicken over, press it down into the wok again, and stir-fry until the chicken begins to brown, about 1 minute. Add the tamarind sauce and stir-fry for 1 minute. Add the chicken stock and sugar and stir-fry for 30 seconds. Add the fish sauce and stir-fry for 1 minute. Stir in the scallion, cover, and remove from the heat.

To fry the eggs: Pour the oil into a wok or deep saucepan to a depth of 1½ inches. Set over medium heat and bring the oil to 360°F. (To test the oil temperature, dip a wooden spoon in the hot oil. The oil should bubble and sizzle gently around the bowl of the spoon.) Add the garlic and cook until it is golden brown, stirring occasionally, about 1 minute. Remove with a wire skimmer or slotted spoon and drain on paper towels.

Add the shallots and fry, stirring frequently, until they are crisp and brown, about 2 minutes. Remove with a wire skimmer or slotted spoon and drain on paper towels.

Return the oil to 360°F. Carefully add two or three eggs, one at a time, to the hot oil. Cook until golden brown and crisp on all sides, about 7 to 8 minutes, turning occasionally to keep them afloat in the hot oil. Remove with a wire skimmer or slotted spoon to a bowl lined with paper towels. Fry the remaining eggs as above.

Place a bowl of the warm chicken-tamarind sauce in the center of a large serving platter. Halve or quarter the eggs lengthwise and arrange them, yolk-sides up, around the bowl of sauce. Sprinkle them with the fried garlic, crispy shallots, and sliced chilies. Tear sprigs of cilantro over the eggs and serve warm or at room temperature.

N O T E : You can make the sauce several hours in advance and keep it covered at room temperature. Warm it over low heat just before serving.

ROYAL THAI CRAB CAKES
WITH PIQUANT DIPPING SAUCE

Khao Tod Neua Pu Talay

Makes about 28 appetizer-size crab cakes

———

R ice, in place of bread crumbs, makes these crab cakes a light, sophisticated beginning to a meal.

Although crabmeat is expensive, a pound makes two dozen or more of these appetizer-sized treats, enough for eight guests. The sweet-and-sour dipping sauce perfectly complements the salty bits of ham found in each crab cake.

SAUCE

½ cup water

½ cup distilled white vinegar

1 cup golden-brown sugar

¾ teaspoon salt

1 large cucumber (about ¾ pound)

1 medium shallot, thinly sliced

6 Thai red pickled chilies (*phrik daeng dong*) or fresh small Thai chilies (*phrik khee nu*), finely sliced

CRAB CAKES

1 pound fresh lump crabmeat

¼ pound Virginia ham, finely diced

2 large eggs, lightly beaten

4 tablespoons all-purpose flour

2 tablespoons sweetened condensed milk

2 cups cold cooked jasmine rice (*khao hom mali*) or any long-grain white rice

1 cup plain dried bread crumbs

Vegetable oil for deep-frying

To make the sauce: Combine the water, vinegar, and sugar in a small saucepan set over medium heat. Bring the mixture to a boil, stirring occasionally. Stir in the salt, return the mixture to a boil, and cook for 2 minutes, stirring occasionally. Reduce the heat and cook at a gentle boil until the sauce begins to reduce and thicken slightly, about 10 to 12 minutes. Remove from the heat and cool to room temperature.

Peel the cucumber and cut it in half lengthwise. Scrape out the seeds with a spoon and cut the halves crosswise into thin slices. Put the cucumber, shallot, and chilies in a small serving bowl. Pour the cooled sauce over them and mix well. Set aside.

To make the crab cakes: In a large mixing bowl, combine the crab, ham, eggs, flour, condensed milk, and rice. Blend with your hands until well mixed. Pour the bread crumbs onto a shallow plate. Take a small handful of the crab mixture and form it into a patty about 2½ inches in diameter. Press each side of the patty into the bread crumbs and coat well. Set the patty aside on a tray or cookie sheet. Continue making patties until you've used up all the crab mixture.

Pour the oil into a wok or a deep, heavy skillet to a depth of 1 inch. Set over medium heat until the oil is sizzling hot, 360 to 375°F. (To test the oil temperature, dip a wooden spoon in the hot oil. The oil should bubble and sizzle gently around the bowl of the spoon.) Fry about three crab cakes at a time until golden brown, about 30 seconds. Remove with a wire skimmer or slotted spoon and drain on a cookie sheet lined with paper towels.

Arrange the crab cakes on a large serving platter and serve at once with the dipping sauce.

NOTE: You can make the crab cake mixture up to a day in advance and keep it covered and refrigerated.

STIR-FRIED CHICKEN WITH SWEET-AND-SAVORY COCONUT CREAM

Phat Kai Kati

Serves 4 to 6

I developed this recipe after reading an interview, in a Thai women's magazine, with an older member of a noble family, in which some great banquets of days gone by were recalled.

This is a stir-fry—not at all a difficult dish to prepare—but the fine balance of flavors results in an elegant taste.

I can (19 ounces) unsweetened coconut milk

I pound boneless, skinless chicken breast, cut into 2 × ¼ × ¼-inch strips

I tablespoon Thai fish sauce (*nam pla*)

I tablespoon crushed yellow bean sauce (*tao jiew dam*)

2 tablespoons sugar

I tablespoon distilled white vinegar

I cup drained, finely cut shreds of pickled ginger (*khing dong*) or fresh peeled ginger, julienned

6 scallions, including the green tops, angle-cut into 1½-inch pieces, bulbs cut in half lengthwise

4 small Thai chilies (*phrik khee nu*), cut lengthwise into fine slivers (optional)

Sprigs of cilantro

Skim the thick cream from the top of the canned coconut milk into a small bowl and reserve.

Pour half of the remaining coconut milk into a medium saucepan. Reserve the rest for another recipe. Warm the coconut milk over high heat. Add the chicken pieces and bring to a low boil. Cook for 1 minute. Remove from the heat and set aside.

Put the reserved coconut cream in a wok and bring to a boil over medium-high heat, stirring occasionally. Lift the chicken pieces from the pan with a wire skimmer or slotted spoon and transfer them to the wok. Add the fish sauce, yellow bean sauce, and sugar, stirring after each addition. Stir in the vinegar and the ginger. Add the scallions and chilies, if desired. Stir-fry just until the scallions are cooked through but crisp-tender, about 30 seconds.

Transfer to a serving platter. Tear sprigs of cilantro over the dish and serve with steamed jasmine rice.

CURRIED MUSSELS WITH SWEET PINEAPPLE AND THAI BASIL

Kaeng Kua Hoy Meng Phu Supparod

Serves 4 to 6

S eldom seen in restaurants or in cookbooks, this is a fabulous, spicy dish with the sweetness of pineapple and basil. My mother made it often.

Because the fresh pineapples found in American markets aren't always as sweet as this dish requires, it's fine to use canned pineapple. Thai lemon basil is preferred here, but any basil will do.

12 large New Zealand mussels, placed in a bowl or sink full of cold water (see Note)

1 can (19 ounces) unsweetened coconut milk

½ cup Kua Curry Paste (page 45)

1 can (20 ounces) crushed pineapple in unsweetened pineapple juice, drained

2 tablespoons coconut-palm sugar or golden brown sugar

3 tablespoons Thai fish sauce (*nam pla*)

2 cups loosely packed Thai lemon basil (*bai mangluk*) or the more commonly available Thai basil (*bai horapha*) or Italian basil

Agitate the water in which the mussels are soaking. Live mussels open and close to breathe. Any mussels that don't eventually close should be discarded. Scrub and debeard the mussels, then drain. Gently pry open the mussels, breaking them apart at the hinge ends. Discard the upper shells, reserving the mussels on their half shells.

Place all of the ingredients within easy reach of the cooking area.

Skim the thick cream from the top of the canned coconut milk into a soup pot, reserving the milk. Set the pot over medium-high heat. Stir in the curry paste until blended and bring to a low boil. Cook, stirring constantly, for 2 minutes. Add the mussels in their half-shells and cook, stirring occasionally, for 30 seconds. Stir in the pineapple. Add the sugar and stir until it's dissolved and blended into the sauce. Stir in the reserved coconut milk and the fish sauce and bring to a boil, stirring occasionally.

Turn off the heat. Stir in the basil and cook for a few seconds, just until the basil begins to wilt.

Transfer to a serving bowl or covered casserole and serve with plenty of steamed jasmine rice.

NOTE: Always buy a few extra mussels, in case one or two have to be discarded.

CRISPY SWEET RICE NOODLES, PALACE STYLE

Mee Krob Saweoy

Serves 6 to 8

*M*ee krob is familiar to anyone who has ever visited a Thai restaurant: crispy noodles that crackle as you bite them, served in a tangy-and-sweet sauce that's studded with shrimp and bits of pork. That's the everyday version. But there's also a tradition of wonderfully elaborate *mee krob*, served palace-style—in a special presentation with a host of condiments and side dishes.

The sweet, sticky sauce lets you present the noodles in a tall cone shape, which looks regal enrobed with a lacy egg net and topped by a chili flower.

For these modern times, I've kept the side dishes down to just one—the delicious and savory Sweet Pork.

⅓ cup honey

⅓ cup distilled white vinegar

11 tablespoons sugar

⅛ teaspoon red food coloring

1 tablespoon Tamarind Sauce (page 61) or liquid tamarind concentrate

4 cups vegetable oil for deep-frying

2 large eggs, lightly beaten

½ pound very thin dried rice-stick noodles (*sen mee*)

⅔ cup small dried shrimp (*kung haeng*)

2 small heads Pickled Garlic (page 64) or commercially made pickled garlic

½ pound bean sprouts

2 small limes, cut into thin wedges

3 or 4 Scallion Brushes (page 389)

1 cut Chili Flower (page 387)

Sweet Pork (page 135)

Combine the honey, vinegar, sugar, food coloring, and tamarind sauce in a wok or medium saucepan. Set over medium-high heat and bring the mixture to a boil, stirring occasionally. Cook the sauce until it thickens, stirring often, about 2 to 3 minutes. Remove from the heat and set aside.

Pour the oil into a large wok or a deep, wide pot set over medium-high heat and bring it to 360°F. (To test the oil temperature, dip a wooden spoon in the hot oil. The oil should bubble and sizzle gently around the bowl of the spoon.)

Put a bowl with the beaten eggs nearby. Dip your fingers and palm into the beaten egg and wave your hand back and forth about 12 inches above the surface of the hot oil with unhurried, even strokes. The beaten egg will trail off your fingers in fine, liquid threads. Dip your hand back into the eggs, this time trailing the egg at right angles to the first threads, making a crosshatch pattern. Repeat this technique until you've used up all the beaten egg.

Cook until the egg net is light golden on the bottom and thoroughly set, about 30 seconds. Carefully turn it over with a wire skimmer and cook until the other side is also light golden, about 30 seconds. Lift the net from the oil and set it aside to drain on paper towels.

Reserve the oil in the wok for frying the noodles.

Gently pull the dried rice-stick noodles apart, breaking them into handfuls. They're brittle and wiry, and little pieces will tend to go flying, so you may want to hold the noodles in a grocery bag while pulling them apart.

Return the oil to 360°F. Place the noodles, and one or two cookie sheets lined with paper towels, within easy reach of the cooking area. Drop a piece of rice-stick noodle into the hot oil to test the temperature. It should drop below the surface, then instantly come back up, puffed up to three or four times its original size.

Drop a handful of the noodles into the hot oil. Turn them with two long-handled slotted spoons or skimmers. In just a matter of seconds, they will puff up and turn a very pale gold. Lift them out and drain them on paper towels.

Repeat this frying technique until all the noodles are cooked.

Fry the dried shrimp in the same hot oil for 30 to 45 seconds. Lift them out with a slotted spoon and place them on paper towels to drain.

Set the pot of honey-tamarind sauce over medium heat. Add the fried shrimp and bring the mixture to a boil, stirring occasionally. Boil for 1½ minutes to thicken the sauce. Remove the pan from the heat.

Place about one fourth of the crispy noodles in a wide, deep bowl. Spoon about one fourth of the sauce over them. Toss them together with two forks, being careful not to crush the noodles. Repeat the above two steps until all the noodles and sauce are thoroughly combined.

Mound the sauced noodles into a tall cone shape on a large serving platter.

Trim away any stem on the pickled garlic and cut the bulb crosswise into thin rounds. Scatter the pickled garlic slices over the noodles. Drape the egg net over the top and arrange the bean sprouts in a ring around the base. Surround the bean sprouts with a circle of lime wedges. Arrange the Scallion Brushes attractively around the mound, curly tops up. Perch the Chili Flower upside down, like a cap, on the top of the noodle mound.

Serve the *mee krob* at room temperature, accompanied by the Sweet Pork.

YELLOW PEPPERS STUFFED
WITH CRAB AND CHICKEN
IN GREEN CURRY

Kaeng Phrik Sod Sai

Serves 4

These are traditionally offered to guests in the royal palace. We make them in Thailand with a pepper known as *phrik yuak*. Very similar peppers can be found here under the names *banana pepper* and *Hungarian wax pepper*.

8 cloves garlic

½ cup loosely packed chopped cilantro, including the stems

1 pound ground chicken

1 pound fresh crabmeat

2 teaspoons white pepper

1 tablespoon granulated sugar

½ pound small (4- to 6-inch-long) yellow chilies (about 12)

1 can (19 ounces) unsweetened coconut milk

¾ cup Fresh Green Chili Curry Paste (page 28)

4 tablespoons Thai fish sauce (*nam pla*)

3 tablespoons golden brown sugar

1 cup loosely packed Thai basil (*bai horapha*) or purple or Italian basil

Prepare a seasoning paste with the garlic and cilantro:

Mortar-and-pestle method: Put the garlic and cilantro in a mortar and pound them to a mash.

Alternate method: Crush the garlic with the side of a chef's knife. Mix the chopped cilantro with the crushed garlic and finely chop.

Combine the seasoning paste, chicken, crab, white pepper, and granulated sugar in a mixing bowl and mix well. Cut the tops off the chilies and reserve. Remove the seeds and ribs from the chilies. Spoon the chicken-crab mixture into the chilies and put the tops back on. Set aside.

Skim the thick cream from the top of the canned coconut milk into a wok or a wide saucepan, reserving the milk. Set the pan over medium-high heat. Stir in the curry paste until blended and bring to a low boil. Cook, stirring constantly, for 2 minutes. Add the reserved coconut milk and cook for 45 seconds, stirring often. Add the fish sauce and sugar and stir until the sugar is dissolved and blended.

Place the stuffed chilies in the simmering sauce and cook until the chilies are tender, about 15 to 20 minutes. Lift them out of the sauce with a slotted spoon and place them on a serving platter.

Remove the sauce from the heat. Stir in the basil and cook for a few seconds, just until the basil begins to wilt. Pour the sauce over the platter of chilies and serve at once with plenty of steamed jasmine rice.

ROYAL LADIES' LUNCH

Khanom Chine Nam Phrik

Serves 6 to 8

There are many *khanom chine* dishes in Thai cuisine—one-dish meals of fine white noodles coiled into nests and topped with a curry sauce. This is the queen of them all.

Its sophistication comes from the elaborate, varied, and abundant selection of condiments. Of course, preparing them requires extra work and rare ingredients, befitting a very special occasion.

The banana blossoms, in Thailand, would be fresh. Here we must use canned blossoms, which vary greatly in quality. You may wish to substitute marinated artichoke hearts, which are less exotic but have an intriguing flavor.

For a royal touch, a pinch of turmeric in the water used to blanch the bean sprouts gives them a pleasing golden color.

continued

CURRIED SHRIMP SAUCE

½ pound medium shrimp, peeled and roughly chopped

1½ cups canned, drained yellow hominy

1 cup Classic Red Curry Paste (page 26)

3 cans (14 ounces each) unsweetened coconut milk

4 tablespoons Thai fish sauce (*nam pla*)

7 tablespoons coconut-palm sugar or golden brown sugar

½ cup fresh lime juice (reserve the lime rinds)

NOODLES

1 pound Japanese *somen* noodles or angel hair pasta

1½ cups loosely packed Thai basil (*bai horapha*) or purple or Italian basil

CONDIMENTS

1¾ cups vegetable oil for frying

⅓ cup thinly sliced garlic (about 18 cloves)

⅔ cup thinly sliced shallots (about 5 to 6)

10 small, dried Japanese chilies

½ pound water spinach (*pak bung*) or common spinach

Pinch turmeric (optional)

¾ pound bean sprouts

1 can (1 pound, 3 ounces) banana blossoms in salted water, drained and cut crosswise into ½-inch pieces, or 1 jar (6 ounces) marinated artichoke hearts, sliced crosswise into ½-inch pieces

3 chicken or duck eggs, hard-boiled, shelled, and sliced, or 8 quail eggs, hard-boiled, shelled, and left whole (optional)

To make the curried shrimp sauce: Combine the chopped shrimp, hominy, curry paste, and one can of the coconut milk in the bowl of a food processor fitted with a metal blade. (If your machine is small, process the mixture in two batches.) Process until the mixture is coarsely blended, stopping occasionally to scrape down the sides of the work bowl.

Transfer the mixture to a medium saucepan set over medium-high heat. Cook for 2 minutes, stirring often. Add the remaining two cans of coconut milk and cook for 2 minutes, stirring occasionally. Add the fish sauce and sugar and cook for 30 seconds. Stir in the lime juice and cook for 1 minute. Add the reserved lime rinds and cook for 1½ minutes. Discard the lime rinds, cover the sauce, and remove from the heat.

To cook the noodles and form them into nests: Fill a large pot with about 3½ quarts of water. Bring the water to a boil, add the noodles, and cook until al dente (1½ to 2 minutes for *somen* noodles; 2 to 2½ minutes for angel hair pasta), stirring occasionally to keep the noodles from sticking to the bottom of the pot.

Drain immediately in a colander. Rinse well until the noodles are cool, tossing and stirring them with a wooden spoon to remove excess starch. Drain the noodles and transfer them to a mixing bowl.

Set a large serving platter on a counter or work surface, along with the bowl of noodles and the basil.

Take a handful of cooked noodles and coil them around two fingers of your other hand to make a 3- to 4-inch mound shaped like a little bird's nest. Put the nest on the serving platter. Repeat until all the noodles have been formed into nests.

Arrange a few basil leaves in the hollow of each nest and set the platter aside.

To prepare the condiments: Pour the oil into a wok or a heavy saucepan set over medium-high heat and bring it to 360°F. (To test the oil temperature, dip a wooden spoon in the hot oil. The oil should bubble and sizzle gently around the bowl of the spoon.) Add the garlic and cook until it is golden brown, stirring occasionally, about 1 minute. Remove with a wire skimmer or slotted spoon and drain on paper towels.

Return the oil temperature to 360°F and fry the shallots, stirring frequently, for about 2 minutes. Remove with a wire skimmer or slotted spoon and drain on paper towels. Add the Japanese chilies and cook, stirring occasionally, just until they deepen in color, about 30 seconds. Remove with a wire skimmer or slotted spoon and drain on paper towels.

Trim off all but the top third of the long stems from the water spinach. Chop the spinach into 2½- to 3-inch lengths. Blanch the spinach in plenty of boiling water for 30 seconds. Transfer the spinach with a wire skimmer or slotted spoon to a bowl of cold water, then drain and set aside.

Return the water to a boil. Add the turmeric, if desired, then blanch the bean sprouts for 20 seconds and drain them immediately.

Arrange all the condiments attractively on a large serving platter. Set it on the table along with the platter of noodles.

Slowly reheat the curried shrimp sauce over medium-high heat. (Heat it through without letting it come to a boil.) Transfer to a serving bowl and serve with the bird's-nest noodles and condiments.

THAI SERVING STYLE: Serve each guest three or four bird's nests and sprinkle them with some of the fried garlic and crispy shallots. Generously ladle the curried shrimp sauce over the noodles. Let the guests help themselves to whatever other condiments they desire.

KING RAMA V'S
FRIED RICE

Khao Phat Kapi

Serves 8

R ama V, also known as King Chulalongkorn, described *khao phat kapi* in his journals as one of his favorite dishes. The shrimp paste gives it a pungency, but it becomes a background note to the myriad condiments, including sliced cucumbers, green mango, lime, chilies, shallots, julienned omelet, and the addictive Sweet Pork.

FRIED RICE

3 tablespoons shrimp paste (*kapi*), wrapped neatly in a double layer of aluminum foil

1 cup plus 1 tablespoon vegetable oil

4 ounces extra-large dried shrimp (*kung haeng*)

6 cups cold cooked jasmine rice (*khao hom mali*) or any long-grain white rice

10 cloves garlic, pounded to a mash or crushed and chopped

3 tablespoons sugar

4 scallions, including the green tops, finely sliced

CONDIMENTS

1 green mango (about 1 pound), or 1 large green apple

1 tablespoon vegetable oil

3 eggs, lightly beaten

1 cucumber, carved into pinwheels (page 389)

2 small limes, cut into thin wedges

1 cup finely sliced shallots

4 serrano chilies, finely sliced

½ cup loosely packed chopped cilantro, including the stems

Sweet Pork (page 135)

To make the fried rice: Set a small skillet over medium heat. Place the foil-wrapped shrimp paste in the skillet and roast it for about 5 minutes, until aromatic, turning the packet over once or twice. Remove the packet from the skillet and set it aside to cool.

Pour 1 cup of the oil into a wok or a wide, heavy skillet. Set over medium-high heat and bring the oil to 360°F. (To test the oil temperature, dip a wooden spoon in the hot oil. The oil should bubble and sizzle gently around the bowl of the spoon.) Deep-fry the dried shrimp in the hot oil until crisp and golden, about 1 to 1½ minutes. Remove with a wire skimmer or slotted spoon and drain on paper towels.

Put the rice in a large mixing bowl and knead it gently through your fingers to separate the grains. Unwrap the shrimp paste and add it to the bowl. Mix the shrimp paste into the rice with your hands until well blended.

Set a wok over medium-high heat. When it is quite hot, add the remaining tablespoon of oil. Rotate the wok a bit so the oil coats the sides. When the oil is hot, add the garlic and stir-fry briefly, just until golden and aromatic.

Add the rice and press it down into the bottom of the wok. Turn the rice mixture over, press it down into the wok again, and stir-fry for 1½ minutes. Add the sugar and stir-fry for 30 seconds. Remove the pan from the heat and mix in the scallions and fried shrimp. Cover and set aside.

To prepare the condiments: Slice the stem end off the mango. With a sharp knife, score the skin lengthwise into quarters, first on one side then the other. Pull the skin off, using the scored sections as a guide. Hold the peeled mango in the palm of one hand, exposing half the fruit, and make a series of quick parallel cuts, slicing into the flesh almost to the seed. When the surface is fully scored, slice crosswise to release the fruit, creating julienne strips. Repeat, scoring the mango down to the seed and slicing off the remaining fruit. Turn the mango over and repeat the tap-cut technique to julienne the rest of the fruit. Set aside.

If using a green apple, peel, core, and cut crosswise into thin slices. Stack the slices and cut them into julienne strips. Set aside.

Add the oil to a medium nonstick or cast-iron skillet and set over high heat. Tip the skillet so the oil coats the surface. When the oil is sizzling hot, add the beaten eggs and rotate the skillet so the whole surface gets coated with egg. As the omelet begins to set, gently push the cooked edges back with a spatula and tip the skillet so that any liquid can reach the skillet's surface. Turn off the heat when the omelet is just set on the bottom, then slide it onto a cutting board. Slice into julienne strips and set aside.

To assemble the dish: Mound the fried rice down the center of a large serving platter. Arrange the cucumber pinwheels along one side and the lime wedges along the other. Sprinkle the sliced shallots down the centerline of the mound. Arrange the julienned mango on each side of the centerline to cover the rest of the mound. Shower the julienned omelet over all.

Put the sliced chilies in a saucer and the chopped cilantro in a small serving bowl. Gently rewarm the Sweet Pork, if necessary, and place it, with its juices, on a small serving platter.

Set the fried rice and condiments on the table and serve.

THAI SERVING STYLE: Take a serving of fried rice and condiments from the large platter. Sprinkle with some sliced chilies, if desired. Top with some of the warm Sweet Pork with its juices and garnish with cilantro. Add a squeeze of lime, if desired. Between bites, pick up a cucumber pinwheel to refresh your palate.

SWEET SNACKS
and
DESSERTS

Khong Wan

I n Thai cookery, we have sweet treats rather than desserts, dishes that are meant to be eaten any time of the day. And in the tropical climate of Thailand, we often want a snack that's both sweet and thirst-quenching—especially in midafternoon. That's why we've developed a tradition of sweet snacks at teatime.

A traditional Thai meal ends with a simple fruit dessert, such as a platter of seasonal fruits carved into flower or leaf shapes.

With so many kinds of fruit to choose from—rambutan, longan, guava, lychee, jackfruit, papaya, durian, mangosteen, several varieties of mango, and at least twenty varieties of banana—it's only natural that they would inspire most of our sweet treats. Typically, these fruits are enhanced with fresh coconut cream, custard, or ice cream and decorated with flower petals (we love our desserts to have fragrance) or even a bit of gold leaf.

In our climate, Western-style pies or cakes would be rather heavy at the end of a big meal. However, the ice creams and sorbets that we learned about from the West, and which we have come to adore, are very suitable to Thai cuisine. You'll find four of them among this chapter's recipes. Fragrant Rose-Petal Sorbet, Fresh Ginger Sorbet, and Sugarcane Sorbet are made especially aromatic by their principal ingredients.

Mango season is a highlight of the year, awaited with great anticipation. When the fruit begins to ripen, we have tons of it—literally—and happily devour it all. One of the most popular of all traditional Thai desserts is Sweet Sticky Rice with Mangoes and Coconut Cream.

One dessert form we've borrowed from Westerners is the custard. Thai versions include Coconut-Cream Custard, which goes nicely with sweet sticky rice.

Our concept of sweet snacks and desserts is different from that of Western cuisines. Many Thai desserts would, for Western palates, confuse the distinction between "sweet" and "savory." But in this chapter I've emphasized the sweet aspect of Thai desserts. We have a very broad range of these treats to offer. On the whole, they're just a little bit lighter than the desserts you may be used to. If you're like me—someone who wouldn't want to go through life without lots of sweet treats—that's very good news.

Kaffir limes

Accentuate the citrusy flavor of ceviche with slivers of fresh Kaffir lime leaves, or use a little of the zest in desserts like lemon meringue or Key lime pie.

FRESH ORANGES IN SWEET ROSE WATER

Som Loy Geow

Serves 6 to 8

This is a refreshing, easy-to-make fruit dessert. It's perfect on a hot summer day, especially after a spicy Thai dinner.

6 oranges

2¾ cups water

1¼ cups sugar

4 teaspoons rose water

Crushed ice

Fragrant rose petals, from unsprayed flowers (optional)

Peel and segment the oranges, taking care to remove all the skin and pith. Place the segments in a glass bowl, cover, and refrigerate.

Combine the water and sugar in a medium saucepan and bring to a boil over medium-high heat, stirring occasionally to dissolve the sugar. Boil gently until the mixture becomes slightly syrupy, about 15 minutes. Stir in the rose water and blend well. Remove the pan from the heat, let cool to room temperature, and chill.

At serving time, arrange the orange segments in a shallow serving bowl. Pour on the chilled syrup and add several handfuls of crushed ice. Shower with rose petals, if desired, and serve at once.

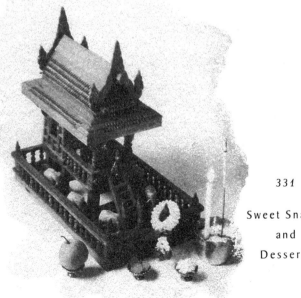

331

Sweet Snacks
and
Desserts

MOLDED TROPICAL-
FRUIT JELLIES

Woon

Makes about 36 small jellies

This summer dessert traces back to the turn of this century, the time of King Rama V. Thai people make these jellies in special molds. The shapes can be fanciful—fruits, vegetables, animals, and flowers, for example—geometric, or even abstract.

Agar-agar, made from seaweed, is the tropical equivalent of gelatin. Its great advantage is that even in sultry climates like Thailand's, it won't melt.

The rosy pink color of jellies made with guava nectar is very appealing, but you can use any tropical fruit nectar. Lacking miniature jelly molds, you can use French tartlet molds, small madeleine pans, plastic sheet candy-making molds, or miniature foil baking cups.

I stick fancy white agar-agar (from a 4-ounce package of two)

2½ cups water

I cup sugar

I can (12 ounces) guava nectar or any tropical fruit nectar

Miniature molds of your choice

Break up the stick of agar-agar and soak in 1 cup of the water until soft, about 5 minutes, pressing occasionally with your fingers to speed absorption.

Combine the sugar and half the guava nectar in a small saucepan. (Reserve the remaining nectar.) Cook over medium-high heat, stirring, until the sugar is dissolved and blended, about 3 minutes. Set aside.

In a medium saucepan set over high heat, bring the remaining 1½ cups of water to a boil. Drain the agar-agar and squeeze out the excess water with your hands. Add the agar-agar to the pot of boiling water and stir until it is dissolved and well blended into a clear liquid, about 4 minutes. Stir in the guava syrup and the reserved guava nectar.

Cook for 3 minutes, stirring occasionally. Remove the pan from the heat and let the mixture cool for 10 minutes.

Place the molds on a cookie sheet, then spoon the fruit gelatin into the molds. Let them cool for 10 minutes, then refrigerate until completely set, about 15 minutes.

Unmold the jellies and serve.

SWEET CORN CUPCAKES WITH COCONUT TOPPING

Khanom Khao Phod

Makes 8 cupcakes

In my childhood, we lived near rice fields. When rice wasn't in season, the farmers raised corn. One of my favorite after-school snacks was this treat, made with fresh corn from the nearby fields.

These cupcakes are only moderately sweet and are delicious with tea or coffee. Serve them at room temperature or slightly warm—never cold.

½ cup rice flour

2 tablespoons tapioca starch

1 tablespoon *salim* flour (mung-bean starch)

¾ cup unsweetened coconut milk

½ cup sugar

⅛ teaspoon yellow food coloring

1 cup corn kernels (fresh or frozen, defrosted, and well drained)

⅔ cup finely grated fresh coconut or dried unsweetened coconut flakes, finely chopped

Pinch or 2 of salt

8 foil baking cups (cupcake size)

To make the batter, combine the rice flour, tapioca starch, *salim* flour, and coconut milk in a medium mixing bowl and whisk until well blended. Add the sugar, food coloring, and corn kernels and mix well.

To make the topping, mix the coconut and salt in a small bowl. Set the batter and topping mixtures aside.

Fill the base pot of a tiered aluminum steamer about one-third full of water. Cover and bring the water to a boil over medium-high heat.

Fill the baking cups about three-quarters full of batter. Place them on a steaming rack, set the rack over the pot, cover, and steam for 5 minutes. Uncover and sprinkle each cupcake with some of the coconut topping. Cover and steam for another 25 minutes. Remove the cupcakes from the steamer and let them cool for 15 to 20 minutes. Unmold the cupcakes and set them on a serving tray.

Serve warm or at room temperature, with a pot of tea or coffee, if desired.

PUMPKIN IN SWEET COCONUT MILK

Fak Thong Kaeng Buat

Serves 4 to 6

Though sweet, this dish is also nourishing. Send your kids off to school with this at breakfast time, or serve it as a comforting dessert in the evening. In the tropics we serve it chilled, but it would also be nice warm on a cool day.

This is often given to monks at ceremonies, perhaps because the color of the kabocha floating in the coconut milk is similar to the color of the monks' robes.

¾ pound kabocha (see Note)
2½ cups unsweetened coconut milk

3 tablespoons coconut-palm sugar or golden brown sugar

Scoop out and discard the seeds and fibers from the kabocha. With a sharp, heavy knife or cleaver, chop it into quarters. Cut off most of the peel and slice the flesh into thin, bite-size pieces (about 1 by 1 by ¼-inch). You should have about 2 cups.

Bring the coconut milk to a boil in a medium saucepan. Boil for 1 minute. Add the sugar and stir to dissolve. Add the sliced kabocha and simmer until it is cooked through and tender, 8 to 10 minutes.

Serve warm, at room temperature, or chilled.

NOTE: You need a ¾-pound piece of kabocha for this recipe. Most Asian markets sell kabocha whole and by the piece. If your market sells only whole kabocha, buy a small one and reserve the rest for another recipe. You may also substitute butternut or acorn squash.

TROPICAL-FRUIT
TEA CAKES

Khanom Polamai

Makes 8 tea cakes

This is the epitome of a Thai-style teatime snack—spongy, light, and airy, just cake-like enough on the outside to contain the moist, tender, tropical fruit–flavored insides. These would also be terrific at a child's birthday party. For a large gathering you could make three batches, using three different fruits for a rainbow mix of colors and flavors.

I can (I pound, 4 ounces) tropical fruit in syrup, such as jackfruit, mangosteen, or lychees

⅓ cup rice flour

⅓ cup *salim* flour (mung-bean starch)

⅓ teaspoon tapioca flour

⅔ cup sugar

½ teaspoon baking powder

2 drops food coloring (yellow for jackfruit, red for lychees, green for mangosteen)

8 foil baking cups (cupcake size)

Pour the canned fruit with its syrup into a blender and process until smooth and liquid. Measure out 1⅔ cups. (Reserve the rest for a fruit smoothie or other use, if desired.) Pour the liquid into a small mixing bowl and add the three flours, sugar, baking powder, and food coloring. Whisk well, until smooth.

Fill the base pot of a tiered aluminum steamer about half full of water. Cover and bring to a boil over medium-high heat.

Fill the baking cups about three-quarters full of batter. Place them on a steaming rack. Set the rack over the pot, cover, and steam until set, about 25 to 30 minutes. Remove the rack from the pot and let cool to room temperature.

Transfer the tea cakes to a serving tray. Serve in their cups and eat with a spoon, or unwrap them and eat with your hands.

STICKY RICE WITH COCONUT SAUCE

Khao Niao Man

Serves 6

F or this rich, satisfying dish, fresh-steamed sticky rice is marinated in a bath of sweet coconut-cream sauce, which is absorbed by the rice as it cools.

Khao niao man is always paired with sweet or savory side dishes. In mango season, juicy-ripe mangoes are served alongside. This and other examples of sweet combinations follow this recipe.

STICKY RICE

1½ cups Thai sticky rice (*khao niao*)

2 quarts water

Cheesecloth

6 pandanus leaves (*bai toey*) from a 4-ounce package of frozen leaves, defrosted (optional)

Spray bottle filled with water

COCONUT SAUCE

1 can (19 ounces) unsweetened coconut milk

¼ teaspoon salt

3 tablespoons sugar

To prepare the sticky rice: Soak the rice in cold water to cover by 2 inches for at least 6 hours or up to 24 hours. Drain, rinse the rice well, and drain again. Pour the 2 quarts of water into the base pot of a tiered aluminum steamer. Cover and bring the water to a boil over high heat.

Line a steamer rack with a double thickness of thoroughly dampened cheesecloth. Spread the rice out evenly over the cheesecloth. If using pandanus leaves, mix them in with the rice so they're evenly distributed and mostly covered by the rice. When the water reaches a boil, set the rack over the pot, cover, and steam for about 15 minutes.

Uncover and spray the surface of the rice with about fifteen short blasts of water from a spray bottle. Cover and let steam for 5 minutes, then spray the rice again. Cover and steam for 5 minutes, then spray the rice a third time. Cover and steam for 5 more minutes, or until the rice is soft and sticky enough to be pressed into little balls. Meanwhile, make the coconut sauce.

To make the coconut sauce: Skim the thick cream from the top of the canned coconut milk into a small bowl. Measure out ¾ cup. (Reserve any leftover cream and the coconut milk for another recipe.)

Combine the coconut cream, salt, and sugar in a medium saucepan. Bring to a boil over medium-high heat, stirring well to dissolve the sugar. Cover and remove the pan from the heat.

Transfer the rice to a large mixing bowl. If you used pandanus leaves, discard them. Pour in the coconut-cream sauce. Stir well to blend, then cover with plastic wrap and set aside to marinate for 30 to 40 minutes so that the rice absorbs the sauce.

The finished dish can be kept, covered, at room temperature for 6 to 8 hours. Don't refrigerate it, however, or the rice will harden.

Serve at room temperature with your choice of side dishes.

STICKY RICE CANDY-CAKES WITH SESAME

Khao Niao Kao

Makes 8 candy-cakes

Originally made in banana-leaf wrappers folded into cups, these candy-cakes are easily portable and therefore great for picnics and other outdoor feasts. They're chewy and crunchy inside, satisfying to the sweet tooths yet nourishing, too. A little food coloring gives them a nice caramel shade.

¾ cup Thai sticky rice (*khao niao*)	1 drop red food coloring
1½ cups water	2 drops yellow food coloring
1 cup unsweetened coconut milk	8 foil baking cups (cupcake size)
1 cup sugar	2 teaspoons sesame seeds

Combine the rice and water in a large saucepan. Cook over medium-high heat, stirring frequently as the mixture boils, for about 8 minutes. Stir in the coconut milk and cook for 3 minutes. Add the sugar and stir well to mix. Cook for 7 minutes, stirring frequently. Stir in the food colorings and lower the heat to medium. Cook for 10 minutes, stirring constantly to keep the rice from scorching on the bottom. The rice should still be a bit crispy and the mixture somewhat sticky. Remove the pan from the heat.

Fill the baking cups about three-quarters full of the sweet rice mixture. Sprinkle each cup with ¼ teaspoon of sesame seeds. Cool to room temperature, then chill until set, about 10 minutes.

Serve at room temperature. Peel off the wrappers and eat out of hand.

SWEET STICKY RICE WITH MANGOES AND COCONUT CREAM

Khao Niao Mamuang

Serves 6

This dessert, a much-appreciated highlight at the end of the hot days of mango season, is composed of Sticky Rice with Coconut Sauce, served with the ripest, juiciest mangoes available. For added texture, crunchy toasted sesame seeds or mung beans can be sprinkled on top.

If ripe mangoes are unavailable, use peaches or any other juicy fruit at its peak.

Sticky Rice with Coconut Sauce
(page 336)

4 ripe, sweet mangoes, peeled and cut
into fat slices or carved into leaves
(page 393)

2 tablespoons sesame seeds or split dried
mung beans, toasted in a dry skillet
until golden brown (optional)

Prepare the Sticky Rice with Coconut Sauce.

Slice or carve the mangoes just before serving. Mound portions of the sweet sticky rice on individual dessert plates and fan out a few slices of mango, or one or two carved mango leaves, alongside. Sprinkle on some toasted sesame or mung beans, if desired. Serve at room temperature.

SWEET STICKY RICE WITH COCONUT-CREAM CUSTARD

Khao Niao Na Sankaya

Serves 6 to 8

———

T hai coconut custard, although light in texture, is quite rich. We like to serve it in small portions alongside a mound of sweet sticky rice in coconut cream. They combine as naturally as kissing does with hugging.

I can (19 ounces) unsweetened coconut milk

4 eggs, beaten

¾ cup coconut-palm sugar or golden brown sugar

Sticky Rice with Coconut Sauce (page 336)

To make the custard: Skim the thick cream from the top of the canned coconut milk into a small bowl. Measure out ¾ cup. (Reserve the leftover cream and coconut milk for another recipe.) Combine the coconut cream, eggs, and sugar in a medium bowl. Whisk or beat well with a wooden spoon to dissolve all of the sugar. The mixture should be smooth and well blended. Pour the liquid into a small heatproof bowl or a cake pan large enough to hold the liquid comfortably, with about 1 inch of clearance at the top.

Fill the base pot of a tiered aluminum steamer about one-third full of water. Cover and bring the water to a boil over medium-high heat.

Set the pan of custard on a steaming rack. Cover the pan with a double thickness of cheesecloth to catch any condensation from the steam. Set the rack over the pot, cover, and steam for 30 minutes. The custard will puff a bit and be firm around the edges, with a soft center.

Turn off the heat and carefully remove the lid to keep excess moisture from dripping down. Discard the cheesecloth and let the custard cool to room temperature.

Cover and refrigerate the custard while you prepare the Sticky Rice with Coconut Sauce.

When ready to serve, mound portions of the sweet sticky rice on individual dessert plates. Spoon on some coconut custard, either chilled or at room temperature, and serve.

Sweet Snacks
and
Desserts

COCONUT ICE CREAM

I-Tim Kati

Makes a scant 2 quarts

This dessert has no dairy products, but the coconut milk and young coconut give it such a rich taste, everybody just calls it "ice cream."

Coconut ice cream is often served with fresh corn kernels or tropical fruit blended through, as in this recipe. For extra texture and flavor, top a scoop of ice cream with roasted peanuts or shreds of Toasted Coconut.

1 pound frozen shredded young coconut, defrosted and drained

2 cans (19 ounces each) unsweetened coconut milk

¾ cup superfine sugar or granulated sugar

⅓ cup fresh corn kernels, or chopped, canned jackfruit, or any fresh or canned tropical fruit

Toasted Coconut (page 62) or roasted unsalted peanuts (optional)

In a large mixing bowl, combine the young coconut, coconut milk, and sugar. Stir until the sugar is dissolved and blended. Add the corn or fruit and mix well. Cover and chill until cold.

Freeze the mixture in an ice-cream maker, following the manufacturer's instructions.

Before serving, temper the ice cream in the refrigerator until it is no longer icy-hard and becomes smooth and easy to scoop.

Scoop the ice cream into dessert bowls and top with Toasted Coconut or peanuts, if desired.

SUGARCANE SORBET

I-Tim Oi

Makes 1 quart

I n Thailand, a young man might call his sweetheart "little sugarcane." After tasting this delicious treat, you'll know why it's such a compliment. Sugarcane Sorbet is snow white, delicate and sweet, but not sugary. For the purposes of this recipe, the canned sticks of sugarcane found in Thai and Asian markets are almost as good as fresh-harvested cane.

1 can (20 ounces) sugarcane	2 cups sugar
5 cups water	1½ teaspoons fresh lemon juice

Drain the sugarcane. Cut each stick in half lengthwise, then slice the halves crosswise into ¼-inch pieces. Place the sliced sugarcane in the bowl of a food processor fitted with a metal blade. Process until finely chopped. You should have about 3½ cups.

Combine the water and sugar in a medium saucepan and bring to a boil. Boil for 5 minutes.

Remove the pan from the heat. Add the chopped sugarcane and let the mixture steep for 30 minutes. Strain the syrup into a mixing bowl, pressing down on the pulpy sugarcane with a wooden spoon to extract all the juices. Stir the lemon juice into the syrup, cover, and chill until cold.

Freeze the mixture in an ice-cream maker, following the manufacturer's instructions.

Before serving, temper the sorbet in the refrigerator until it is no longer icy-hard and becomes smooth and easy to scoop.

Scoop the sorbet into dessert bowls and serve.

N O T E : Purée some fresh strawberries for a pretty topping sauce, if desired.

FRESH GINGER SORBET

I-Tim Khing

Makes 1½ quarts

Ginger is a flavor that should be enjoyed in its full, feisty intensity. This sorbet, though cooling, is refreshing in a stimulating way. It lets the peppery, fragrant taste linger on your tongue.

5 cups water

2½ cups sugar

⅓ cup minced fresh ginger

⅓ cup fresh lime juice

Combine the water and sugar in a medium saucepan and bring to a boil. Boil for 5 minutes. Remove the pan from the heat. Add the minced ginger and let the mixture steep for 10 minutes.

Strain the syrup into a mixing bowl. Stir in the lime juice, cover, and chill until cold.

Freeze the mixture in an ice-cream maker, following the manufacturer's instructions.

Before serving, temper the sorbet in the refrigerator until it is no longer icy-hard and becomes smooth and easy to scoop.

Scoop the sorbet into dessert bowls and serve.

FRAGRANT ROSE-
PETAL SORBET

I-Tim Dok Gulab

Makes about 1 pint

On special occasions in Thailand, this sorbet might arrive at your table decorated with candied rose petals or curls of edible silver or gold leaf.

Begin by choosing ready-to-bloom roses (pesticide-free, of course) with the deepest color and fragrance you can find. Red, crimson, and fuchsia-colored petals will give you the most deep-hued and flavorful results.

3½ cups water

1 scant cup sugar

1 cup tightly packed fresh rose petals (unsprayed), deep in color and fragrance (see Note)

2 teaspoons fresh lemon juice

Additional rose petals or candied violets for decoration (optional)

Combine the water and sugar in a medium saucepan and bring to a boil. Boil for 5 minutes. Remove the pan from the heat. Stir in the rose petals and let the mixture steep for 25 minutes. The syrup should be infused with flavor and have a distinct rosy hue.

Use a wire skimmer or slotted spoon to strain out and discard the petals. Stir in the lemon juice, cover, and chill until cold.

Freeze the mixture in an ice-cream maker, following the manufacturer's instructions.

Before serving, temper the sorbet in the refrigerator until it is no longer icy-hard and becomes smooth and easy to scoop.

Scoop the sorbet into dessert bowls, sprinkle on a few fresh rose petals or candied violets, if desired, and serve.

NOTE: Rinse the roses under cold water. Gently shake away the excess water, then snip off the blooms and let the petals dry on paper towels before measuring.

BEVERAGES

Kreung Deum

If you were to ride a train through Thailand, north from Bangkok to the old capital at Ayutthaya, for example, at every station you'd see dozens of local boys darting along the platform, busily offering passengers creamy Thai iced coffee in straw-equipped plastic pouches.

Even while walking a remote jungle trail, you're likely to come upon a coconut vendor patiently standing at the crossroads, ready to machete open the fibrous tops of fresh green coconuts for thirsty customers.

In a humid tropical environment like Thailand's, liquid refreshment is a constant need. Fortunately, our country grows an immense variety of tropical fruits, coffees, teas, herbs, and flowers to juice, steep, and brew for our native drinks. Pineapples and sugarcane are crushed in old-fashioned presses to extract their fresh, clear juice. Other fruits and herbs, such as lemon grass, mangoes, guavas, and longans, are made into blended drinks sweetened with sugar.

The drinks featured in this chapter have bright, clear, natural flavors, with a moderate sweetness. Some are also aromatic, such as Fresh Ginger Drink, or herbaceous, such as Pandanus Leaf Iced Tea, made from the naturally perfumed fronds of the pandanus tree. You'll also find flavor combinations that are novel to American tastes, such as the added trace of salt in Thai Limeade, or the citrus accent of Watermelon-Lime Cooler.

In addition to the homemade drinks you'll learn to make in this chapter, Thai markets always have a wide selection of carbonated fruit sodas with flavors such as lychee and young coconut.

Our coffees and teas, which may be served hot or iced, are typically blended with grains and sweet spices to mellow their naturally pungent natures. They are brewed strong, then made ultra-creamy with canned evaporated milk, which is the tropical cook's equivalent of half-and-half.

If you were to open the refrigerator in a typical Thai household, you'd see row upon row of bottled colas, fruit sodas, and other cold drinks. Fresh meat and produce will always be abundant at tomorrow's market, and daily marketing is a traditional part of life. In the minds of Thai people, the magic of refrigeration isn't keeping your groceries fresh, it's simply having a cold drink handy whenever you want one.

Beverages even have a spiritual side in our culture. Monks are allowed just two meals daily; the final one is before noon. From then on, they must refrain from solid food but can still partake of liquids. Therefore, people who wish to "make merit" by offering nourishment to a Buddhist priest can extend the gift of a delicious drink at any hour.

Of course, beer has long been a favorite of Thai diners—since the turn of the century, in fact, when Bangkok entrepreneurs hired German "brewmeisters" to reveal the secrets of their art. Now we have several highly regarded Thai lagers and ales. There is even a special class of hors d'ouevres, known as *kap glaem*, or "drinking food," meant to be eaten alongside pungent sips of whiskey or beer. Wine is very expensive in Thailand, but more and more Americans have learned that it can also be elegantly matched with Thai food. A Sauvignon Blanc or Gewürztraminer is a great partner with many Thai recipes.

Whatever drinks you choose to accompany your Thai dishes, I hope they'll always feel as refreshing as a long, cool sip of iced coffee in the middle of a train ride through the tropics.

FRESH GINGER DRINK

Nam Khing Sod

Serves 6 to 8

As the summer rainy season progresses, shoots of young ginger grow abundantly. With them we create this sweet, peppery, refreshing drink. It's typically served iced but is also delicious and soothing served hot. When I offer it at parties, everyone remarks on how well it goes with a variety of dishes and how pleasant it is to discover a new, lively, nonalcoholic drink.

Mixed with a little sparkling water, Fresh Ginger Drink becomes homemade gingerale.

½ pound baby ginger or mature ginger ¾ cup sugar
   (about 1 large branch)
9 cups water

With a chef's knife or cleaver, cut the unpeeled ginger into long pieces about the size and shape of french fries.

Bring the water to a boil in a large saucepan. Add the sliced ginger and keep at a gentle boil for 10 minutes. Turn off the heat and transfer the ginger with a wire skimmer or slotted spoon to a large, heavy mortar for crushing. Cover and reserve the pot of hot water. Gently pound the ginger with the pestle until all the pieces are lightly crushed. (Or you can seal the ginger in a large Ziploc bag and beat it with a mallet or rolling pin until lightly crushed.)

Return the crushed ginger to the pot of hot water. Cover and let steep for 15 minutes. Lift the ginger out with a wire skimmer or slotted spoon and discard. Add the sugar and stir to dissolve.

To serve hot: Fill a teapot with the ginger drink and pour through a tea strainer into individual cups or mugs.

To serve cold: Cool to room temperature and pour through a sieve into a large pitcher. Cover and refrigerate until chilled. Serve in tall glasses over ice.

THAI LIMEADE

Nam Manao

Serves 6 to 8

The tropical heat and humidity of a Bangkok afternoon are intense. So are the flavors of a typical Thai meal. That's why we like our limeade especially sweet and tangy, with a salty bite. To gain that extra depth of flavor, we steep the lime rinds to release their essential oils and add a pinch of salt for every glass.

American taste buds may be startled by the presence of salt in a glass of limeade—that's why I've listed it as an optional ingredient. But if you crave the authentic Thai taste, give it a try.

1 cup fresh lime juice (reserve the rinds)	6½ cups water
Sugar Syrup (recipe follows)	1 teaspoon salt, or to taste (optional)

Combine the lime juice and sugar syrup in a large pitcher. Set aside.

Bring the water to a boil in a large saucepan. Remove the pan from the heat. Add the reserved lime rinds and steep for 10 minutes. Strain the liquid and add it to the pitcher of sweetened lime juice. Stir well. Taste, and add salt if desired.

Cover and refrigerate until chilled. Serve in tall glasses over ice.

SUGAR SYRUP

Nam Chuam

Makes about 1¾ cups

1½ cups sugar	1½ cups water

Bring the sugar and water to a boil in a small saucepan. Reduce the heat and simmer for 5 minutes. Set aside to cool.

LEMON GRASS TEA

Nam Takrai

Serves 4 to 6

This herb tea is another Thai drink that tastes equally good hot or cold. Although the flavor is lemony, lemon grass does not have the tang or astringency of citrus fruit. Instead, it imparts a delicate, herbaceous character. Only a small amount of sugar is needed to complement its soothing taste.

Sun-dried lemon grass is sold in cellophane packages at your local Thai market or health food store.

8 cups water   ¼ cup sugar
I cup dried lemon grass (2 ounces)

Bring the water to a rolling boil in a large saucepan. Add the lemon grass and turn off the heat. Stir, cover, and let steep for 15 minutes. Strain the liquid and add the sugar. Stir until the sugar is dissolved and blended.

To serve hot: Fill a teapot with the tea and pour into individual cups or mugs.

To serve cold: Cool to room temperature and pour into a large pitcher. Cover and refrigerate until chilled. Serve in tall glasses over ice.

Coconut-Palm Sugar

Sweeten your tea with this tropical sugar in place of honey or white sugar. Or mix some coconut-palm sugar and grated coconut into your next batch of pancake batter.

PANDANUS LEAF
ICED TEA

Nam Bai Toey

Serves 6 to 8

P andanus is a palm-like tropical tree with long, sweet, spear-shaped leaves. Some people call it "Asian vanilla." This tea, made with fresh frozen pandanus leaves, has a soft, smooth taste that is at once sweet and slightly smoky.

Even after defrosting, the pandanus leaves retain their sweet mellow scent and fresh-picked flavor. Thai markets here in America now carry both the fresh frozen leaves and bottled extract used to make this drink.

10 cups water

1 package (4 ounces) fresh frozen
    pandanus leaves (*bai toey*)

1 teaspoon pandanus extract
    (*krin bai toey*)

1 cup sugar

Bring the water to a boil in a large saucepan.

Meanwhile, defrost the pandanus leaves and cut them into 6-inch lengths. Add the pandanus to the boiling water. Stir well, cover, and boil for 10 minutes.

Remove the pan from the heat. Lift out the pandanus leaves with a wire skimmer or slotted spoon and discard. Add the pandanus extract and sugar and stir until the sugar is dissolved and blended. Cool to room temperature and pour through a strainer into a large pitcher.

Cover and refrigerate until chilled. Serve in tall glasses over ice.

SWEET LONGAN DRINK
WITH WHOLE FRUITS

Nam Lamyai Bai Toey

Serves 10 to 12

Longans are a prized delicacy grown in northern Thailand, around Chiang Mai and Chiang Rai. Each year's harvest is celebrated in local festivals and eagerly anticipated throughout the country.

The fruit, which ripens in late summer, is soft to the touch, with pale, juicy flesh similar to a peeled grape. Some of the crop is preserved by drying, like raisins, and some is canned in light syrup.

Like the fruit itself, this drink is sweet, mellow, and refreshing, with a haunting, slightly musky taste.

10 cups water

1 box (3 ounces) dried seedless longan

1 can (1 pound, 4 ounces) whole longan in syrup (see Note)

1¼ cups sugar

¼ teaspoon pandanus extract (*krin bai toey*)

Pour the water into a large saucepan. Add the dried longan, working the individual fruits loose from the pack with your fingers. Add the canned longan with its syrup. Cover and bring the mixture to a boil. Add the sugar and stir well to dissolve. Reduce the heat and simmer for 5 minutes.

Remove the pan from the heat. Stir in the pandanus extract and let the mixture cool to room temperature.

Pour the drink, with its whole and dried fruits, into one or more large pitchers. Cover and refrigerate until chilled.

Pour into tall glasses over ice. Include some of the whole fruits with each glass and serve with iced-tea spoons to retrieve and enjoy the fruits in between sips.

NOTE: Dried longan will keep indefinitely in the refrigerator, but the canned fruit, once opened, is more perishable. Since this recipe makes several servings, you may wish to cut it in half. If so, refrigerate any leftover canned fruit and use it within 3 to 4 days.

WATERMELON-LIME COOLER

Nam Tangmoo Manao

Serves 6 to 8

Most everyone has cooled off in the summertime with a fragrant slice of watermelon. Thai people love this drink, which uses a bit of sugar syrup and just enough lime juice to bring out the delicate, flowerlike aspect of the melon's flavor.

7 pounds watermelon (about half a medium-sized fruit), seedless if available

7 tablespoons or more fresh lime juice

7 tablespoons or more Sugar Syrup (recipe follows)

Slice the rind off the watermelon and cut the fruit into 1-inch cubes. (If the watermelon is not seedless, pick out and discard the seeds.) You should have about 15 cups of cubed watermelon. Purée the fruit in a blender, a few cups at a time, until smooth and liquid.

Strain the liquid through a fine-mesh sieve into a large pitcher. You should have about 8 cups of juice. Add 7 tablespoons each lime juice and sugar syrup. Stir well. Taste, and add more lime juice and/or syrup if desired.

Cover and refrigerate until chilled.

When ready to serve, stir well to reblend and pour into tall glasses over ice.

SUGAR SYRUP

Nam Chuam

Makes a generous ½ cup

½ cup sugar

½ cup water

Bring the sugar and water to a boil in a small saucepan. Reduce the heat and simmer for 5 minutes. Set aside to cool.

THAI ICED TEA

Cha Yen

Serves 4 to 6

Of all the offerings at a typical Thai restaurant, Thai iced tea is one of the first things people fall in love with. It's a native-grown red-leafed tea that's spiced with star anise, cinnamon, and vanilla. We brew it strong, to be blended with a rich swirl of evaporated milk.

Thai tea and the traditional cloth filter (*tung tom kah fe*) used to brew it can be found in any Thai market. Although there's no substitute for this particular tea, you can brew it with a coffee filter or a fine-mesh strainer.

6 cups water

I cup Thai tea (*cha Thai*)

I cup sugar

I to I½ cups evaporated milk or half-and-half

Thai brewing style: Bring the water to a rolling boil in a large saucepan. Fill a Thai-style cloth coffee filter with the tea and set it in a heatproof container, such as a large coffee carafe or pitcher. Pour the boiling water over the tea in the cloth bag, letting it course through the tea and into the carafe. Set the bag in the carafe and steep for 2 minutes. Lift out the tea strainer to drain, then dunk it back down into the brew. Dunk several times, for about 1 minute, and ladle some of the liquid back through the cloth strainer once or twice. As the brew becomes stronger, it will deepen in color to a vivid orange. Strain out the tea in the cloth bag, pressing out as much liquid as you can (a pair of tongs works well here). Discard the tea leaves and rinse out the bag. Add the sugar to the hot tea and stir to dissolve. Cool to room temperature, cover, and refrigerate until ready to serve.

Alternate brewing style: Bring the water to a rolling boil in a large saucepan. Add the tea and remove the pan from the heat. Stir gently to submerge all the tea leaves in the water. Steep for about 5 minutes. The liquid should turn bright orange and have a strong, clean taste with no hint of bitterness. Pour the brew through a coffee filter or a fine-mesh strainer into a large pitcher. Add the sugar to the hot tea and stir to dissolve. Cool to room temperature, cover, and refrigerate until ready to serve.

At serving time, fill tall glasses with crushed ice or ice cubes. Add enough of the Thai tea to fill the glasses about three-quarters full, then float 3 to 4 tablespoons of evaporated milk over the ice in each glass.

Serve with iced-tea spoons, so your guests can blend the contrasting white milk and dark tea into the inviting terra-cotta color of Thai iced tea.

THAI ICED COFFEE

Kah Fe Yen

Serves 4 to 6

E ven something as basic as coffee can't escape the Thai penchant for spicing to create additional layers of flavor. Thai iced coffee is based on a blend of ground coffee, roasted corn, sesame, and spices we call *oliang*.

As with Thai Iced Tea (page 353), I've given you two brewing methods. One uses the traditional cloth strainer, called a *tung tom kah fe*, the other a standard coffee filter or fine-mesh strainer.

6 cups water	1¼ cups sugar
⅔ cup Thai coffee powder (*oliang* powder)	1 to 1½ cups evaporated milk or half-and-half

Thai brewing style: Bring the water to a rolling boil in a large saucepan. Fill a Thai-style cloth coffee filter with the coffee and set it in a heatproof container such as a large coffee carafe or pitcher. Pour the boiling water over the ground coffee in the cloth bag, letting it course through the coffee and into the carafe. Set the bag in the carafe and steep for 10 minutes, occasionally lifting the bag out to drain back into the brew. Strain out the coffee in the cloth bag, pressing out as much liquid as you can (a pair of tongs works well here). Discard the coffee grounds and rinse out the bag. Add the sugar to the hot coffee and stir to dissolve. Cool to room temperature, cover, and refrigerate until ready to serve.

Alternate brewing style: Bring the water to a rolling boil in a large saucepan. Add the Thai coffee, stir just long enough to blend, and immediately remove the pan from the heat. Steep for 10 minutes. Pour the brew through a coffee filter or a fine-mesh strainer into a large coffee carafe or pitcher. Add the sugar to the hot coffee and stir to dissolve. Cool to room temperature, cover, and refrigerate until ready to serve.

At serving time, fill tall glasses with crushed ice or ice cubes. Add enough of the Thai coffee to fill the glasses about three-quarters full, then float 3 to 4 tablespoons of evaporated milk over the ice in each glass.

Serve with iced-tea spoons so your guests can stir the contrasting white milk and dark coffee together into a creamy blend.

Thai Iced Tea

(page 353)

This rich drink already tastes like dessert in a glass. Go one step further and make it into a simple Italian granita. Freeze Thai Iced Tea in a cake pan and scrape with a fork into shavings, or freeze it in ice-cube trays, then crush the cubes in a food processor. Serve in chilled goblets or dessert bowls.

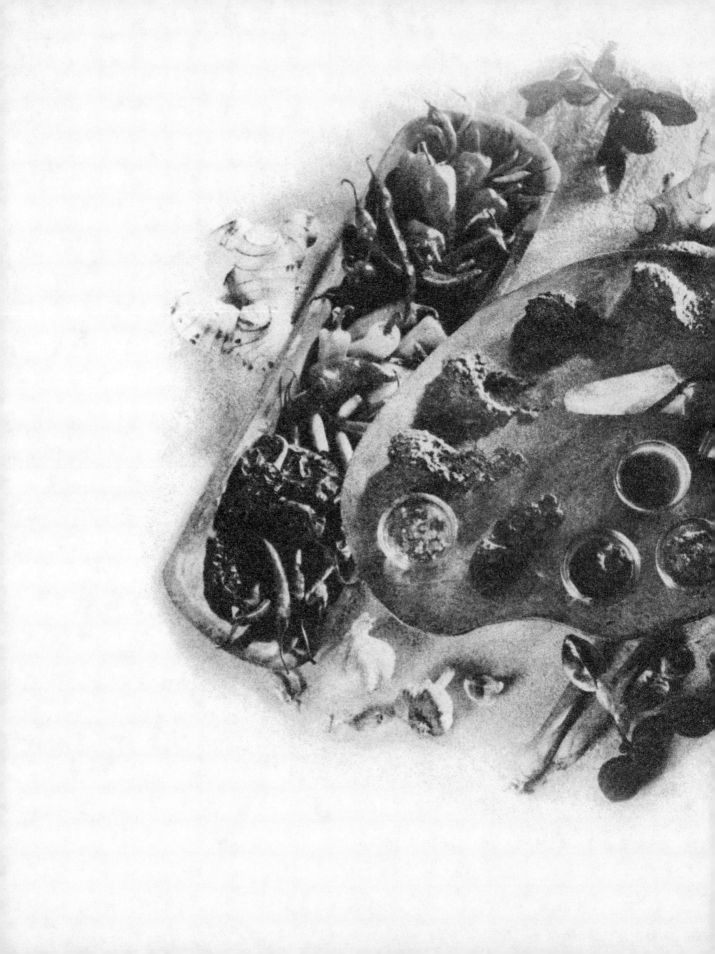

COOKING WITH A THAI ACCENT

Ahan Thai Pasom Ahan Farang

A restaurant critic once commented generously on the "sophisticated overtones of Italian and French cuisines" in my cooking. In fact, it's always been in the nature of Thai chefs to borrow and adapt from other kitchen traditions.

A guiding principle of Thai life is that the things you do should be *sanuk* or "fun." For us as Buddhists, the ultimate goal in life is to achieve nirvana, supreme happiness. Having fun in the things you do proves that you're on the right path.

Thai cooking is *sanuk*, and never routine, because we're always ready to assimilate new ideas. When large numbers of American tourists began appearing in Thailand, streetside food vendors evolved American Fried Rice, a brand-new recipe that included bite-size chunks of hot dogs.

Of course, most of our inventions are more elegant than that. We've absorbed a lot of influence from our neighbors—China, Burma, India, and Malaysia. When French colonists were in Southeast Asia, their cuisine also influenced our own. And we love Italian food, with all its rice and noodle dishes, which fit our eating traditions like a glove.

Perhaps the best way to introduce a chapter on Thai-style improvising is through the experiences of my co-authors, Theresa Volpe Laursen and Byron Laursen. Like you, they love Thai food, but were relative newcomers to Thai ingredients and cooking techniques. While testing this book's recipes, they gradually developed an independent sense of how to "play" with the new flavors that had found their way into their kitchen. They became ready, as you soon will, to take a free hand with Kaffir lime leaves, Thai basil, coconut milk, curry pastes, and the many other flavorful components we Thai chefs use. They began improvising ways to incorporate the Thai tastes and ingredients they loved with their own cooking style.

In fact, all the recipes in this chapter are their inventions, based on knowledge they gained while testing traditional Thai dishes. Therefore, I want to step aside here and let them complete these words of introduction to "Cooking with a Thai Accent."

LETTER FROM THE TEST KITCHEN

The key to this chapter was learning the natures of a few key Thai ingredients. As Byron and I became more familiar with those flavor sources, we began to use them in Western-style dishes for ourselves, friends, and family.

The more well versed we became, the more new recipes followed.

Our first step was an impromptu stir-fried rice made for a quick supper. Early in the recipe testing, we'd noticed that whenever the combination of crushed garlic, pepper, and cilantro stems hit the hot surface of a wok, a heady aroma filled the kitchen that instantly reminded us of our first visit to a Thai restaurant. Clearly, this three-part harmony provided some of the key notes inherent to Thai cuisine. From that realization, we improvised Fragrant Fried Rice.

Later, for a barbecue with friends, I concocted Bangkok Burgers with Grilled Marinated Onions and Spicy Thai Ketchup.

Thai cooks respect personal expression and creative ingenuity. Victor was especially taken with our Panang Pizza, flavored with authentic Thai curry paste and daubed with coconut cream.

This chapter's East-meets-West entrées, side dishes, condiments, and desserts will encourage you to begin cooking and thinking like a Thai chef. Once you've known the pleasures of working with aromatic Thai herbs and spices, they become less mysterious and more like new friends you can call on any time you cook. Eventually, you'll blend what you've learned with your own kitchen traditions. I promise you, the experience will be *sanuk.*

BANGKOK BURGERS WITH GRILLED MARINATED ONIONS AND SPICY THAI KETCHUP

Makes 6 burgers

This is really three recipes in one. You can enliven a plate of french fries or a meatloaf recipe with the Spicy Thai Ketchup, and the Grilled Marinated Onions will be equally heady served with a thick steak. You can also serve the burgers in conventional American style—with mustard, relish, and plain ketchup.

BANGKOK BURGERS

½ teaspoon black peppercorns

2 large cloves garlic

½ cup loosely packed chopped cilantro, including the stems

1½ pounds ground beef

GRILLED MARINATED ONIONS

¼ cup Thai soy sauce with mushroom (*see-eu khao het hom*) or a Chinese brand, such as Pearl River Bridge

½ tablespoon coconut-palm sugar

2 large onions (about 1¼ pounds), sliced

1½ tablespoons vegetable oil, if stir-frying onions

SPICY THAI KETCHUP

Bottled Thai chili sauce (*sriracha*)

6 sesame-seed hamburger buns

To make the burger patties: Make a seasoning paste from the peppercorns, garlic, and cilantro:

Mortar-and-pestle method: Pound the peppercorns to a powder. Add the garlic and cilantro stems and pound the mixture to a mash.

Alternate method: Coarsely grind the peppercorns in a spice mill. Crush the garlic with the side of a chef's knife. Mix the cilantro, pepper, and garlic together and mince.

Put the ground beef in a large mixing bowl and work in the seasoning paste, kneading the mixture with your hands just until blended.

Form six patties from the seasoned ground beef. Keep refrigerated until ready to grill.

To marinate the onions: Combine the soy sauce and sugar in a large mixing bowl, stirring until the sugar is dissolved and blended. Toss the sliced onions in the marinade, breaking the onion slices into rings. Mix well until all the onion rings are basted with the marinade. Cover and set aside while you make the Spicy Thai Ketchup and fire up the grill.

To make the Spicy Thai Ketchup: For a moderately spiced ketchup, mix 1 part Thai chili sauce to 2 parts ketchup. For very spicy ketchup, mix them in equal amounts. Set aside.

To grill the onions and burgers: Build a medium-hot charcoal fire or preheat a gas grill. If your grill is large enough, you can grill the onions on the side in a hinged basket as you tend to the burgers. Otherwise, you can stir-fry the onions in a wok: Set a wok over high heat. When it is quite hot, add the oil. Rotate the wok a bit so the oil coats the sides. When the oil is hot, add the onions with their marinade and stir-fry until soft and well browned, about 5 to 8 minutes. Keep covered until ready to serve.

Grill the burgers to taste, about 4 to 5 minutes on each side for rare, slightly longer for medium or well done.

Split and toast the buns on the grill.

Top the burgers with the grilled onions and serve with Spicy Thai Ketchup.

Cooking
with a
Thai
Accent

THAI-STYLE
TUNA SALAD

Serves 6 to 8 as a side dish, or 4 as a one-dish meal

Thais often make a quick meal by mixing fresh aromatic herbs and vegetables into a soup or salad made with a convenient pantry item like canned sardines. Tuna in cans has the same appeal to busy American cooks, many of whom grew up on tuna-salad sandwiches, tuna melts, and tuna casseroles. But unlike those mayonnaise-based recipes, this light concoction features the citrusy, herbal Thai flavorings of fresh lemon grass and mint, plus a lemony traditional Thai dressing that's brightened with palm sugar and fresh chilies.

SALAD

1 large can (12½ ounces) chunk light tuna, packed in water

1 large stalk lemon grass, tough outer leaves discarded, lower stalk trimmed to 6 inches and finely sliced

1 large ripe tomato, chopped

1 small red onion, cut in half and finely sliced

2 scallions, including the green tops, finely sliced

¾ cup loosely packed chopped fresh mint

½ head each Boston lettuce, romaine, and radicchio

DRESSING

½ cup fresh lemon juice

1½ tablespoons coconut-palm sugar

1½ tablespoons Thai fish sauce (*nam pla*)

4 small Thai chilies (*phrik khee nu*), finely chopped

4 cloves garlic, chopped

Drain the canned tuna, pressing out all the water so it won't dilute the salad dressing. Put the tuna, lemon grass, tomato, red onion, scallions, and mint in a large mixing bowl. Tear the lettuce and radicchio into bite-size pieces. (You should have about 8 cups.) Add the torn salad greens to the bowl. Mix well.

Combine the dressing ingredients in a blender and process until the sugar is completely dissolved and the dressing is smooth and well blended.

Pour the dressing over the salad, toss, and serve.

FRAGRANT FRIED RICE

Serves 2 to 4

Once you've sampled the aroma of crushed garlic, pepper, and cilantro sizzling together, you'll possess a primary Thai flavor secret. This recipe makes a great quick snack or a nice side dish with roasted chicken, beef, or pork.

3 cups cold cooked rice

1 bunch cilantro

5 cloves garlic

½ teaspoon black peppercorns

2½ tablespoons vegetable oil

½ cup chopped onion

3 tablespoons Thai fish sauce (*nam pla*)

1 tablespoon coconut-palm sugar or golden brown sugar

Bottled Thai chili sauce (*sriracha*)

Put the rice in a large mixing bowl. Separate the grains by gently crumbling the rice through your fingers. Set aside.

Chop the cilantro stems, reserving the leaves.

Make a seasoning paste from the garlic, cilantro stems, and black pepper:

Mortar-and-pestle method: Put the garlic, chopped cilantro stems, and black peppercorns in a mortar and pound them to a mash with a pestle.

Alternate method: Crush the garlic with the side of a chef's knife. Coarsely grind the peppercorns in a pepper mill or spice grinder. Mix the cilantro stems with the garlic and black pepper, and finely chop.

Set a wok over medium-high heat. When it is quite hot, add the oil. Rotate the wok a bit so the oil coats the sides. When the oil is hot, add the seasoning paste and stir-fry for a few seconds until it is aromatic. Add the onion and stir-fry until tender, about 1 minute. Add the cooked rice and stir-fry for 1 minute. Add the fish sauce and sugar and stir-fry for about 2½ minutes.

Transfer the fried rice to a serving dish. Top the rice with some of the reserved cilantro leaves and serve with Thai chili sauce.

PANANG PIZZA

Makes three 8-inch pizzas

This recipe delivers all the flavors of a chicken satay on a chewy pizza crust that cooks as nicely on an outdoor grill as it does in the oven.

Curried Peanut Satay Sauce, one of the most addictive condiments in all of Thai cooking, is spread over the dough, then topped with tender, bite-size chicken-breast pieces in a curry-coconut marinade. Finally, the pizza is dotted with small dollops of coconut cream and slender sprigs of cilantro.

The pizza-dough recipe was adapted from one originated by Abby Mandel and published in the *Los Angeles Times*.

MARINADE

½ cup unsweetened coconut milk

2 tablespoons Panang Curry Paste (page 32), or 1 tablespoon canned Panang curry paste

1 tablespoon dark brown sugar

1 tablespoon Thai fish sauce (*nam pla*)

½ tablespoon whole coriander seed, ground

½ pound boneless, skinless chicken breast

PIZZA DOUGH

1 package dry yeast

2 teaspoons honey

1 cup plus 2 tablespoons warm water (105 to 115°F)

2 cups bread flour

1 cup all-purpose flour

1¼ teaspoons salt

2 tablespoons olive oil

TOPPING

9 long (12-inch) bamboo skewers (if grilling the pizza), soaked in a tray of cold water for at least ½ hour

Olive oil for brushing the pizza dough

¾ cup Curried Peanut Satay Sauce (page 55)

Coconut cream, from the top of 1 small can (5.6 ounces) of unsweetened coconut milk

Sprigs of cilantro

To marinate the chicken: Combine the marinade ingredients in a bowl and mix well. Slice the chicken breasts in half lengthwise to make thin, flat slabs, then cut them into 3 by 1-inch strips. Add the chicken to the marinade, stirring to coat all the pieces. Cover and refrigerate for at least 3 to 4 hours or up to 24 hours.

To make the pizza dough: Stir the yeast and honey into the warm water. Let stand until foamy, about 5 minutes.

To knead the dough in a food processor or electric mixer, place both flours and the salt in the work bowl of a food processor fitted with a metal blade (or dough blade), or into the bowl of a mixer fitted with a dough hook. Turn the machine on.

Add the yeast mixture and oil. Process or beat until the dough is moist but still cleans the sides of the bowl. Add flour by the tablespoons if the dough is too wet; add water by the teaspoon if the dough is too dry.

Mix until the dough is supple and elastic, about 40 seconds in a processor, or 6 to 8 minutes in a mixer.

Place the dough in a large Ziploc (1-gallon size) bag. Seal at the top. Let the dough rise in a warm place until doubled, about 1 hour. Punch the dough down. (The dough can be used immediately, refrigerated for up to 5 days, or frozen for up to 3 months.)

To prepare the pizza:

Grilling method: Build a medium-hot charcoal fire or preheat a gas grill. Meanwhile, thread the marinated chicken onto the soaked bamboo skewers, about two pieces per skewer. Grill the skewered meat until partially cooked, about 1 minute per side. Remove the meat from the skewers and set aside.

Divide the dough into thirds. Form the first piece of dough into a ball and roll it out on a floured work surface. Pick it up to shape it with your hands, stretching it gently to make a circle. Brush both sides well with olive oil and set the shaped pizza dough on the grill. Cover and cook for about 4 minutes. The pizza dough should puff and have grill marks on the underside. Turn the pizza round over.

Spread on ¼ cup of the satay sauce and arrange about one-third of the grilled chicken pieces on top. Cover and cook about 4 minutes more.

Remove the pizza from the grill and dot the surface with about one-third of the coconut cream. Tear sprigs of cilantro over the pizza and serve.

Make the other two pizzas.

Oven method: Preheat the oven to 500°F. If using a pizza stone, place it in the upper third of the oven.

Divide the dough into thirds. Form the first piece of dough into a ball and roll it out on a floured work surface. Pick it up to shape it with your hands, stretching it gently to make a circle. Place the shaped dough on a well-floured wooden peel, a pizza pan, or a cookie sheet.

Brush the edges of the dough with olive oil and spread on ¼ cup of the satay sauce. Lift about one-third of the chicken pieces out of the marinade and arrange them on top.

Bake the pizza on its pan, or slide it off the peel onto the heated stone. Bake it in the upper third of the oven for about 8 to 12 minutes. (Pizza cooks more quickly on a stone than in a pan.) The pizza crust should be crisp and browned on the bottom and around the edges.

Remove the pizza from the oven and dot the surface with about one-third of the coconut cream. Tear sprigs of cilantro over the pizza and serve.

Make the other two pizzas.

Fresh Corn Sauté with Coconut Milk and Thai Basil

Serves 4

This is a tropical interpretation of an American standard—creamed corn. The sauce, although much lighter, still clings nicely to the corn and accents each bite with fresh pepper and licoricey Thai basil.

4 large ears white corn, or 1 pound frozen corn kernels, defrosted

2 tablespoons butter

⅓ cup unsweetened coconut milk

½ teaspoon freshly ground black pepper

⅓ cup loosely packed Thai basil (*bai horapha*)

Salt

Husk the corn and remove the silk. With a cleaver or sharp knife, cut the corn off the cobs and scrape the cobs to release the milk. Set aside.

Melt the butter in a small saucepan over medium heat. When the butter begins to sizzle, add the corn and sauté, stirring constantly, for 2 minutes. Add the coconut milk and cook, stirring often, for about 2 minutes, or just until the corn is cooked through. Turn off the heat. Stir in the pepper and the basil and cook for a few seconds, just until the basil begins to wilt. Season with salt to taste and serve.

MASHED POTATOES WITH GARLIC, CILANTRO, AND WHITE PEPPER

Serves 6

This all-American comfort-food favorite takes on a Thai nuance from the versatile flavor trio of garlic, pepper, and cilantro.

6 russet potatoes (about 3¾ pounds), peeled and cut into quarters

6 cloves garlic, peeled

6 tablespoons (¾ stick) butter, softened

½ cup hot milk or half-and-half

½ cup loosely packed chopped cilantro, including the stems

½ teaspoon white pepper

Salt

Combine the potatoes and garlic in a large saucepan and add enough water to cover. Bring the water to a boil and cook until the potatoes are fork-tender, about 20 minutes. Drain well.

Add the butter and hot milk. Mash, then beat with a wooden spoon until well blended. Mix in the cilantro and white pepper. Season to taste with salt and more white pepper, if desired, and serve.

THAI-SPICED
POTATO CHIPS

Serves 6

I n Thailand, street vendors serve homemade potato chips coated with a sugary glaze. We've turned the tables and spiked these chips with chili fire.

A mandolin or vegetable peeler is the perfect tool for making wafer-thin potato slices.

6 russet potatos (about 3¾ pounds), peeled and sliced wafer-thin

2 quarts vegetable or peanut oil for frying

1 teaspoon salt

½ teaspoon Thai chili powder (*phrik pon*) or other ground red chili to taste, such as New Mexico chili powder or cayenne

Soak the potato slices in a large bowl of ice water for 1 hour.

Preheat the oven to 300°F.

Heat the oil in a large, heavy pot or a deep-fat fryer to 350°F.

Mix the salt with the chili powder and set aside.

Drain the potato slices and pat them dry with paper towels. Working in batches to avoid overcrowding, fry the potato slices until crisp and golden brown, about 1 minute. Drain on paper towels, then spread out on a baking sheet. Sprinkle the chips with some of the spice mixture and place in the oven to keep crisp while you fry and season the remaining slices.

SPICY THAI SALSA

Makes about 3 cups

This chunky fresh-tomato salsa is spiced with the complex flavors of *sriracha*, Thailand's favorite hot sauce, instead of chopped fresh chilies. Kaffir lime leaves, cut into fine slivers, give a concentrated bite of fresh lime flavor and fragrance.

This salsa is delightful with such Mexican-American favorites as guacamole and chips, tacos, and quesadillas. It's also wonderful with Thai recipes, such as Sweet Corn Fritters (page 261).

1¾ pounds ripe plum tomatoes, roughly chopped

1 small red onion, chopped

1 clove garlic, crushed and chopped

6 (3 pairs) fresh Kaffir lime leaves (*bai magroot*), finely sliced into slivers

1 teaspoon coconut-palm sugar

½ teaspoon coarsely ground black pepper

2 teaspoons or more bottled Thai chili sauce (*sriracha*)

½ cup loosely packed chopped cilantro, including the stems

Salt

Combine all of the ingredients except the cilantro and salt in the bowl of a food processor fitted with a metal blade. Process until well blended but still chunky. Transfer the mixture to a strainer set over a bowl. Let stand for a minute or two to drain out some of the excess liquid. If you wish, sip the drained liquid for a spicy tomato juice cocktail.

Transfer the salsa to a serving bowl and mix in the chopped cilantro. Add salt to taste and more ground pepper or *sriracha*, if desired, and serve.

Covered and refrigerated, this will keep for about 1 week.

HERBAL THAI MAYONNAISE

Makes about 1 cup

This will give a welcome flavor lift to almost any recipe that uses standard mayonnaise.

Spread some on a fresh tomato sandwich, layering in anise-scented Thai basil leaves. Or fry soft-shell crabs and tuck them into French rolls spread with a little of the mayonnaise, adding paper-thin slices of lemon to create a Thai-style Louisiana po' boy. Spicy Thai Ketchup (page 360) on the side takes the place of the traditional rémoulade.

2 cloves garlic, chopped

¾ cup plus 2 tablespoons safflower oil

2 tablespoons toasted sesame oil

2 egg yolks

½ teaspoon salt

¼ teaspoon white pepper

2 tablespoons fresh lemon juice

¼ cup loosely packed chopped cilantro, including the stems

Combine the chopped garlic, safflower oil, and toasted sesame oil in a blender and process until the garlic is puréed and blended with the oils. Transfer to a small bowl and set aside.

Put the egg yolks, salt, pepper, and lemon juice in a mixing bowl and whisk until smooth and well blended. Whisk in the garlic oil very slowly, adding it in a thin trickle at first. Beat briskly. When the mixture begins to thicken, add the oil in a steady stream. Beat briskly until all the oil is incorporated. Mix in the cilantro.

Stored in an airtight container in the refrigerator, this will keep for about 1½ weeks.

TROPICAL-FRUIT SALAD
WITH TOASTED COCONUT

Serves 6

We've suggested some of the most readily available tropical fruits, but you can take a more exotic direction with lychees, starfruit, rambutan, or any other rare tropical fruit. Or simply substitute a big bowl of summer berries. Another time, carve mango slices into leaf shapes, using the method on page 393, and serve them with the Toasted Coconut on the side.

1 pineapple, Tahitian if available	1 pint strawberries
1 mango	A few lime wedges (optional)
1 papaya	Honey (optional)
1 large banana	Toasted Coconut (page 62)

Peel and core the pineapple, then cut the fruit into bite-size cubes.

Slice the stem end off the mango. With a sharp knife, score the skin lengthwise into quarters, first on one side, then the other. Pull the skin off, using the scored sections as a guide. Hold the peeled mango in the palm of one hand, exposing half the fruit, and make a series of quick parallel cuts, slicing almost to the seed. When the surface is fully scored, slice crosswise to release the fruit, creating julienne strips. Repeat, scoring the mango down to the seed and slicing off the remaining fruit. Turn the mango over and repeat the tap-cut technique.

Peel the papaya and cut it in half lengthwise. Scoop out the seeds and cut the fruit into bite-size pieces.

Peel the banana and slice it crosswise.

Hull the strawberries and cut each one in half or, for large berries, in quarters.

Combine all of the fruit in a large bowl. Squeeze some fresh lime juice over the salad and drizzle on some honey, if desired. Toss, and divide the salad into individual serving bowls. Top each bowl with a generous handful of Toasted Coconut and serve.

Cooking
with a
Thai
Accent

JASMINE MADELEINES

Makes thirty-six 3¼-inch madeleines

The Thai love of scented desserts in fanciful shapes inspired this adaptation of the classic French sponge cookie. Victor thought it made a perfect Thai-style "tea-time sweet."

Do as the French do, and dip these seashell-shaped cookies into a hot cup of tea.

4 eggs, at room temperature

⅔ cup sugar

2 teaspoons grated orange peel

1 cup all-purpose flour, sifted

½ teaspoon baking powder

10 tablespoons (1¼ sticks) unsalted butter, melted and cooled

1¼ teaspoons vanilla extract

½ teaspoon jasmine essence (*krin mali*)

Confectioners' sugar

Beat the eggs and sugar together with an electric hand mixer or a whisk for 12 to 15 minutes, until the mixture reaches a thick, batterlike consistency and has a light lemon color.

Add the orange peel.

Sift the flour and baking powder together and very gently fold them into the egg mixture. Fold in the melted butter, vanilla, and jasmine essence. Let the batter rest in a cool (not refrigerated) place for 1 hour.

Preheat the oven to 375°F. Brush madeleine pans with melted butter, coating all the grooves, then dust with flour. Spoon the batter into the madeleine pans, filling them three-quarters full. Bake until light golden, about 8 to 10 minutes.

Unmold the madeleines and set them on wire racks, pattern sides up, to cool completely. (The madeleines should release easily from the molds when you press their narrow ends lightly.) Let the madeleine pans cool. Butter and flour them again before refilling them with batter.

Dust the madeleines with confectioners' sugar and serve with a pot of tea, if desired.

NOTE: Madeleine pans come in a variety of sizes and shapes. Standard pans have molds about 3¼ inches long. Petite pans have molds about 1¾ inches long. Using different sizes yields a charming mix of shapes.

PAPAYA BAKED IN GINGER CREAM

Serves 2

Here's a treat that's light, comforting, and mellow. Serve it for breakfast, for dessert, or as an evening snack alongside a cup of tea.

This recipe was inspired by a baked pear recipe in Martha Stewart's book *Entertaining.*

I ripe papaya (about I pound)	⅛ teaspoon freshly grated ginger
Butter for the pan	3 tablespoons half-and-half
I tablespoon sugar	Freshly grated nutmeg

Preheat the oven to 375°F.

Peel the papaya and cut it in half lengthwise. Scoop out the seeds. Generously butter a baking dish just large enough to hold the papaya halves. Sprinkle the baking dish with half the sugar. Put the papaya halves, cut-sides down, in the dish and sprinkle with the remaining sugar. Bake for 15 minutes.

Meanwhile, mix the grated ginger with the half-and-half. After 15 minutes, remove the pan from the oven and pour on the spiced half-and-half, then dust each papaya half with freshly grated nutmeg. Return the pan to the oven and cook for 10 more minutes.

Let the baked papayas cool slightly before serving.

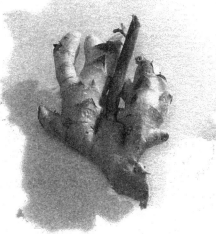

CHERIMOYA ICE CREAM

Makes about 2 quarts

Cherimoyas are plentiful and well loved in Thailand, where they are called *noi na*. They remain a somewhat expensive delicacy in America. This recipe makes a generous amount, however, so its per-serving cost is moderate. And the taste and texture are out of this world.

An ever-increasing number of California farmers have begun growing this fruit, whose creamy, mild, and flavorful flesh has inspired people to call it "custard apple."

3 pounds very ripe cherimoya	I cup whipping cream
¾ cup superfine or granulated sugar	½ cup water
2 tablespoons fresh lime juice	

Cut the cherimoya in half and scoop the creamy flesh into a sieve placed over a bowl. Push it through with a wooden spoon or pestle. Release the pulp that clings to the seeds. Discard the seeds. Scrape all the pulp from the outside of the sieve as well. You should have 3 cups.

Process all the ingredients in a blender or food processor fitted with a metal blade just until blended.

Transfer the mixture to a covered container and chill in the refrigerator until cold.

Freeze in an ice-cream maker following the manufacturer's instructions.

Temper the ice cream in the refrigerator for about 15 minutes before serving so it reaches a smooth scooping consistency.

MENU-PLANNING GUIDE

Ohk Bamp Raikan Ahan

For an easy introduction to Thai food, just present one or two signature dishes the next time you cook for family or friends. Many Thai favorites, such as Chicken-Coconut Soup or the Classic Thai Noodles (*phat Thai*), can be easily matched with home-cooked American dishes. One-dish meals or antipasto-like salads, such as Chiang Mai

Noodle Curry, and Coconut, Lemon, and Ginger Salad, are perfect for casual home entertaining. During the year-end holiday season, Fresh Ginger Drink, Curried Pumpkin-Fried Rice, or Pumpkin in Sweet Coconut Milk will add a complementary liveliness to traditional fare.

Sooner or later, though, a time will come when you're inspired to make a complete Thai menu. This guide is meant to provide you with a wealth of suggestions and "entry points" for your explorations of Thai cuisine. Once you've grasped the basics, let your imagination and creativity take over. There are few strict rules and lots of personal freedom.

REGIONAL THAI MENUS

NORTHERN THAILAND: A CHIANG MAI PICNIC

The slightly cooler climates of the mountainous north are perfect for growing garlic, coffee, tea, and, a more recent introduction, strawberries.

Sticky rice is great for a picnic. It rolls conveniently into little balls, which are easy to eat out of hand. Grilled chicken and sausages, a Chiang Mai specialty, can be barbecued on site or cooked first and brought along. The grilled meat aromas are a perfect counterpoint to the sweet-hot, citrusy flavors of the Green Mango Salad.

Menu serves 6

Coconut, Lemon, and Ginger Salad
with Sweet Shrimp Sauce

Barbecued Chicken, Chiang Mai Style

Spicy Chiang Mai Sausages

Green Mango Salad, Chiang Mai Style

Issan Sticky Rice

Iced Lemon Grass Tea

Basket of Strawberries

HEARTLAND:
A BANGKOK CELEBRATION

The full moon of the twelfth lunar month usually occurs in November. It's the occasion of our Loy Krathong festival. We gather by canals and along riverbanks under the full moon, setting loose small homemade *krathongs* on the water. They are little folded-leaf crafts, some simple and some quite elaborate, bearing lit candles and good-luck coins. They carry our wishes for the coming seasons downstream, along with any cares of the past year that we wish to discard. If the *krathong's* candles stay lit, we know that our prayers will be answered.

This is a menu to be served and enjoyed at any festive occasion. If you actually were in Bangkok during Loy Krathong, you'd invite guests to gather after they'd sent their wishes and their worries down the river. At your household pavilion they'd enjoy predinner drinks and appetizers as the procession of lights streamed through the city.

Menu serves 6

Cocktails

Golden Money Bags
with Sweet-and-Spicy Dipping Sauce

Hot-and-Sour Shrimp Soup

Whole Lobster in a Sea of Curry

Winged Bean Salad with
Toasted Coconut and Crispy Shallots

Steamed Jasmine Rice

Fresh Ginger Drink

Cherimoya Ice Cream

NORTHEASTERN PROVINCES: CLASSIC ISSAN FLAVORS

Issan, which has always been our poorest region, has nonetheless given a gift to the entire country. It's this classic flavor trio, which is loved throughout Thailand.

Menu serves 4 to 6

Barbecued Chicken, Issan Style

Green Papaya Salad with Thai Chili and Lime

Issan Sticky Rice

COASTAL THAILAND: A SEAFOOD FEAST

From the southeastern gulf, on the island called Ko Samui, come the sweetest coconuts in all of Thailand. In fact, the long strip of land linking Thailand and Malaysia is home to hundreds of lush coconut plantations. And, since that peninsular stretch has ocean on both sides, seafood is incredibly plentiful throughout the region. This coastal menu features seafood that is raw, grilled, and stir-fried, along with other southern delicacies—jackfruit, pineapple, and cashews.

Menu serves 6 to 8

Pineapple-Ginger Soup

Roasted Cashews

Southern-Style Seafood Barbecue

Fresh Oyster Salad on the Half Shell

Mixed Seafood Stir-Fry,
Gulf Port Style

Steamed Jasmine Rice

Cold Thai Beer

Coconut Ice Cream
with Jackfruit and Toasted Coconut

Typical Thai Lunch and Dinner

A classic Thai meal is a feast of tastes and textures. Our passion is to slowly savor a fine dinner with good company and conversation. This calls for a meal of many courses, enjoyed at leisure.

The same care and attention to balancing flavors is part of even the simplest meal. All Thai cooks have a handy repertoire of quickly prepared dishes.

A simple lunch at home typically incorporates whatever's on hand in the kitchen into a hastily made stir-fry, such as Pork-Fried Rice or Rice-Stick Noodles with Chicken and Vegetables. Or it might be leftover curry from the previous night's dinner, such as Seafood Dumplings with Chu Chee Curry, served with steamed jasmine rice.

Lunch is often eaten on the go from a street-vendor's cart, or wrapped in banana leaves and carried by a farmer into the fields in a woven basket.

Family Dinner for Six

Sweet Corn Fritters with Dipping Sauces

Bangkok Fisherman's Soup

Cellophane-Noodle Salad
with Shrimp, Chicken, and Pork

Barbecued Chicken, Bangkok Style,
with Sweet-and-Spicy Dipping Sauce

Shrimp-Fried Rice

Fresh Oranges in Sweet Rose Water

DINNER PARTY FOR EIGHT

Chicken in Pandanus Leaves
with Sweet Black Bean Sauce

Carved Pineapple Centerpiece

Curried Pumpkin-Coconut Soup with Thai Basil

Green Curry with Mixed Vegetables, Tofu, and Thai Basil

Pork with Garlic and Crushed Black Pepper

Deep-Fried Pomfret with Hot Chili
and Sweet Bell Pepper Sauce

Steamed Jasmine Rice

Fresh Ginger Sorbet

HOME-STYLE DINNER
FOR TWO

Pork and Eggplant Stir-Fry

Classic Shrimp Paste and Chili Sauce
with Fresh Vegetable Crudités

Steamed Jasmine Rice

HOME-STYLE DINNER
FOR FOUR

Chicken-Coconut Soup
with Siamese Ginger and Lemon Grass

Crispy Catfish Curry

Hot-and-Sour Salty Egg Salad

Steamed Jasmine Rice

VEGETARIAN THAI MENUS

VEGETARIAN LUNCHEON BUFFET
Menu serves 6

Tropical-Fruit Wontons with Green Peppercorns

Tofu Salad with Toasted Rice Powder and Mint,
Served in Lettuce Cups

Khanom Chine with Curried Vegetables and Thai Basil

Lemon Grass Tea

Sugarcane Sorbet

VEGETARIAN FAMILY DINNER
Menu serves 4

Vegetarian-Style Pumpkin-Coconut Soup
with Savory Tofu and Thai Basil

Fried Rice with Walnuts and Raisins

Stir-Fried Napa Cabbage with Garlic and Yellow Bean Sauce

Tossed Green Salad with Thai Citrus Vinaigrette

VEGETARIAN DINNER PARTY
Menu serves 6 to 8

Pineapple-Ginger Soup

Vegetarian Spring Rolls with Spicy Cucumber Relish

Massaman Curry with Sweet Potato,
Fried Tofu Squares, and Peanuts

Vegetarian-Style Green Papaya Salad

Steamed Jasmine Rice

Sweet Corn Cupcakes with Coconut Topping

SPECIALTY DISHES

FIRE AND SPICE: THE HOTTEST THAI RECIPES

For those who love the pleasurable pain of chili heat, here's a selection of some the spiciest curries, noodles, stir-fries, and salads, including a few condiments that will set fire to any dish.

Fiery Jungle Curry with Grilled Beef,
Herbs, and Vegetables

Fiery Jungle Curry, Vegetarian Style

Red Curry with Beef and Green Peppercorns

Green Curry with Beef, Eggplant, and Green Chili

Mahogany Fire Noodles

Chicken with Green Chili and Holy Basil

Spicy Stir-Fried Squid with Red Chili and Holy Basil

Fiery Grilled Beef Salad

Classic Chili Dipping Sauce

Fresh Lemon-Chili Sauce

Chilies-in-Vinegar Sauce

FRUIT *and* VEGETABLE CARVING *and* THAI FAVORS

Salak Polamai leh Pak leh Khong Chom Ruay

If you've ever seen traditional Thai dancers, you were probably amazed by their grace, attention to line, and skillfully practiced movements.

That same kind of patient, loving dedication is also expressed in the ancient Thai art of fruit and vegetable carving.

Fruit and vegetable carvers originally worked exclusively for the royal family. And to this day, artists who live within the walls of the palace are always on call to enhance the royal table.

Since our king and queen often dine informally, the royal food carver also prepares centerpieces and other works to order for individual citizens.

Practically every meal served in Thailand has at least some small decorative touch—from banana or *ti* leaves lining a platter to simple leaf and flower shapes carved from carrots, chilies, or cucumbers.

There are many traditional fruit and vegetable carving forms, but no set rules. Imagination is allowed to play the biggest part. When a Thai woman was selected as Miss Universe just a few years ago, a watermelon was fashioned into a regal crown for the centerpiece at the Bangkok reception in her honor.

Whatever the form, the message is always the same: The food before you was prepared with loving care, and you will find it to be delightful.

It's also practical, as all the carved food is meant to be eaten. A centerpiece of fruits carved into flowers will become dessert. Leaves carved from eggplants or carrots will find their way into the next day's stir-fried rice.

While expert carvers, like expert traditional dancers, have trained since childhood, a newcomer can quickly learn enough basic food carving to achieve beautiful results.

In my family, my mother and sisters are the carving experts. My own skills are rather basic. But the simple carving forms in this chapter will add a touch of liveliness and extra charm to your meals.

The floral arts also have ancient roots. The history of Thai flower arranging goes back well over six hundred years. But it was under the influence of Rama V, our king in the earliest part of this century, that garland making became the national passion that it is today.

Bracelet-sized garlands—known as *pyan mali*—are most often made from jasmine, roses, and orchids. They are strung in a circle, with a multistranded tassel of coordinating blossoms. We use garlands as tokens of greeting, to convey respect and wishes for good luck. You'll see them draped around family shrines, hanging in windows and doorways, and presented to heads of state and to students at graduation.

In this chapter you'll learn the easy steps for creating strikingly beautiful, yet simple, fresh flower garlands. They can beautify your dinner table, or be given as gifts, or they can add their scent to a guest's bedroom. You might even want to use a garland as an exotic alternative to a bridesmaid's bouquet.

I believe you'll be pleasantly surprised by how these traditional Thai decorations will make your servings as inviting to the eye as they are to the palate.

CHILI FLOWERS

A pair of scissors is all you need to make these stylized flowers. A chili of any size can easily be cut into thin strands to make a fringe of petals. The petals begin to open up, like a budding flower, when left to soak in a bowl of ice water. Slender chilies create thin, spidery petals for a tropical look. Smaller ones become pleasing, rounded flowers with gently curving petals.

1. Choose smooth, bright-colored chilies with pointed tips and intact stems.

2. Hold a chili by the stem. Take a pair of scissors and cut straight through the chili, lengthwise, from the point to the stem. Rotate the chili and cut through the two halves to create four spears.

3. Either remove the center ribs and seeds or pinch them free of the spears with your fingers. The seeds then stand out as a separate cone in the center, creating a "pistil" for your chili flower.

4. Depending on your patience and the size of your chili, you can continue to bisect the spears until they are finely cut into lengthwise shreds.

5. Drop the chili into a bowl of ice water and set aside until the petals curl out.

NOTE: Be careful when handling chilies. Don't touch your face or your eyes while you're making a chili flower, and wash your hands thoroughly after you finish.

Fruit and
Vegetable
Carving and
Thai Favors

CARROT LEAVES

These are among the simpler carved vegetable leaves. The design is characterized by gently curving beveled edges and crisply etched veins. Carrot leaves can be made a day in advance if kept refrigerated in cold water.

1 large, plump carrot

1. Scrape the carrot clean and trim off the stem. Cut a 3-inch-long section from the widest end.

2. Halve the carrot section lengthwise.

3. Hold one of the halves on end and slice off the round side so you have a large, oblong piece of carrot. Reserve the other half.

4. Hold the carrot piece in your hand and pare off the top edge all the way around to create a beveled edge.

5. Hold the knife at a 45-degree angle and carefully cut a shallow, gently curving, S-shaped vein down the center. Make another cut parallel to the first, creating a V-shaped channel. Pick out the carrot flesh from the channel cut and you have the leaf's vein.

6. Create smaller veins extending from the center vein. Cut three on each side, using the same channel-cut technique. Space them irregularly for a natural appearance.

7. Create a second leaf from the remaining piece of carrot.

SCALLION BRUSHES

S callion tops, when finely sliced and dropped into an ice-water bath, become a plump, curly tangle of greens that will remind you of curlicued gift-wrap ribbon. For the showiest, tightest curls, make your scallion brushes several hours or even a day ahead and keep them refrigerated in cold water.

1 long, plump scallion

1. Cut off the bulb end at a point about 1 inch below where the green tops branch out, so the tops remain in one piece.
2. Trim off the tops so you have a 6- to 8-inch piece.
3. Place the scallion piece on a flat work surface and hold it by the stem end. With the point of a sharp knife, slice the green tops lengthwise, starting where they branch out from the stem, all the way to the end. Fan out the slices a little so you reach all the strands. Cut them as finely as possible for maximum curling effect.
4. Drop the scallion brush into a bowl of ice water and set aside until the strands tangle up into curls.

CUCUMBER PINWHEELS

C ucumber slices turn into pinwheels when the vegetable has been striped with a series of long, shallow cuts.
These can be made in advance and kept refrigerated in cold water.

1 well-formed, smooth-skinned cucumber

1. Hold the knife at a 45-degree angle. Carefully make a shallow cut down the full length of the cucumber. Make another cut parallel to the first, creating a V-shaped channel. Pick out the cucumber flesh from the channel. Turn and repeat the channel cuts about ¼ inch apart (or as close as patience allows) until you have encircled the cucumber, creating a striped effect.
2. Cut the cucumber into thin crosswise slices to make pinwheels.

CARVED PINEAPPLE
CENTERPIECE

Imagine a glistening golden-yellow pineapple standing upright, etched with twirling rows of channel cuts. It looks tricky, but the "eyes" of the pineapple provide an easy connect-the-dots pattern to guide your carving. At serving time the pineapple is cut into bite-size pieces yet still retains an artful shape.

Carved pineapple makes a sweet, refreshing finish to a meal. You can also pair it with something savory, such as grilled shrimp, for a sumptuous appetizer.

I pineapple (see Note)

1. With a large, sharp knife, trim just enough from the base of the pineapple to allow you to stand the fruit upright on a flat work surface. Examine the outer skin of the pineapple. You'll find that the "eyes" run in diagonal rows, spiraling all around the fruit.

2. Remove the tough pineapple skin by slicing straight down with a sharp knife. Work your way all around the fruit, being careful to retain the dark "eyes."

3. Lay the pineapple on its side. Pare the tough skin from the curving base and the top surrounding the greens.

4. Stand the pineapple upright and go over it once more, carving off all traces of skin or green rind while leaving the "eyes" exposed.

5. Clean off the work surface. Starting at the top of the pineapple, begin carving out the "eyes" along a naturally winding spiral. Hold a small, sharp knife at a 45-degree angle and make two shallow cuts, above and below the first set of three "eyes," creating a shallow, V-shaped channel. Pick out the pineapple flesh from the channel. Continue removing the "eyes," three at a time, with this channel-cut technique, until one spiral is complete from top to bottom. Begin again at the top of the pineapple and continue to carve out the "eyes" until they've all been removed and the fruit is etched with winding spiral cuts all around.

6. At this stage, the pineapple can be presented in its upright position as a centerpiece.

7. When you're ready to convert your centerpiece into servings, stand the fruit upright and cut it into two equal halves. Carve right through the topknot and straight down to the bottom. Use a large, sharp knife and cut with a back-and-forth sawing motion. Lay the pineapple halves, curved sides down on a work surface, exposing the core. Remove the core with the same channel-cut technique. Make the cuts quite shallow, so the pineapple will hold together after further cuts are made in the following steps.

8. Turn the pineapple halves over, exposing the spiral cuts. Starting just below the topknot, cut each half lengthwise into thirds, angling your knife to the center as you make the two cuts. The fruit will still be joined at the top, and the pineapple halves will retain their rounded shapes. Hold the pineapple halves gently in place as you cut them crosswise into ¾-inch slices.

9. Carefully slide the two halves onto a serving platter. Arrange them so that the topknots are at opposite ends. Serve at once, or insert toothpicks in each piece of fruit for a spiked effect.

NOTE: Choose a large, well-formed pineapple with a good topknot of leafy greens. The pineapple should be ripe and fragrant, but not too soft. It should just yield to a firm touch.

FRESH-FLOWER GARLANDS

There are endless varieties of Thai garlands. The favorite, seen everywhere, is the small welcoming garland made of deeply scented jasmine blossoms strung in a circle and decorated with flowery tassels. Visitors to our country will see these garlands dangling from the rearview mirrors of every taxicab.

One of these wristlet-sized garlands, hung on a bedpost or placed on a table, will scent a whole room.

Tropical jasmine isn't widely available in America, but with the simple instructions below, you can fashion a beautiful Thai-style garland using more readily available blossoms, bought from a florist or picked from your garden.

Thai people use a very long, slender needle to make their garlands, but a 5-inch needle known as a "doll-making," or "upholstery," needle, works well and can be found at the notions counter of most fabric shops. Use the strong and wiry cotton thread called "button thread."

1. Choose small, fragrant flowers, such as baby roses or miniature carnations, for the garland, and carnation buds for the tassels. To make a garland 16 to 20 inches around with five tassels, you need about thirty-five blossoms and twenty-six unopened buds.

continued

2. Thread a 5-inch doll-making needle with a 3-foot length of heavy button thread. Knot the end.

3. Using scissors, cut the flowers off their stems right at the base, or calyx, of the blossoms.

4. Hold the first flower with the blossom end facing left. Thread it onto the needle by piercing it straight through the base. Keep it in position on the needle and thread the second flower so it faces the opposite direction. (Throughout the making of the garland, continue threading the flowers in alternate directions.)

5. Position two or more blossoms on the needle at a time, then carefully push them down the thread together. Don't push them to the end of the thread; leave about 6 inches free above the knot for later use as a tie.

6. When you have thirty of the flowers threaded (reserve five for the tassel ends), push them relatively close together and slip the needle from the thread. Bring the two ends together and tie them so the garland forms a circle. Make three tight knots to keep it secure. Trim the ends. Set aside while you make the tassels.

7. Cut the carnation buds off their stems.

8. For the long center tassel, use one reserved flower and six carnation buds. Re-thread the needle with an 18-inch length of thread and knot the end. Run the needle through the center of the reserved flower, starting from the blossom end and coming out through the center of the base. Push the flower right down to the knotted end.

9. Run the needle through the blossom end of a carnation bud, going lengthwise, straight through the center and out through the opposite end. Push the bud down the thread to meet the blossom. Thread the remaining buds so they meet each other end to end. Unthread the needle, leaving the last several inches of thread for later use as a tie. Set aside.

10. Make four tassels to surround the long central tassel: Rethread the needle, again using 18 inches of thread. Make a tassel as directed above, but using one reserved flower and just five carnation buds. Make three more tassels in the same manner.

11. Hold the tassels up by their threads. Adjust the four shorter tassels to uniform length, with the longer tassel in the center. Lay the tassels down, keeping two shorter tassels on each side of the longer one. Cut a short length of thread and slip it under the tassels where they meet at the top. Tie the short thread to keep the tassels securely positioned. Hold the threads of the tassels together and wrap them twice around the garland, keeping the carnation buds close to the garland's flowers. Tie off the tassel threads. Trim the ends.

12. If the garland is not to be used immediately, layer it gently between two sheets of dampened paper towels and place in the refrigerator. Depending on the flowers you've used, it should keep fresh this way for several hours, or even overnight.

MANGO LEAVES

J ust a few quick, easy cuts accentuate the natural leaf shape inherent in a plump mango half.

Carved mango leaves make colorful, edible decorations for a platter of fresh tropical fruits, or they can be the main attraction in Sweet Sticky Rice with Mangoes and Coconut Cream (page 338).

I large, ripe mango

1. Neatly slice off the stem end of the mango.

2. Hold the fruit gently while removing the peel, to keep the rounded shape of the mango intact. If the mango is completely ripe, you can pull the skin off in strips. Start at the top, where the stem end has been removed. If the mango is too firm to peel by hand, slice off the skin with a sharp knife, being careful to follow the natural curves of the fruit.

3. Cut off the flesh in two thick slices, one from each side of the flat center seed.

4. Set the two halves, cut sides down, on a work surface. Each should resemble a natural leaf shape, with a rounded stem end and a gently pointed tip. (Trim the "leaves" a bit here and there to define their shapes, if needed.) Hold the knife at a 45-degree angle and carefully cut a shallow diagonal line from the stem end of one leaf to the point near the center where the fruit is thickest. Make another cut parallel to the first, creating a V-shaped channel. Pick out the mango flesh from the channel cut. Cut another shallow diagonal line from the channel down toward the tip of the leaf. Make a parallel cut, creating a second V-shaped channel. Pick out the mango flesh from the second channel cut and you have the leaf's vein.

5. Create smaller veins extending from the center vein. Cut three on the widest side of the leaf, using the same channel-cut technique. Cut the first from the high midpoint of the center vein. Space the other two irregularly for a natural appearance.

6. Create a second leaf from the remaining mango half.

Fruit and
Vegetable
Carving and
Thai Favors

MAIL-ORDER SOURCES FOR THAI INGREDIENTS, COOKWARE, SEEDS, and PLANTS

Thai Ingredients and Cookware

The Chile Shop
109 E. Water Street
Santa Fe, NM 87501
505-983-6080
(Several varieties of New Mexico chili powder)

The CMC Company
P.O. Drawer B
Avalon, NJ 08202
800-262-2780
(Thai staples, including unsweetened dried coconut, dried Guajillo chilies, dried New Mexico chilies, fish sauce, and coconut-palm sugar)

DeWildt Imports, Inc.
RD #3
Bangor, PA 18013
215-588-4949
800-338-3433
(Numerous Thai staples and spices; cookware)

Hot Stuff Spicy Food Store
227 Sullivan Street
New York, NY 10012
212-254-6120
(Thai staples, including Lee Kum Kee chili-garlic sauce)

La Cuisine
323 Cameron Street
Alexandria, VA 22314
703-836-4435
800-521-1176
(Numerous Thai staples; cookware, including bamboo skewers, fanciful candy molds for making Thai desserts, RCW electric ice-cream makers, and much more)

Le Saucier, Inc.
35 Eldridge Road, Suite 209
Boston, MA 02130
617-323-5015
(Thai staples)

Mo Hotta-Mo Betta
P.O. Box 4136
San Luis Obispo, CA 93403
805-544-4051
800-462-3220
(Thai staples, including coconut milk, pickled garlic, and the preferred brand of *sriracha*—no English translation, but the Thai script looks like "FISSION")

Nancy's Specialty Market
P.O. Box 327
Wye Mills, MD 21679
800-462-6291
(Thai staples, including mushroom soy sauce and rose-flower water)

The Oriental Pantry
423 Great Road
Acton, MA 01720
508-264-4576
800-828-0368
(Fresh specialty ingredients, such as freshly cut stalks of lemon grass, Hawaiian ginger, and baby ginger; Thai staples, including hard-to-find Thai tea; cookware includes sturdy stainless-steel cutters in floral shapes for Thai toast)

Pendery's
1221 Manufacturing
Dallas, TX 75207
214-741-1870
800-533-1870
(Dried red California, Guajillo, and New Mexico chilies for making curry pastes)

Spice Merchant
P.O. Box 524
Jackson Hole, WY 83001
307-733-7811
(Numerous Thai staples, including coconut milk, Thai chilies, light soy sauce, Golden Mountain sauce, rice sticks, coconut-palm sugar, and much more; cookware includes rice cookers, spice mills, and 14-inch nonstick woks)

Taylor & Ng
1212B 19th Street
Oakland, CA 94607
415-834-2754
800-255-3129
(Cookware, including nonstick woks, up to 14-inch size, nonstick tiered steam pots, wok utensils, and Chinese cleavers)

Thai Seeds and Plants

The Cook's Garden
P.O. Box 535
Londonderry, VT 05148
802-824-3400
(Seeds for cilantro, purple basil, and Thai chilies)

De Giorgio Seeds
6011 N Street
Omaha, NB 68117-1634
402-731-3901
800-858-2580
(Seeds for holy basil, Thai lemon basil, cilantro, kabocha, and Thai eggplant)

Nichols Garden Nursery
1190 North Pacific Highway
Albany, OR 97321
503-928-9280
(Seeds for Thai basil, holy basil, cilantro, baby corn, flowering bok choy, baby bok choy, bitter melon, winter melon, and yard-long beans)

Oriental Vegetable Seeds
Evergreen Y.H. Enterprises
P.O. Box 17538
Anaheim, CA 92817
714-537-3319
(Seeds for yard-long beans, all kinds of Chinese cabbage, baby corn, Thai eggplant, Thai basil, cilantro, Thai chilies, and kabocha)

Sandy Mush Herb Nursery
316 Surrett Cove Road
Leicester, NC 28748
704-683-2014
(Can ship live lemon-grass divisions; seeds include anise basil, dark opal basil, and holy basil)

Seeds of Change
1364 Rufina Circle, #5
Santa Fe, NM 87501
505-438-8080
(Seeds for bok choy, Thai basil, holy basil, and serrano chilies)

Mail-Order
Sources for Thai
Ingredients,
Cookware, Seeds,
and Plants

INDEX